D0842277

*British Theatre
and the Other Arts,
1660–1800*

"*The Scene open'd; is presented a Hell, in which* Pluto, Proserpine, *and other Women-Spirits appeared seated, attended by Furies; the Stage being fill'd on each side with* Crimalhaz, Hamet, Q. Mother, *and all the Court in Masquerade. After soft Musick Enter* Orpheus." (*From Elkanah Settle's* The Emperor of Morocco. *London: William Cademan, 1673.*)

British Theatre and the Other Arts, 1660–1800

Edited by
SHIRLEY STRUM KENNY

FOLGER BOOKS
Washington: The Folger Shakespeare Library
London and Toronto: Associated University Presses

© 1984 by Associated University Presses, Inc.

Associated University Presses
440 Forsgate Drive
Cranbury, NJ 08512

Associated University Presses
25 Sicilian Avenue
London WC1A 2QH, England

Associated University Presses
2133 Royal Windsor Drive
Unit 1
Mississauga, Ontario, Canada L5J 1K5

Library of Congress Cataloging in Publication Data
Main entry under title:

British theatre and the other arts, 1660–1800.

    "Folger books."
    Includes bibliographical references.
    1. Theater—Great Britain—History—17th century—
Addresses, essays, lectures.   2. Theater—Great Britain—
History—18th century—Addresses, essays, lectures.
3. Arts—Great Britain—Addresses, essays, lectures.
I. Kenny, Shirley Strum.
PN2592.B74   1984   790.2′0941   82-48158
ISBN 0-918016-65-7

Printed in the United States of America

FOLGER INSTITUTE SYMPOSIA

Compiled by the Folger Institute
of Renaissance and Eighteenth-Century Studies
and Published by the Folger Shakespeare Library

FOLGER INSTITUTE CENTRAL EXECUTIVE COMMITTEE

An influential collaborative enterprise founded in 1970 and now co-sponsored by twenty-one major universities, the Folger Institute is a rapidly growing center for advanced studies in the humanities. Through support from such agencies as the National Endowment for the Humanities and the Andrew W. Mellon Foundation, the Institute offers a complex interdisciplinary program of seminars, workshops, symposia, colloquia, and lectures. The physical center of the Institute is the Folger Shakespeare Library, an independent research library administered by the Trustees of Amherst College and located on Capitol Hill in Washington. Since 1969 the Library's Director has been O. B. Hardison, Jr.

Contents

Preface

Scholarship on Restoration and eighteenth-century British theatre has flourished in the last two decades. The pioneering work in *The London Stage, 1660–1800* and the *Biographical Dictionary of Actors, Actresses, Musicians, Dancers, Managers, and Other Stage Personnel in London, 1660–1800* has made accessible primary materials never before available in easily usable form. Excellent new editions have provided both texts and information about individual plays, enriching research possibilities. Important new critical works have developed from the expanded awareness of scholars thinking about drama in terms of the theatre.

The opening of research possibilities in the drama of the period has revealed a closeness between theatrical dynamics and other aspects of British culture by no means fully explored in times past. We have long discussed the connections between politics and the theatre and the social implications of theatrical trends, and we have at least hinted at the relationships between the theatre and the novel; we have recognized dramatic poets as the darlings of the Restoration court and the scapegoats of Augustan poets; we have known that plays were important to the reading public as well as to theatregoers. We have considered pit, box, and gallery as the site of social interaction and intrigue, as the essayists, novelists, and poets reiterated throughout the period. With the new tools of research now available, we are beginning to be able to trace and evaluate the impact of the theatre on the culture with considerable precision, and we can now recognize how many research possibilities lie ahead.

The present volume deals with one of the most interesting aspects of the relationship of theatre to other facets of London life—the interconnections between theatre and other arts, specifically the musical, visual, and fictive arts. No attempt has been made either to provide comprehensiveness (an impossible task in the scope of the volume) or to narrow the focus. Taken together, the essays included here are intended to provide important new information and also to suggest some of the kinds of research and some of the directions that are now possible.

The volume evolved from a conference on English Theatre and the

Sister Arts, 1660–1800, sponsored by the Folger Institute of Renaissance and Eighteenth-Century Studies, with the aid of a grant from the National Endowment for the Humanities. Seven of the essayists were speakers at the conference (Professors Scouten, Milhous, Lincoln, Hook, Knapp, Burnim, and Halsband); the other eight essays have been written especially for this volume.

A note of thanks is due to Professor Philip H. Highfill, with whom I planned and co-chaired the conference. Eileen Moye typed the manuscript with incredible efficiency, accuracy, and editorial skill. Sara Friedlander helped with the typing, Grace Depp and James May helped check footnotes, and Joan Wood helped all of us.

—SHIRLEY STRUM KENNY

Abbreviations for Frequently Cited Sources

Biographical Dictionary	Philip H. Highfill, Jr., Kalman A. Burnim, and Edward A. Langhans. *A Biographical Dictionary of Actors, Actresses, Musicians, Dancers, Managers, and Other Stage Personnel in London, 1660–1800.* Carbondale: Southern Illinois Univ. Press, 1973—
Cibber	Colley Cibber. *An Apology for the Life of Colley Cibber,* ed. B. R. S. Fone. Ann Arbor, Mich.: University of Michigan Press, 1968.
Dennis	John Dennis. *The Critical Works of John Dennis,* ed. Edward Niles Hooker. 2 vols. Baltimore: Johns Hopkins Press, 1939–43.
Fiske	Roger Fiske. *English Theatre Music in the Eighteenth Century.* London: Oxford University Press, 1973.
Georgian Playhouse	Iain Mackintosh. *The Georgian Playhouse, Actors, Artists, Audiences, and Architecture, 1730–1830.* London: Arts Council of Great Britain, 1975.
Hume	Robert D. Hume. *The Development of English Drama in the Late Seventeenth Century.* Oxford: Clarendon Press, 1976.
The London Stage	*The London Stage 1660–1800,* ed. William Van Lennep, Emmett L. Avery, Arthur H. Scouten, G. W. Stone, Jr., and Charles Beecher Hogan. 5 parts in 11 vols. Carbondale, Ill.: Southern Illinois University Press, 1960–68.
Milhous	Judith Milhous. *Thomas Betterton and the Management of Lincoln's Inn Fields, 1695–1708.* Carbondale, Ill.: Southern Illinois University Press, 1979.
Paulson	Ronald Paulson. *Hogarth: His Life, Art, and Times.* 2 vols. New Haven, Conn., and London: Yale University Press, 1971.
Price	Curtis A. Price. *Music in the Restoration Theatre.* Studies in Musicology, No. 4. Ann Arbor, Mich.: UMI Research Press, 1979.

11

*British Theatre
and the Other Arts,
1660–1800*

"*A State is presented, the King, Queen, and* Mariamne *seated;* Muly-Hamet, Abdelcador *and Attendants, a Moorish Dance is presented by* Moors *in several Habits, who bring in an artificial Palm-tree, about which they dance to several antick Instruments of Musick; in the intervals of the Dance, this Song is sung by a Moorish Priest and two Moorish Women; the Chorus of it being performed by all the* Moors." (*From Elkanah Settle's* The Emperor of Morocco. *London: William Cademan, 1673.*)

1

Theatre, Related Arts, and the Profit Motive: An Overview

SHIRLEY STRUM KENNY

In the Restoration and increasingly in the eighteenth century, theatre was business as well as art. Profitable art was welcomed in theatrical houses; so was profitable claptrap. The works of Purcell and Handel were enthusiastically supported by theatrical management; so was William Joy, the Strong Man of Kent, who could lift a weight of 2,240 pounds.[1] Dr. Johnson was not the first to note that "The Drama's Laws the Drama's Patrons give": the century is full of references to the cheapening of dramatic art in order to fill houses. Playwrights who aspired to the purest classical tragedy found themselves writing domestic comedy in order to see third-night profits. Critical theory focused primarily on tragedy, but since the successful new plays were usually comedies, the repertory itself contained more comedies than tragedies.[2] The theatre did not differ, in the profit motive, from theatre now, or, for that matter from today's television fare—in order to survive, the management had to sell what the audience would buy. Formulas for successful seasons developed: comedies predominated, with the plays of the turn-of-the-century playwrights (Farquhar, Etherege, Vanbrugh, Cibber, Steele) the strongest eighteenth-century component; Shakespeare and Fletcher prospered; spectaculars in the form of operas or elaborately mounted tragedies appealed to the taste for the exotic; modern tragedy, adorned by the best actors, gave the rare "quality" touch; afterpieces (light and fluffy farces, pantomimes, or sometimes processions or pageants) rounded out programs when the main pieces might not guarantee a house; and interruptive and inappropriate entr'acte singing, dancing, and specialty acts proved reliably popular. Managers carefully calculated audience response, and the competition among the theatres, like movie and television competition now, resulted in the coupling of fierce striving for originality on the one hand and slavish imitation of success on the other.

The commercial calculations that determined the repertory and thereby influenced what authors wrote prompted enterprising artists and musicians to participate in theatrical productions; such calculations also encouraged enterprising businessmen outside the theatre to exploit the popularity of stage productions. Although imprinted T-shirts, posters, and original-cast recordings were centuries away, printed libretti, engravings of scenes, porcelain figurines of actors and actresses, and even playing cards with actors' pictures on them were designed for public consumption. Theatre proved thoroughly, energetically commercial.

J. H. Plumb says that in England the commercialization of leisure "can be discerned in the 1690s, and in 1750 and 1760, leisure was becoming an industry with great potentiality for growth." He appropriately emphasizes the importance of the growing market for printed materials, "for reading implies time to spare and money to spend."[3] The links between theatre and print are manifold. Although play texts had been printed for more than a century before the Restoration, regular publication developed during the Restoration, and the pace quickened in the 1690s.[4] Playwrights ordinarily received small but reliable profits from selling their publication rights, and booksellers stood to make a considerable profit from successful plays. On at least one occasion a suppressed play, Gay's *Polly,* brought significant profits in print. Moreover, a steady market developed for reprints of popular plays, often produced in a smaller format than the standard quarto or octavo first edition.[5] Duodecimos, sometimes bound in sets, were printed and reprinted, often reusing frontispiece engravings from earlier editions. Profits were enticing enough to encourage booksellers to join forces to publish plays.

The merchandising of the theatre relied on advertising, and the newspapers were involved in almost all aspects of the trade. Newspapers carried notices of theatrical performances. Daily advertising began when the *Daily Courant* was founded in 1702; two years later, daily notices of the evening's performances began to appear regularly. Advertisements were often followed by notices from publishers of the availability of printed texts: "These plays are sold by . . ." or "On Tuesday next will be publish'd . . ." or "This Day is publish'd . . ." So frequent were the advertisements that Knapton and Lintott, for example, followed daily theatrical advertisements with the formula "This Play is sold by . . ." Very popular plays warranted advertisements not only for the first edition but for subsequent ones as well. For example, the first edition of *The Recruiting Officer* was advertised in April 1706, then the corrected second edition between July and September, and the third in November and December; the texts were also regularly noted ("These plays are sold by . . .") in advertisements of performances.

Newspapers and periodicals also carried teasers, puffs, and gossip from the theatres. As early as the 1690s, Peter Motteux's *The Gentleman's Journal* commented frequently on theatrical events. Prologues, epilogues, and songs were sometimes printed in periodicals, presumably to sell the periodical rather than to bring audiences to the theatres, but both effects probably occurred. Duels, riots, and personal encounters in the theatres were covered by the press; puffs announcing the excellence of pieces in rehearsal helped swell the crowds for performances. Richard Steele's *The Conscious Lovers,* for example, had been publicly touted, according to John Dennis, as "the very best that ever came upon the *English* stage" before it even opened.[6] Whether it was the puffs or Dennis's prepremiere attacks that prompted attendance, certainly the power of print accounted in part for the eighteen-night opening run. The play "had such a Reputation before it was known," the *Freeholder's Journal* reported on 14 November 1722, "that a Man of no great Curiosity would have ventur'd to squeeze into the Crowd that went to see it the first Night."[7]

Print also magnified the effects of importing visual and musical arts into the theatre. The bills advertised song and dance. Scenery and costuming were puffed as well as lighting effects. Until midcentury, costumes and sets, sufficiently noted in print, served as justification for raising ticket prices for elaborately mounted productions—surely nothing more clearly exposes the commercial motivation behind the visual and musical stage arts.

Print was, in addition, the medium that allowed the theatre to be sold for home consumption in many forms: printed plays to be performed at home or savored in the privacy of the closet, engravings to be collected and admired, music to be played and sung at home. The acceleration of theatre-related printing in the period speaks eloquently of the growing commercialism associated with the theatre. From editions of single plays grew collected works of popular authors and then collections of miscellaneous plays such as *The English Theatre* and *Bell's British Theatre.* Periodicals as diverse as *The Gentleman's Journal, The Diverting Post,* the *Tatler* and the *Spectator,* and the *Gentleman's Magazine* refer frequently to the theatre. The reason for such substantial coverage is obvious: the audience of these periodicals enjoyed reading about the stage, as readers of publications as diverse as *Time* and the *Times Literary Supplement (TLS)* do now. The publication of critical reviews obviously also met a deeply felt need on the part of readers. Drama was part and parcel of the developing emphasis on leisure that Plumb traces; as such, it was perfect for commercial exploitation.

The Visual Arts

In the United States in the second half of the twentieth century, movie and television performers, both as individuals and as characters from films and television series, have been hawked in many forms—as posters, T-shirt decorations, plastic dolls, to name a few. Big moneymaking films often flagrantly subordinate characterization and plot to the mechanical tricks of "special effects." Peter Pan has delighted generations of audiences by flying, and in Las Vegas elaborately bedecked showgirls year after year descend in golden birdcages or sail above the stage on silver moons. Inside the theatre and outside, salable visual "art" is created for public consumption.

The extravagances of the 1970s were fully anticipated in the Restoration and eighteenth century. The excitement of exhilarating theatrical effects was thoroughly exploited by playwrights and managers. Flying, disappearing, and other magical feats were greatly appreciated by audiences, who also enjoyed the "special effects" created by instantaneous changes of elaborate scenery in plain view. Moreover, by the 1690s artists outside the theatre were discovering the marketability of theatrical memorabilia in the form of paintings and prints, and during the eighteenth century images of actors were created in other forms as well, as figurines, plaques, even heads of canes. Obviously, the impetus for using theatrical subjects for this burst of creativity, much of which expressed itself in inexpensive media capable of easy reproduction, was commercial.

One cannot argue that the emphasis on scenes and machines came solely as a response to commercial drives. Rather, the impulse was, at least in the beginning, theatrical. Throughout the Restoration and eighteenth century, critics declaimed against the emphasis on spectacle; a play, after all, acts no better before splendid scenes, although an audience may well be willing to settle for inferior drama if it is elaborately staged. Throughout the 140-year period, scenes, machines, lighting, and costumes encouraged audiences to come to the theatre. Richard Cumberland in 1806 ruefully complained that "The splendor of the scenes, the ingenuity of the machinist, and the rich display of dresses aided by the captivating charms of music, now in a great degree supercede the labours of the poet."[8] His regrets echoed those of commentators throughout the period. Although the mission from first to last was identical—to awe the audience through lavishness and magical transformations of the stage—skills improved throughout the period, so that the technological accomplishments and the artistic excellence of the scenes consistently approached the unbelievable. The Restoration theatre was as full of marvels in its day as the theatre of the 1790s, and audiences throughout the period were struck with admiration.

Painted scenes, used from earliest Restoration times, embodied both magnificence and realism; as an innovation in the public theatre, they provided strong incentives for attendance. According to Sybil Rosenfeld, the Restoration companies preferred public and private interiors and formal parks and gardens; landscapes "were of the familiar baroque type of three-perspective cypress alleys and a rockbound shore."[9] Scenes were stored and reused, and inventories built up in the theatres. But new scenes, particularly those which realistically detailed recognizable prospects and landmarks and those which staggered the audience with their grandeur, were cause for considerable excitement. For example, two new sets were constructed for the premiere of *The Conscious Lovers* in 1722, depicting Charing Cross and the Mall: ". . . you may see as far as from *White-Hall* to *Temple-Bar*, and the Shops and all: Then, there is the very Centry Box, the old Soldier, my Lord's Chair, and the Trees, just as tho' they were all alive."[10] For a performance of *Julius Caesar* on 24 September 1723, a prospect of ancient Rome was devised. For Aaron Hill's production of Handel's *Rinaldo* in 1711, a prospect of mountains, complete with rocks, caves, and waterfalls, engulfed the stage from front to back, and water actually cascaded. The opera, Addison wrote, "is filled with Thunder and Lightning, Illuminations, and Fireworks; which the Audience may look upon without catching Cold, and indeed without much Danger of being burnt; for there are several Engines filled with Water, and ready to play at a Minute's Warning."[11] The use of wings as well as shutters provided a sense of perspective which gave the illusion of "previously undreamed of loftiness and vastness" in scene painting.[12] Act drops were devised; scenes were cut to reveal other scenes behind.

A landscape tradition also developed, with scenes often painted by easel landscapists such as George Lambert, John Inigo Richards, Nicholas Thomas Dall, and others. Rosenfeld classifies landscape scene painting into two categories, a quiet pastoral tradition that approached realism more closely than European scenes and the "wild romantic scenes that put England in the lead."[13] The most notable creative force in the latter tradition, of course, was Philip James de Loutherbourg, friend of Boucher and Servandoni, who, having left Paris for London in 1771, soon revolutionized London theatre with his artistic direction of all visual aspects including the scenery, lighting, and mechanical systems, as well as the costuming for productions. De Loutherbourg worked miracles never before attempted on the English stage; he designed forest foliage that turned from green to "blood colour"; he made a palace tumble into ruins and a grand naval review with real masts and riggings move in time with music. But if his skill in scenic painting and mechanical manipulation was new, his success was a response to the audience's century-long craving for elaborate staging.

Machines provided the epitome of exciting staging, and they were most heavily used in operas and other spectaculars. Incredible machines provided for ascents and descents, flying chariots and flying witches and goddesses, ghosts appearing and disappearing, Jupiter being transformed into a bull, and the Lancashire Witches' brooms marching off and fetching bottles. Part illusion, part mechanical ingenuity, the trickery never failed to please audiences and rarely failed to displease dramatic critics.

Needless to say, scenes and machinery cost dearly. Add to the costs the acquisition, rental, and cleaning expenses of properties and costumes, and one begins to wonder if the profit motive should not have encouraged modesty in scale. However, there were several commercial reasons for the heavy expenditures. In the first place, during most of the period keen competition raged among companies. Presumably tricks to bring an audience into one house robbed another of customers, thus doubly affecting the competition. Therefore if one theatre gained auditors through staging, the other was tempted to try to gain them by the same method. Moreover, until midcentury, new scenes and costumes were sometimes used as a rationale for raising ticket prices.[14] Since scenes could be reused, newly painted scenery could become an asset for later productions.

To the artist, of course, the financial aspect was appealing. Scene painting kept numerous young artists from going hungry as they attempted to establish their reputations in other genres. Some painters, notably de Loutherbourg, found the stage irresistible. Not only was de Loutherbourg well paid; so successfully had he created a following that he was able during his last year at Drury Lane to open the "*Eidophusikon; or*, Various Imitations of Natural Phenomena represented by Moving Pictures," on a stage six feet wide and eight feet deep. The scenery was there—dawn at Greenwich Park, noon in Tangier, sunset near Naples, the moon rising over the Mediterranean, and a shipwreck. Music was also there, including songs by Michael Arne and J. C. Bach.[15] The next year a new series of six scenes—including Niagara Falls, the moon rising with a waterspout off a rocky Japanese coast, and Milton's Satan arraying his troops on the back of the fiery lake with the raising of the Palace of Pandemonium—was offered, with music by Mr. Burney. In effect, theatre without actors or plays was successfully being marketed.

As the artist was brought into the theatre for commercial reasons, so the theatre as a subject became profitable to artists and artisans outside the houses. Actors and actresses posed for portraits, often portraits undramatic in conception. Even some portraits of actors as stage characters—Reynolds's Garrick as Kitely, for example—lack highly dramatic qualities. One can scarcely distinguish the portraits of many actors and actresses from the portraits of other men and women of sufficient means to pay for a sitting. What is different, and significantly different, is the number of theatrical portraits translated to engravings for "mass" production and "mass" merchandising. A portrait of Nell Gwyn by Lely, for example, was engraved in a mezzotint by Peter Van Bleeck, and the practice of engraving portraits became increasingly popular during the period. Later in the period, David Garrick was not only painted by numerous artists, including Hogarth, Zoffany, Reynolds, Batoni, Pine, Van Loo, and others, but oil portraits were in turn engraved. Garrick's likeness appeared in terra cotta, cast busts, watercolors, etchings, pencil, pen and ink, and wash pictures, as well as on medals (mulberry wood, copper gilt), wall hangings, Wedgwood jasperware, a hair picture, Liverpool Delft tiles, playing cards, and refreshment tokens for the Jubilee at Stratford.[16] The creative spirit alone did not inspire artists to such Garrickmania; the commercial impulse quickened their pens, pencils, brushes, fingers, knives, styluses, and assorted other tools. Garrick pieces sold.

Garrick was the century's favorite theatrical subject—Kalman A. Burnim has located more than 450 likenesses—but he was by no means unusual in being memorialized through engravings as well as paintings. If oils were commissioned by the rich, engravings could be purchased by the less affluent, and they were marketed regularly. Not only were portraits of actors, actresses, and playwrights popular, but more directly theatrical subjects were chosen as well. Actors were depicted in favorite roles. Stages, scenes, audiences, and dramatic moments from performances became popular. The engravings from the 1673 edition of Elkanah Settle's *The Empress of Morocco,* showing elaborate scenes, machines, costumes, and a production number of the Moorish dance, opened a door on popular publication of art, but not until several decades later did engravings of theatrical scenes become common.

By the 1720s, engraved frontispieces for printed plays were multiplying. Ordinarily, first editions did not contain frontispieces; the rapidity of press work probably made them an impossibility, and the plays would sell anyway because they were new. Later editions, however, regularly had plates, often kept and reused, copied in piracies, and imitated in new engravings when the old plates finally wore out or new publishers bought rights to a play. A market also developed for theatrical prints such as Hogarth's scenes from *The Tempest, The Indian Emperor, The Beggar's Opera, Henry the Eighth,* and *Henry the Fourth,* his portraits of Quin and Garrick, and his offstage prints, such as *The Laughing Audience* and *Strolling Actresses Dressing in a Barn.*[17]

The multiplicity of theatrical prints and the interest in copies of the works of outstanding artists bespeak a commercialism tempered by recognition of who the good artists were. A few examples of engravings of the paintings of Johann Zoffany will illustrate the point: R. Sayer engraved his *Cymbeline* (ca. 1764) in 1770; John Finlayson engraved *The Provok'd Wife* (1765) in mezzotint in 1768 and *A Scene in The Devil upon Two Sticks* in 1769; many engravers did Zoffany's portrait of Macklin as Shylock (ca. 1768), including two dated 1769; Johann Gottfried Haid engraved *The Farmer's Return* (1762) and *The Mayor of Garratt* (1764) in mezzotint (1766, 1765); and James MacArdell's 1764 mezzotint of Zoffany's Garrick and Mrs. Cibber in *Venice Preserv'd* (1763) was so popular that a number of copies in oil apparently were produced subsequently. The list could be greatly extended, but these examples suggest the popularity of theatrical engravings. Purchasers wanted not only the best actors but the best painters copied in their engravings.

Given the multiplicity of frontispieces and other engravings of theatrical personages and scenes, there can be little surprise that the theatrical genre became appropriate as a structure and metaphor for viewing English social and cultural life. William Hogarth, according to Ronald Paulson, "recognized the stage as a useful compositional unit for the sort of graphic scene that interested him and a source of expressive faces. . . . The very nature of the London stage was significant to Hogarth the painter as it was to Gay the dramatist."[18] Hogarth's *Beggar's Opera* series reflects the entertainment in the theatre in 1728. His *Marriage a la Mode* is entirely theatrical in conception: scenic in design, the series embodies a plot carefully developed through characterization (including the portrayal of stock characters), with intense care to details of sets, costumes, and gesture. The same theatrical quality permeates his other great series, *The Rake's Progress* and *The Harlot's Progress;* the theatrical experience of the audience is part of the allusional backdrop for appreciation of the prints. As Paulson has acutely pointed out, Hogarth "thought of his pictures in terms of a stage representation—a succession of scenes, with lines spoken and gestures—rather than a book."[19] His audience would have immediately responded to the stage qualities; they had, in a sense, been programmed to respond to the evocation of theatrical echoes. *Marriage a la Mode* was appropriately dramatic not only because of the progression of the action but also because courtship and marriage plots all but monopolized the comic repertoire. The Progresses successfully employ the dramatic format because of the ironic interplay between the Rake's and Harlot's downfalls and tragic drama. Hogarth's exacting detail in "scenery" and "costuming" are also "theatrical" in convention. Hogarth and his admirers shared an understanding of the theatrical reverberations in his works.

For Hogarth and increasingly for later satirists such as Thomas Rowlandson and James Gillray, the theatre became a microcosm for depicting the follies of the British, in taste, in affectations, even in politics and social theory. Scenes from plays were a medium of contemporary satire; for example, Rowlandson's depiction of the auction scene of *The School for Scandal* with the Prince of Wales (later George IV) as Charles Surface was etched and published by V. M. Picot in 1788 as a direct political satire. In such satirical prints, the artist economically brought a wealth of allusion to his works. Rowlandson, as well as others, also turned his attention to the spectators, not only satirizing English crassness and crudity, but introducing recognizable caricatures into his drawings of Box-lobby Loungers or Vaux-hall promenaders. The focus was changed. No longer was the stage scene and dramatic structure the key; instead, the theatre as social and cultural phenomenon was central, with the audience becoming as important a subject as the actors and sets. The centrality of theatre in British cultural life and the marketability of prints based on theatrical scenes continued to encourage artists to produce prints based on the theatre, even if the prints had little to do with actual productions.

Theatre's impact on the artistic vision shows one side of the commercial connection between theatre and art—that is, the evolving of structural and metaphorical strengths in graphics. But another side of the relationship of artists and the theatre involved purely financial interests. Many artists, particularly landscapists and engravers, found sustenance in the theatrical trade. Hogarth and others profited from engraving ephemera such as benefit tickets. Landscapists painted theatrical scenes until they established reputations as easel artists. The book-publishing trade employed engravers to do frontispieces. Porcelain and pottery makers created figures of actors and stage characters in porcelain figures, busts, statuettes, medallions, plaques, cheap tiles with transfer pictures, and household objects such as tea services and snuff boxes. Fire screens reportedly carried images from *The Beggar's Opera,* and playing cards still exist with four theatrical knaves: Garrick as Tancred; an actor, perhaps Quin, as Falstaff; Woodward as Captain Bobadil; and a Harlequin.[20] In a sense, the theatrical-souvenir business evolved during the period. There was money to be made on theatrical wares, and some of those who made it became important English artists later in their careers.

Music and Dance

As Curtis A. Price points out, London in the late seventeenth and eighteenth centuries saw a "thoroughly musical" theatre.[21] Operas and other musical novelties engrossed audiences, and the ordinary comedies and tragedies were also graced with music in many forms—songs written for the plays, including new songs for productions of old plays, snatches of old songs, short pieces played between the acts, musical interludes that served as finales for plays. The examples are numerous even if one looks no further than the play texts: the songs by Henry and Daniel Purcell, John Eccles, Richard Leveridge, and others; the dances that closed plays such as *The Country Wife* and *The Beaux Stratagem;* the violin sonata by Carbonelli that Steele felt constrained to substitute in *The Conscious Lovers* when no actor could be found to sing his new "Love-sick Maid." Stage directions often tell us that a character sings or hums a tune even when no particular tune is suggested. If playwrights did not include enough music, sometimes supplementary tunes were added during rehearsals, within the scenes as well as between the acts. Three songs were added during rehearsals, for example, to Farquhar's *Love and a Bottle,* which already contained songs and dancing. Musical decisions were not in the author's hands; songs could be set, added, or omitted after the play had entered rehearsal. Authors came to expect musical tinkering.

Critical reaction against musical theatre—that is, operas, masques, and other ornate presentations—was intense by the turn of the eighteenth century. Prologues and epilogues from both houses also condemned not only excessiveness in staging but the importation of musicians. The prologue to Mary Pix's *The Deceiver Deceived,* at Lincoln's Inn Fields in 1697, complained that

> With Powderle-Pimp of Dance, Machine and Song,
> They'll spin ye out short Nonsense four hours long:
> With Fountains, Groves, Bombast and airy Fancies
> Larded with *Cynthias,* little Loves and Dances:
> Which put together, makes it hard to say,
> If Poet, Painter, or Fidler made the Play.

Music, song, and dance were categorized along with elaborate scenery as decadent and anti-intellectual, as appealing only to the senses, not the intellect.

As the eighteenth century progressed, music remained an important part of theatrical performances, but increasingly it was assigned to the interstices of performances. The playhouse musicians entertained with selected pieces before the curtain rose; entr'acte entertainment included instrumental solos, songs, and especially dances, as well as such additional entertainments as juggling acts, rope or ladder dancing, acrobatics, and other feats of strength and skill. Thirty-six of the seventy performers at Drury Lane in 1730–31 were advertised as dancers, although many were primarily actors, and in 1741–42, twenty-eight of the eighty-eight Covent Garden company members were employed only to dance.[22] For a long time dancing remained the most popular entr'acte entertainment, but Charles Beecher Hogan shows that in the 1780's songs began to compete more regularly.[23]

Furthermore, incidental music remained important. The Covent Garden account books list twenty-one orchestra members in 1757–58 and 1760–61; the Drury Lane treasurer's books list twenty-three for 1778–79.[24] George Winchester Stone records that the annual budget for music at Covent Garden was about £700 up to 1766–67, or about 5 percent of total expenditures, then grew to an average of £1,450 a year, closer to 7 or 7.5 percent, including salaries for performers, purchase of compositions, maintenance of instruments, music copying, etc.[25]

Instrumental music written specifically for the purpose was used to cover transitions between scenes and acts. In the Restoration new act tunes adorned new plays and often revivals of old ones. Each play had its own set of act tunes, seldom reused for other plays. The pieces were brief and sometimes all but indistinguishable from others, but they were regularly original for premieres and important revivals. Nine tunes were usually composed: the first and second music, played before the curtain opened, ordinarily consisted of two pieces each; after the prologue another piece followed as the overture or "curtain tune" to accompany the curtain's rising; four other tunes were written to signal the conclusion of each of the first four acts, for the curtain did not normally ring down until the end of the play. The pieces were short and varied, such as slow airs, brisk airs, gavottes, hornpipes, jigs (gigues), rondeaus ("Round O's"), sarabands, minuets, courantes, allemandes, marches, and chaconnes. They were played by theatre orchestras that ranged at various times from a few musicians to more than thirty.[26] In the eighteenth century, the rage for new act tunes died down,[27] but the principle of covering intermissions with music, albeit increasingly with familiar rather than new music, continued.

In the late 1690s, when the dissolution of the United Company had precipitated feverish competition between Drury Lane and Lincoln's Inn Fields, the theatres began vying for foreign musical talents as a means of winning the battle for audiences. Foreign singers and dancers were imported at ruinously high salaries. The French dancer Balon had a five-week engagement for a stipend of 400 guineas in 1699. Singers also commanded exorbitant salaries that year: the castrato Signor Clementine, for example, earned a reported salary of £500 and another eunuch, Francisco, reportedly earned 120 guineas for five performances. Bernacchi earned £1,200 in 1729–30, Senesino £1,400 in 1730–31.[28] Gradually singers became regular performers at the theatres: Margarita de l'Epine, for example, plus Jemmy Bowen, Maria Gallia, Catherine Tofts, and many more. For the 1698–99 season the known members of Rich's company numbered thirty-eight, nine of whom were singers; of the forty-one known members during the following season, six were singers and four were dancers.[29]

Whereas music had been used within and between scenes in the Restoration, in the 1690s English opera became very important; by 1705 the rage for Italian opera had drastically changed the nature of theatrical seasons. During most of the eighteenth century, the audience's taste for operatic entertainment was indulged to the extent of fifteen to twenty percent of the repertoire. A sampling of London performances in every fifth season from 1714–15 to 1769–70 shows a range from about six percent of the total in 1719–20 to more than thirty percent in 1764–65. In four of the twelve seasons (1714–15, 1724–25, 1759–60, 1769–70) musical performances comprised approximately twenty percent of the total, and in five others (1729–30, 1734–35, 1739–40, 1749–50, 1754–55) approximately fourteen to sixteen percent. In other words, opera was thoroughly entrenched in the theatres, with oratorios and burlettas also popular. The operas of the early period, with music by such composers as Purcell, Eccles, Bononcini, and others, were followed by works of Handel and others such as Arne and Pepusch. By the end of the century, the leading contributors were composers such as Didbin, Shields, and Storace.

The relentless addition of musical accouterments to plays, the importation of ruinously high-salaried foreign singers and dancers, and the constant attempts to mount operas would suggest that music was the best way to sell tickets. Yet Judith Milhous' research into the financing of operas[30] gives pause: if making money at opera was so close to impossible, why did theatre managers continue to try? If famous foreigners drained coffers unreasonably, why were they imported? Although raising ticket prices for musical performances was an accepted practice, the annual opera budget had to be supplemented in many ways: through royal gifts (George I paid an annual £1,000 for seven years); by subsidy from the Royal Academy of Music; and by some ingenious subscription schemes. The opera continued to rely on heavy subsidies to meet its deficits; the annual deficit in the 1740s reached £4–5,000. There were, of course, financial hopes for musical productions of all sorts, the eternal hope that the genre would become self-supporting, the desire to rob the other houses of auditors who would then become devotees of opera:

> Get some She Monster some sixteen Foot high,
> Get some subscription, tho' you don't know why:
> Get some fam'd Opera, any how translated,
> No matter, so the t'other House don't get it.[31]

But the productions were too elaborate, the performers too expensive, and opera never became a steady moneymaker.

Still there were occasional bonanzas. *The Beggar's Opera* truly did make Gay rich, netting him almost £700 from his four benefits, 90 guineas for the copyright to the play and the *Fables,* and a total that has been estimated as high as £2,000. Theatrical manager John Rich probably netted £4,000 or more.[32] Moreover, its success paved the way for Gay's profiting by *Polly,* even though the sequel was never allowed to be staged. Some operas, the popular *Camilla,* for example, had enormously successful runs that raked in huge profits. But taken as a whole, opera could not meet the commercial challenge; it never became a satisfactory business proposition, despite the occasional pots of gold.

Theatrical music was, however, profitable to artists in the theatres, and not only to the most famous imported singers but also to the composers, singers, and dancers who were part of the regular companies. Enterprising playwrights such as Peter Motteux made money writing operas and other novelties; songwriters and composers, not only Henry Purcell but his brother Daniel Purcell and many other lesser talents, cranked out songs for plays; later composers even reset songs from entrenched plays with more contemporary versions; performers such as Jemmy Bowen and Richard Leveridge regularly sang; the playhouse musicians, the many violinists as well as drummers, kettle-drummers, trumpeters, oboists, flautists, lutenists, and others, had regular jobs. The best musicians were connected with the theatres in various ways—English music and theatre were inextricably linked during the period, although concert halls, pleasure gardens, and other entertainments also provided outlets for musical talents.

Theatrical music was profitable to artists and businessmen outside the theatres. Music publishing became an industry of considerable scope. Before the end of the seventeenth century, engraving became the standard method of musical printing, a practice that continued into the nineteenth century.[33] The unrivaled John Playford had engaged printers to set music from movable type until he died in 1686; the pioneer in changing to the far more beautiful process of engraving was Thomas Cross, who not only popularized copper and later other metal engraving, but also "set a standard of artistic workmanship that was rarely equalled by his contemporaries and successors."[34] The 1690s became the watershed for music publication. Competition encouraged publishers such as Cross, John Walsh, and others to apply "high pressure methods to the publication of musical scores—large cheap editions, wide-scale advertisement and considerable surreptitious puffing in the newspapers."[35] Engraving was cheapened by substituting pewter plates for copper; inferior "punched" engravings were used to save money; considerable piracy of foreign music supplemented English publishers' stocks. That the efflorescence of theatre music and of music publishing came simultaneously is by no means coincidental. Cross, "practically the inventor of sheet music," issued many songs from the theatre on inexpensive half-sheet broadsides that "must have come forth in enormous numbers."[36] Cross and Walsh both sometimes published the same theatrical songs, and sometimes other competitors joined them. Moreover, popular songs were reissued from the old plates to meet the demand. Single songs, cheap, attractive, and readily available, were sometimes collected into volumes, headed by elaborately engraved title pages. Walsh was particularly adept at collections, in which he included engravings of songs also sold separately. The broadsides and collected songs ordinarily included the vocal line, the words, and the flute accompaniment.

Engravings of both vocal and instrumental theatrical music were issued during the late seventeenth and early eighteenth centuries. Walsh published more than fifty sets of act music for plays and dramatic operas in the first decade of the eighteenth century, mostly as separate numbers in *Harmonia Anglicana, or the Musick of the English Stage*.[37] Other collections also included act tunes, for example, Henry Purcell's *A Collection of Ayres, Compos'd for the Theatre* (1697). But after the first decade of the century, publication of overtures and act tunes abated, and for many years few were published, although Handel's still appeared. In the 1740s two pantomime overtures were published, and in the 1750s a few opera overtures appeared. During the 1760s and 1770s publication of instrumental scores increased, but it declined in the 1780s and 1790s; only one English opera overture of that period survives.[38]

From 1743 to 1762 full scores were published for eleven operas; only two more full scores appeared during the next twenty years. However, vocal scores, complete with choruses, were widely published after 1763; Fiske counts at least eighty. Full scores provided the orchestration necessary for performances in provincial towns, but they proved too expensive to be profitable; the vocal scores on two or three staves, whether complete with choruses or not, found a steady market because they allowed the songs to be sung and accompanied at home.

The engraved scores usually appeared a month or more after the stage premieres. Fiske says that the delay was caused by the time required for engraving. Theatre companies made agreements with playwrights not to publish play texts until after the first run, and opera publication may sometimes have been influenced by similar considerations, although "reading" an opera would not have replaced hearing it.

According to Fiske, all but the most famous composers paid for the engraving, printing, binding, and paper for publishing their scores. Engraving was considerably more expensive than setting type: vocal scores for full-length productions sold for 10s. 6d., those for afterpieces for about 6s. By 1783, James Harrison was trying to win business by bargains: he offered the *New Musical Magazine*, with a sixteen-page vocal score as a supplement, for a mere 1s. 6d., with the complete vocal score of the *Messiah* as the bonus for having purchased five consecutive issues.[39]

Large-scale music publication appears to have been profitable. Walsh is said to have cleared £1,500 on Handel's *Rinaldo* in 1711, and he left a fortune of £30,000 at his death. His son John Walsh, also a music publisher, left £40,000.[40] By the end of the century, John Longman paid William Shield a thousand guineas for *The Woodman* and Storace 500 each for most of his operas, a generosity that Fiske believes may have contributed to the publisher's bankruptcy in 1798.[41] From the half-sheet broadsides of Cross to the operas of Longman, the business of publishing theatrical music had enriched publishers and sometimes subsidized composers.

Libretti were also published, often sold in the theatre, sometimes given to opera subscribers. The words of theatrical songs were published in periodicals such as *The Muses Mercury* and collected in volumes such as *Pills to Purge Melancholy*. Gagey found 123 published ballad operas, mostly in the 1730s.[42] Perhaps the most unusual form of publication was the printing of various airs from *The Beggar's Opera*, complete with the lyrics, the flute line, and a notation of the character who sang each, on a pack of playing cards.

London theatre spawned provincial performances, not only of the plays and operas but of the music. Both through popularization in the theatre and through the medium of print, the music found its way to all parts of the kingdom, and musicians and home hobbyists took advantage of it. The economic ripples from theatrical music spread.

Fiction

The relationship between drama and fiction is, of course, of a different kind from that between theatre and the visual and musical arts. Fiction involves only the medium of print; the two arts borrowed from one another, but they could not be melded into a single performance. Drama was first and foremost public; the reading of fiction was private. Yet the influence of each on the other and the shared commercial necessities in publication caused close connections between the two genres.

Interrelationships between fiction and drama were cultural, social, and commercial. Plays and fiction were directed toward the same audience, published in the same inexpensive, large-scale operations, and rewarded by the same kinds of usually modest compensation. Authors wrote for an audience that both attended the theatre and read fiction, and often the authors themselves had experience in both genres. Successful stage gimmicks were incorporated into fiction, and vice versa.

Seventeenth-century fiction, as Charles C. Mish has shown, divides into two genres, romantic fiction of refined love and grand adventures, aimed at the polite, and realistic short tales of "rough and lively doings of middle-class actors in everyday settings, aimed at the vulgar."[43] But the audience of the eighteenth-century novel was aimed at the polite, the moneyed middle class and women of some education and leisure. The novels shared with the romances first of all the need for ample reading time. The evolution in reading tastes is illustrated by comparing two well-known featherbrained readers, Biddy Tipkin of Steele's *The Tender Husband* (1705) and Lydia Languish of Sheridan's *The Rivals* (1775). Biddy's head is "full of Shepherds, Knights, Flowery Meads, Groves and Streams" from French romances such as *Cassandra, Astraea,* and *Clelia,* all of which had multivolume English translations. (The same romances were listed in Leonora's library in *Spectator* No. 37, with *Clelia* opening "of it self in the Place that describes two Lovers in a Bower.") Lydia's acquisitions from the circulating library include a great variety of recent novels: *The Fatal Connection* by Mrs. Fogerty: *The Mistakes of the Heart* by Treyssac de Vergy, and *The Tears of Sensibility* by Baculard d'Arnaut, the latter two both translated from the French; *The Delicate Distress* by Elizabeth Griffith and *The Gordian Knot* by her husband Richard Griffith (published together as *Two Novels in Letters*); and other romantic folderol, as well as *Peregrine Pickle, Humphry Clinker,* and the second volume of *The Sentimental Journey.* Lydia is in many ways a direct descendant of Biddy; each reads the fiction fashionable in her own time, and although the fiction is considerably different, each suffers the same romantic ideas as a result. The fact that Lydia, doubtless by mistake, borrows Smollett and Sterne as well as romantic novels punctuates the ironies of her reading list.

As plays contain references to fiction, eighteenth-century novels contain numerous references to the theatre. A few examples will suffice: Fielding's Partridge in *Tom Jones* sees Garrick perform in Drury Lane; he is not impressed—the man was not acting, he really *was* afraid of Hamlet's ghost. Evelina effuses, "Well may Mr. Garrick be so celebrated, so universally admired—I had not any idea of so great a performer." Pamela writes a critique of Steeles's *Tender Husband,* first staged and printed thirty-five years earlier, deploring its improbability, unnaturalness, and lack of morality.[44] The play's heroine, Biddy, is quoted or paraphrased in both *Clarissa* and *Sir Charles Grandison,* and Clarissa finds a copy of Steele's plays in Madame Sinclair's library. George Primrose, son of the Vicar of Wakefield, takes a turn at being a strolling actor. Why, one must wonder, were such references included? To test Evelina's London poise at the theatre is entirely understandable, since the theatre was central to cultural and social life. But why did Fielding go out of his way to compliment Garrick in a scene scarcely indispensable to the novel? Why did Richardson choose to have Pamela discuss *The Tender Husband* or indeed any other play? Part of the answer to all these questions must be that the theatre was so familiar to the audience of the novel that references were particularly allusive.

A surprising number of writers of fiction tried their hands at drama, and dramatists tried theirs at fiction. Both Congreve and Farquhar wrote short "novels"; Congreve's *Incognita* was published in 1692 before his first play appeared in October 1693; Farquhar's *Adventures of Covent Garden* was issued a fortnight before his first play *Love and a Bottle* was published and probably about a fortnight after it had opened. The first of Aphra Behn's nineteen plays was staged in 1670; her first novel appeared in 1684. Fielding's fictional career began only after his theatrical career came to an abrupt halt with the Licensing Act of 1737. Goldsmith's novel preceded his first play by six years. Smollett gave tragedy a try shortly before his first novel appeared in 1748. By 1749 he had received £100 for an English opera, *Alceste;* Handel wrote the music and Servandoni painted the scenes for an opening at Covent Garden in 1749–50., but the opera was never performed.[45] His two-act farce, *The Reprisal,* on the other hand, was a great success at Drury Lane in 1757. After establishing herself as a novelist, Charlotte Lennox wrote *The Sister,* but it was treated so harshly when it opened at Covent Garden in 1767 that she withdrew it after the first night; *Old City Manners,* her adaptation of *Eastward Hoe*!, fared much better at Drury Lane in 1775, and despite a few hisses the first night, survived a healthy run.[46] Even Dr. Johnson tried his hand at both genres: *Irene* was staged at Drury Lane in 1749, and *Rasselas* appeared in 1759.

Moreover, fictional materials were turned into drama. Farquhar used some of his farcical material from *The Adventures of Covent Garden* as subplot in *The Constant Couple*. Some of Aphra Behn's novels were metamorphosed into drama; for example, Thomas Southerne based *The Fatal Marriage* on her *The Unhappy Vow-Breaker* in 1694 and wrote *Oroonoko*, based on her novel, the following year, and Catherine Trotter's dramatization of *Agnes de Castro* appeared the same season. Thomas D'Urfey brought adventures of Don Quixote on stage in three parts in 1694 and 1695. Joseph Reed turned *Tom Jones* into a comic opera, which opened in 1769. Lillo even took a tale from the old ballad of George Barnwell as material for *The London Merchant* in 1731. The prose version of *The Tempest* printed in this volume is a rare example of drama becoming material for prose fiction.

The close interrelationships between novels and drama are in part explicable because they were written for the same audience, primarily the gentry and middle class with enough leisure to attend the theatre and read books and with enough money to afford the two forms of entertainment. Published plays and novels were marketed to the same groups of people and were assigned the same relative importance in libraries.

Booksellers took seriously their responsibility to publish and market respectable tomes—scientific repositories, ecclesiastical works, law books, histories, dictionaries, and other prestigious works—and they did so on heavy paper in large formats. Herbals, travel books, and other volumes using handsome plates grew in popularity. "How-to" manuals became another important although less distinguished area of publication, including books on how to be a good wife, how to cure ailments, and how to cook. Fiction and drama fit into the category of books considered less significant, advertised less consistently, and printed with less loving care. Addison describes in Leonara's library "That Part of the Library which was designed for the Reception of Plays and Pamphlets, and other loose Papers." Plays were often sold unbound, and fiction could also be published in this inexpensive, casual fashion. Both plays and fiction could in some instances be purchased in parts; Shakespeare's plays, for example, were issued in parts in the 1730s by Jacob Tonson and Robert Walker at a price of a mere penny a sheet or approximately four pence a play, during the great Shakespeare publishing war.[47]

Play publication was directly related to performance, and as a result a group of theatre-related conventions developed: the title page usually stated that the play was printed "As it was Acted at" a given theatre; the original cast was listed in the Dramatis Personae; prefaces sometimes carried commentary about the theatrical problems or successes of the piece. Reading a play could help someone visualize a performance he had not seen. Or it could provide an effective way to reconstruct a performance the reader had attended and gain the verbal resonances perhaps lost in the theatre.[48] Booksellers decreased the time between the premiere and publication of plays as a merchandising strategy to capitalize on the interest in the staged production, and on occasion copies were sold in the theatres. Published editions could also serve as prompt books for productions.

But whereas published music could only be enjoyed when used as a performance text, in fact published plays were also literary texts, meant for enjoyment in the quiet of one's closet as surely as novels were. To the reading public, the published play became not only a way to reconstruct a specific theatrical performance or a promptbook for mounting a new one; it became a way to read and visualize a story, and in that sense the function of published plays greatly resembled the function of printed fiction. With the exception of the folios of a few distinguished playwrights such as Shakespeare and Jonson, plays, like novels, were not considered serious literature. Yet cheap, unpretentious, and eminently readable as they were, they sold well.

Women read plays and fiction, a fact often considered worthy of comment. To many minds women who read resembled bears who danced; even so, if women were to read, prudence suggested they should address works that taught them religious devotion and housewifery. Alas, they tended to show some considerable interest in works of the imagination as opposed to *The Ladies Calling* by the author of *The Whole Duty of Man* or *The Fifteen Comforts of Matrimony* or indeed other works considered useful and appropriate. Therefore women were satirized, even by proponents of their education such as Addison and Steele, for preferring plays and fiction. In *Spectator* No. 92, Addison's attempt to compile a lady's library begins with recommendations of the publishers (their own publications) and suggestions of husbands (books advocating virtue, recipes for food and medicine, *Wingate's Arithmetick*, etc.) before turning to the choices of the ladies, who prefer romances, principally *Pharamond* and *Cassandra*, and Restoration tragedies, including Dryden's *All for Love* and *Aureng-Zebe*, Southerne's *The Fatal Marriage*, and Lee's *Sophonisba, Mithridates King of Pontus, The Rival Queens*, and *Theodosius*. Addison claims to take his task seriously because most books are "calculated for Male Readers, and generally written with an Eye to Men of Learning." Eustace Budgell in *Spectator* No. 365 jokingly warns about the dangers of the month of May, "which infuses a kindly Warmth into the Earth, and all its Inhabitants," and specifically warns women that during May they should be careful "how they meddle with Romances, Chocolate, Novels, and the like Inflamers" and continues, "As for that part of the Fair Sex, who stay in Town. . . . If they cannot forbear the Play-house, I would recommend *Tragedy* to them, rather than *Comedy;* and should think the *Puppet-show* much safer for them than the *Opera,* all the while the Sun is in *Gemini.*"

As the century progressed, novels and plays were often mentioned as the favorite reading matter of women, but men certainly read them too. The consumer's attitude toward novels and plays was somewhat akin to the modern attitude toward paperbacks—people read them with great frequency but did not consider them important library acquisitions. A strong market existed, not only for early, quickly printed editions, but also for reprints, and in the case of some works, frequent reprints. Both plays and novels were illustrated, and the same artists created plates for both: Hogarth, for example, created five frontispieces for the five-volume translation of the romance *Cassandra* (third edition, 1725) and drew two illustrations for *Tristram Shandy* in 1760, as well as illustrating theatrical pieces as diverse as James Miller's *The Humours of Oxford* (1730), Fielding's *The Tragedy of Tragedies* (1730–31), Joseph Mitchell's opera *The Highland Fair* (1731), Joseph Huggins's oratorio *Judith* (1733), and Garrick's interlude *The Farmer's Return from London* (1762).[49] Many of his 1730s illustrations were engraved by Gerard van der Gucht. With both multivolume fiction and collections of plays, frontispieces became standard by the 1730s, at least in reprints and collections.

Although drama and fiction were closely interrelated throughout the period, a number of events in the late 1730s and 1740s culminated in even closer relationships and more favorable conditions for publication. The Licensing Act of 1737, first of all, limited legitimate theatre to the two patent houses and required that plays be licensed by the Lord Chamberlain's office. Opportunities for writers were considerably lessened, and the repertory relied even more heavily on Shakespeare and the turn-of-the-century comic writers than it had in years past. The plays of Congreve, Vanbrugh, Cibber, Farquhar, and Steele, for example, jumped from eighteen percent of the total repertory in 1734–35 to twenty-seven percent in 1739–40 and twenty-eight percent in 1744–45.[50] Henry Fielding, manager of the company in the Little Theatre in the Haymarket, left the theatre altogether. The time was ripe, certainly, for application of creative talents to a new genre, the novel.

Moreover, the business world was ready for the novel. Publishers had for a long time developed a clientele of readers for works of the imagination. Through their experience with plays and other popular literature, they had geared themselves for economical printing of materials that appealed to a large audience. Circulating libraries had become well established by the 1740s, large ones in London as well as a network in spas and provincials centers. If novels, because of their length, might be considered expensive to purchase, they could be borrowed with ease; they were the most popular items in circulating libraries, with plays following as second.[51]

Not surprisingly, then, shared literary traditions enriched both genres, with the theatre deeply influencing the conventions of the early novel. Dramatic subject matter, characterization, plot development, dialogue, and visual effects found their way into fiction, not only the short fiction of the early period, but the novels we think of as characteristic of the English tradition.

The comic novels were most deeply affected by the theatre. They usually have a courtship plot as a central action. Although they do not necessarily emulate drama in the common pattern of two young couples, a serious pair and a pair of amatory gamesplayers, they sometimes do, and, like stage comedies, they sometimes contain a pair of young servants who comically echo the serious love plot. Adventures and rescues are interspersed with delicate drawing-room scenes in both genres, and closure usually comes with the promise or consummation of the marriage vows, often of more than one couple.

Heroes frequently resemble the rash but goodhearted young men that populate the comedies. They win the heroines by a process of maturation: that is, they vow to discard their not terribly wicked ways in favor of a sincere, sedentary, faithful marriage. The heroines are either paragons reminiscent of Steele's Indiana or more spirited and headstrong girls reminiscent of Farquhar's Sylvia; Fielding's Amelia is a married version of the first, Sophia Western a prime example of the second.

Stock characterizations in the novels also echo stage traditions. Heavy fathers, country bumpkins, sly servants and faithful servants, unctuous, unappealing suitors, antiquated virgins—the list is extensive. Fictional heroines, like dramatic ones, tend not to have mothers, although they are often blessed with aging spinster aunts eager to provide good advice on courtship and matrimony: Barsheba Tipkin in *The Tender Husband* and Mrs. Western in *Tom Jones* share some surprising verbal similarities, and Tabitha in *Humphry Clinker* is a sister character. Squire Western is cut from the same cloth as Steele's Sir Harry Gubbin and other antecedent country squires, irascible, unreasonable parents, who despise London and cannot cope with intrigue. Matthew Bramble, softened and sentimentalized, also owes something to the stage tradition of pleasurably eccentric country gentlemen. Comic servants are descended from generations of theatrical forebears. The parallels are multitudinous, the similarities too strong to be denied.

The courtship plots also move in analogous ways: courtships involve some duplicity between lovers, often necessary and sometimes unintentional. They are resolved through highly improbable plots of trickery and disguise, with misdirected letters, unkept assignations, unrealized mistaken identities, and happy endings. Sons and daughters rediscover long-lost parents; lovers are reunited against overwhelming odds; old offenses are forgiven in a spirit of unstinting benevolence.

Novels rely to some extent on dialogue, and the dialogue carries theatrical overtones, complete sometimes with what amounts to stage directions. *Tom Jones* contains excellent examples of the kind of dialogue, speech indications, and "stage directions" that evoke stage scenes:

"Inclinations!" cries the Aunt, with some Warmth. "Inclinations! I am astonished at your Assurance. A young Woman of your Age, and unmarried, to talk of Inclinations! But whatever your Inclinations may be, my Brother is resolved; nay, since you talk of Inclinations, I shall advise him to hasten the Treaty. Inclinations!"

Sophia then flung herself upon her Knees, and Tears began to trickle from her shining Eyes. . . .

"I hope, Madam," cries *Sophia*, with a little Elevation of Voice, "I shall never do any Thing to dishonour my Family; but as for Mr. *Blifil*, whatever may be the Consequence, I am resolved against him, and no Force shall prevail in his Favour."

Western, who had been within hearing during the greater Part of the preceding Dialogue, had now exhausted all his Patience; he therefore entered the Room in a violent Passion, crying, "D——n me then if *shatunt* ha' un, d——n me if *shatunt*, that's all—that's all—D——n me if *shatunt*."[52]

The reader of plays is well prepared to read and visualize the dialogue.

Fielding captured the fervor of the wonder-filled stage denouement when he used the verb "cries" for seven successive speeches in his discovery scene:

"Hast nut gin thy Consent, *Sophy*, to be married To-morrow?" "Such are your Commands, Sir," cries *Sophia*, "and I dare not be guilty of Disobedience." "I hope Madam," cries *Allworthy*, "my Nephew will merit so much Goodness, and will be always as sensible as myself, of the great Honour you have done my Family. . . ." "Yes," cries *Western*, "but if I had suffered her to stand shill I shall I, dilly dally, you might not have had that Honour yet awhile; I was forced to use a little fatherly Authority to bring her to." "I hope not, Sir," cries *Allworthy*. "I hope there is not the least Constraint." "Why there," cries *Western*, "you may bid her unsay all again, if you will. Do'st repent heartily of thy Promise, do'st not *Sophy?*" "Indeed, Papa," cries she, "I do not repent, nor do I believe I ever shall, of any Promise in favour of Mr. *Jones*." "Then, Nephew," cries *Allworthy*, "I felicitate you most heartily; for I think you are the happiest of Men. And, Madam, you will give me leave to congratulate you on this joyful Occasion: indeed I am convinced you have bestowed yourself on one who will be sensible of your great Merit, and who will at least use his best Endeavors to deserve it." "His best Endeavors!" cries *Western*, "that he will I warrant un."[53]

The denouement has a familiar ring to those who see and read plays.

Furthermore, the use of eccentricities of speech—speech tags, dialect indicated by orthographical conventions, malapropisms, slang, and colloquialisms given to particular characters—derived from stage conventions. Direct quotations of speech in novels allowed authors to use the stage conventions of dialogue to produce effects that could not be created through paraphrase. Quoted dialogue in novels reads like the printed dialogue in published plays.

The novel also carefully sets scenes and costumes characters, through description rather than visual evocation. Props are used—one is reminded of Sophia's muff in *Tom Jones,* for example, not to mention the swords and cudgels, mirrors, and masks that give clues to character and figure prominently in the action of novels.[54]

The interrelationships between the theatre and the novel, then, truly were cultural and social as well as commercial. The audience was, by and large, the same: individuals with enough leisure and money to enjoy the theatre and read published plays and fiction. A group of writers with experience in both genres were prominent creators of both kinds of literature. A group of publishers, using mass-production methods based on cheap printing, produced salable materials, enhanced in later editions with engravings by the finest hands (Rowlandson, for example, illustrated Smollett's novels). As a result, dramatists and novelists drew from a common store of conventions, not only in plot materials but also in devices of dialogue, characterization, setting, costume, and gestures. Comedies were short and comic novels were often long, but they both described a familiar world; domestic tragedies perhaps prepared the way for tragic or serious novels; operas appealed to the craving for the exotic, satisfied by romances. And reprints in duodecimo made both plays and novels easily and economically available to an ever-growing group of readers.

Mackintosh describes the Georgian era as a Golden Age because the fine and theatre arts were so closely intertwined.[55] It was an era of expansion for truly popular theatre. It was also, as Plumb shows, a time of astonishing expansion in the development and marketing of leisure. The resulting growth of interest in theatre and the other arts resulted in the intertwining of artistic efforts. The audience of the theatre bought engravings if not paintings, played from sheet music and sang at home, read novels. Artists and businessmen in all genres seized the opportunity to coordinate their efforts for art and profit. And the profits were certainly there. The hope for windfalls sprang eternal. Modest sums were available for those who participated in publication—writers, artists, engravers, composers, printers, and certainly the booksellers who encouraged reproductions of words, music, and pictures. Small sums fell to the creators of porcelain figures and plaques with actors' portraits, the builders of sets, the costumers, and presumably the cleaners of feathers. But those who profited the most perhaps were the consumers, whose lives were enriched by the ready accessibility of theatre and the other arts.

Notes

1. *The London Stage, 1660–1800,* ed. William Van Lennep, Emmett L. Avery, Arthur H. Scouten, George Winchester Stone, and Charles Beecher Hogan (Carbondale, Ill.: Southern Illinois University Press, 1960–68), part 1, 522. All information on performances is taken from *The London Stage* unless otherwise noted.

2. George Winchester Stone, Jr., "The Making of the Repertory," in *The London Theatre World, 1660–1800*, ed. Robert D. Hume (Carbondale, Ill.: Southern Illinois Univ. Press, 1980), pp. 181–209.

3. J. H. Plumb, *The Commercialisation of Leisure in Eighteenth-Century England* (Reading: University of Reading, 1973), pp. 3–4.

4. Judith Milhous and Robert D. Hume, "Dating Play Premières from Publication Data, 1660–1700," *Harvard Library Bulletin* 22 (1974), 374–405.

5. By the early 1720s octavo first editions had become common. See Shirley Strum Kenny, "The Publication of Plays," in *The London Theatre World*, p. 324.

6. John Dennis, *A Defense of Sir Fopling Flutter, A Comedy Written by Sir George Etherege*, in *The Critical Works of John Dennis*, ed. Edward Niles Hooker, 2 vols. (Baltimore: Johns Hopkins University Press, 1939–43), 2 : 241.

7. *The London Stage*, part 1, p. lxxxiv.

8. Richard Cumberland, *Memoirs of Richard Cumberland Written by Himself* (1806; repr. Philadelphia: Parry and McMillan, 1856), p. 387.

9. Sybil Rosenfeld, "Landscape in English Scenery in the Eighteenth Century," in *Essays on the Eighteenth-Century English Stage*, ed. Kenneth Richards and Peter Thomson (London: Methuen, 1972), p. 171.

10. *Freeholder's Journal*, 28 November 1722.

11. *Spectator* No. 5, quoted from *The Spectator*, ed. Donald F. Bond, 5 vols. (Oxford: Clarendon, 1965), 1 : 24–25. All quotations are from this edition.

12. Kalman A. Burnim, "Some Notes on Aaron Hill and Stage Scenery," *Theatre Notebook* 12 (1957): 30.

13. Rosenfeld, p. 177.

14. Judith Milhous, "Company Management," in *The London Theatre World*, pp. 17–18.

15. *A Biographical Dictionary of Actors, Actresses, Musicians, Dancers, Managers, and Other Stage Personnel in London, 1660–1800*, ed. Philip H. Highfill, Jr., Kalman A. Burnim, and Edward A. Langhans, vol. 4 (Carbondale, Ill.: Southern Illinois University Press, 1975), pp. 308–11.

16. See Kalman A. Burnim, "Looking upon His Like Again: Garrick and the Artist," pp. 182–218 below. Also *The Georgian Playhouse, Actors, Audiences, and Architecture, 1730–1830*, exhibition catalogue; exhibition devised by Iain Mackintosh assisted by Geoffrey Ashton (London: Arts Council of Great Britain, 1975), parts 3, 4.

17. For Hogarth's theatrical work, see Mary F. Klinger, "William Hogarth and London Theatrical Life," in *Studies in Eighteenth-Century Culture*, vol. 5, ed. Ronald C. Rosbottom (Madison, Wisc.: University of Wisconsin Press, 1976), pp. 22–27.

18. Ronald Paulson, *Hogarth: His Life, Art, and Times*, 2 vols. (New Haven, Conn., and London: Yale University Press, 1971), 1 : 182.

19. Ronald Paulson, "*The Harlot's Progress* and the Tradition of History Painting," *Eighteenth-Century Studies* 1 (1967): 85.

20. *Georgian Playhouse*, item 80.

21. Curtis A. Price, "Music as Drama," in *The London Theatre World*, p. 210.

22. *The London Stage*, part 3, 1 : clv.

23. Ibid., part 5, 1 : lxxxiii.

24. Ibid., part 4, 1 : cxxvii.

25. Ibid., p. cxxix.

26. Curtis A. Price, *Music in the Restoration Theatre*, Studies in Musicology, No. 4 (Ann Arbor, Mich.: UMI Research Press, 1979), pp. 53–81.

27. Roger Fiske, *English Theatre Music in the Eighteenth Century* (London: Oxford University Press, 1973), p. 259.

28. *The London Stage*, passim.

29. Ibid., part 1, pp. 501–2, 514.

30. Judith Milhous, "The Multimedia Spectacular on the Restoration Stage," pp. 41–66 below.

31. Epilogue, *The Temple of Love, A Pastoral Opera* by Peter Motteux, 7 March 1706.

32. Edmond McAdoo Gagey, *Ballad Opera* (New York: Columbia University Press, 1937), p. 36.

33. Charles Humphries and William C. Smith, *Music Publishing in the British Isles* (London: Cassell and Company, 1954), p. 14.

34. Ibid., pp. 14–15.

35. Plumb, *Commercialisation*, p. 8.

36. *Grove's Dictionary of Music and Musicians*, 5th ed., ed. Eric Blom (1954; rpt. New York: St. Martin's Press, 1968), 6:825.

37. Price, *Music in the Restoration Theatre*, p. 237.

38. Fiske, pp. 298–99.

39. Ibid., pp. 293–301.

40. *Grove's Dictionary*, 9: 152, 153.

41. Fiske, p. 300.

42. Gagey, pp. 237–43.

43. Charles C. Mish, *Short Fiction of the Seventeenth Century* (New York: New York University Press, 1963), pp. vii–xvi.

44. *Pamela in Her Exalted Condition*, Volume 4, Letter 15.

45. *The London Stage*, part 4, 1:97, 179.

46. Ibid., 3:1386.

47. Giles E. Dawson, "Robert Walker's Editions of Shakespeare," in *Studies in Renaissance Drama*, ed. Josephine Waters Bennett, Oscar Cargill, and Vernon Hall, Jr. (New York: New York University Press, 1959), pp. 58–81.

48. See Peter Holland, *The Ornament of Action, Text and Performance in Restoration Comedy* (Cambridge: Cambridge University Press, 1979), pp. 99–137.

49. Hanns Hammelmann, *Book Illustrators in Eighteenth-Century England*, ed. T. S. R. Boase (New Haven, Conn., and London: Yale University Press, 1975), pp. 56–57.

50. Shirley Strum Kenny, "Perennial Favorites: Congreve, Vanbrugh, Cibber, Farquhar, and Steele," *Modern Philology* 73 (1976): S6.

51. Plumb, *Commercialisation*, p. 8.

52. Henry Fielding, *Tom Jones*, ed. Martin C. Battestin and Fredson Bowers, 2 vols. (Middletown, Conn.: Wesleyan University Press and Oxford: Clarendon Press, 1975), 1:333–35.

53. Fielding, *Tom Jones*, 2:975–76.

54. See, for example, Leo Hughes, "Theatrical Convention in Richardson: Some Observations on a Novelist's Technique," in *Restoration and Eighteenth-Century Literature*, ed. Carroll Camden (Chicago: University of Chicago Press, 1963), pp. 239–50.

55. *Georgian Playhouse*, introduction.

Theatre, Music, and Dance

2

The Multimedia Spectacular on the Restoration Stage

JUDITH MILHOUS

"English opera," or "semi-opera" as Roger North sourly dubbed it, remains largely forgotten and ignored. There are reasons for this neglect. We possess no scene designs for these productions, and we lack even a floor plan for the Dorset Garden Theatre, in which they were staged. The music which has been preserved is for the most part frustratingly incomplete.[1] Staging has not been a major preoccupation of students of Restoration drama. Most ordinary Restoration comedies and tragedies (*The Country-Wife* and *All for Love,* for example) make no very great technical demands on a theatre. When thinking of a "fancy" production from this period, critics tend to refer to *The Conquest of Granada,* whose "very glorious scenes and perspectives" impressed John Evelyn when it was staged at the Bridges Street Theatre in 1670–71.[2] Yet the works that extended the technical capacities of the Restoration theatre to their utmost are what may best be called the "Dorset Garden spectaculars," a series mounted under Betterton's direction between 1673 and 1692. These works include the "operatic" versions of *Macbeth* and *The Tempest* staged in 1673 and 1674, Shadwell's *Psyche* (1675), Charles Davenant's *Circe* (1677), Dryden's *Albion and Albanius* (1685), Betterton's *The Prophetess* (1690), Dryden's *King Arthur* (1691), and *The Fairy-Queen* (1692), attributed to Settle. Taken together, these shows constitute a significant sub-genre: they, not the heroic plays, were the blockbuster efforts of the most successful Restoration theatre companies. The Dorset Garden spectaculars took the Restoration theatre into a whole new realm.

"English opera" is hard to define precisely. Such a work combines spoken dialogue with music and dance, fancy scenery, and special staging effects. Given that many Restoration plays employ all these elements, we must grant that the difference is often one of degree rather than kind. But as I will demonstrate, the scale of production puts these shows in a special category. Indeed, they were not technically feasible until the 1670s. Scenery was important in the 1660s, of course: after Davenant opened Lincoln's Inn Fields with its changeable scenery, Killigrew had to counter by building the Bridges Street Theatre. But Pepys often speaks of going to "hear" a play, and John Downes, prompter throughout the period, mentions scenery only four times in relation to productions before 1673. To judge by his reports, once the initial novelty of scenery had worn off, the companies put money into costumes.[3]

The building of the Dorset Garden Theatre in 1671 gave the Duke's Company the sort of venue for music, dance, and scenic display of which its founder, Davenant, had dreamed back in the 1630s.[4] Probably Thomas Betterton arranged the theatre's elaborate machinery after making a trip to France to study Continental practices.[5] The theatre was apparently not fully rigged for machine productions until 1673, when Settle's *The Empress of Morocco* was mounted and promptly drew an energetic if disjointed travesty from the rival King's Company.[6] The kind of staging accorded Settle's play was soon exploited in more elaborate and more expensive productions, and the Duke's Company (the United Company after 1682) maintained a predilection for "opera" which lasted as long as Betterton had Dorset Garden available to him.

Any study of these operas suffers from the double problem of missing music and limited literary merit.[7] These works now lie very dead on the printed page—in part a result of the common practice of creating operas by cutting down old plays to make space for spectacle and song. But from the standpoint of what these shows meant to the Restoration theatregoer and to the management, there is much to be learned from the evidence we do possess.

The Nature of the Dorset Garden Spectacular: Some Questions of Effect, Scale, and Cost

The key factors that differentiate the Dorset Garden spectacular from ordinary plays are the extent of the use of music, the size of the cast, and the elaborateness of the staging—in particular the use of fancy machines and flyings. Some sense of the visual element can be conveyed by quoting two representative stage directions. Machines are used sparingly in *Circe*, but as an integral part of the plot, rather than just as decoration. For example, in act 3:

> The *Scene* opens to the inward part of the Temple; *Orestes* is discovered crown'd, as to the Sacrifice; with him *Diana's* Priests bearing her Images, *Pylades*, Guards and Attendants. . . . As [the priests] go to kill *Orestes*, two

Dragons rise out of the Earth, and bear him away; *Circe* appears in a Chariot drawn by Dragons. . . . [and] Flyes away.[8]

The Prophetess is an altogether more complex production, one sequence of which is a vision produced by Delphia for Dioclesian:

> She waves her Wand thrice. Soft Musick is heard. Then the Curtain rises, and shews a stately Tomb: *Aurelia* lying in the midst of it, on a Bed of State. . . . *Delphia* stamps, and it vanishes: behind it is seen a large *Cupola*, supported by *Termes* on Pedestals. The Prophetess waves her Wand, the *Termes* leap from their Pedestalls, the Building falls, and the *Termes* and *Cupola* are turn'd into a Dance of Butterflies. (pp. 46–47)

This sort of exuberant display is one of the defining characteristics of the English opera.

At this juncture a knotty problem must be faced. Just how literally can we take stage directions? As Edward A. Langhans's *Restoration Promptbooks* shows, the theatres did not always do what the printed quartos called for.[9] In performance of ordinary plays, the companies tended to simplify, and for them most scenery and costumes were drawn from stock. But for operas we have good evidence that Dorset Garden could and did produce the dazzling effects described. As early as *The Tempest* in 1674 a pamphlet libretto of the songs and masques was either distributed free or sold to the audience during the first run—a device unprecedented in the English theatre. *The Songs in Circe* was licensed for publication while that opera was playing. The libretto of Dryden's *Albion and Albanius* was available to the audience, with his word that the printed descriptions of special effects were provided by Betterton, who devised and staged them.[10] For Betterton to describe something other than what the audience was seeing would have rendered the performance ridiculous. Stage directions must be treated cautiously. They are evidence not necessarily of what *was* done but of what could be done—and for operas, probably was.

The attractiveness of the staging tricks characteristic of the operas is evident in the "machine farce" boom of the 1680s. Such plays as Shadwell's *The Lancashire Witches* (1681), Behn's *The Emperor of the Moon* (1687), Mountfort's *Dr. Faustus* (1688), and Dryden's *Amphitryon* (1690) abandon the quasi-realism of more familiar Restoration comedies and indulge freely in fantasy and the supernatural. These plays were obviously written to capitalize on the staging capacities of Dorset Garden without incurring the sort of expense an opera entailed.

One further indication of the attractiveness of the operas is the revival of scenes from them as afterpieces or added attractions after 1700. Even the original scenery from the 1670s seems to have retained some appeal. In the summer of 1704 the Drury Lane Company (which had removed a lot of scenery from the largely abondoned Dorset Garden Theatre, damaged in the great storm of November 1703) suddenly began advertising "original" scenery for the thirty-year-old *Empress of Morocco*, and assured potential patrons of *Psyche:* "All the Scenes and Flyings as they were formerly presented" (9 June).[11]

Performing "Ordinary" Plays

Before we turn to a survey of the major spectaculars, some grounds for comparison with "ordinary" plays need to be laid out. Evidence is hard to accumulate, but only by looking into such matters does one get a sense of what was special about the Dorset Garden spectacular.

In a normal season a company played around 200 days.[12] If each of four new productions succeeded to the extent of a ten-day run over the course of the season (a highly optimistic assumption), there would still be 160 days to fill with stock plays. Twenty-five productions, old and new, averaging eight days apiece, would fill an ideally balanced season. In the decade 1669–70 to 1678–79, we know about the performance of 132 plays by the Duke's company, 73 of them new. For the King's Company, we know of 92 productions, 45 of them involving new scripts.[13] The King's Company ran fewer plays longer than the Duke's Company, which was always more experimental.

The size of the company necessary to mount the standard repertory remained quite steady. Seven of the Duke's Company's more successful plays, evaluated on the basis of Downes' reports and performances recorded in *The London Stage*, indicate the basic company for stock plays. A certain amount of doubling to cover minor characters is probable, but these numbers cannot be much reduced.

The Villain	11 men	5 women	servants, fiddlers, etc.
Sir Martin Mar-all	5 men	5 women	a carrier, bayliffs, other servants
The Sullen Lovers	11 men	5 women	sargent with musketeers, waiters, fiddlers, etc.
She wou'd if she cou'd	6–7 men	6 women	waiters, fiddlers, and other attendants
Don Carlos	6 men	4 women	attendants, guards
Titus & Berenice	5 men	2 women	no attendants mentioned
plus *Scapin*	7 men	2 women	no attendants mentioned
The Orphan	7 men	4 women	no attendants mentioned

Not surprisingly, most plays called for roughly the number of performers the company had on hand. More could be added for group scenes, but by and large these plays do not include crowds that participate in the action, so that, except for the speaking characters and a small retinue of attendants, crowds could be painted.[14]

Any amount of delay might occur between the time a script was written and the time it was produced. Most scripts do seem to have been staged within about six months of acceptance. Both normal rehearsal time and a much shorter period are illustrated by a notorious case at the turn of the century, Craufurd's *Courtship a la Mode* (July 1700). The author reports in his preface that Lincoln's Inn Fields had had his script in rehearsal for six weeks without making any progress on it, when he withdrew the play and offered it to Drury Lane, where it was accepted in two days and performed in less than twenty. Twenty days was a tight schedule; the thirty-six working days in six weeks was not. Actors who performed together most days and who were responsible for memorizing lines outside rehearsal needed comparatively little time to work out details of a new production.[15] Scenery and costumes drawn from stock caused no delay. Nor did they really involve any expense beyond the normal daily "house charges." Downes's occasional comment, "New Cloath'd," suggests that to outfit the whole cast for a new play was unusual, a mark of confidence and a special effort. In virtually every respect, from lead time and cast size to investment and potential loss, operas were different.

The Early Opera Experiments

The first four operas Betterton produced were experiments of rapidly increasing complexity. My discussion will focus on elements that contributed most to the development of the "English opera" idiom.

We can deduce little about the operatic version of *Macbeth* in comparison to the original Lincoln's Inn Fields production because only one script was published.[16] Downes says, "Being drest in all it's Finery, as new Cloath's, new Scenes, Machines, as flyings for the Witches; with all the Singing and Dancing in it . . . it being all Excellently perform'd, being in the nature of an Opera, it Recompenc'd double the Expence; it proves still [i.e., about 1706–8] a lasting Play."[17] He implies a perceptibly larger-scale production than the Davenant version; but we can identify no precise lead time. In the cast for this opera we have eight actors' names, but twelve named male characters, plus soldiers and attendants. There are three women plus one or more female servants. The sex of the Witches is uncertain, but since Heccate was played by Sandford, the other three were probably also male.[18] There is no large chorus mentioned. We cannot estimate cost or profit, having only Downes's remark to go on.

The earliest example of an opera made out of a play for which we can compare the scripts is the 1674 *Tempest*.[19] Downes specifies "all New in it; as

Scenes, Machines . . . not any succeeding Opera got more Money" (pp. 34–35). The opera does not appear to have used more complicated equipment than other productions to date, but there were more visually heightened moments than before. We have no way to estimate the lead time it took to get this opera mounted. The 1674 quarto lists no actors' names, but the script could be played by about a dozen men plus extra mariners, guards, and spirits to attend Prospero, and five women (if Hippolyto, Ariel, and Milcha were all played by women).[20] Caliban is surely male, and if Heccate is any indication, Sycorax was probably also played by a man. The overture is described as being played by twenty-four violins, though that may only represent Shadwell's dream. Charles II loaned the company some singers from the Chapel Royal for the first run—a most unusual proceeding.[21] Prices were doubled even six months later, whereas for an ordinary play prices were raised only for the first run. The cost of the production is not known, but Elkanah Settle does tell us that *The Tempest* cost "not one third" as much as the next opera, *Psyche*.[22]

Several stage directions in the Dryden-Davenant *Tempest* are so laconic as to prohibit comparison: the actual effects may have been much more impressive than the directions indicate. At three points, however, we can see clearly how the new facilities of Dorset Garden changed the production.

In act 3 Davenant had introduced "eight fat spirits" to dance before Alonzo, Antonio, and Gonzalo, who then espy offstage "A Table . . . set out and furnisht / With all varieties of Meats and fruits" (Q 1670, p. 37). These fat spirits were not one of Davenant's higher inspirations, and Dent points out that they drew snide comment in *The Rehearsal*.[23] Remembering them, we can see part of the reason the trick table in the opera remained in Downes's memory. But the 1674 quarto indicates that a table was used twice in the play: once for the noblemen, when spirits flew away with it, and a second time in the fourth act for the lower plot characters, Trinculo and his cohorts, when it sank through a trap (Q 1674, pp. 47–48 and 59). The first disappearance serves the same purpose Davenant's had, to lure the nobles offstage to end a scene, but their mirage was made manifest. The second has neither practical nor thematic relevance, though Trinculo's response to the vanishing apparently made it memorable for Downes. Intentionally or not, the similarity of the incidents links the two groups of characters (although the tables may not have been the same). Repetition of effects was a pitfall Betterton thereafter sought to avoid.

The third effect to be considered in the operatic *Tempest* is important because it represents a complete departure from the Davenant production, not just a development of it. Having agreed to Prospero's final instructions, Davenant's Ariel sang "Where the Bee sucks" and danced a saraband with his counterpart, Milcha. So far as we can tell from stage directions, they remained grounded, however joyous. A benediction from Prospero ended the play (Q 1670, pp. 81–82). By contrast, the opera includes two scene changes within the last five pages: it ends with a nautical masque and an apotheosis of the newly freed Ariel (Q 1674, pp. 77–81). The effect of this scene must have been quite powerful; decades later, Downes recorded it even before the trick table. It is a particularly good example of visual enhancement. For the first time in the opera the merely human characters see Ariel fly, and the audience at the same time sees not only their wonder but also a tableau of the liberated Ariel soaring before the rising sun. Spirits had flown, of course, in *Macbeth*—but here Betterton had found a way to relate trick and theme in a brilliant finale.

Psyche continues the pattern of basing a production on an existing play, but this time not one that English audiences had seen. Betterton did not skimp in presenting Shadwell's adaptation of the 1671 French tragédie-ballet of the same name: there is at least one major staging feat in each act. Downes's comment on this opera is particularly revealing:

> The long expected Opera of *Psyche* came forth in all her Ornaments; new Scenes, new Machines, new Cloaths, new *French* Dances: This Opera was splendidly set out, especially in Scenes; the Charge of which amounted to above 800*l*. It had a Continuance of Performance about 8 Days together, it prov'd very Beneficial to the Company; yet the *Tempest* got them more *Money*. [pp. 35–36]

The stage directions for *Psyche* are among the most frequently cited in discussions of fancy staging in this period. Scholars use them confidently because Shadwell credits the production staff which brought his script to the stage, specifying that "in those things that concern the Ornament or Decoration of the Play, the great industry and care of Mr. *Betterton* ought to be remember'd, at whose desire I wrote upon this Subject."[24] However, he also says proudly that he has "not alter'd six lines in it since it was first written," sixteen months earlier. In September 1673 Betterton had set Shadwell to work translating the source play. Several members of the Duke's Company were involved in the court production of *Calisto*, which finally came on in the middle of January 1675, a month before *Psyche*, no doubt interfering with rehearsals for the opera. All the new "Ornaments" and conflicting commitments explain why *Psyche* was "long expected."

We need particularly to compare the scale of this opera with that of the earlier experiments. The quarto again provides no Dramatis Personae, but from numbers mentioned in stage directions and the score, I would venture some guesses. At a minimum, with much doubling and few attendants, the production demands five women in speaking roles plus six who sing and dance and four men in speaking roles plus ten who sing and dance. Fifteen women and fifteen men, plus musicians, would come closer to what the script calls for. Extra attendants could certainly have been used. But we can safely conclude that *Psyche* involved a company much larger than normal.

The script calls for nine different settings, three or four of which might conceivably have been drawn from stock. Downes does not say that all the scenes were new.[25] The £800 he specifies was for scenery alone; the total cost of the production must have been distinctly higher. Isaac Fuller's 1670 answer to the King's Company's lawsuit against him gives us some notion of a contemporary price scale: he claimed to have spent £100 for materials and assistants to paint one fancy scene for *Tyrannick Love*.[26] Even if Fuller exaggerated, and even if Betterton used a "house" painter rather than someone outside the theatre, £800 would not have been a disproportionate cost for opera scenery.

We have no basis on which to estimate costume expenses.[27] Prices were tripled for the first performance, though probably only doubled after that. The king was charged the highest price he ever paid for theatregoing at the premiere of *Psyche*, but a doubled price when he returned two perform-ances later.[28] The humorless and envious Elkanah Settle, replying to an attack on his *Empress of Morocco*, asserts that

> I have often heard the Players cursing at their oversight in laying out so much on so misliked a Play; and swearing that they thought they had lost more by making choice of such an *Opera-writer*, than they had gained by all his Comedies; . . . and that for the future they expect the *Tempest*, which cost not one Third of *Psyche*, will be in request when the other is forgotten.[29]

What did the audience get for its high-priced tickets, and what did the company put its money into? The descriptions in the text are more elabo-rate than those in the 1674 *Tempest*, but they could reflect Shadwell's im-aginings rather than what actually happened on the stage of Dorset Garden. A survey of these productions enables us to say that what *Psyche* calls for is by no means out of line with operas later in the sequence.

Splendor escalates markedly in this production. *Psyche* lends itself to clearly developed contrasts between, for example, the ornate Temple of Apollo Delphicus and "a Rocky Desart full of dreadful Caves, Cliffs, and Precipices" in act 2, or that between Hell and a sort of Mount Olympus in act 5. When Jupiter summons "all / The pow'rs of Heaven to keep a Fes-tival" at the end of the opera, the masque serves as a gorgeous and appro-priate conclusion to the preceding spectacle. Precise timing is essential in *Psyche*. Within a page in act 5, Venus "mounts her Chariot and flies away"; ten lines later, "*Venus* being almost lost in the Clouds. *Cupid* flies up and gets into her Chariot, and brings her back"; and after ten more lines "*Jupi-ter* appears upon his Eagle."[30] In *The Tempest*, even when both Ariel and Milcha fly, their actual motions are not specified except that they "cross in the air" (Q 1674, p. 11). The company's machinists had gained some expe-rience from earlier "flyings," but *Psyche*, having been transferred out of a theatrical milieu much more advanced than England's, must have been quite a test for them. *Psyche* is, from our point of view, a giant step toward the development of a visual idiom for these productions, and a reflection of what was happening on the Continent.

Circe, the last of the Dorset Garden spectaculars produced in the seventies, has received little attention from scholars, though it is in fact a considerable achievement.[31] Unified effort is the feature of this production to be emphasized. Downes called it an opera (although the title page bears the word "Tragedy"), and he records that "all the Musick was set by Mr. *Banister,* and being well Perform'd, it answer'd the Expectation of the Company" (pp. 36–37). The script is the only one by Charles Davenant, then Patentee of the Duke's Company. Presumably he could avail himself of the theatre's facilities and the Company's resources. While there is less description in the stage directions of gilded palaces and flying spirits than in *The Tempest* and *Psyche,* there is an unusually detailed outline of business for the attendants of the principal characters. Perhaps Davenant is only specifying standard theatrical practice in plays about royalty, but Circe's maids, spirits, priests, and magicians are used as extensions of her: they participate in the action. For example, rather than bring dangerous herbs with her to the spot where she conjures up Pluto, she sends a spirit for them; and her whole train helps with the masque intended to seduce Orestes. Her attendants have major responsibilities in each act.[32]

As the title indicates, the play revolves around Circe. In her ambition for her son, she is a typical wicked queen, but her powers as a sorceress not only give motion to all but one of the spectacular elements of the play, they also determine the cataclysmic end of a civilization. Taken as a struggle between the powers of Light (Love) and Darkness (Death), the play offers no hope for Love. That starkness is the outcome of Circe's inability to love, but young Davenant shows a discipline unusual in his time by not rescuing Scythia, or at least allowing Iphigenia and Pylades to escape the holocaust.

From the point of view of structure, the spectacular elements are particularly well woven into this script, making the spirit realm visible and omnipresent. At Circe's command, Pluto rises in a chariot drawn by black horses to foretell the future (1. 5). She has "two dragons rise out of the earth, and bear [Orestes] away" from the altar where he is about to be sacrificed, while she hovers over the scene in a dragon chariot (3. 6). She arranges an elaborate masque to seduce her captive and protects him from her husband in a magic bower (4. 1–3). At her order, Orestes is driven mad after he deserts her. He is tormented by the minions of the God of Sleep, one of his hallucinations taking the form of the ghost of Clytemnestra (5. 6). Too late, Circe calls for medicines to make him sane. When she offers to embrace him, Orestes, under the impression he is once again killing his mother, stabs her and then stabs himself (5. 9). The mortally wounded but still raging queen has the city set aflame ("Spirits bearing Torches flie cross the Stage"). Rejecting future existence in all its forms, she succumbs, while the city blazes behind her.

The integration of effects in this production is an instance of the gulf between operas as the Duke's Company conceived them and ordinary plays with a fancy scene or two such as *The Rival Queens* (Drury Lane, 1677). On the other hand, *Circe* may well have cost less to produce than *Psyche*. The scenes could easily have been pulled from stock (Circe's Cave, the Greek fleet, a temple, a garden, "some publick Place of the City"). The costumes, though not described, are also likely to have been standard "classical," at least some of which might have come from the current wardrobe. The principal effects depend on machines rather than on full sets, except for the City afire during Circe's last speech.

In respect of cast size as well as machine display, *Circe* deserved to be called an opera. It contains speaking roles for four men and three women, and stage directions in acts 4 and 5 indicate choruses of from ten to fifteen men and eight to twelve women. (At least four members of each chorus dance as well as sing.) More men to play soldiers and other attendants would have been useful. The bare minimum cast amounts to fourteen men and eight women. Lead time is again undeterminable. Once John Bannister had written the music, if scenery were indeed stock, lead time would have been largely a matter of coordinating special effects and crowd scenes. Prices were doubled, as we know both from a bill to Charles II and a prologue reference to "5s worth of wit." The results were gratifying: three weeks after *Circe* opened, the company declared the highest shareholders' dividend in two years.[33]

Downes implies that all the operas mentioned so far made money; we know that two did much better than that. Why, then, did a gap of eight years occur before the next production? Theatrical hard times were brought on by the Popish Plot and the Succession Crisis, an obvious deterrent. Amalgamation with the bankrupt King's Company in 1682, and Betterton's absorption in new repertory possibilities are a second factor.[34] The scanty records suggest that at least three of these operas continued to be performed during these eight years, so the genre did not disappear, it merely remained static.[35]

Reflecting on the three major operas from the seventies, we can make certain generalizations. In cast size, scenic expense, lead time, and complexity of machine staging these are extraordinary productions. The Duffett burlesques mounted by the King's Company indicate their exceptional nature. His *Empress of Morocco* (August 1673) parodies Settle but also takes a crack at the operatic *Macbeth* in the epilogue. *The Mock-Tempest* and *Psyche Debauch'd* follow in 1674 and 1675. (Drury Lane would probably have mounted something along the lines of *Circe Transform'd* if Duffett had not been in prison in 1677.) No ordinary play ever drew such a response from the rival company in this period.

The 1674 *Tempest* in particular demands recognition for its enormous and lasting popularity. Moore calls it "the most popular play of the Restoration"[36]—an overstatement, since we lack the records to prove it, but quite possibly true, and certainly not far off the mark. Modern readers inevitably have trouble seeing it as anything but a vulgarization wrought upon a bastardization of Shakespeare, but Restoration audiences loved it, and from the theatre managers' viewpoint, it was a durable moneymaker. Little wonder that they were ready to underwrite further ventures in this expensive but alluring genre.

The Major Extravaganzas

During the season of 1682–83, the managers were busy with the details of the union, but by the summer of 1683 they were evidently ready to consider another operatic venture, and Charles II seems to have felt secure enough to interest himself once again in such matters. On 25 August 1683 Lord Preston wrote to the earl of Sunderland, "I have received the honour of your lordship's by Mr. Betterton with his Majesty's commands to me to assist him in treating with some persons capable of representing on [sic] opera in England."[37] There must have been some real public interest in this project. On 14 August the Newdigate Newsletter had noted that "the Managers of ye Kings Theatre intend wth in short time to pforme an Opera in like manner of yt of ffrance. Mr. Batterton wth other Actors are gone over to fetch ye designe."[38] Whether Betterton tried to persuade a French company to visit London we do not know; he wound up commissioning a collaboration between Dryden and Louis Grabu.

A good deal of confusion surrounds the circumstances in which *Albion and Albanius* was written and produced. The matter has been further clouded by Edward L. Saslow's recent suggestion that it received its premiere in May 1684.[39] Saslow's evidence is a reference in the Newdigate Newsletter of 24 May 1684: "his Majesty is Entertained with Mr Drydens new play the subject of which is the last new Plott."[40] This is usually taken as a reference to Dryden and Lee's *The Duke of Guise* (first performed in December 1682), although that would not be a very new play.[41] *Albion and Albanius* could perhaps have been "read" or given some kind of concert performance at Windsor in May 1684, but it could not have been staged there, since the theatre was not rigged for such a production. Further, we know that the opera was still only in rehearsal on 1 January 1685, as *The London Stage* records. Dryden himself says in the "Postscript" to the preface that Charles "had been pleas'd twice or thrice to command, that it shou'd be practic'd, before him, especially the first and third Acts of it." And in the Dedication of *King Arthur* (1691) Dryden says that "*Albion and Albanius,* was often practis'd before Him at *Whitehal.*" Another piece of evidence to consider is Dryden's letter of circa August 1684 in which he says "and for the Act wch remaines of the opera, I believe I shall have no leysure to mind it," and a few lines later, "I desire to know whether the Dukes house are makeing cloaths & putting things in a readiness for the singing opera, to be playd immediately after Michaelmasse."[42] Ward doubtfully suggests that the "opera" was *Albion and Albanius* and the "singing opera" *The Tempest,* but this does not make sense. The only "singing opera" (as opposed to semi-opera) Dryden ever wrote was *Albion and Albanius.* I would suggest, therefore, that the "opera" on which Dryden was still working was *King Arthur,* which he claimed to have written "seven Years ago" when it was finally published in 1691, i.e., in 1684. *Albion and Albanius,* I deduce, was complete, and Dryden was expecting a production at Dorset Garden by the United Company in late October or November. Given the complexity of the preparations, the company fell behind schedule, held rehearsals in December and January, and was not quite ready for public performance at the time of Charles's death in February 1685.

Albion and Albanius is an anomaly in the series of English operas at Dorset Garden. It is the only one that is something like an opera in the modern sense of the term, all sung. In every respect it was a radical departure. Even before music was added, the text was unlike anything known in London theatres during Charles's reign. Here French precedents are of interest to the scholar, but they would have had no bearing on the response of most audience members in 1685. Serious plays in the active repertory the previous two seasons include *Constantine the Great, Valentinian, The Disappointment, The Duke of Guise, All for Love, The Conquest of Granada,* and *Rollo.* None of them could be said to prepare the way for *Albion and Albanius.* Allegorical display of living royalty is difficult to plot through three whole acts, and Dryden apologizes for the weakness of the "Fable," which veers from abstract to real events and back several times. Such shifts might not have disconcerted the original audience as much as they do the twentieth-century reader, but knowledge of the convention would have had to be gained outside the theatre. Dryden also found that words written to be sung must fit together differently from stage speech, a difficulty exacerbated by collaboration with a composer working outside his native language. And however much the king appreciated French music, English musicians by and large opposed it, even forming a faction against the interloper Grabu.[43]

The stunning profusion of complex scenes and machines described in the stage directions is not just the playwright's pipedream. Dryden says in his preface, "The descriptions of the Scenes, and other decorations of the

Stage, I had from Mr. *Betterton,* who has spar'd neither for industry, nor cost, to make this Entertainment perfect, nor for Invention of the Ornaments to beautify it." In other words, the scene descriptions were provided by the man who executed them. Since we lack scene designs for all these productions and must depend on stage directions to describe what occurred onstage, we need to identify a standard of feasibility by which to judge the descriptions. *Albion and Albanius* provides that standard. Even satirical comments admit that the production was eyecatching.[44]

The visual challenge of this opera was to combine recognizable places and identifiable persons with a wide range of allegorical figures and pagan deities. Recognizable locales had been called for in comedies at least as early as Sedley's *The Mulberry Garden* (1668),[45] but serious plays rarely depended on particular London settings. Within its genre, *Albion and Albanius* is unique in proclaiming recognizable locations. To the twentieth-century reader, the supernatural and relatively realistic elements seem to be pulling in opposite directions. Some examples of the antithetical stage directions will illustrate this tension.

Act 1 opens on "a street of Palaces, which lead to the Front of the *Royal Exchange;* the great Arch is open, and the view is continued through the open part of the *Exchange,* to the Arch on the other side, and thence to as much of the Street beyond, as could be properly taken."[46] Into the midst of London descends Mercury in a chariot drawn by ravens, to converse with Augusta and Thamesis; Juno now appears in the new peacock machine, the displayed tail of which "is so Large, that it almost fills the opening of the Stage between Scene and Scene."[47] Yet a third machine is to materialize, presumably further downstage. The circles that frame the "celestial phenomenon" on which Iris rides were the rainbows that satirists mention in their descriptions. But the audience in the theatre could hardly know that the design for Iris's machine was based on something real, a helion which a sea captain had observed and sketched and passed on to the playhouse.[48] Here we have a direct pairing of a pagan goddess with the fruits of scientific inquiry—though it probably communicated about as unevenly as the stage direction now reads. To complete act 1 the 1660 Restoration is recalled by versions of "the 4 Triumphal Arches erected at his Majesties Coronation."

Act 2 begins in a typical "Poetical Hell," complete with dancing devils. (Charles II did not care as much for this act as for the first and third, according to Dryden.) Scene 2 is "a Prospect taken from the middle of the Thames," and was a view any playgoer could check the next time he was on the river between York Buildings and Whitehall. Both Mercury and Apollo appear in this act, which Neptune and his followers bring to a close with a nautical masque.

Dryden suddenly becomes more particular and satiric in act 3, which opens on a view of Dover, where allegorical but recognizable choruses of political dissidents dance and fight. The classical element reasserts itself when "the Cave of *Proteus* rises out of the Sea":

> *Albion* [i.e., Charles II] and *Acacia* [i.e., Innocence] seize on him [Proteus], and while a Symphony is playing, he sinks as they are bringing him forward, and changes himself into a Lyon, a Crocodile, a Dragon, and then to his own shape again: He comes toward the front of the Stage, and Sings.

Though the direction does not tell us how this series of transformations was accomplished, one practical way would be for Albion to wrestle supernumeraries costumed in Proteus's animal guises out of one or more of the stage traps, while Proteus himself made his way under the stage to a trap further forward, out of which he could emerge and sing. However it was accomplished, such a maneuver requires careful coordination to execute in time to music. Later in this scene walls of fire (perhaps reused from *Circe*) protect Albion from various attacks. Then Venus rises out of the sea, bringing Albanius (i.e., James II) with her. Apollo reappears, this time on a throne, not in the sun chariot, and participates in the apotheosis of Albion. The final scene is again described as a recognizable place, "that part of *Windsor,* which faces *Eaton,*" surmounted in the scenic stage by "a Vision of the Honors of the Garter, the Knights in Procession, and the King under a Canopy." The satiric element recurs visually in this scene. As if the setting were not complex enough, "*Fame* rises out of the middle of the Stage, standing on a Globe; . . . On the Front of the Pedestal is drawn a Man with a long, lean, pale Face, with Fiends Wings, and Snakes twisted round his Body"—the vanquished Shaftesbury, complete with tap in his side. A song from Fame and a grand dance of twenty-four end the opera.

How this bravura display of Dorset Garden's technical potentialities would have fared had Charles lived to enjoy its public performance through the winter and spring of 1685, it is idle to speculate. Delayed by the king's death, *Albion and Albanius* finally received its premiere 3 June 1685. On 13 June the news of Monmouth's invasion reached London and ruined its run. Downes reports that the opera was "perform'd on a very Unlucky Day, being the Day the *Duke* of *Monmouth,* Landed in the *West*: The Nation being in a great Consternation, it was perform'd but Six times, which not Answering half the Charge they were at, Involv'd the Company very much in Debt" (p. 40). This assessment is questioned by the editors of the California Dryden, who say that "contrary to its reputation, the opera seems to have been a reasonably successful venture," and call it "a popular piece."[49] They are quite right in pointing out the evident success of the printed text and music, and the surprising number of extant scores suggests considerable interest in the music. But however shaky on dates and details, Downes seems to have had an excellent memory for profitability.

And we have no records of any revival. Indeed, as the California editors observe, after the Revolution of 1688 revival would not have been feasible.

Obviously *Albion and Albanius* had a very long lead time. The opening Dryden had expected in October or November was delayed at least two months before the king died. Official mourning and further script revisions delayed the premiere until June. Even before the intervention of Fate, gossip had reported that the opera "pleaseth mightily, but the rates proposed will not take soe well, for they have set the boxes at a guyny a place, and the Pitt at halfe. They advance 4,000*l*. on the opera, and therefore must tax high to reimburse themselves."[50] The total cost named is mind boggling. An audit of United Company accounts for the decade 1682–92 provides a basis from which we can make some rough comparisons.[51] During that time production costs had totaled £85,394. In a normal performance year of 200 days, more or less, £4,000 would represent an investment of about half the company's annual expenses just for this one production. The decor was unusually elaborate, and probably none of it was already on hand. Stage directions indicate singing roles for between eight and ten men and four and six women as principals; a chorus of twelve to twenty-four, at least some of whom could both sing and dance, is also necessary. Even without knowing specific costs, we can see that this opera must have been far more expensive than its semi-opera predecessors.

How else might we assess the rumored figure? We can consider it in relation to the actual disaster. We can look at it as a projection of what might have happened if all had gone well. We can also question it altogether.

To make £4,000 in the six days the opera actually ran (ignoring, for the moment, house charges, which must have been higher than usual), the company would have had to take in over £660 each day. At single prices £100 a day was a high receipt.[52] Even if quadruple prices had produced £400 for each of the six days, the company would not have come close to breaking even. Had they been able to play a dozen times to full houses at these extraordinary prices, they could have cleared all expenses (£400 for 10 days = £4,000 plus two more days to make up house charges for the run).

Quadruple prices seem incredible, even under ideal conditions, and King James in fact paid only double when he saw a performance on 3 June 1685.[53] What do the figures look like if we assume the managers planned to do as they had done with *Psyche* and reduce prices after the premiere? Then they might have projected £400 the first day and £200 thereafter (if houses remained full), which would have necessitated a run of twenty-one days to clear costs.[54] Had they been able to open in February as they once seemed nearly ready to do—had the king not died—they would still have gotten tangled up in the customary hiatus of Lent and Easter. Twenty-one performances seems an overly optimistic projection.

Having suggested a revision of the quadruple prices report, we might as well examine the £4,000 rumor also. If true, that investment makes *Albion and Albanius* the biggest plunge of Betterton's career. Most of the money went for surface decoration, not new equipment: except for the peacocks' tails, the machines of Dorset Garden were more than adequate for the effects we read of. Rumor may have exaggerated the money spent, a hypothesis we cannot test. But Dryden's biographer Ward has suggested another possible explanation.[55] Since this production was designed at King Charles's behest by his principal actor-manager, his poet laureate, and a composer imported for him, might the United Company not reasonably have expected a token of his approval if the results pleased him? A subsidy of £1,000 (such as he had contributed to the theatre's construction fund in 1671) would have cut five days off the projected run at double prices, figuring the premiere at triple prices. And while a projected run of sixteen days was optimistic, it was not inconceivable. Downes mentions eight-, ten-, twelve-, and fourteen-day runs prior to this opera (although admittedly for plays and at single prices).

Whatever the real investment and loss, an inspection of the company's payments to the managers suggests that they negotiated with their creditors for long-term repayment of loans or settlement of bills. Except for the period of official mourning and for the disastrous month of June, the treasurer continued to pay salaries and low but regular dividends.[56] In 1684–85 the theatre was open 156 days (plus some undetermined number in June, for which there are no records). At best this is a short season in which to earn a living for a whole year; to make up the opera investment in that time looks impossible. *Albion and Albanius* must be taken as a grandiose overextension of means, any way we assess it.

The United Company spent 1685–86 and 1686–87 recouping its fortunes. By that time the political climate was sufficiently threatening to make expensive operas seem like a bad idea, and we should feel no surprise that until William and Mary were firmly established on the throne, the company did not venture another major spectacular. Its stopgap was machine farce: this hiatus is the time when *The Emperor of the Moon, Faustus,* and *Amphitryon* were produced. The last three Dorset Garden spectaculars staged by Betterton—*The Prophetess, King Arthur,* and *The Fairy-Queen*—occurred at yearly intervals beginning in 1690. They have in common a return to the old, safer style of semi-opera, and the immense advantage of music by Henry Purcell. Why *King Arthur* was not the first in the series we do not know. Perhaps the managers, wanting to take no chances, preferred to go with something less innovative.

Downes tells us that *The Prophetess,* staged in June 1690, was "wrote by Mr. *Betterton;* being set out with Coastly Scenes, Machines and Cloaths: The Vocal and Instrumental Musick, done by Mr. *Purcel;* and Dances by Mr. *Priest;* it gratify'd the Expectation of Court and City; and got the Author great Reputation" (p. 42). We have no information about lead time for this opera, nor do we have any specific figures about the cost. But by this date "opera" implied heavy expenditure and a considerable risk. Dryden issued the standard complaint about expense in his prologue, printed in the January 1707 *Muses Mercury:*

> WHAT *Nostredame* with all his Art can guess
> The Fate of our Approaching Prophetess?
> A Play that like a Perspective set right,
> Presents our vast Expences close to sight,
> But turn the Tube and then we sadly view
> Our distant Gains, and those uncertain too:
> A sweeping Tax, which on our selves we raise,
> And all like you, in hopes of better days.
> When will our Losses warn us to be wise?
> Our Wealth decreases, and our Charges rise.
> Money, the sweet Allurer of our Hopes,
> Ebbs out by Oceans, but comes in by Drops.
> We raise new Objects to provoke Delight,
> But you grow sated at the second sight.

Betterton treats his audience to a conjuration, a dragon chariot, a vision instantly transformed (this time, because the play is a tragicomedy rather than a tragedy, into a dance of butterflies, not nightmares). Summers identified the "farther Curtain" in act 3 as the first use of a drop on the Restoration stage.[57] The final masque develops around a new machine that adds four small but practical playing levels to that of the stage floor. On the other hand, "A Pallace" in acts 1 and 5, a "Forest" in act 2, and the encampment scene in act 4 might well have come from stock. Costume demands are not unusual except for the eight dancing butterflies in act 4,[58] though of course any amount of money could have been spent on clothes. The script has speaking roles for at least six men and four women. In the final scene we can identify twelve women and as many men singing and dancing, in addition to the seven speaking characters who observe the masque. More could have been used as attendants.

The special glory of *The Prophetess* is the addition of Purcell's music. The masque alone comprises "half of Purcell's score and takes three-quarters of an hour to perform," according to Moore.[59] *The Prophetess* returned to several old patterns—an existing script, a fantasy world, production numbers paced toward a concluding masque—but added the excitement of music by an ambitious young composer. The production team was satisfied enough to repeat the formula twice more. How remunerative *The Prophetess* was we cannot tell, but this production remained the standard of operatic grandeur for some fifteen years.[60] All the signs point to its being solidly and lastingly profitable.

The success of *The Prophetess* probably encouraged the company to proceed with *King Arthur*. Dryden had been at work on it back in 1684, but it was "deferr'd," he says in the preface to *Albion and Albanius*, by "some intervening accidents."[61] In his 1691 dedication he mentions that extensive rewriting was necessary before the piece could be produced, but we have no way of knowing what was changed. The premiere probably occurred about the first week of June 1691.[62] Downes says cheerfully, "It was Excellently Adorn'd with Scenes and Machines: The Musical Part set by Famous Mr. *Henry Purcel;* and Dances made by Mr. *Jo. Priest:* The Play and Musick pleas'd the Court and City, and being well perform'd, twas very Gainful to the Company" (p. 42). Cibber offers another opinion, often quoted: "Though the Success of *The Prophetess* and *King Arthur* . . . was in Appearance very great, yet their whole Receipts did not so far balance their Expence as to keep them out of a large Debt. . . . Every Branch of the Theatrical Trade had been sacrific'd to the necessary fitting out those tall Ships of Burthen that were to bring home the Indies" (*Apology,* 1:187). But Cibber had only joined the company as a salaried actor the previous year, and he wrote this recollection nearly fifty years later. I suspect that here, as in so many places, Cibber conflates and blurs: he is probably remembering *The Fairy-Queen.* Downes is much more likely to have known precisely what made money and what did not.

Cost and lead time for *King Arthur* are unknown, and again we have no way of telling how much of the scenery and costumes were new, though the "Frost Scene" was created for it. "Scene a deep Wood" and "pavilion scene" (3.1. and 2.2.) are described as if they were on hand. Nine men and three women have speaking parts; many more men appear as soldiers. The singers and dancers number at least eighteen. As usual, prices were doubled, and remained so even long after the first run.[63]

Dryden's stage directions for *King Arthur* are frustratingly terse and underwritten. For example, after the Frost Scene in act 3, no return to the forest is indicated, but surely the rape threat took place somewhere other than in the frozen north. Act 4 shows no location either, until twenty-nine lines into the scene we are told, "Scene of the Wood continues."[64] This probably just implies, of course, that, as in *Albion and Albanius,* Dryden left implementation to Betterton, and in this instance did not bother to obtain written descriptions from him for the printed quarto.

King Arthur is explicitly tied to the *Albion* prologue by the final victory masque, which celebrates the glory of Britannia and the Order of the Garter. Two innovations figure in visualizing this production, one easier to assess than the other. Dryden was proud of the research he had put into this script, and some attempt may have been made to convey an "old English" milieu in scenery and costume, though he left us no hints as to how this might be done. The other innovation was the great Frost Scene conjured up by the wicked magician Osmond. The unique "prospect of Winter in Frozen Countries," combined with Purcell's music, brilliantly performed by Mrs. Butler as Cupid with a chorus of "Cold People," remained such an attraction that it was played as an excerpt long after the production as a whole had dropped out of the repertory.[65]

Downes says that *King Arthur* proved "very Gainful," and though we cannot be sure either how much it cost or made, at least it succeeded well enough for the United Company to go ahead with an even more lavish production the next season. *The Fairy-Queen* had its premiere 2 May 1692. Purcell provided the music; Priest did the dances; the rewriting necessary to adapt *A Midsummer-Night's Dream* to operatic purposes is sometimes said to have been done by Elkanah Settle.[66] Downes emphasizes the cost and scale of the production. "This in Ornaments was Superior to the other Two; especially in Cloaths, for all the Singers and Dancers, Scenes, Machines and Decorations, all most profusely set off. . . . The Court and Town were wonderfully satisfy'd with it; but the Expences in setting it out being so great, the Company got very little by it" (pp. 42–43).

What were these "superior Ornaments"? The first act begins in what could easily have been a stock "Palace" scene, then changes to "a Wood, by Moonlight." Fairyland in act 2, at least as described, would call for a form of *scena per angolo* painting; and the contrast between it and the unparticularized Wood was worth spending money to achieve:

> The Scene changes to a Prospect of Grotto's, Arbors, and delightful Walks: The Arbors are Adorn'd with all variety of Flowers, the Grotto's supported by Terms, these lead to two Arbors on either side of the Scene, of a great length, whose prospect runs toward the two Angles of the House. Between these two Arbors is the great Grotto, which is continued by several Arches, to the farther end of the House.[67]

The enchanted Lake of act 3 is fairly standard, and might have been stock or new, though, as part of a routine transformation sequence (swans into dancers), a dragon bridge vanishes and "Trees that were Arch'd" over the water "raise themselves upright." Two stage directions in act 4 are noteworthy. The sun is seen to rise—mists clear away from in front of it—and since Purcell wrote music to accompany this effect, it presumably happened. In the center of the sunlit garden is a fountain "where the Water rises about twelve feet." (Alas, we have no hint as to whether the fountain here, or the one in act 5, was practical.) Juno in her peacock chariot covers the change in the last act to the final scene, "a transparent prospect of a *Chinese* Garden."

Eleven men in all have speaking parts, though five of the "Comedians" (excepting Bottom) might have been doubled by chorus members. Assuming Robin Goodfellow to have been a woman's role, there are four women who speak. The chorus of twenty-four includes at least four sopranos, three altos or countertenors, three tenors, and two basses, if the score was followed in casting. Dancers are hard to separate from singers, except that the six monkey dancers do not sing as a group. The Dramatis Personae implies that twenty-four Chinese dance the Grand Dance; if this does not include the monkeys, the total cast would come to between forty and forty-five.

What did all this cost? Narcissus Luttrell tells us that "a new opera, called The Fairy Queen: exceeds former playes: the clothes, scenes, and musick cost 3000£."[68] We cannot place too much reliance on this report. Luttrell was a gossipmonger, not a theatrical insider. But in conjunction with Downes, this does suggest a very heavy investment. The Betterton-Purcell-Priest team evidently felt great confidence in its ability to make the formula work. Public response seems to have been enthusiastic. The *Gentleman's Journal* for May 1692 (licensed 14 May) implies that *The Fairy-Queen* had run twelve consecutive days, "and continues to be represented daily." A month later Princess Anne's attendance was reported in the Newdigate Newsletter. At double prices (which the queen was still paying in February 1693), fifteen large (£200) houses would have been necessary to repay the investment; with an allowance for even minimal house charges, the time to recoup becomes eighteen or twenty days. Since the opera remained in the repertory well into the next season, it probably did break even, but why it never proved "gainful" is easy to see. And the house charges are likely to have been high. The anonymous author of the preface to the 1692 edition comments, "we cannot reasonably propose to ourselves any great advantage, considering the mighty Charge in setting it out, and the extraordinary expence *that attends it every day 'tis represented*" (italics added).

There is an inevitable tendency to see *The Fairy-Queen* as the final stage of a progression, an evolutionary end product that sank under its own weight. It makes a logical halting point for this study because it was Betterton's last opera at Dorset Garden; only once again, with Granville's *The British Enchanters* at the Haymarket in 1706, was he able to indulge his penchant for this genre. There is good evidence, however, that had Betterton and the senior actors stayed with the Patent Company, he would have gone on mounting such productions. Sometime during 1694 Purcell wrote most of the music for an operatic *Indian Queen,* and Betterton was paid the startling sum of £50 to supervise the staging, but he did not do so before the actors' walkout in December 1694.[69] Had Christopher Rich not seized control of the Patent Company the preceding December, we would probably have several more full-scale English operas from the turn of the century.

Conclusion

Lead time of between six months and two years, casts easily twice as large as normal, decor that could consume as much as half of a season's production budget—if the costs as reported are even close to accurate, they are out of all proportion to the risk involved. Why did the company take such chances?

The external justification was the effect the sheer scale of these operas had on the audience. Regular theatregoers, used to seeing the same old costumes and scenery, were treated to a crowd of new faces among the old, exotically dressed characters moving on more levels than were ordinarily used and in environments unique to these shows. As the introduction of primitive moveable scenery at Lincoln's Inn Fields had once been enough to entice people who otherwise did not attend the theatre, so the vocal and visual display of operas almost certainly drew some occasional spectators. Native patrons were not the only audience, however. Major cities on the Continent had long been producing shows at least as large. When visiting ambassadors expressed an interest in theatre, these were the productions they were taken to see, as we learn from newsletter and newspaper reports over a period of three decades. Whether the diplomats were genuinely impressed (and what their standards were) is less important than the sense that to make a name for herself in the realm of contemporary culture, England needed to prove she too could mount machine plays.

Within the company itself, the scale meant all sorts of differences in working conditions. The spoken and sung portions of many of these operas could be rehearsed separately at first, but eventually the pieces had to be brought together, especially where effects required complex coordination. For some regular company members, opera might be a chance to show off the range of their talents. Sustained singing and dancing call for different abilities and pacing than the single lute song or witty jig. The best singers and dancers were kept very busy, as we can see by folowing Bowman and Mrs. Butler through *King Arthur*.[70] For the whole company, an opera meant working with more people than usual, some of whom must have been comparatively inexperienced and in need of supervision. For salaried employees, it probably meant little if any more money; for shareholders, it might well mean loss, though these was always the hope of another perennial moneymaker such as *The Tempest*.

The scenes and machines used in operas were both exceedingly expensive and not readily reusable in ordinary comedies and tragedies. Supernatural trappings have no place in realistic "London" comedies, and have only limited viability in serious plays. A cloud machine from the fifth act of *Psyche* (1675) which carries "richly Habited" musicians as well as Apollo cannot be readily jobbed into *The Man of Mode* or *Don Carlos* (both 1676) to help recoup the investment. A fancy prison scene or an elaborately appointed boudoir might, in sharp contradistinction, be employable in several new plays and many revivals over a period of years: such an apartment was one of the scenes in *Don Carlos*.[71] Once launched, however, the operas fed into one another. Juno's peacocks and Apollo's sun chariot from *Albion and Albanius* reappear five years later in *The Prophetess*. The dragon chariot in *Circe, The Prophetess,* and *King Arthur* is probably one vehicle. The Honor of the Garter, part of the last scene of *Albion and Albanius,* also ended *King Arthur.*

The stimuli of novelty and complexity enlivened these productions for the whole company. For the producers (so to speak) the appeal lay in how to mount these shows in the first place, given the cost involved, and how to make each different. The process brought its own rewards if the mechanics worked; financial success was desirable but could hardly have been the primary goal. More than just money was lost on *Albion and Albanius:* a major experiment failed. By contrast, the brilliant team that put together the last three Dorset Garden spectaculars had every reason to plan more, as there is evidence they were doing.[72]

An ordinary play could be mounted in a month, and most regular plays simply drew on stock scenery and costumes. English operas placed a wholly different burden on the theatre. Handicapped by the lack of scene designs and costume renderings, we have trouble appreciating their magnificence. For the Restoration audience they had the kind of thrill that Technicolor added to film spectaculars. The sheer scale of production, the cost and conspicuous lavishness, appealed to the audience. The semi-operas represent a special and short-lived synthesis of music, drama, and spectacle. Early in the eighteenth century Italian opera absorbed the theatre's musical energies and the fantasy element of the semi-operas, while farce (and later pantomime) inherited the fancy staging tricks Dorset Garden was built to produce. As literature, the Dorset Garden spectaculars are entirely forgettable. As theatre, they are important because they expanded the definition of theatre for English audiences, capitalizing on the technical resources of the Restoration stage. Betterton's motto appears to have been "THINK BIG," and his results were evidently dazzling.

Notes

1. For music-oriented evaluations, see *Roger North on Music,* ed. John Wilson (London: Novello, 1959); Edward J. Dent, *Foundations of English Opera* (1928; rpt. New York: Da Capo, 1965); Robert Etheridge Moore, *Henry Purcell and the Restoration Theatre* (1961; rpt. Westport, Conn.: Greenwood Press, 1974); and Richard Luckett, "Exotick but rational entertainments: the English dramatick operas," in *English Drama: Forms and Development,* ed. Marie Axton and Raymond Williams (Cambridge: Cambridge University Press, 1977), pp. 123–41. On the day to day importance of music, see Price.

2. John Evelyn, *Diary,* 9 February 1671.

3. In *Roscius Anglicanus* (1708: rpt. Los Angeles: Augustan Reprint Society, 1969) John Downes lists the following pre-1673 productions as having new or especially fine "cloaths": *Love and Honour, The Adventures of Five Hours, Henry VIII, Mustapha,* Orrery's *Henry V,* and *Charles VIII of France.*

4. The preface to the 1692 *Fairy-Queen* quotes from Davenant's *The Siege of Rhodes* as proof that he intended to build a machine theatre. On those plans see John Freehafer, "Brome,

Suckling, and Davenant's Theater Project of 1639," *Texas Studies in Language and Literature* 10 (1968): 367–83. For detailed discussion of the Dorset Garden Theatre, see Edward A. Langhans, "A Conjectural Reconstruction of the Dorset Garden Theatre," *Theatre Survey* 13 (1972): 74–93; John R. Spring, "Platforms and Picture Frames: A Conjectural Reconstruction of the Duke of York's Theatre, Dorset Garden, 1669–1709," *Theatre Notebook* 31 (1977): 6–19; and Robert D. Hume, "The Dorset Garden Theatre: A Review of Facts and Problems," *Theatre Notebook* 33 (1979): 4–17.

5. Betterton probably went to France in 1662 and again either in 1669 or 1671, according to the *Biographical Dictionary*, 2:76, 79. Dates and details of these trips remain problematical.

6. Langhans, "A Conjectural Reconstruction of the Dorset Garden Theatre," p. 79.

7. On the literary merits, see (under titles of the operas) Robert D. Hume, *The Development of English Drama in the Late Seventeenth Century* (Oxford: Clarendon Press, 1976). Hazelton Spencer denounces those pieces based on Shakespeare in *Shakespeare Improved* (1927; rpt. New York: Ungar, 1963). No one has yet given these productions the kind of treatment accorded serious drama by Philip Parsons in "Restoration Tragedy as Total Theatre," in *Restoration Literature: Critical Approaches*, ed. Harold Love (London: Methuen, 1972), pp. 27–68.

8. *Circe* (1677), pp. 25 and 30–31. References are to the first London edition of each play unless otherwise specified.

9. See Edward A. Langhans, *Restoration Promptbooks* (Carbondale, Ill.: Southern Illinois University Press, 1981), especially p. xxiii.

10. See J. G. McManaway, "Songs and Masques in *The Tempest*," *Theatre Miscellany: Six Pieces connected with the Seventeenth-Century Stage*, Luttrell Society Reprints No. 14 (Oxford: Blackwell, 1953), pp. 71–96. On *Circe*, see *The London Stage*, part 1, p. 257. The book for *The Prophetess* was available by 3 June 1690, when Luttrell purchased a copy. The score did not appear until March 1691—according to Purcell, because of the expense and difficulty of printing music. For *Albion and Albanius*, see *The Works of John Dryden*, Vol. 15, ed. Earl Miner and George R. Guffey (Berkeley, Calif.: University of California Press, 1976), p. 11.

11. Advertisements are quoted from *The London Stage*, part 2.

12. Edward A. Langhans, "New Restoration Theatre Accounts, 1682–1692," *Theatre Notebook* 17 (1963): 118–34.

13. Since most authors, unlike their Elizabethan counterparts, published their plays, we can be confident that we know of most new productions. But we have no good way even to guess how many old plays were revived and kept in the repertory.

14. Montague Summers in *The Playhouse of Pepys* (1935; rpt. New York: Humanities Press, 1964), pp. 43, 62 assumes that Davenant followed French practice and painted crowds. In 1709, Christopher Rich removed from Drury Lane some scenery that included "a scene of a multitude" (Richard Hindry Barker, *Mr. Cibber of Drury Lane* [1939; rpt. New York: AMS, 1966], p. 83).

15. See the complaint in Gildon's *Life of Mr. Thomas Betterton* (1710; rpt. New York: Augustus M. Kelley, 1970), p. 15, that young actors "now scarce ever mind a Word of their Parts but only at *Rehearsals*."

16. For a complete discussion, see the introduction to Christopher Spencer, *Davenant's Macbeth from the Yale Manuscript* (New Haven, Conn.: Yale University Press, 1961), especially p. 16.

17. *Roscius Anglicanus*, p. 33.

18. The music for *Macbeth* published in 1770 was reworked, and it is only doubtfully attributed to Matthew Locke. Changes include an incomplete switching of Heccate from bass to soprano, which suggests that the witches were male. See Rosamond E. M. Harding, *A Thematic Catalogue of the Works of Matthew Locke* (Oxford: Blackwell, 1971).

19. Both versions are reprinted in facsimile in George Robert Guffey's *After The Tempest* (Los Angeles: William Andrews Clark Memorial Library, 1969). They will be cited hereafter as Q 1670 and Q 1674.

20. Ariel is assumed to have been played by a woman, and the prologue for the 1670

production refers to a woman playing a man, usually taken to mean Hippolyto. See the cast in the entry for 7 November 1667 in *The London Stage,* part 1.

21. On the singers from the Chapel Royal, see *The London Stage,* 16 May 1674. The double prices are recorded in Charles II's bills for theatregoing, printed by Allardyce Nicoll, *A History of English Drama 1660–1900,* 6 vols., rev. ed. (Cambridge: Cambridge University Press, 1952–59), 1:348.

22. *Ibrahim the Illustrious Bassa* (1677), preface, p. [6].

23. Dent, p. 145. The Fat Spirits appear on p. 37 of Q 1670.

24. Thomas Shadwell, Preface to *Psyche* in *The Complete Works,* ed. Montague Summers (1927; rpt. New York: Blom, 1968), 2:279–80.

25. The Wood in act 1, Lovers' Leap in act 2, the city street in act 3, and the Desert in act 4 seem to me likely to have been pulled from stock if anything was. As late as 1709 two of the settings for this production seem to have been extant: see the "twelve scenes of Cupids' wings" (act 3) and "twelve scenes of orange wings" (act 4) mentioned in Barker, *Mr. Cibber,* p. 83.

26. For the text of the Fuller suit, see John Dryden, *Works,* Volume 10, ed. Maximillian E. Novak and George R. Guffey (Berkeley, Calif.: University of California Press, 1970), appendix.

27. In regard to the size of the cast and the elaborateness of the costumes, we may note that Duffett's *Psyche Debauch'd* calls for about twenty characters plus supernumeraries, and that he burlesques costume by having many of his characters appear half-dressed. The identity of mythological figures in Shadwell's script may not always have been clear to the audience: one of Duffett's characters is called "Woossat."

28. Nicoll, 1:348. Normal prices were 4s. and 2s. 6d; doubled were 8s. and 5s.; tripled were 12s., and 7s. 6d. The prologue to *Psyche Debauch'd* jeers at a price of a crown (5s.) apiece, though two years later the Duke's Company itself refers to tripled prices in the prologue to *Tunbridge Wells.*

29. *Ibrahim the Illustrious Bassa,* preface, p. [6].

30. Shadwell, *Works,* 2:335.

31. Summers gives an energetic plot summary in *The Playhouse of Pepys* (pp. 445–47), although he glosses over the less savory aspects of act 5. Hume is misled in expecting the *Iphigenia in Tauris* story, a mere digression in this play (*Development of English Drama,* p. 314). Musicologists look at the opera to lament that Purcell set only one scene for the 1685 revival (see Dent, pp. 139, 154–56 and Moore, pp. 13–14, 176–77).

32. Syrens enchant the Greek strangers at Circe's behest, making them easy to capture (2. 1). We learn by report that Circe has also had her spirits incite her husband to molest Iphigenia, a crime she plans to use against him (2. 2 and 3. 1).

33. See my "Duke's Company's Profits, 1675–1677," *Theatre Notebook* 32 (1978): 76–88, especially p. 81.

34. See my "Annotated Census of Thomas Betterton's Roles," *Theatre Notebook* 29 (1975): 33–43, 85–94.

35. *The London Stage,* part 1, lists in November 1677 *The Tempest,* in June 1680 *Macbeth,* in the spring of 1682 *Macbeth, The Tempest,* and *Circe* or *Psyche* (from conflicting sources). The only known revival of one of the Duffett burlesques also occurred in 1682.

36. Moore, p. 178.

37. Historical Manuscripts Commission, *Seventh Report,* part 1 (London, 1879), appendix, p. 288.

38. John Harold Wilson, "Theatre Notes from the Newdigate Newsletters," *Theatre Notebook* 15 (Spring 1961): 79–84.

39. "Dryden in 1684," *Modern Philology* 72 (1975): 248–55. Cf. Robert D. Hume, "Thomas Shipman's *Henry the Third of France:* Some Questions of Date, Performance, and Publication," *Philological Quarterly* 55 (1976): 463.

40. John Harold Wilson, "More Theatre Notes from the Newdigate Newsletters," *Theatre Notebook* 16 (Winter 1961–62): 59.

41. The writer of the Newdigate Newsletters is not always reliable about such details. For example, on 11 January 1694 he calls *The Prophetess* (1690) "the New Opera."

42. *The Letters of John Dryden*, ed. Charles E. Ward (1942; rpt. New York: AMS, 1965), No. 11 (Dryden to Tonson).

43. See Franklin B. Zimmerman, *Henry Purcell, 1659–1695* (London: Macmillan, 1967), pp. 23–27, 49, and 118.

44. See "The Raree-show, from Father HOPKINS" in the entry on Grabu in the *Biographical Dictionary*, 6:293, which credits the machines to Betterton (possibly on the authority of the libretto) and mentions rainbows and peacocks. Hugh Macdonald in *John Dryden: A Bibliography* (1939; rpt. London: Dawsons, 1966), pp. 127–28, note 3, also cites "A Journal from Parnassus," which mentions rainbows, flutes, and peacocks' tails, calls the opera a "gaudy Project," and emphasizes that the players lost money by it.

45. For a discussion of scene locations that seem to have remained in stock, see Montague Summers, *The Restoration Theatre* (1934; rpt. New York: Humanities Press, 1964), pp. 219–21, 223, and 225–26.

46. Dryden, *Works*, 15:19. All stage directions are quoted from this edition.

47. Whether the peacock was single or double is unclear: compare the description in act 3 with note 44 above, which suggests more than one peacock. If this is the machine described in *The Fairy-Queen*, the plural is more likely yet.

48. On the design, see the illustration reprinted in Dryden's *Works*, 15:28 and discussed on p. 372.

49. Dryden, *Works*, 15:323 and 329.

50. Edward Bedingfield to the countess of Rutland, 1 January 1684/85, cited in the *London Stage*, part 1, p. 334.

51. See Hotson, p. 288.

52. Compare the report of £130 as the all-time high at single prices (at Drury Lane) for Shadwell's *The Squire of Alsatia* (Downes, p. 41). Isaac Fuller claimed that the King's Company had taken in £100 a day for *Tyrannick Love* (see note 26).

53. Nicoll, 1:350.

54. £4,000 investment

  − 375 received at premiere (£400 less minimum house charges)

  £3,675 costs, divided by £175 (double prices, less house charges), yields a run of 20
     days beyond the premiere to recoup.

55. Charles E. Ward, *The Life of John Dryden* (Chapel Hill, N.C.: University of North Carolina Press, 1961), pp. 329–32.

56. See my "United Company Finances, 1682–1692," *Theatre Research International*, 7 (1981–82): 37–53, especially p. 39.

57. Summers, *Restoration Theatre*, p. 101.

58. "Eight Dancing Dresses in Imitation of Butterflies" are listed in the inventory of costumes made after Christopher Rich's death in 1714, published by Sybil Rosenfeld in *Theatre Notebook* 5 (1950): 15–19, and Betterton owned what appear to have been renderings for the costumes when he died (*Pinacotheca Bettertonaeana* [1710], Prints & Drawings, No. 55, "Eight Butterflies curiously drawn in Colours").

59. Moore, p. 145.

60. See *The London Stage*, part 2, for performances in whole or in part. For some attempts to surpass *The Prophetess*, see Robert D. Hume's essay, chapter 3 below.

61. In the preface to the Purcell Society edition of *King Arthur*, Margaret Laurie suggests that Dryden wrote the opera and prologue originally "to celebrate the twenty-fifth anniversary of the Restoration," but she offers no evidence for this statement (*The Works of Henry Purcell*, 25 [London: Novello, 1971]).

62. See Milhous and Hume, "Dating Play Premieres," pp. 374–405.

63. Nicoll, 1:350. Christopher Rich's inventory (note 58) lists "Eighteen Singers and Dancers Dresses for King Arthur."

64. *Dryden: The Dramatic Works*, ed. Montague Summers, 6 vols. (London: Nonesuch, 1931–32), 6:275. All quotations from *King Arthur* are from this edition.

65. See *The London Stage*, part 1, p. 395, and part 2, 1:52, 246, 249, and 339.

66. Robert D. Hume and I question the attribution to Settle in "Attribution Problems in English Drama, 1660–1700," *Harvard Library Bulletin* 31 (1983): 5–39.

67. *The Fairy-Queen* (1692), p. 14.

68. Cited in *The London Stage*, part 1, p. 408.

69. See Judith Milhous, *Thomas Betterton and the Management of Lincoln's Inn Fields, 1695–1708* (Carbondale, Ill.: Southern Illinois University Press, 1979), p. 241.

70. A slightly less tidy example can be seen if one traces the use of any single voice type through the scores of most of these productions. Sopranos and basses are clearest. However, composers' designations did not always correspond to the actual casts.

71. The 1709 scenery list cited in note 14 contains "Don Carlos' chamber." A scene in *Squire Oldsapp* (1678) is identified the same way: see Summers, *Restoration Theatre*, p. 217.

72. Not only was *The Indian Queen* ready for production, but Purcell wrote new music for *The Tempest* in 1695, and we may suppose that Betterton had been planning a new production of his first great operatic success. If George Granville was telling the truth when he said that his *British Enchanters* (1706) was inspired a dozen years before it appeared on the stage, then it too might have found a place in the series of Betterton's late productions at Dorset Garden.

3

Opera in London, 1695–1706

ROBERT D. HUME

My starting point is a hardy cliché, the gist of which may be stated thus: the death of Purcell in 1695 marked the end of the "English opera" tradition that had flourished in the Restoration and left a void, ultimately filled by imported Italian opera circa 1705. Most thumping clichés have some element of truth in them, and for this one we must grant that English opera in the Betterton tradition did indeed die out, and that a craze for Italian opera swept the London theatre early in the eighteenth century. That the English opera tradition ended with Purcell in 1695 is, however, entirely false. Nor was there anything like a musical void in the London theatre prior to the opening of Vanbrugh's Haymarket in 1705.

Writing in 1963, Stoddard Lincoln observed that "the sixteen years from the death of Henry Purcell in 1695 to the advent of George Frideric Handel in 1711, hardly noticed by scholars of drama and neglected by musicologists, are usually considered an interregnum between the consummation of the musical ideals of the Restoration, which stemmed from primarily French sources, and the establishment of the Italian music that dominated eighteenth-century England. Actually these sixteen years are as rich as they are confusing."[1] In the last two decades scholars have made considerable advances in this realm. Lincoln's thesis gave us a thorough treatment of Eccles's contributions to the theatre. Roger Fiske has provided—again from an essentially musical point of view—a survey of most of the relevant works written and produced in London.[2] Theatre management, largely neglected since Leslie Hotson's sketchy survey at the end of *The Commonwealth and Restoration Stage* (1928), has recently been intensively studied by Judith Milhous, who has dispelled many myths by returning to primary documents in the Public Record Office.[3] The theatrical circumstances that helped give rise to the "invasion" by Italian opera have been well analyzed in an important article by Curtis A. Price.[4]

What we still lack—and what I will try to provide here—is a clear sense of why the theatres operated as they did, musically speaking. Analysis of the music itself I willingly leave to musicologists, but we are faced by a real puzzle. English opera, far from disappearing with the death of Henry Purcell, flourished in the years immediately after 1695. As late as 1706 Granville's *The British Enchanters* was a booming success—*after* the production of Italian opera in London. Italian opera—excepting *Camilla* in 1706—was far from a financial success at any point in its early history in England. Why, then, did it displace a healthy and popular native tradition?

The custom of jumping straight from Purcell to Handel was established by Burney in 1789 and is one not likely to be abandoned by popular historians of the opera. Donald Jay Grout, in an influential *Short History*, says that "Purcell's death in 1695 put an end to all hope for the future of English musical drama. London was even then full of Italian musicians; audiences became fascinated with Italian opera, and English composers did no more than follow the trend. The success of . . . *Camilla* . . . in 1706 marked the capitulation, and the fashion was completely established by the time of Handel's arrival and the performance of his *Rinaldo* in 1711."[5] This is, in essence, the position taken by almost all opera historians.[6] In part this is explicable simply in terms of the difficulty of discovering what operas were mounted in the intervening period. Alfred Loewenberg's *Annals of Opera* (acknowledged as a selective list) includes *none* of the twenty-two "operas" I propose to discuss here.[7] Of these I would count nine as "masques," and two or three more are perhaps really just old plays fitted out with an unusual amount of music. But at least ten are genuine operas as the English public then understood the term. And Loewenberg does enter such generically similar works as the Shadwell-Locke *Psyche* (1675), the Dryden-Purcell *King Arthur* (1691), and the Anon.(?)-Purcell *The Fairy-Queen* (1692). Even *The London Stage,* though it enters most of these works in its daily performance calendar, does not always make clear that they are operas. Given this dearth of readily accessible information, early scholars quite naturally concentrate either on the Davenant-Betterton tradition, which produced the Dorset Garden spectaculars of the seventies, eighties, and early nineties,[8] or on the Italian operas mounted at Vanbrugh's Haymarket after 1705.[9] The inaccessibility—or total disappearance—of much of the music from the period under discussion here has naturally contributed to its neglect. The first good list of operas (omitting masques) produced in London between 1695 and 1705 was published by Eric Walter White in 1951.[10] In his text, White jumps straight from Purcell at the end of chapter 1 to "The Handelian Catastrophe" in chapter 2, but in a survey covering some 300 years this is perhaps to be expected. White did at least clearly establish the existence of English operas during this musical interregnum.

One considerable awkwardness in any study of the present subject is inevitable confusion over what is meant by "opera." Many of the works involved might well be termed "masques." Some of them were mounted as entities unto themselves (Congreve's *The Judgment of Paris*); others were staged in tandem with a play, though without much attempt at connecting the two (*Peleus and Thetis* in Granville's *The Jew of Venice*); some are tied into the companion work after a fashion (*The Loves of Mars and Venus*, given with Ravenscroft's *The Anatomist*); occasionally one is tightly integrated thematically and dramatically (*Ixion* in Ravenscroft's *The Italian Husband*). Even those full-length works which occupy a performance date by themselves (the 1674 *Tempest*, *King Arthur*, *The Virgin Prophetess*, and others) strike us as plays with a lot of incidental music rather than as "operas." To Purcell, however, an "opera" was a spoken play into which musical masques were interpolated. Recitative was rarely employed: the "story" was carried on by means of spoken dialogue.

However inexact the terminology of the time, we can probably make some rough distinctions. Used in its broadest sense, "opera" simply means drama with a considerable amount of added music, or a masque. During the 1690s some writers seem to make a distinction between "opera" and "masque" basically in terms of scale. Blockbuster Dorset Garden productions such as *Psyche* and *Circe* were "operas," while shorter or less elaborate productions amounted merely to "masques." Sneering at the pretentions of Rich's company, the prologue to Motteux's *The Loves of Mars and Venus* gibes: "And what we call a Masque some will allow/To be an Op'ra, as the World goes now." The production of *Arsinoe* in 1705 was genuinely revolutionary in the London theatre. Though translated into English, it was "Italian opera" in the sense that it contained no spoken dialogue and it presented none of the fancy scenic and machine effects long associated with English opera as staged by Betterton. Writing ex post facto, old Roger North describes "the introduction of Semioperas" under Betterton's sponsorship: "a sort of plays, which were called Operas but had bin more properly styled Semioperas, for they consisted of half Musick, and half Drama." The vogue for Italian opera, he remarks, finally "forc't" the semioperas "to yeild and give place to their betters the compleat operas."[11] For the sake of clarity, I will use "English opera" or "semi-opera" to designate full-length works on the mixed model; "masque" to describe shorter works of the English sort; and "Italian opera" (whether sung in English or Italian) to refer to works that were all sung.

My aims may be simply stated. I propose first to give some account of the last of the Dorset Garden spectaculars—works almost wholly neglected by theatre historians. Second, I wish to survey the flurry of masques mounted in the mid-1690s. This renewed competition in the London theatre after the actors' rebellion of 1695 culminates in the great opera collision in the season of 1698–99 between Lincoln's Inn Fields's *Rinaldo and Armida* and Drury Lane's *The Island Princess*. And third, I wish to consider the heated competition between Vanbrugh and Rich circa 1705—a competition in which opera was a key factor. I want to call attention to the sheer volume of operatic entertainment getting staged in London during this alleged "interregnum," to suggest that many of these works were interesting, successful, and worthwhile, and finally to offer the heterodox opinion that the triumph of Italian opera was by no means as foreordained and inevitable as it is usually considered to have been.

Major Productions by the Patent Company

Because the English operas staged at Dorset Garden by the Duke's and United Companies have been so heavily associated with Betterton—and rightly so[12]—there has been a tendency to assume that after he decamped to Lincoln's Inn Fields in 1695 the Patent Company turned to other kinds of attractions. This view is, in fact, quite untrue. In its first two seasons after the secession of the rebels, Rich's company mounted six new opera productions, and it produced three more in the next four seasons. Such tactics are, indeed, what we might expect. As Cibber says in an often-quoted passage,[13] the remnants and youngsters left to Rich were no match for the veteran stars of Lincoln's Inn Fields in the standard repertory. Consequently, Rich tried to capitalize on new plays, and his possession of Drury Lane and Dorset Garden. Stuck in the cramped old Lincoln's Inn Fields Theatre, Betterton—whose company had no capital at all—was in no position to mount shows such as *King Arthur* (1691) or *The Fairy-Queen* (1692), productions on which he had lavished thousands of pounds. That Rich should want to take advantage of his superior physical theatre facilities makes a great deal of sense.

The first major production of a "new" show by the Patent Company was Henry Purcell's operatic reworking of Dryden and Howard's *The Indian Queen* (1664). Exactly when this production reached the stage we do not know. It was probably written by the summer of 1694 at latest. In the "Reply of the Patentees" (10 December 1694), Rich complains that Betterton "has had 50*11* for his care & trouble to gett up ye Indian Queen though he hath not yett done itt"[14]—striking testimony to Betterton's immense value in producing such works. At this time £50 was an annual salary for all but a few top actors in the London theatre: Betterton himself probably drew less than £150 for his acting. The editors of *The London Stage* place performance of *The Indian Queen* in "mid-April" of 1695.[15] This dating seems to me improbable. On Cibber's testimony, the company was struggling just to recast a few standard repertory plays—*Abdelazer, Hamlet, The Old Batchelour, Othello, Julius Caesar.* Could they—would they have tried to—get up a large and complicated musical show from scratch? Even assuming that a minimum of money was spent and that the elaborate scenic effects favored by Betterton were downplayed, such an effort seems unlikely. A more logical date for the opera is sometime between late October and December 1695.[16]

Rich's strategy seems obvious. If his scrubs could not compete with the senior actors on equal terms, they could at least turn Betterton's specialty back on him. We have solid evidence that *The Indian Queen* was a lasting success. Gildon tells us so: "*The Indian Queen* . . . formerly Acted with general Applause, at the Theatre royal, but now turn'd into an Opera, and many times of late represented at the same Theatre, with the like Success."[17] Our scanty performance records amply bear out this assertion. We know of performances in April 1696 (for the Venetian ambassadors), March, June, and December 1697 (in the last instance, for visiting Russian nobles). Use of the show to entertain visiting dignitaries suggests that it was considered in a class with *The Prophetess* and *King Arthur.* Our lack of a definite performance date in 1695 is frustrating, but the publication of Daniel Purcell's "Additional Musick to the *Indian Queen*" (the masque in act 5), advertised in the *Post-Boy,* 29 February–2 March 1696, suggests a date late in the year.

The Indian Queen was not, however, Rich's first attempt to turn Betterton's operatic specialty against the rebel actors. Retaining the potentially invaluable services of Henry Purcell and good theatre buildings, Rich quite naturally took advantage of them with an adaptation of Fletcher's *Bonduca,* which probably reached the stage before the end of September 1695. No exact date can be assigned, but a prologue reference to *She Ventures and He Wins,* which had failed at Lincoln's Inn Fields by 19 September, makes the September date likely.[18] *Bonduca* is a distinctly minimal opera—a cut version "With a New Entertainment of Musick, Vocal and Instrumental," as the title page says—and one which reused old scenery. George Powell (Rich's leading actor) signed the dedication but disclaimed responsibility for the adaptation, said to have been done by "a Friend of mine." In all likelihood Powell did the not very fancy staging. *Bonduca* is a quick, cheap, relatively simple "opera," but it did allow the young Drury Lane Company to capitalize on some of its strengths. The old Dorset Garden Theatre was in a dilapidated state, but as the prologue to *Bonduca* observes, the company was "bringing / Machines, Scenes, Opera's, Musick, Dancing, Singing; / Translated from the Chiller, Bleaker *Strand,* / To your Sweet *Covent-Garden's* Warmer Land"—i.e., from Dorset Garden to Drury Lane.[19]

To employ Henry Purcell to the utmost was obviously a good idea for a struggling company of journeymen and beginners. Purcell contributed all or part of the additional music for the five new productions known to have been staged at Drury Lane between its reopening in April 1695 and his death the following November—*Abdelazer* (1676—long out of the repertory), *The Mock Marriage, The Rival Sisters,* part 3 of *Don Quixote,* and *Oroonoko.* In addition to these sets of incidental music and the two operas already mentioned, there is at least some possibility that Purcell also provided a new score for Betterton's first great operatic triumph, the 1674 (or "Shadwell") version of *The Tempest*. This would have been turning Betterton's own guns on him with a vengeance. John Bannister had written music for the original 1667 production; Locke, Draghi, Humphrey, and Pietro Reggio all contributed to the 1674 revamping, often called the most popular play of the Restoration period. We have no definite record of a performance between February 1682 and May 1697. Republication of the text in 1695 is, however, a probable indication of revival, and the publication of a song by Purcell in *Deliciae Musicae* (1696) seems to bear this out. Whether Purcell actually wrote the new music (published much later) is at best questionable. R. E. Moore treats it as definitely his, but a strong countercase has been made by Margaret Laurie, who ascribes it to Weldon.[20] But whether with new music or old, *The Tempest* certainly became a mainstay in the repertory of Rich's young company. A recast production in the fall of 1695 seems highly likely.

Scholars have noted in recent years that Rich's company was forced to rush out a large number of new plays in its first difficult seasons after the split.[21] The importance of operas in the company's competitive efforts should not, however, go unnoticed. The three substantial musical productions in the fall of 1695 were a key part of Rich's effort to survive and compete against a popular veteran company. The lack of new operatic productions later in the season I would attribute to the obvious—Purcell's death on 21 November. That stunning loss to the Patent Company, coupled with the availability of earlier operas for revival *(Psyche, Circe, The Prophetess, King Arthur)*, probably accounts for the abrupt cessation of new opera productions. Performance records are so sparse that we have no idea when these other operas entered the Drury Lane repertory, or what older plays and operas Rich relied upon during the spring of 1696. For those months we have exactly *one* recorded performance of anything but new plays (most of which are dated by publication)—*The Indian Queen* on 29 April. That Rich was using some of the older operas seems highly likely: we have definite proof that by the spring of 1697 at least *Psyche* and *The Prophetess* were back in the repertory.

During the season of 1696–97 Rich's company tried three more original operas. Two of them were relatively cheap and simple shows; the third, Settle's ambitious *The World in the Moon,* was an expensive fiasco that came just at the end of an already mediocre season. The first opera of the year, *A New Opera Called Brutus of Alba,* was very much the sort of show *Bonduca* had been. This opera is a patchwork put together from a number of sources, including Tate's play of 1678. Powell and Verbruggen signed the dedication, in which they imply that they would welcome "visitors" on benefit nights, but they were probably responsible for no more than the staging. Daniel Purcell was the composer; only a few songs survive. The show probably received its premiere on 26 October, but what sort of run it had, or whether it was later revived, we have no records to show.[22] As literature, the piece has few merits. I termed it a "vulgar mishmash" some years ago, and on rereading it I see no reason to alter my low opinion.[23] If the show failed, it got what it deserved.

The company's second opera of the season, Durfey's *Cinthia and Endimion*, was apparently a flat failure. The identity of the composer is unknown. One song by Clarke survives, and Fiske offers the plausible suggestion that he was collaborating with Daniel Purcell. Fiske comments sourly that both *Brutus of Alba* and *Cinthia and Endimion* "have uninteresting and badly written librettos," and I entirely agree with him. Durfey's lyrics are as lovely as usual, but the story is sodden and the staging was apparently entirely simple and routine. Fiske says that *"Cinthia and Endimion* was presented at Court before it was given at Drury Lane," but this is an error. The title page says, "Designed to be Acted at Court, before the late Queen; and now Acted at the Theatre Royal." In other words, the opera was probably written by the fall of 1694, and the company had been in no hurry to produce it. The intended court venue, however, may account for the very simple staging. The date of the Drury Lane production is not exactly known. *The London Stage* puts it in December 1696, but since operas were usually published simultaneously with the premiere, and publication was advertised 16 January 1697, a mid-January date seems likely. A copy in the Library of Congress has a manuscript date of "16 Januar." and since Saturday is the commonest day for a premiere, I would hypothesize that Saturday, 16 January is the premiere. That *Cinthia and Endimion* got produced at all is testimony to the difficulty the two theatre companies were having in finding good new plays. Old scripts refused by the United Company were being pulled out of bottom drawers, dusted off, and given a try.

Perhaps as a result of the disappointing showing of these two cheap operas Rich decided to plunge heavily on a fancy, expensive opera. Settle's *The World in the Moon* is a most interesting experiment. The company employed the Dorset Garden Theatre, and evidently made a serious attempt to put its potentialities to use in an innovative way. Preparatory puffs appeared in the newspapers about two weeks before the show opened. The *Post-Boy* of 12–15 June 1697 reported:

> Great Preparations are making for a new Opera in the Play-house in Dorset-Garden, of which there is great Expectation, the Scenes being several new Sets and of a moddel different from all that have been used in any Theatre whatever, being twice as high as any of their former Scenes. And the whole Decoration of the Stage not only infinitely beyond all the Opera's ever yet performed in England, but also by the acknowledgement of several Gentlemen that have travell'd abroad, much exceeding all that has been seen on any of the Foreign Stages.

The opera probably received its premiere on Friday, 25 June or Saturday,

26 June (having been published the twenty-fifth), and it achieved a benefit night for "the Undertaker" (Christopher Rich) on 1 July. The *Post-Boy* of that date advertised the benefit with the comment that "The new Opera . . . is acting with great applause." Perhaps so, but the show enjoyed almost no further vogue in its entirety. A few bits do seem to have been chopped out and cannibalized as entr'actes after the turn of the century—for example, on 23 October 1702 and 22 June 1703. The opera was never reprinted, and a handful of performances in the slack summer season of its premiere cannot have more than started to repay the high costs of such a production.

Settle's dedication to Rich was clearly written before performance, and hence tells us nothing about reception. Settle did, however, make very plain the degree of "Labour, and Expense" involved. "Never was such a Pile of Painting rais'd upon so Generous a Foundation; especially under all the Hardships of so backward a Season of the Year (our Misfortune, not Fault)." In other words, Rich gambled a lot of money on a production that did not reach the stage until the weather was hot and the town sparsely populated.

The World in the Moon, flop or not, is a unique and fascinating experiment. It consists of a normal, quasi-realistic "London" comedy, part of which is set in the Dorset Garden Theatre, thus making an excuse for introducing large chunks of an opera in "rehearsal." The integration of play and musical spectacle is unusual and clever, and has roused some modest enthusiasm among recent critics.[24] About ten of the songs by Daniel Purcell and Clarke survive; they are unremarkable. The company put its money and effort into fancy scenery. Settle boasts in his dedication "that the Model of the Scenes of this Play, are something of an Original: I am sure I have removed a long Heap of Rubbish, and thrown away all our old *French* Lumber, our Clouds of Clouts, and set the Theatrical Paintings at a much fairer Light. . . . I dare confidently averr, the Prospect of this Stage will put all the old Rags out of Countenance."[25] As Milhous observes, this sounds like a deliberate attempt to outdo the grandiosities of Betterton's *Prophetess*—and it cannot have been anything but a financial disaster. Rich's company had been staging *The Indian Queen, The Prophetess,* and *Psyche* during the spring of 1697, and we can hardly imagine that they would have gambled on Settle's spectacular if those shows had not been making money.

After the misfire with *The World in the Moon,* Rich prudently stuck to revivals and plays for a while. In the 1697–98 season we find *The Prophetess, The Indian Queen, King Arthur,* and *The Tempest* definitely in the repertory. The actors put on *The Island Princess* at their own expense in 1699 (an episode to be discussed in section 2 below): not until February 1700 did Rich underwrite even another cheap opera. Oldmixon's *The Grove,* with music by Daniel Purcell, was mounted in late January or February 1700, probably as a counterattraction to Lincoln's Inn Fields' *Measure for Measure* (adapted by Gildon), into which Henry Purcell's *Dido and Aeneas* (1689) was interpolated between the acts.[26] The failure of *The Grove* may well be attributed to cuts and a sloppy production. Oldmixon's text is by no means without merit—a "pastoral" with more than usual character interest. Oldmixon's "Preface" tells us that the music was well received, and Fiske praises it. Oldmixon blames ill success in the theatre on factors beyond his control. "The Persons . . . who thought the Catastrophe was not enough prepar'd, and that the discovery in the last Act was huddled and in confusion . . . will now see if what he had writ had been spoken, everything wou'd have appear'd clear and natural, which, to shorten the Entertainment, had been before broken and disorder'd." Such claims are now difficult to assess, but I can see no intrinsic reason that this should not have been a popular show.

The great success of *The Island Princess* in February 1699 must certainly have suggested to Rich that money was to be made in English operas—or he would not have kept on underwriting them. About *Alexander* (a revamping of Lee's *The Rival Queens*, 1677, with music by Daniel Purcell and Godfrey Finger) we know very little, even though we possess the full score; indeed, few theatre historians seem to have been aware that there was such an opera. It does not appear in White's appendix A, and *The London Stage* fails to differentiate it from Lee's original play.[27] My best guess is that the opera production received its premiere around 20 February 1701. Lady Morley—an enthusiastic operagoer—attended it on Thursday the twentieth and Saturday the twenty-second. On 5 April she went to "The Rivall Queene" at Drury Lane—presumably still the operatic form.[28] We have no other definite performance dates before or during this season. By January 1703 the original form of Lee's play was in the repertory at Lincoln's Inn Fields,[29] and later performances at Drury Lane (e.g., 13 June 1704, 19 December 1705) appear from the newspaper bills to be the straight play, not the operatic adaptation.

Alexander was clearly not a major effort. One hint of its scale can be deduced from the Morley lawsuit: "ordinary" rather than "raised" prices were charged. For a seat in a box at *The Prophetess, The Indian Queen, Psyche, King Arthur, The Island Princess, The Virgin Prophetess,* and even *The Grove* five shillings was the usual price, even many years after the premiere. But for *Bonduca, Cinthia and Endimion, The Tempest,* and *Alexander,* only four shillings were charged. This is a clear indication of production scale.

During the 1700–1701 season Rich was evidently having excellent luck with English operas. Scanty though our performance records are for this period, we have definite evidence that the following operas were in Drury Lane's active repertory: *The Prophetess, The Island Princess, The Tempest,* and *King Arthur.* Small wonder that Rich, despite such disappointments as *The World in the Moon* and *The Grove,* was proceeding full blast with another blockbuster production—*The Virgin Prophetess*. He probably hoped to get it mounted during the fall of 1700. The *Post-Boy* of 14—16 May 1700 announced:

> Great Preparations have been making, for some Months past, for a New Opera to be acted next Term at the Theatre Royal, which, for Grandeur, Decorations, Movements of Scenes &c. will be infinitely superior to *Dioclesian* (*The Prophetess*) which hitherto has been the greatest that the English Stage has produced, that probably 'twill equal the greatest Performance of that Kind, in any of the foreign Theatres. The Musick is compos'd by the Ingenious Mr Finger, and the Paintings made by Mr Robinson.

Once again poor old Elkanah Settle seems to have dreamed of outdoing Betterton. Finger's music is relatively short—the emphasis in "This costly Play" (as the prologue terms it) is on staging as fancy as the Drury Lane Theatre was capable of producing. (Dorset Garden was in very bad repair by this time, and Rich had been turned out of it for nonpayment of rent.) This grand showpiece appears to have run three to six nights in mid-May 1701. Parts of the staging must have been truly spectacular—in particular the "Dome scene," which occasionally turns up in later seasons as an entr'acte or afterpiece (e.g., 27 December 1703, 12 November 1705). The music is nothing special, and the libretto is testimony only to Settle's mediocrity as a writer. The late spring premiere once again cannot have helped the run. Nonetheless Drury Lane's long-awaited opera may well have made Lincoln's Inn Fields nervous: the production of *The Mad Lover* during the 1700–1701 season and the appearance of *Circe* in the Lincoln's Inn Fields repertory in June 1701 suggest a concerted attempt to fight opera with opera.

The Virgin Prophetess sank almost without trace, and it was Rich's last venture in that variety of opera. The quiescence of the theatres, operatically speaking, during the next three years is not hard to understand. There was no topflight composer available to Drury Lane; Dorset Garden was almost unusable; Settle had cost Rich's company a great deal of money on a pair of horrendous flops. Competition between the two companies diminished drastically during the years after 1701, which no doubt reduced pressure on the managers to mount financially risky operas.[30] We should not suppose, however, that the failure of Settle's cumbrous shows represents a rejection of English opera by an audience increasingly familiar with vocal and instrumental Italian music. A look at performance records for 1702–1703 and 1703–1704 shows the following English operas in the active repertory: *The Tempest* (at both theatres—possibly using different scores), *The Prophetess*, *The Island Princess*, *The Fairy-Queen* (act 1 alone—much of the music apparently having been lost very early), *Psyche*, and *Circe*. Far from being despised and neglected, these English operas show all the signs of being perennial favorites. Italian opera did not flourish in England because of a vacuum, and, some misfires notwithstanding, Rich appears to have got a substantial competitive advantage out of "Bettertonian" opera. At this point, then, we need to inquire how Betterton and his fellow rebels met the challenge.

Masques at Lincoln's Inn Fields—and the Great Collision of 1698–99

While Drury Lane staged old and new "Bettertonian" operas, what of Lincoln's Inn Fields? In the ten years the rebel company spent there prior to the opening of Vanbrugh's Haymarket in 1705 it mounted exactly two "operas" of the sort we have been discussing at Drury Lane. Instead of full-dress operas we find a series of short masques at Lincoln's Inn Fields. Some scholars have imagined that this turning away from opera was a matter of choice. Richard Luckett says that "Betterton seems for a time to have concentrated on . . . 'masques' within plays" in the years around 1700.[31] Fiske says that "full-length operas . . . were for the most part" written for Rich's company, while "at Lincoln's Inn Fields Betterton preferred the single interpolated masque with a mythological plot," a kind of entertainment that "must have been much closer to Italianate opera."[32] The truth of the matter, as Judith Milhous has demonstrated in her account of the Lincoln's Inn Fields Company, is that Betterton had to abandon the opera that was his trademark because of a physically inadequate theatre and harsh financial constraints.

The cramped Lincoln's Inn Fields Theatre had been abandoned by the Duke's Company in 1671, used by the King's Company after the burning of Bridges Street until the completion of Drury Lane in 1674, and not employed as a theatre since then. It had never been designed for fancy machine staging or large-scale shows: little wonder, then, that Betterton should feel compelled to move toward a form in which singing rather than staging was paramount. When he did manage to mount a small-scale opera in 1698, Dennis's *Rinaldo and Armida*, "this surpriz'd not only *Drury-lane*, but indeed all the Town, no body ever dreaming of an *Opera* there . . . [though] they had heard of *Homer*'s Illiads in a Nut-shel, and Jack in a Box, and what not."[33]

Financial limitations must have been equally compelling. The actor-sharers had no capital at all, and their "sharers' agreement" specifically forbade the involvement of outside investors. They had left behind their entire stock of scenery and costumes, and they had to pay for the conversion of a tennis court to a theatre. Cibber says that "many People of Quality came into a voluntary Subscription of twenty, and some of forty Guineas a-piece, for erecting a Theatre within the Walls of the Tennis-Court in *Lincoln's-Inn-Fields*."[34] That the company could have raised much over a thousand pounds this way seems unlikely—and Betterton had been known to spend three and four thousand pounds on a single opera production at Dorset Garden. For him to go on as he had done was physically and financially impossible: hence the turn to masques. Until the company paid for its theatre renovations and built up a stock of scenery and costumes, no other option was open to them.

Rich's success with revivals of older operas, and his obvious inclination to try new ones, probably made the rival company anxious to reply in kind as best it could. They had a kind of model available to them in *The Rape of Europa by Jupiter,* a masque produced sometime during 1694 in the last year of the United Company. The circumstances in which this little piece was staged are maddeningly vague. Eugene Haun asserts that it is by William Ranson, and that, like *The Judgment of Paris* (1701), it "seems to have been performed" as a "single" production. On both counts this seems to me quite wrong. The attribution to Ranson Haun derives from Wing, but this is in fact a misreading derived from alphabetical juxtaposition.[35] And however elaborately set, a narrative masque of eight pages cannot have supplied an evening's entertainment by itself. Stoddard Lincoln has suggested on stylistic grounds that the author was Peter Motteux, and this seems highly plausible.[36] And what might this piece have been added to? Lincoln suggests—on what evidence I do not know—that it was written for a revival of Rochester's *Valentinian* in late 1694. We have evidence that *Valentinian* was revived sometime that year, and *The Rape of Europa by Jupiter* does seem a highly suitable interpolation for the masque called for in act 4. It could well have been written to replace Francis Fane's uninspired original (1684). The Dorset Garden location specified on the title page, however, is a problem. The 1685 quarto of *Valentinian* says, "Acted at the Theatre Royal"—i.e., Drury Lane—and while such a move is by no means impossible, it would be highly unusual.[37] At any rate *The Rape of Europa by Jupiter* made a convenient model for the Lincoln's Inn Fields Company. Eccles was their house composer, and Motteux was working for them in the first three seasons after the split.

The triumphant opening of Lincoln's Inn Fields in April 1695 with *Love for Love* probably left the rebel actors feeling too secure to worry much about finding special musical additions as a competitive device. Their employment of one circa September 1695 was more a matter of topical convenience than deliberate competition against *Bonduca* and Drury Lane's operatic attractions to come. *The Taking of Namur and His Majesty's Safe Return,* with words by Motteux and music by Eccles, celebrates King William's successful siege of Namur, which surrendered on 26 August 1695. How much staging this piece was accorded we have no way to determine—probably not a great deal. *The Taking of Namur* was presumably an entirely inorganic addition to one of the company's repertory plays—perhaps as masque or entr'acte, perhaps as afterpiece. It is, however, a significant step toward Lincoln's Inn Fields's characteristic form of added musical attraction.

During the 1695–96 season the Lincoln's Inn Fields Company contented itself, musically speaking, with many added songs. We possess music by Eccles for eight of the nine new plays they staged that season. The last of them, Motteux's *Love's a Jest* (June 1696), is a sort of potpourri, generously stuffed with songs and "dialogues" set to music by Eccles. The considerable success of this piece seems to have spawned an immediate imitation at Drury Lane—*The Cornish Comedy,* a similar bit of fluff brought to the stage by George Powell with music by Clarke.

By the season of 1696–97 Lincoln's Inn Fields was a bit more serious about competition. Drury Lane had survived a rocky first year and had enjoyed a pair of major successes in *Oroonoko* and *Love's Last Shift,* as well as a lastingly popular opera in *The Indian Queen.* The rebel actors riposted with an interesting experiment—Ravenscroft's *The Anatomist* (November 1696), a cheerful farce into which they interpolated *The Loves of Mars and Venus* in three separate pieces. Motteux provided words; Eccles set acts 1 and 2; Finger set act 3. Stoddard Lincoln has offered a detailed analysis.[38] For our purposes here the most striking fact about this odd conglomeration is its considerable success—"owing to the Musick," *A Comparison between the Two Stages* tells us. This opinion is confirmed by Gildon: "This play met with extraordinary Success having the Advantage of the excellent Musick of *The Loves of Mars and Venus* perform'd with it."[39] In various guises the show enjoyed a considerable vogue on the eighteenth-century stage. A significant part of its attraction was probably the dancing. Lincoln offers the plausible suggestion that Sorin did the original choreography—he had signed a contract with Betterton during the summer of 1696. The only other musical show staged during this season was *Hercules,* a masque by Motteux and Eccles which served as act 3 of Motteux's miscellany, *The Novelty.* This medley—a pastoral, a one-act comedy, a masque, a one-act tragedy, and a "short Farce after the Italian [Commedia dell'Arte] manner"—was staged with considerable success in late May or June 1697. Most of the music for *Hercules* is lost, but from the text I would suppose it to have been a delicious little masque in a comic mode.

The success of these masques naturally led the Lincoln's Inn Fields Company to try more of them during 1697–98. The more than welcome Treaty of Ryswick, signed at the end of September 1697, provided an occasion for *Europe's Revels for the Peace.* The premiere may well have been at court, on King William's birthday (4 November). Some confusion has surrounded this occasion. *The London Stage* reports a reference in the Lord Chamberlain's papers "to a performance given jointly by both companies."[40] But since this short masque (the usual Motteux-Eccles collaboration) cannot have been the whole evening's entertainment, and since all of the performers named in Q 1697 are from Lincoln's Inn Fields, I would hypothesize that Drury Lane's contribution was entirely separate. *Europe's Revels* is a joyous romp with very flashy martial music—a seventeenth-century "forerunner of Beethoven's *Wellington Symphony* and Tchaikowsky's *1812 Overture*," as Lincoln observes.[41] In all probability Lincoln's Inn Fields added this piece to various plays during the winter.

The considerable success of *The Anatomist* with its musical additions the previous fall seems to have stimulated Ravenscroft to try a more ambitious project. *The Italian Husband* (probably premiered in December 1697) is a short, stark, highly effective "Continental"-style tragedy in three acts. What makes it unusual, beyond its brevity, is its full situational and thematic integration of music into the tragedy. The wedding anniversary entertainments of act 1 work in well, while the *Ixion* masque in act 3 is an exact thematic anticipation of the catastrophe into which it leads. Coming at a time when the trend was toward completely unrelated musical additions and entr'actes, *The Italian Husband* is a striking reminder that serious use could be made of music if dramatists wanted to take the trouble. Apart from Stoddard Lincoln, hardly anyone has taken notice of this remarkable tragedy. Fiske mentions it only to ascribe the masque to Taverner (an ascription suggested in the 1812 *Biographia Dramatica*) and to say that the music to *Ixion* is lost. But since incidental music by Eccles for the play is preserved, we are probably safe in supposing that he provided music for the masque. The librettist for *Ixion* is not stated in the quarto of 1698: lacking an explicit ascription, Ravenscroft himself seems the likeliest candidate. In all probability, *The Italian Husband* failed outright. It ran counter to current taste in tragedy (note Gildon's angry denunciation), and there is no record of revival or reprinting.[42] So little known is this musical experiment that no hint of *Ixion*'s presence in the evening's entertainment is to be found in *The London Stage*.

Early in the season of 1698–99 Lincoln's Inn Fields made a major effort to put on a real opera, enjoyed a fair success with it, and then found its success wiped out by a hastily mounted counterattraction at Drury Lane. This direct collision between operas at the rival houses marks the only such head-on conflict in the period under consideration, and it was a deeply disappointing setback for Lincoln's Inn Fields. The story has been clouded by a confusion on the part of the generally reliable author of *A Comparison between the Two Stages*, who has Drury Lane's *The Island Princess* coming first, to be ineffectually "answered" by *Rinaldo and Armida* at Lincoln's Inn Fields.[43] This view was quite naturally adopted by the editors of *The London Stage*, but it is demonstrably erroneous, and it obscures a most interesting chapter in the history of the competition.[44]

Rinaldo and Armida is a serious attempt to advance the mode developed a year earlier in *The Italian Husband*. With Dennis as the author this would almost have had to be the case: his hostility to works of "mere sensual

Pleasure" was longstanding,[45] and certainly he had little love for random musical additions to serious drama. The title page of the 1699 edition calls the work simply "A Tragedy," and makes no mention of the musical component. Some two weeks before the quarto appeared there was published *The Musical Entertainments in the Tragedy of Rinaldo and Armida*, "All Compos'd by Mr. John Eccles, and Writ by Mr. Dennis."[46] Dennis's preface to the *Musical Entertainments* addresses the generic question directly. "Though the Tragedy of *Rinaldo* and *Armida*, of which the following Lines are a Part, has gone in the World under the Name of an *Opera*; yet is neither the Dramatical Part of it, like the Drama of our usual *Opera*'s, nor the Musical part of it like that which is Sung and Play'd in those Entertainments: For all the Musick in this Play, even the Musick between the Acts, is part of the Tragedy, and for that Reason the Musick is always Pathetick." Here is the key: "all the Musick . . . is part of the Tragedy." Dennis goes on to commend Eccles for having "so throughly enter'd into my design"—i.e., expressing such passions as "Love and Joy, Anger, Compassion, Terror, Grief, Horror, Astonishment and Despair." Dennis is no great tragedian, but in concept this is an impressively forward-looking work. A variety of evidence cited in the *London Stage*—letters, poems, and pamphlets— suggests that *Rinaldo and Armida* enjoyed a good initial run.[47] When Elizabeth Barry wrote to Lady Lisburne on 5 January 1699, "I never knew a worse Winter only we have had pretty good success in the Opera of Rinaldo and Armida," she certainly seems to have been implying that Lincoln's Inn Fields had done well with its opera. For December and January the performance records suggest that Drury Lane was feeling its rivals' musical success. Drury Lane countered first with French singers, then with a Eunuch, and finally with a visiting Italian, "Don Segismondo Fideli."[48]

Drury Lane evidently felt hard enough pressed to rustle up an opera of its own posthaste. *The Island Princess . . . Made into an Opera* ("All the Musical Entertainments, and the greatest Part of the Play New, and Written by Mr. *Motteux*") was probably rushed into performance 7 February 1699 when Lady Morley first attended it. Leveridge, Clarke, and Daniel Purcell all contributed music. At the end of act 5 "A Musical Interlude" called "The Four Seasons or Love in every Age" is simply tacked on, "Set to Music by Mr. Jeremy Clarke." A note in the published text says cheerfully: "This Entertainment is perform'd at the End of the last Act, but was design'd for another Season, and another Occasion: And what is mark'd thus (") is omitted" (p. 37). I have previously termed Motteux's rehash of Tate's 1687 revamping of the 1669 version of Fletcher's play (1621) "a thundering melodrama, trashy but effective."[49]

However patchy a show, musically and dramatically, *The Island Princess* was a tremendous success, and it remained popular for more than a quarter of a century. (Fiske calls it "by far the most successful English opera before *The Beggar's Opera*,"[50] though *The Tempest* seems an equally plausible candidate.) The Drury Lane actors, under heavy competitive pressure and getting little help from their master Rich, struck it lucky. How they inveigled Motteux away from Lincoln's Inn Fields (where he had previously done all his work) we do not know. Milhous points out that the prologue implies that the performers had to underwrite the cost of the scenery themselves—a piece of penny-pinching that apparently did not prevent Rich from trying to deny Motteux the traditional author's "third day" profits.[51] Rich probably felt badly enough burned by his expensive fiasco with *The World in the Moon* back in June 1697 that he wanted to take no chances. If the actors were frightened enough by Lincoln's Inn Fields' success with *Rinaldo and Armida* to put up their own money for an opera, well and good. Rich benefited, however, from the great popularity of *The Island Princess:* performances continued right through the spring; the music got republished in various forms and was heavily advertised—signs of an altogether exceptional success. This triumph in head-on competition finally established the Drury Lane Company as a serious threat to the veteran stars at Lincoln's Inn Fields. The author of *A Comparison between the Two Stages* puts the point thus: the opera competition constituted "the great Turn which seem'd to decide the Fates of *Rome* and *Carthage*. . . . The Quality, who are always Lovers of good Musick, flock hither [to Drury Lane], and by almost a total revolt from the other *House*, give this new Life, and set it in some eminency above the *New;* this was a sad mortification to the old Stagers in *Lincoln's-Inn-Fields*."[52] Though confused about the sequence of the competition, the author seems absolutely right in seeing this as a crucial defeat for Lincoln's Inn Fields.

By the season of 1699–1700 the Lincoln's Inn Fields Company was in serious disarray, and by November of the 1700–1701 season the situation was so serious that the Lord Chamberlain had to intervene in the company's internal affairs.[53] Giving Betterton more executive authority does seem to have put the company back on the road to reasonable stability, but in the meantime its competitive efforts were minimal. The smashing success of Farquhar's *The Constant Couple* (November 1699) at Drury Lane was a serious blow. Lincoln's Inn Fields did manage to counter *The Grove* with *Dido and Aeneas* (the sequence is undeterminable), but the only new musical additions of importance this season were to Drury Lane's revival of *The Pilgrim* (April 1700), in particular Dryden's *Secular Masque*, with music by Daniel Purcell and Finger.

That Betterton should have turned to opera when given increased authority at Lincoln's Inn Fields is in no way surprising. About *The Mad Lover* we know frustratingly little.[54] It appears to have been a kind of imitation of *The Island Princess*—a rewrite of a Fletcher play done by Motteux, in this case with music by Eccles and an added masque, *Acis and Galatea*. The text was not published; parts of the music reached print during the spring of

1701. *Acis and Galatea* was published in 1701, and it remained popular until the Handel-Gay resetting of 1732. Lincoln estimates a premiere in December 1700, but this seems too close to the administrative reorganization at Lincoln's Inn Fields (ordered 11 November). I would offer the hypothesis that Betterton, once given more power, turned immediately to an imitation of the sort of patchwork opera that had given Drury Lane such success two seasons earlier. The first publication of music from *The Mad Lover* occurred in February 1701, which is about where I would place the premiere. Success was probably limited or nil—by June parts of the music were being used as added attractions for *Circe*.

After this the two companies increasingly settled into something like peaceful coexistence. The most delightful of all the masques, Congreve's *The Judgment of Paris* (March 1701), was set in competition by Eccles, Finger, Daniel Purcell, and Weldon. The special genesis of the work removed it from ordinary competitive circumstances: first played independently at Dorset Garden, it was used by both companies as an afterpiece in later seasons.[55] In the years after 1700 both Drury Lane and Lincoln's Inn Fields seem to have decided that completely disjunct musical entertainments (both instrumental and vocal) were preferable to masques. Probably separate music was less trouble, especially when they found that they needed to advertise added music and dancing with essentially every performance. There are almost no masques after 1700. *Peleus and Thetis*—interpolated into Granville's *The Jew of Venice* in January 1701 at Lincoln's Inn Fields—is probably the last of the breed.

The dearth of operas and masques between 1701 and 1705 can in large part be attributed to the *modus vivendi* established between the warring theatres. Neither company was flourishing, and neither wanted to risk money on expensive new productions or extras. Notions of a new union were bruited about in 1701 and 1702, and in the spring of 1703 Vanbrugh began making plans for a grand new theatre. In all probability both companies envisaged a joining of forces there, as Vanbrugh himself appears to have done.[56] The pacific spirit obtaining by the season of 1703–4 is obvious in the last masque we need to consider. Motteux's *Britain's Happiness, A Musical Interlude,* the title page tells us, was "Perform'd at both the Theatres." Indeed it was—at Drury Lane on 22 February 1704, as set by Weldon, and at Lincoln's Inn Fields on 7 March, as set by Leveridge. Mrs. Tofts appeared on both occasions, something that would not have occurred a few seasons earlier. A newspaper advertisement calls the piece "A new Entertainment of Vocal and Instrumental Musick (after the manner of an Opera)." However remote from our notions of "opera," this sort of entertainment cannot be ignored in studying the subject.

"Italian infiltration" (to borrow Curtis Price's phrase) certainly occurred in the London musical world between 1695 and 1705. One need only read the many concert bills and entr'actes recorded in *The London Stage* to see the truth of this. But did the popularity of Italian vocal and instrumental music necessarily portend the obliteration of the native operatic tradition? The continued popularity of the English operas—documented above makes this at least a questionable proposition.

Vanbrugh versus Rich in 1705 and 1706

In retrospect, the "triumph" of Italian opera has seemed inevitable to music historians. Those writing in English have tended to treat the affair as a tragedy: the death of Purcell robbed native English music of its great white hope, and thus the dominance of hateful foreign opera was assured. Fiske speaks of Italian opera as a "disease," whose "first virulent germs were carried to the country by Thomas Clayton."[57] This attitude is by no means atypical. But the chauvinism seems exaggerated: some of the Italian opera music is quite wonderful, and if an objection is to be raised, it might better be to opera in Italian than to Italian opera.

If, in 1705 or 1706, someone had asked people in theatrical and musical circles in London whether entertainment in a language almost no one understood would put English opera off the stage and stand by itself as the sole business of an entire opera company, the idea would probably have been received with incredulity and derision. The initial conflict was not so much between "English" and "Italian" opera as between "semi-opera" and "all-sung" opera. Everyone assumed that a foreign opera would have to be translated into English to be acceptable to London audiences—and for some years "Italian" operas were duly performed in English, or as bilingual hybrids if visiting Italian stars were included in the cast.

The familiar story, told and retold in opera histories, is extremely simple. Vanbrugh planned to open the Haymarket with an excitingly different "Italian" opera; Rich stole it; Rich's huge success with *Camilla* in 1706 paved the way for the arrival of Handel in 1711. End of story.

The reality is rather more complicated.[58]

Vanbrugh's plan was to open the Haymarket with a pair of exotic operas. "The Play-House in the Hay-Market . . . is almost finish'd, in the mean, time two Opera's translated from the Italian by good Hands, are setting to Musick, one by Mr. Daniel Purcell, which is called Orlando Furioso, and the other by Mr. Clayton, both Opera's are to be perform'd by the best Artists eminent both for Vocal and Instrumental Musick at the Opening of the House."[59] But the theatre was far from ready, and the wily Christopher Rich slipped in and arrogated Clayton's *Arsinoe* unto his own theatre, where it opened with considerable success on 16 January 1705. Since Daniel Purcell's *Orlando Furioso* was apparently never completed, this left Vanbrugh scrambling frantically for an appropriate counterattraction. He settled on "a Foreign Opera, Perform'd by a new set of Singers, Arriv'd from *Italy;* (the worst that e're came from thence) for it lasted but 5 Days, and they being lik'd but indifferently by the Gentry; they in a little time marcht back to their own Country."[60] The opera was Jakob Greber's *The Loves of Ergasto,* as the dual-language edition of 1705 dubs it. Some mystery continues to surround this production. Who were the singers? Did they actually perform in Italian?[61] That *Ergasto* was a humiliating failure, however, there is no room to doubt. I agree with Price and Milhous that the performance was almost undoubtedly in Italian—and I would take the failure of *Ergasto* as implying—at least at this stage—a rejection of foreign-language opera.

Clayton's *Arsinoe* really was a radical departure in several respects. It was all-sung, and it entirely dispensed with the machines and scenic effects which are so prominent in semi-opera. Clayton trumpeted his imitated innovations in his preface. "The Design of this Entertainment being to introduce the *Italian* manner of Musick on the *English* Stage, which has not been before attempted; I was oblig'd to have an *Italian* Opera translated. . . . The Musick being Recitative, may not, at first, meet with that general Acceptation, as is to be hop'd for from the Audience's being better acquainted with it: But if this Attempt shall, by pleasing the Nobility and Gentry, be a Means of bringing this manner of Musick to be us'd in my Native Country, I shall think all my Study and Pains very well employ'd."[62] Fiske's contempt notwithstanding ("It is tragic that playhouse audiences were taken in by this nonsense . . . the silliness of both words and music passing unnoticed"),[63] *Arsinoe* must have seemed excitingly fresh and different.

What would the 1705–6 season bring? Vanbrugh tried three operas at the Haymarket: a traditional semi-opera (Granville's *The British Enchanters*), a pseudo-Italian opera in translation *(The Temple of Love),* and a radical experiment in the semi-opera tradition (Durfey's *The Wonders in the Sun*). Rich replied with another Italian translation, *Camilla.* At the end of the season only the possessor of a crystal ball would have known that no more semi-opera would be produced in London. *The British Enchanters,* staged in late February, was a resounding success.[64] It is a highly traditional semi-opera staged by Betterton—who had a theatre physically capable of mounting this sort of show for the first time since the actors' rebellion of 1694. The music—only part of it extant—was composed by Eccles and William Corbett. The work has attracted rather little commentary. Fiske barely notes it in passing, calling it "a modest success."[65] This is quite misleading. *Camilla,* staged five weeks later at Drury Lane, ran only ten nights its first season. And if we look at Drury Lane's offerings in the interim we can see that Rich countered with *King Arthur, The Tempest,* and *The Island Princess,* as well as with *Arsinoe.* The season totals for 1705–6 show *The British Enchanters* 12, *Europe's Revels* 6, *The Island Princess* 13, *Bonduca* 2, *King Arthur* 2,

The Indian Queen 2, and some single performances, versus 16 for *Arsinoe* and 10 for *Camilla*. English opera was still competitive, and given the reception of the Haymarket's Italianate opera, Vanbrugh might well have concluded that semi-opera was still the best bet.

The Temple of Love (words by Motteux, music by Saggione), "consisting all of Singing and Dancing . . . lasted but Six Days, and answer'd not their Expectation."[66] Thus the Haymarket tried an anglicized "Italian" opera on the model of *Arsinoe*, though with heavier emphasis on dancing, and had very poor success with it. The failure of Durfey's delightful *The Wonders in the Sun* (April) is probably explicable in terms of its peculiarity. Downes tells us that it ran only six days and failed to return half the cost of the production.[67] Much of the music consists of the sort of traditional tunes used so well in *The Beggar's Opera* twenty-two years later: in 1706 this must have been a startling innovation. But the bottom line was that in three tries the Haymarket had done well only with a semi-opera; Rich had done about equally well with an Italianate opera.

One of the puzzles attaching to *The British Enchanters* is why Vanbrugh did not open the Haymarket with it in April 1705. We have strong evidence that the piece was ready for production as far back as November 1704—indeed, that immediate performance at Lincoln's Inn Fields was contemplated. *The Diverting-Post* announced "Amadis de Gaul an Opera in French, Set to Musick by Baptista de Lully, and translated into English by the Honorable G. Granville Esq; now set to Musick by Mr. Eccles: The Parts are all dispos'd, and will speedily be perform'd at the New Theatre in little Lincoln's-Inn-Fields."[68] Brief reflection tells us why the plan for a production at Lincoln's Inn Fields was abandoned: the theatre could not provide the kind of staging appropriate to the show, and to invest in expensive scenery that would not fit the new theatre made no sense. Why not just hold *The British Enchanters* for the opening of the Haymarket then? What need the frantic search that produced the ill-fated *Loves of Ergasto*? We have, indeed, Downes's forcefully worded opinion that "had they Open'd the House at first, with a good new *English* Opera, or a new Play; they wou'd have preserv'd the Favour of Court and City, and gain'd Reputation and Profit to themselves."[69] Downes may be a biased source—he had been Betterton's prompter for more than forty years—but the success of *The British Enchanters* a year later does suggest that it might have got the Haymarket off to a much better start. The reasons for bypassing it are fairly obvious. Vanbrugh was frantically anxious to get his long-delayed theatre going, and it was not fully rigged and operational when he opened it in April 1705. In the middle of July the company moved back to Lincoln's Inn Fields, "till Her Majesty's Theatre in the Hay-Market be intirely finish'd" as their advertisement in the 19 July *Daily Courant* explains.[70] Not until 30 October 1706 was the Haymarket properly ready for occupancy. Under the circumstances, if Vanbrugh wanted to open in April, he had to do so with an opera that made absolutely minimal demands for scenes and machines.

What the season of 1706–7 might have brought in the way of renewed competition we can only speculate. But as things fell out, a change in the competitive circumstances put the Haymarket entirely out of the opera business. Fiske assumes that "the comparative failure of *Wonders in the Sun* turned the Queen's Theatre against operas."[71] In actuality, the lack of operas at the Haymarket was a matter of formal agreement. In essence Vanbrugh tried to force a union, failed, and settled for a trade: Rich's best actors in return for exclusive rights to opera and special musical entertainments at Drury Lane.[72]

This "union" (as Downes terms it) gave the Haymarket a greatly strengthened position in legitimate drama, but left opera entirely to Rich, who quite naturally went with the formula that had proved so successful for him. *Camilla* received 23 recorded performances this season; *The Island Princess* 7, *The Tempest* 4, and *Arsinoe* 3. The two new operas were both Italian-style in English. *Rosamond* (March 1707) lasted only three nights. Addison's libretto is a good one, but Clayton's music—succinctly described as "cretinous" by Fiske[73]—ruined the show. *Thomyris* (April) managed a respectable seven nights. The music was good—selected from Scarlatti, Bononcini, and others, with English words to fit the tunes by Motteux—but the real significance of this opera lies in Rich's importation of the Italian castrato Valentino Urbani to perform in it. Valentino was the first international star (albeit a second-rank one) to appear in opera in London. His singing in Italian (while the rest of the cast sang in English) does not seem to have disturbed the fascinated audience. Valentino proved, however, merely the thin end of the wedge.

During 1706–7, Rich mounted both Italianate opera and semi-operas: although his acting company had been greatly weakened in the September 1706 trade-off, he still had one, and regular plays remained his staple fare. In the fall of 1707, however, Vanbrugh maneuvered for and finally brought about an absolute generic split. As of 13 January 1708, by order of the Lord Chamberlain, the Haymarket was forbidden to produce plays and Drury Lane was forbidden to mount operas.[74] Vanbrugh, suffering under the peculiar delusion that there was a fortune to be made in opera, was anxious to import flashy Italian stars, a policy carried on by his successor Owen Swiney, who managed to sign the celebrated Nicolini for the 1708–9 season. All of the operas at the Haymarket after the 1708 union are Italianate—for the very good reason that without an acting company Vanbrugh was physically unable to produce semi-opera. And even had the managers at Drury Lane wished to rejoin with English operas they were absolutely prohibited from putting on any sort of opera.

Under these circumstances the "triumph" of Italianate opera was indeed assured. The circumstances, however, were far from inevitable. The smashing success of *Camilla*[75] fired Vanbrugh's greed, and he happened to possess the personal and political connections which enabled him to engineer a monopoly for himself. The financial bath he took in 1708 was hardly what he had in mind. Swiney struggled along until 1713, when he went broke and fled abroad. Even the presence of Handel from 1711 on did not make Italian opera more than a marginal operation. Had George I not come to the throne Italian opera might have had a rather short and dismal history in England. It was given a tremendous boost by the establishment of the munificently funded Royal Academy of Music in 1719—but even that did not keep it solvent for long.

The move into all-sung opera entirely in Italian, which so baffled and offended Addison, was a more or less inevitable result of the importation of foreign stars. Nicolini was fabulously expensive, and of course he was useless in any wholly English entertainment. Coupled with a government-ordered company structure that made semi-opera impossible, all-sung opera in Italian—starting with *Idaspe* (*Hydaspes*) in 1710—seems logical enough. And after 1714 royal snob appeal helped keep it going.

Some peculiar opinions continue to haunt this whole subject. Semi-opera is often regarded as unnatural—a brontosaural form left behind by evolution. And yet what is *The Magic Flute?* What are the operettas of Gilbert and Sullivan? Recitative is a rather peculiar convention itself. Likewise the notion that the "triumph" of Italian opera was a "tragedy," a great misfortune for English music, seems excessive. Exactly twenty years after Vanbrugh so cleverly contrived his own financial downfall, *The Beggar's Opera* revivified the whole London theatre and contributed substantially to Handel's eventual financial ruin. In ballad operas and burlettas there is a whole world of English theatre music, largely neglected until recent years, but nonetheless a major prop of the theatre in eighteenth-century London.[76]

Notes

1. Stoddard Lincoln, "John Eccles: The Last of a Tradition" (diss. Wadham College, Oxford, 1963), p.1.

2. Fiske, passim.

3. Milhous, passim.

4. Curtis A. Price, "The Critical Decade for English Music Drama, 1700–1710," *Harvard Library Bulletin* 26 (1978): 38–76.

5. Donald Jay Grout, *A Short History of Opera*, 2d ed. (New York: Columbia Univ. Press, 1965), p. 146.

6. For example, Leslie Orrey, *A Concise History of Opera* (London: Thames and Hudson, 1972), pp. 57–59; Stelios Galatopoulos, *Italian Opera* (London: Dent, 1971), p. 29.

7. Alfred Loewenberg, *Annals of Opera 1597–1940*, 3d ed. (1943; rpt. Totowa, N.J.: Rowman and Littlefield, 1978).

8. See especially Dent, *Foundations of English Opera*, and Judith Milhous, "The Multi-Media Spectacular on the Restoration Stage."

9. Two essays that have been particularly influential are W. J. Lawrence's "The Early Years of the First English Opera House," *Musical Quarterly* 7 (1921): 104–17, and Allardyce Nicoll's "Italian Opera in England: The First Five Years," *Anglia* 46 (1922): 257–81. See also J. Merrill Knapp, "Eighteenth-Century Opera in London Before Handel, 1705–1710," following.

10. Eric Walter White, *The Rise of English Opera* (London: Philosophical Library, 1951), Appendix A (covering 1590 to 1951).

11. *Roger North on Music*, pp. 306–7, 353.

12. See, for example, Richard Luckett, "Exotick but rational entertainments: the English dramatick operas," *English Drama: Forms and Development*, ed. Marie Axton and Raymond Williams (Cambridge: Cambridge University Press, 1977), pp. 123–41. Luckett stresses "the extent to which dramatick opera was Bettertonian opera" (p. 133).

13. Cibber, pp. 109 ff., especially p. 112.

14. P.R.O. LC 7/3. Quoted from Milhous, Appendix B, p. 241.

15. *The London Stage*, Part 1, p. 444.

16. The appearance of *The Songs in the Indian Queen* (Day and Murrie 137) with a 1695 date strongly implies a production that year. See Cyrus Lawrence Day and Eleanore Boswell Murrie, *English Song Books 1651–1702: A Bibliography* (London: Bibliographical Society, 1940). The title page of the *Songs* implies that Purcell is alive—an argument for an October or November date. From the only full text we possess (British Library Add. MS. 31, 449) we can make some deductions. All of the performers named would have been available in Rich's Company in either the spring or the fall of 1695. There is no reason to suppose that the manuscript list represents a tentative cast from before the rebellion, a suggestion made by the editors of the California Dryden and picked up by the editors of *The London Stage*. The California editors assume that the "Bowen" named was William Bowen, who jumped to Lincoln's Inn Fields in March 1695—but the person meant was almost certainly "Jemmy" Bowen, a boy singer who had previously worked with Purcell. See *The Works of John Dryden*, vol. 8, ed. John Harrington Smith and Dougald MacMillan (Berkeley: University of California Press, 1962), p. 325. Had the elder actors been available, several would almost certainly have been named—John Bowman and Anne Bracegirdle in particular.

17. Charles Gildon, *The Lives and Characters of the English Dramatick Poets* (London: Leigh and Turner [1699]), p. 75.

18. See Maximillian E. Novak, "The Closing of Lincoln's Inn Fields Theatre in 1695," *Restoration and Eighteenth-Century Theatre Research* 14 (1975): 51–52.

19. This use of opera as a competitive device was first remarked upon, I believe, by Robert Etheridge Moore, *Henry Purcell and the Restoration Theatre* (1961; rpt. Westport, Conn.: Greenwood, 1974), chapter 5, especially p. 149.

20. "Did Purcell set *The Tempest?*" *Proceedings of the Royal Musical Association* 90 (1963–64): 43–57.

21. See Shirley Strum Kenny, "Theatrical Warfare, 1695–1710," *Theatre Notebook* 27 (1973): 130–45, and Milhous, chapter 4.

22. On the dating problems, see Milhous and Hume, "Dating Play Premieres," pp. 374–405, especially p. 398. On matters of authorship see Milhous and Hume, "Attribution Problems in English Drama, 1660–1700."

23. Hume, p. 428.

24. See Fiske, p. 9; Hume, pp. 428–29; Milhous, pp. 94–95.

25. For a discussion of the scenery, see Sybil Rosenfeld, *A Short History of Scene Design in Great Britain* (Oxford: Blackwell, 1973), pp. 55–57.

26. See Eric Walter White, "New Light on *Dido and Aeneas*," in *Henry Purcell 1659–1695: Essays on His Music*, ed. Imogen Holst (London: Oxford University Press, 1959), pp. 14–34.

27. For much the best account of this mysterious operatic *Alexander*, see Curtis A. Price, "Eight 'Lost' Restoration Plays 'Found' in Musical Sources," *Music and Letters* 58 (1977): 294–303, especially 297–99.

28. Leslie Hotson, *The Commonwealth and Restoration Stage* (1928; rpt. New York: Russell and Russell, 1962), pp. 378–79.

29. See Edward A. Langhans, "New Early 18th Century Performances and Casts," *Theatre Notebook* 26 (1972): 145–46.

30. See Milhous, chapter 6.

31. Luckett, p. 126.

32. Fiske, p. 13.

33. Anonymous, *A Comparison between the Two Stages* (1702), ed. Staring B. Wells (Princeton, N.J.: Princeton University Press, 1942), p. 22.

34. *Apology,* p. 109.

35. Eugene Haun, *But Hark! More Harmony: The Libretti of Restoration Opera in English* (Ypsilanti, Mich.: Eastern Michigan University Press, 1971), pp. 145–48. Cf. Donald Wing, *Short-title Catalogue,* 3 vols. (New York: Columbia University Press, 1945–51), 3:113.

36. Lincoln, pp. 140–41, 219–21. See also Lucyle Hook, "The Rape of Europa by Jupiter," *On Stage and Off: Eight Essays in English Literature,* ed. John W. Ehrstine, John R. Elwood, and Robert C. McLean (Pullman, Wash.: Washington State University Press, 1968), pp. 56–62.

37. The date remains problematical. See *The London Stage,* part 1, p. 427. Luttrell's copy (now in the Huntington Library) is dated "2 Octob. [1694?]"; the edition is dated 1694. Eccles's music (British Library Add. MS. 35,043) was partially published in *Thesaurus Musicus,* The Third Book, which was published with a 1695 date, but was licensed 16 March 1694 and entered in the Stationers' Register on 29 September 1694. (This peculiar collection is Day and Murrie 139.) For further discussion, see Lucyle Hook, "Motteux and the Classical Masque," below. The reduced price paid by Luttrell argues that (contrary to his usual practice) he did not buy his copy hot off the press, but whether the 1694 licensing date is to be trusted we cannot be certain.

38. Lincoln, pp. 229–46.

39. Anonymous, *A Comparison,* p. 20; Gildon, p. 115.

40. *The London Stage,* part 1, p. 488. Cf. P.R.O. LC 5/152, pp. 202 and 220, and Eleanore Boswell, *The Restoration Court Stage* (1932; rpt. New York: Barnes and Noble, 1966), p. 105.

41. Lincoln, p. 248. The manuscript score is preserved in British Library Add. MS. 29,378.

42. See Lincoln, pp. 210–14; Fiske, pp. 13–14; Gildon, p. 116.

43. Anonymous, *A Comparison,* pp. 21–22.

44. For the details of the proper dating and sequence see Milhous and Hume, "Dating Play Premieres," pp. 400–402.

45. See particularly his "Essay on the Opera's after the Italian Manner" (1706) rpt. in Dennis, 1:382–93.

46. See Herbert Davis, "Musical Entertainments in *Rinaldo and Armida:* by John Dennis," *Theatre Miscellany: Six Pieces connected with the Seventeenth-Century Stage,* Luttrell Society Reprints, No. 14 (Oxford: Blackwell, 1953), pp. 99–115. For a significant correction see Eugene Haun, "John Dennis' 'Rinaldo and Armida' confused with Handel's 'Rinaldo,'" *Notes and Queries* 199 (1954): 249–50. The *Musical Entertainments* had escaped the notice of Day and Murrie.

47. *The London Stage,* part 1, pp. 505–7.

48. See the epilogue to Farquhar's *Love and a Bottle* (December 1698).

49. Hume, pp. 457–58.

50. Fiske, p. 11.

51. Milhous, pp. 130–31.

52. Anonymous, *A Comparison,* pp. 21–22.

53. See Milhous, chapter 5.

54. By far the best disentanglement and analysis remains buried in Stoddard Lincoln's "John Eccles," pp. 258–82, a discussion to which I am indebted.

55. For a comparative analysis of the various settings see Fiske, pp. 15–24. See also Hook, below.

56. See Judith Milhous, "The Date and Import of the Plan for a United Theatre Company in P.R.O. LC 7/3," *Maske und Kothurn* 21 (1975): 81–88, and *Thomas Betterton,* chapter 6.

57. Fiske, p. 31.

58. For a detailed contemporary account, see the anonymous "A Critical Discourse on Opera's and Musick in England," published with a translation of Francois Raguenet's *A Comparison Between the French and Italian Musick and Opera's* (London, 1709). The copiously annotated copy in the Cambridge University Library has been reprinted in facsimile with an introduction by Charles Cudworth (Westmead, Farnborough, Hants.: Gregg International, 1968).

59. *The Diverting-Post,* 28 October 1704.

60. John Downes, *Roscius Anglicanus* (1708; rpt. Los Angeles: Augustan Reprint Society, 1969), p. 48.

61. For discussion see Fiske, pp. 33–35, and Price, "Critical Decade," pp. 46–47.

62. *Arsinoe . . . an Opera, After the Italian Manner* (London: Tonson, 1705).

63. Fiske, p. 33. Fiske is in error when he says that "there were twenty-four performances the first season and a dozen more the next." I count sixteen performances in spring 1705, and sixteen more in 1705–06.

64. Granville's later claim of "an uninterrupted Run of at least Forty Days" (*Works* [London: Tonson and Gilliver, 1732], preface to the opera) is of course ridiculous. It ran twelve days during its first partial season.

65. Fiske, p. 40.

66. Downes, p. 49.

67. For favorable commentary see Fiske, pp. 41–44; Hume, p. 479; Milhous, p. 206.

68. *The Diverting-Post,* 28 October–4 November 1704.

69. Downes, p. 48. The identification was made by Stoddard Lincoln in "The Anglicization of *Amadis de Gaul,*" *On Stage and Off,* pp. 46–52. This is the only serious analysis of the opera known to me, beyond what Lincoln has to say in "John Eccles," chapter 13.

70. See Judith Milhous, "New Light on Vanbrugh's Haymarket Theatre Project," *Theatre Survey* 17 (1976): 143–61.

71. Fiske, p. 44.

72. For details, see Price, "Critical Decade," pp. 54–63, and Milhous, chapter 7. A specific illustration is offered by *The British Enchanters,* which was advertised for performance at the Haymarket on 10 December 1706: "without singing & dancing mauger the necessity thereof," wrote the indignant Granville in protesting this "design to murder the Child of my Brain." See *Vice Chamberlain Coke's Theatrical Papers 1706–1715,* ed. Judith Milhous and Robert D. Hume (Carbondale, Ill.: Southern Illinois University Press, 1982), no. 7. Granville's friends in the Lord Chamberlain's office obliged by suppressing the performance.

73. Fiske, p. 47.

74. For the order (discussed by Milhous and Price), see P.R.O. LC 5/154, pp. 299–300 (printed in *Vice Chamberlain Coke's Theatrical Papers,* pp. 49–50).

75. Fully analyzed by Lowell Lindgren in "A Bibliographic Scrutiny of Dramatic Works Set by Giovanni and His Brother Antonio Maria Bononcini" (diss., Harvard University, 1972). For an accessible short form of Lindgren's study, see his "I Trionfi di Camilla," *Studi Musicali* 6 (1977): 89–159.

76. For useful advice and criticism I want to thank Edward A. Langhans, Judith Milhous, Curtis A. Price, Carolyn Kephart, and Jeanne Meekins.

4

Eighteenth-Century Opera in London before Handel, 1705–1710

J. MERRILL KNAPP

Introduction

A surprising number of books and articles have been written on the theatrical history of the opening decade of the eighteenth century in England, and particularly on the years 1705 to 1710. A number of scholars have published articles in *Theatre Survey* and *Theatre Notebook*,[1] and there are fuller accounts by Allardyce Nicoll, Dennis Arundell, W. J. Lawrence, and Roger Fiske.[2] Except for Fiske in his *English Theatre Music in the Eighteenth Century*, however, almost all of these have dealt largely with the theatres themselves, their management, finances, and theatrical seasons rather than with the substance of the repertory. Music was an important part of this "whole show," as Professor George Winchester Stone calls it, whether it was orchestral music before the main piece, incidental songs between the acts, or the all-sung variety. I will only touch on a part of this broad topic—the genre of opera, that slippery term which could mean so many different things in the late seventeenth and early eighteenth centuries: Purcell's *The Fairy-Queen*, George Granville's *The British Enchanters*, or Bononcini's *Camilla*, for instance.

Although theatrical historians might be said to have neglected the music of the interregnum between Purcell and Handel, there is a fairly good reason for their silence: the music is hard to find. With one or two exceptions, there are no full scores of the operas I have listed (see Appendix). The music that does survive is found only in *Selected Songs*, printed by John Walsh and his successors in an abbreviated form, with parts missing (particularly the viola), instrumental sections of a song curtailed, no recitative, and not all of the songs printed. If we had to judge Purcell or Handel in this way, our judgment of them would be quite warped.

Nevertheless, this first large-scale printing of music in the English-speaking world was disseminated widely and helped to establish its authors as well-known figures in English households. Walsh's prints were also designed for harpsichord and recorder and could be performed easily by the eager amateurs who wanted to learn more exactly what the music was like, even if the figured bass had to be realized.

The Operas

All-sung Italian opera on the English stage came about largely by accident in the years 1705–10. There were two important factors, however, that helped it. One was the influence of Italian culture at the beginning of the century in England, whether it was Palladio in architecture, Paolo Rolli in poetry, or the fashion of aristocratic sons traveling to Italy in their *Wanderjahre*. The second was the introduction of Italian singers to London, both women and castrati. These singers were to become enormously popular in the coming decades, and from the beginning they insisted on singing opera in their own language (since most of it was originally in Italian) instead of in English, or in a mixture of English and Italian.

The presence of these singers is well authenticated in *The London Stage*, from the 1680s on: first came the castrato, Siface, who sang at court in 1687, and then others followed, particularly the Franco-Italian soprano, Margarita de L'Epine, who sang regularly between the acts at Drury Lane, probably in Italian, in 1703–4. Such singers were attracted by high English fees and reports on the Continent of English munificence. Their popularity, however, soon caused grumbling from the natives about their presence, and complaints were to rise in a crescendo as time went on.

Already in 1698, the epilogue to George Farquhar's *Love and a Bottle* read:

> When their Male Throats no longer drew your Money,
> We got ye an Eunuch's pipe, *Seignior Rampony*.
> That Beardless Songster we cou'd ne're make much on;
> The Females found a damn'd Blot in his *Scutcheon*.
> An *Italian* now we've got of mighty Fame,
> *Don Segismondo* Fideli.—There's Musick in his Name,
> His voice is like the Musick of the Spheres,
> It shou'd be Heavenly for the Price it bears. [20£. a time][3]

And Steele's famous epilogue to *The Tender Husband* (April 1705) has a further sting:

> Britons, who constant War, with factious Rage,

For Liberty against each other wage.
From Foreign Insult save this *English* Stage.
No more th'Italian squaling Tribe admit,
In Tongues unknown; 'tis Popery in Wit.
The Songs (their selves confess) from *Rome* they bring;
And 'tis High-Mass, for ought you know, they Sing.
Husbands take Care, the Danger may come nigher,
The Women say their Eunuch is a Friar.[4]

The events that led up to the introduction of *Arsinoe,* the first all-sung Italianate opera, are well known. Christopher Rich, the manager at Drury Lane, was a shrewd businessman who saw that music of the Italian variety had become a powerful attraction. He already had on his roster a number of singers, including L'Epine and Catherine Tofts, who could perform an "opera," as well as the instrumentalists who would form the orchestra. There were also rumors that Vanbrugh's new Queen's Theatre in the Haymarket, which was about to be completed, not only would take in Betterton's Lincoln's Inn Fields troupe but would also skim the top off the Drury Lane Company, undertaking Italian opera in the process. Vanbrugh's interest in opera is clearly shown through his letters to the earl of Manchester, English ambassador in Venice, during the years 1707–8, when they both tried to get Italian singers for the Queen's Theatre in London.[5]

Rich may have bribed Thomas Clayton, who had probably intended his new venture in "opera" for the Haymarket, to give it to Drury Lane because construction of the Haymarket Theatre was so slow. At any rate, *Arsinoe, Queen of Cyprus* saw the light of day and was a great success. It was short and was played with either preliminary dancing and singing or a one-act play—*The Quacks* in April and May 1705, *The Old Batchelor* in December 1705.

The text was an English version of an Italian libretto of the same name by Tomaso Stanzani, first heard in Bologna in 1676 with music by Petronio Francheschini. Sonneck says it was a free translation[6]; Cunningham in his book on Motteux says it was a complete rearrangement of the original with the scenes cut in half, the action disconnected, and an awkward text as the result.[7] The plot is more straightforward than most Italian ones of this period, with two pairs of lovers who in spite of intrigue, confusion, and mistaken identity are eventually united. A holdover from the seventeenth century is a pair of comic servants, Delbo and Nerina, who assist their master and mistress in the intrigue and have several quasi-courting scenes to themselves.

In his preface, Clayton is careful to make no claim about writing all the music.[8] He probably gathered various Italian arias together, then may have put in a few of his own, and tried to fit them all to Motteux's words. The result, unfortunately, was bad. The music verges on the incompetent—phrases that go nowhere, arias that begin and end in different keys for no apparent reason, meandering melodies with no shape or form. Clayton had some reputation as a London musician (he had been a member of William and Mary's court band), but he was certainly not a good arranger of other men's music or a composer of his own, as Addison, to his sorrow, was to learn with *Rosamond* later on.

Why then was the work popular? Probably, more than anything else, because of its novelty. The cast was entirely English, including Richard Leveridge and Mrs. Tofts, and they evidently made a hit. Also, the sets were designed by Sir James Thornhill, and this was an added attraction.

The public liked it, but elsewhere it suffered abuse. Addison and Burney later on were scornful and so was Colley Cibber, whose famous paragraph in *The Apology* was probably near the mark:

> The Italian Opera began first to steal into *England;* but in as rude a Disguise, and unlike it self, as possible; in a lame, hobling Translation, into our own Language, with false Quantities, or metre out of Measure, to its original Notes, sung by our own unskilful Voices, with Graces misapply'd to almost every Sentiment, and with Action, lifeless and un-meaning, through every Character.[9]

Solid information about the next opera, *The Loves of Ergasto* (April 1705), is scanty. Questions arise about the nature of the opera, who sang in it, and whether it was sung in Italian or English. There is no surviving music, except an old score in Vienna from which the music may possibly be de-rived, but there is a libretto, a rare copy to be found at Princeton,[10] which shows Italian and English on opposite pages, an epilogue by Congreve which says, "In sweet Italian strains our shepherds sing," and a title that reads, "Represented at the Opening of the Queen's Theatre in the Hay-market." The plot is a simple pastoral with a silly ending in which one of the male lovers turns out to be the long-lost brother of the maiden he is supposed to marry. But the English translations are quite good—much better than what passes for verse in *Arsinoe*—and there is plenty of dancing. Even so, the opera disappeared after five performances.

The most interesting of these early operas is *Camilla* (March 1706), largely because it was the work of one composer. It had the longest inter-mittent run of any all-sung opera in eighteenth-century England. There is a good deal of misinformation about its composer and its background. Like the two Haydn brothers, Michael and Josef, who were always being con-fused, there were two Bononcinis (three if we count their father, who was also a fairly well-known musician). *Camilla* is by Giovanni Bononcini, not his brother, Marc'Antonio, or Antonio Maria, as he is often called. Giovanni, Handel's chief rival in London in the 1720s and fifteen years older (his dates are 1670–1755), was far better known in Europe at this time than his younger contemporary. His operas had been widely per-formed in Rome, Venice, Berlin, and Vienna in the 1690s and early 1700s, and it was not surprising that a work of his would be found desirable in London. Bononcini was a very competent, facile composer who could write a catchy melody, but whose music overall lacks depth and solidity. Nicolo Haym, a German-Italian cellist, composer, librettist, and man of all trades, who was largely responsible for the musical arrangement of many early London operas, made a close adaptation of Stampiglia and Bononcini's *Il Trionfo di Camilla, Regina de' Volsci,* first given in Naples in 1696 and a great success in fifteen Italian cities after that. This London *Camilla* (of which five editions of the libretto were printed by 1726) included fifty-four English versions of fifty-six Italian arias from the first Naples production.[11]

Rich wanted *Camilla* to attain the financial success of *Arsinoe,* since he was very conscious of keen rivalry from the Queen's Haymarket Theatre. A contract between Haym and Rich for the direction of the opera tells how an unnamed person was paid to translate the text into English prose; then a Mr. Northman was paid by Rich to put the prose into English verse to fit the Italian music[12] (Motteux probably had a hand in this also). Haym then copied a new score, putting in alterations and additions he considered necessary, including the English recitative. He was paid £100 for his role as arranger, copyist, impresario, and performer (cellist) in the production.

The complicated text concerns the attempt of Camilla to regain the throne of Volscia, which has been usurped from her father by Latinus, a tyrant. She returns to her country disguised as a shepherdess, Dorinda. Prenesto, son of Latinus, falls in love with Camilla, obviously not knowing who she is. Lavinia, daughter of Latinus, is in love with Turnus, king of Rutilia, who is disguised as a Moorish slave at Latinus's court in order to win back his kingdom from the tyrant. After many complications, the two sets of lovers finally outwit Latinus and win each other, assisted by two comic servants, Linco and Tullia.

The cast was again English except for Lavinia (Joanna Maria). Leveridge made a further reputation as Linco and Catherine Tofts as Camilla. With the music Bononcini is at his best in the lighter vein. One of his pieces is a song to "Fair Dorinda" which is quite attractive:

CAMILLA

hap - py, hap - py, Fair Do - rin - da, hap - py,

hap - py, hap - py, may - est thou ev - er be.

At the beginning of act 2, there is an interesting scene in which Tullia is showing Camilla and Linco through a sumptuous picture gallery, once owned by Camilla's father. Camilla is restrained at first but then works herself into a fury, finally revealing herself as Camilla, the rightful queen. The music builds up through accompanied recitative to revenge aria and is very effective. Bononcini does not let the aria go on too long because length would make it lose its force. The balance between accompagnato and aria is excellent. Addison had fun in *The Spectator* with some of the translations. A comparison of the Italian and the English shows why:

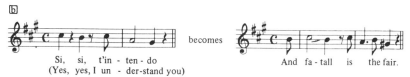

Si, si, t'in - ten - do   becomes   And fa - tall is the fair.
(Yes, yes, I un - der-stand you)

Nevertheless the opera as a whole was deservedly popular. Even the anonymous author of *A Critical Discourse on Opera and Musick in England* (1709), who was generally disparaging about these early operas, had a kind word: "This being a Royal Opera, the Musick admirable, and Perform'd in a more regular Method than any of the former (tho' much of its Beauty was lost in the *English* language) it receiv'd so Universal an Applause, that I don't think it ever met with so good a Reception in any of its first Representations abroad."[13]

During *Camilla*'s initial year, the clamor began to grow against opera as a threat to the spoken drama. John Dennis issued *An Essay on the Opera after the Italian manner, which are about to be establish'd on the English Stage, With some Reflections on the Damage which they may bring to the Publick* (1706). While his fulminations may have largely come about because he was a disgruntled playwright of the older generation, his chief complaint was that opera was a mere sensual delight which had driven out poetry. "Sense upon the stage seems to have given place to Sound," he said (a standard criticism against opera heard through the centuries).

But this plaint did not deter Addison and Clayton from *Rosamond* (March 1707), in which for once there was a literate and original libretto. Addison kept the Italian conventions: six characters, three of each sex; a cloud machine in act 3; and the happy ending (in the original ballad Rosamond died). But there was little dramatic action, and the music was appalling. Unfortunately, Thomas Arne was not yet on hand to breathe life into this libretto, as he did later.

Peter Motteux claimed that *Thomyris, Queen of Scythia* (April 1707) was entirely his own work: "Neither the Words, the Thought, nor the Design owe anything to Italy."[14] Johann Pepusch composed the recitative, and Heidegger chose the arias, among which were some by Alessandro Scarlatti and Giovanni Bononcini. Motteux speaks in the preface of his difficulty "in working so many Airs of different Kinds into one Subject, and in putting Words wholly different from the *Italian*, to Songs so full of pathetick Notes and nice Graces in a Language perhaps too manly for such Composers, if not manag'd with the utmost Art." He pays tribute to Heidegger: "Tho' Music is only his Diversion, the best Masters allow him to be so good a Judge, that I have no reason to doubt but his Collection will be generally approv'd." He also has praise for Pepusch. The plot has many similarities to *Camilla*, which Motteux undoubtedly had in mind as a financial success to be imitated. The heroines are both queens who have trouble gaining or keeping their thrones; there are four lovers eventually united and a pair of comic attendants who spend their time courting.

One special note, however, appears in act 1 of the libretto. When Oronte, who is Thomyris's son and general of her army, enters, there is a note that reads: "The Part of Orontes, being sung by Signor Valentino at the desire of most of the Nobility who subscribed for the first Performance of this Opera, you have here the same in Italian, as it is translated out of English and adjusted to the same Music." The part throughout is in two languages, and undoubtedly Valentini, a castrato, sang it in Italian, as he had in a *Camilla* revival the previous month (March 1707).

Valentini, whose full name was Valentino Urbani, was the first castrato to sing regularly in London. He remained for four seasons, until 1710, and returned again in 1712–14. His voice was an alto of rather restricted range and limited powers, according to Charles Burney, quoting opera-goers of the time, but Colley Cibber thought he was quite a good actor. At any rate, the novelty of hearing a castrato must have accounted for considerable interest in his performance.

Some of Bononcini's arias in *Thomyris* can be traced to two of his operas called *Polifemo* and *Cefalo*, produced in Berlin in 1702.[15] They serve as instructive examples of how Motteux did his work. There is generally little relation between the English and Italian in overall meaning: the Italian of one aria by Oronte, who is thwarted in his love for Clearte, speaks of the cruel rays of his beloved's eyes that have no light for him, while the English talks of the "Chains of Love" Oronte bears. But Motteux does make an effort to keep the same number of syllables in each line, and the rhyme schemes are similar, although obviously with different end-sounds. The music is only fair. Yet some of Motteux's verse can be attractive. Another aria from *Cefalo* for Baldo, the male comic, who sings to his counterpart, Media, reads:

> Farewell Love and every Pleasure
> Honour calls and we must part.
> War from you now claims my Leisure
> I'll go raise my Fame and Treasure.
> Storm and Plunder/ Fight and Thunder
> Then at last I'll bring you under,
> Gold and Conquest gain the Heart.

Valentini himself seems to have been responsible for the next opera, *Love's Triumph* (February 1708), which some believe was modeled on a puppet show called *La Pastorella* by Pietro Ottoboni, others, on an opera called *Il Trionfo d'Amore*. Motteux did the adaptation (his last for the theatre), but the venture was a failure. The previous lack of success with pastoral dramas should have warned the backers what to expect. Mr. X of the *Critical Discourse* said:

> The composition was *Italian,* yet being directed by one who can't compose himself, and is consequently improper for such an Undertaking, being fit only to sing when his Voice will permit him; I say, this Pastoral being stuffed out with Dance and Chorus after the *French* fashion, was so disrelished by the Audience, that the second Night of its Representation, the whole Town . . . forsook it.

Pyrrhus and Demetrius, which followed (December 1708), was to be one of the turning points in the competition between the forms of opera that would prevail in London. It was the first opera to have Nicolini, the finest castrato of his generation, as a star member of the cast. The negotiations of Vanbrugh and Manchester in Italy had borne fruit, and Nicolini, undoubtedly attracted by an offer of £1,000 for two seasons (a very large sum then), sang in all the Italian operas through 1711–12, returned again to London in 1715, and left finally in June 1717. With all the diatribes against the Italian invasion in these years, the severest critics, Addison and Steele particularly, admitted that Nicolini had that rare combination for opera: he could act as well as sing. Cibber appropriated Steele's words in *The Tatler* by writing:

> Nicolini sets off the Character he bears in an Opera, by his Action, as much as he does the Words of it by his Voice; every Limb and Finger contributes to the part he acts, insomuch that a deaf Man might go along with him in the Sense of it. . . . His Voice at this first time of being among us . . . had all that strong, clear, Sweetness of Tone, so lately admired in Senesino. A blind Man could scarce have distinguished them, but in Volubility of Throat, the former had much the Superiority.[16]

Pyrrhus was an adaptation by Owen Swiney of a libretto by Adriano Morselli, the music to which had been set by Alessandro Scarlatti in Naples in 1694. It was one of Scarlatti's earliest successes. Haym adapted the music, adding arias of his own and some of Bononcini's, as well as retaining some of Scarlatti's. Nicolini and Valentini sang entirely in Italian; Tofts sang partly in Italian and partly in English; a singer called "the Baroness" had one scene in Italian; the rest of the cast sang in English. The music was printed in two editions, the first by Walsh, the second by John Cullen, whose title page said: "Songs . . . with the Italian Words Grav'd under the English to such as are sung in Italian and a Table for the ready finding of them." Haym's arias are competent but dull; some of Scarlatti's are first-rate with a drive and energy that matches the best of the time. He was fond of slow sicilianos and fast 3/8 pieces with frequent changes of tempo within either the A part or the B part of the aria. The plot was inordinately complicated and was criticized as such, but evidently the singing swept all before it in triumph.

Clotilda (March 1708) was another attempt to repeat the success of a previous opera, but its performances were far fewer. Heidegger took particular pains to engage the Venetian painter, Marco Ricci—then in London—to paint the sets and to sink more money in costumes ("Spanish Habits" in this case, since the setting was Castile). There was the same mixture of languages in the singing, but this time when the ladies, Mrs. Tofts and Margarite L'Epine, sang in scenes with Nicolini and Valentini they also sang in Italian. Another difference was that, although most of the English recitative was exceedingly skimpy and abbreviated, when it came to scenes for the two castrati, the text suddenly blossomed out into long Italian dialogue, as if the original Italian words had been kept intact and nobody had bothered to cut or change them. The story was the old patient Griselda theme, modified for the available cast.

Vanbrugh and Manchester correspondence shows that operatic backers had impressive aristocratic support: the queen, the duke and duchess of Marlborough, the lord treasurer, and Vice-Chamberlain Coke. An invitation to come to London was even sent to Bononcini, then in Vienna at the height of his fame under Emperor Joseph I, but he refused. If he had come in 1708 or 1709, Handel's subsequent career in England at that early date might have been quite different. Without Bononcini, the nobility had to be content to hear his music in *pasticcios.*

The next work, *Almahide* (January 1710), was about half his, and it seems to have come from Johann Wenzel, Count Gallas, Viennese ambassador in London. The opera was important for several reasons. First, it was sung entirely in Italian. *The Loves of Ergasto* may have preceded it, but *Almahide* firmly established a precedent. Heidegger's notice "To The Reader" in the libretto is unequivocal about this new practice:

Several People of Quality, and Encouragers of the Opera's, having found fault with the Absurdity of those Scenes, where the Answers are made in *English,* to those that sing in *Italian,* and in *Italian* to those that recite in *English,* and it being impossible to have the whole Opera performed in *English,* because the chief Actors would not be able to perform their parts in our Language: I hope I shall be pardoned, if I have made all the Parts in *Italian.* 'Tis a Language with more Vowels, softer and more adapted to Musick than any other; besides for the convenience of those who do not understand it, I have translated the Opera litterally on the other side of the Book. I must only beg their Favour in making Allowances for the *Italianisms,* and the flatness of a literal Translation, when it is known that all Originals suffer, when Translated.[17]

A second unusual feature of the opera was that it contained two English comic interludes interspersed between the first three acts—perhaps because the main work was sung in Italian, perhaps to use the talents of Doggett and Mrs. Lindsey, two favorite players, who were Floro, a Corporal, and Blesa, an Old Woman.

The music is decidedly more Italianate than that of some of the previous operas. Divisions and ornamentation abound for both the castrati and the leading ladies. Almost all the arias are *da capo* with the slow ones superior to the fast ones. Bononcini's overture is Handelian in style (Largo, Presto, Largo, Allegro 12/8-gigue). His fugal Presto dies out after three entries and then alternates *tutti* and solo oboes in thirds and sixths for the rest of the movement.

The author of *The Critical Discourse,* who ceased his specific comment after *Clotilda,* ends his essay by lambasting the *pasticcios,* particularly those put together by Heidegger, which he scornfully designates "Swiss Operas" because of Heidegger's nationality. He adds his own prescription for a successful opera in England; (1) An opera should be written by one person or at least overseen by someone "capable of uniting different styles so artfully as to make 'em pass for one." (2) "The Words ought to be sung in *Italian,* being a Language the most proper for Musick of any other in Europe." (3) Composers ought to learn the capabilities of their performers and write music to fit their various talents. (4) Composers should avoid a servile imitation of Italian compositions, "since an Opera with no more than ten or twelve good Airs in it will pass in *Italy,* whereas here in *England* five or six bad ones are sufficient to damn the whole Composition." (5) It is not enough to have a fine melody in the aria; the instrumental part must also be good. There must be a kind of contest between voice and instrument. (6) "The Airs ought to be studied without being stiff, melancholy without being heavy, and lively without being trivial: there ought to be something new and uncommon, sweet and entertaining in every part."

The next opera, *L'Idaspe Fedele,* or *Hydaspes* (March 1710), as it was called in English, was famous primarily because of Nicolini's fight with a lion, which Addison made notorious a year later in *The Spectator.* Nicolini was evidently responsible for the opera's performance in England; the libretto's Italian dedication signed by him says that the work was "*da me fornito al Regio Teatro*" (furnished by me for the Royal Theatre). The cast was all foreign except for one minor role, and the music was mostly by Francesco Mancini (1679–1739), a Neapolitan composer.

The famous lion scene at the beginning of act 3 may have been ridiculous to Addison as drama, but as music it had its points. Two lovers, Idaspe (Nicolini) and Berenice, are allowed to be married in a public arena by Artaserse, king of Persia. But the king schemes to have Idaspe thrown to a raging lion instead. Idaspe stands along against the lion and strangles it with his bare hands. When their fate is first made known, the two lovers bid farewell in a moving twelve-measure duet. Then Nicolini sings his vehement aria, "*Mostro crudel,*" before strangling the creature. The aria is fine music with contrasted A and B parts in Allegro and Largo. The audience undoubtedly smiled when they read the English translation: "Why dost thou, horrid Monster, pause? / Come on; sate thy rav'nous Jaws / This naked Bosom tear / For thou within shalt find a Heart / Guarded by Flames will make thee start / And turn thy Rage to fear." But opera is filled with such illogical and musical moments, and Nicolini probably brought it off convincingly.

There is little to say about the last opera, *Etearco* (January 1711), which came before Handel's *Rinaldo,* except that it was another *pasticcio* arranged by Haym but taken largely from a Viennese opera of the same title by Bononcini. It did have the distinction of possessing the entire Italian recitative originally written by Bononcini. It was, in fact, probably the only London opera before the 1720s that had this unifying feature.

Italian opera was already established on the English musical stage, then, by the time of Handel's providential arrival—providential in that one able composer could capitalize on the current musical rage and continue to attract an audience. Yet the ascendancy of this kind of opera was largely accidental, even though the popularity of Italian singers and their music caused most of it. By the winters of 1710 and 1711, it was clear that the mixed Italian-English product was no longer viable. If Nicolini and his compatriots were to continue as star attractions at the Queen's Theatre, they were going to sing opera in their own language, particularly if the works were originally Italian. Addison summed it up well in *Spectator* No. 18 by saying:

> At length the Audience grew tir'd of understanding Half the Opera, and therefore, to ease themselves intirely of the Fatigue of Thinking, have so order'd it at Present, that the whole Opera is perform'd in an unknown Tongue.[18]

The Italians had conquered.

Appendix
List of Operas with Date of First Performance and Total Number of Performances

1. *Arsinoe* (Librettists: Motteux/Stanzani—Music: Clayton?) Pasticcio. Drury Lane, 16 January 1705. 36 performances to 1707.

2. *The Loves of Ergasto* (Jacob Greber) Pastoral. Queen's Theatre, Haymarket, 9 April 1705. 5 performances in April.

3. *The Temple of Love* (Motteux/?—Saggione) Pastoral. Queen's Theatre, Haymarket, 7 March 1706. 2 performances in March.

4. *Camilla* (Haym/Stampiglia—Giovanni Bononcini) Drury Lane, 30 March 1706. 112 performances to 1728.

5. *Rosamond* (Addison—Clayton) Drury Lane, 4 March 1707. 3 performances in March.

6. *Thomyris, Queen of Scythia* (Motteux—Italians) Pasticcio. Drury Lane and Queen's Theatre, 1 April 1707. 43 performances to 1728.

7. *Love's Triumph* (Motteux/Ottoboni—Italians) Pastoral pasticcio. Queen's Theatre, Haymarket, 26 February 1708. 8 performances in 1708.

8. *Pyrrhus and Demetrius* (Swiney/Morselli—Haym, Bononcini, A. Scarlatti) Pasticcio. Queen's Theatre, Haymarket, 14 December 1708. 58 performances to 1717.

9. *Clotilda* (Heidegger/David—Italians) Pasticcio. Queen's Theatre, Haymarket, 2 March 1709. 10 performances to 1711.

10. *Almahide* (Heidegger/?—Italians, mostly Bononcini) Pasticcio. Queen's Theatre, Haymarket, 10 January 1710. 25 performances to 1712.

11. *Hydaspes (L'Idaspe Fidele)* (Caudi—Mancini and others) Pasticcio. Queen's Theatre, Haymarket, 23 March 1710. 46 performances to 1716.

12. *Etearco* (Stampiglia—Italians, mostly Bononcini) Pasticcio. Queens Theatre, Haymarket, 10 January 1711. 7 performances in January.

13. *Rinaldo* (Aaron Hill/Rossi—Handel) Queen's Theatre, Haymarket, 24 February 1711. 53 performances to 1731.

Arsinoe, The Temple of Love, and *Rosamond* were sung entirely in English. *The Loves of Ergasto* was probably sung in Italian. *Camilla and Thomyris* were sung at first in English, but from 1708 through 1710 partly in English and partly in Italian. They reverted to English after 1710. *Love's Triumph* was probably in English. *Pyrrhus and Demetrius* and *Clotilda* were partly in English and partly in Italian. From *Almahide* on, the operas were sung entirely in Italian.

All of the libretti for the works listed above, with the exception of Addison's *Rosamond* and possibly *Thomyris,* were adaptations for the English stage of Italian originals.

Notes

1. For example, see Donald C. Mullin, "The Queen's Theatre, Haymarket: Vanbrugh's Opera House," *Theatre Survey* 8 (1967): 84–105; Judith Milhous, "New Light on Vanbrugh's Haymarket Theatre Project," *Theatre Survey* 17 (1976): 143–61; Ronald C. Kern, "Documents Relating to Company Management, 1705–1711," *Theatre Notebook* 14 (1959–60): 60–65; Philip Olleson, "Vanbrugh and Opera at the Queen's Theatre, Haymarket," *Theatre Notebook* 26 (1972): 94–101; Daniel Nalbach, *The King's Theatre, 1704–1867* (London: Society for Theatre Research, 1972); Price, "Critical Decade," pp. 38–76; Lowell Lindgren, "I Trionfi di Camilla." *Studi Musicali* 6 (1977): 89–159.

2. Nicoll, *A History of English Drama, 1660–1900,* 2; Nicoll, "Italian Opera in England. The First Five Years," *Anglia* 46 (1922); Dennis Arundell, *The Critic at the Opera* (London: Ernest Benn, 1957); W. J. Lawrence, "The Early Years of the First English Opera House," *Musical Quarterly* 7 (1921: 104–12; Fiske.

3. Quoted from *The Complete Works of George Farquhar,* ed. Charles Stonehill, 2 vols. (1930; rpt. New York: The Gordon Press, 1967), 1:74.

4. Quoted from *The Plays of Richard Steele,* ed. Shirley Strum Kenny, (Oxford: Clarendon Press, 1971), p. 273.

5. *The Letters of Sir John Vanbrugh,* ed.Geoffrey F. Webb (London: Nonesuch Press, 1928).

6. Oscar Sonneck, *Catalogue of Opera Librettos,* vol. 1 (Washington, D. C.: Government Printing Office, 1914), p. 161.

7. Robert N. Cunningham, *Peter Anthony Motteux* (Oxford: B. Blackwell and Mott, 1933), p. 15.

8. Thomas Clayton, *Arsinoe, Queen of Cyprus, An Opera after the Italian Manner: All Sung As it is Perform'd at the Theatre Royal in Drury Lane By Her Majesty's Servants* (London: Tonson, 1705).

9. Cibber, p. 175.

10. *The Loves of Ergasto, A Pastoral Represented at the Opening of the Queen's Theatre in the Haymarket.* Compos'd by Signior Giacomo Greber (London: Tonson, 1705).

11. Lowell Lindgren, "A Bibliographic Scrutiny," "I Trionfi di Camilla," passim.

12. Nicoll prints this in part.

13. *A Critical Discourse on Operas and Musick in England* (London: 1709).

14. Peter Anthony Motteux, Preface, *Thomyris, Queen of Scythia. An Opera As it is Perform'd at the Theatre Royal in Drury-Lane . . . By P. Motteux* (London: Tonson, 1707).

15. Lindgren, "A Bibliography Scrutiny," passim.

16. Cibber, p. 211.

17 *Almahide. Opera Dedicata A Sua Eccelenza Il Signor Giovanni Wenceslao Conte di Gallasso* (London 1710).

18. Quoted from *The Spectator,* ed. Donald F. Bond, 5 vols. (Oxford: Clarendon Press, 1965), 1:81.

5

Motteux and the Classical Masque

LUCYLE HOOK

Restoration and eighteenth-century drama scholars have argued for years about whether or not an English opera could have finally developed from the spoken play by the addition of the kinds of copious instrumental and vocal music, dancing, and spectacle that were in vogue in the last decade of the seventeenth century. It is generally concluded that Henry Purcell's early death in 1695 put an end to whatever hope there was for a native English opera that might have been strong enough to prevail over the encroaching Italian all-sung opera. When the unthinkable calamity had finally happened with the success of *Arsinoe* in 1705, the critic John Dennis summed up the belief that had been held by proponents of spoken English drama for the past three decades:

> This small Treatise is only levell'd against those Operas which are entirely Musical. . . . We have endeavour'd to shew . . . that the *English* Stage is like to be overthrown by the Progress of these new Operas . . . that the *Italian Opera*, another Entertainment, which is about to be estab-lish'd in the room of Plays, is a Diversion of more pernicious Conse-quence, than the most licentious Play that ever has appear'd upon the Stage.[1]

Ironically, the emergence of Italian opera with all-sung aria and recitative came about in some degree through the economical introduction of theat-rical novelty to old plays, plays that were now embellished with special features from the Continent. Gradually the added vocal and instrumental music, dance, and spectacle became more important than the original play. But this transformation had been taking place over the thirty years from 1675 to 1705 (from Thomas Shadwell's *Psyche* to Thomas Clayton and Peter Motteux's *Arsinoe*). The changes that occurred during the last decade of the seventeenth century are in some ways the most interesting.

As might be expected, many of Shakespeare's plays were among those revived with the addition of music after the Restoration in 1660. Of special importance is the John Dryden–William Davenant version of *The Tempest* in 1667, with additional alterations by Thomas Shadwell in 1674, and music by Matthew Locke. The 1664 Davenant version of *Macbeth* had many revivals, with additional songs and music by a number of composers over a thirty-year period, until all were superseded by the 1696 score by John Eccles and Godfrey Finger, never published but fortunately still in manuscript.[2] *A Midsummer-Night's Dream* was revised in May 1692, with music by Henry Purcell; retitled *The Fairy-Queen*, it was the most elaborate adaptation of all.

But even more popular than Shakespeare in the last decade of the seventeenth century were the revivals of Beaumont and Fletcher (especially Fletcher). Only recently have they come to light. The reasons for their "discovery" and the hitherto unrecognized part they played in the final emergence of an all-sung English opera are of more than passing interest.

Into the theatrical world of such musical adaptations came Peter Anthony Motteux, an educated French Huguenot who arrived in London in the early 1680s. Motteux's transformation from refugee to English citizen was effected by 1686, and he entered the literary life of London with the first issue of the *Gentleman's Journal* in January 1692. Although a minor figure in the annals of drama, Motteux played an important role in the changing world of English theatrical and musical life. In the two decades that saw the seventeenth century out and the eighteenth century in, he occupied a commanding place as an entrepreneur in the transition of theatrical public taste. He used the *Gentleman's Journal* for instruction both intellectual and moral, but he also used it unswervingly for his own advancement. And although the periodical lasted less than two years, by the end of that time Motteux had secured a firm foothold in theatrical and musical circles in London.

In the January 1692 issue, Motteux commenced the education of his English readers in what was to be a decade-long effort to persuade them to favor Italian or all-sung opera. He led into the subject boldly:

> I must tell you that we shall have speedily a New Opera, wherein something very surprising is promised us; Mr. *Purcel* who joyns to the Delicacy and Beauty of the *Italian* way, the Graces and Gayety of the *French*, composes the Music, as he hath done for the *Prophetess*, and the last Opera called *King Arthur*. . . . Other Nations bestow the name of Opera only on such Plays whereof every word is sung. But experience hath taught us that our English genius will not rellish that perpetual Singing. . . . In several other Countries I have seen their Opera's still Crowded every time, tho long and almost all Recitative. . . . But our *English* Gentlemen, when their Ear is satisfy'd, are desirous to have their mind pleas'd, and Music and Dancing industriously intermix'd with Comedy and Tragedy. . . . All this however doth not lessen the Power of

Music, for its Charms Command our attention when used in their place, and the admirable Consorts we have in *Charles Street,* and *York buildings,* are undeniable proof of it. . . . These Opera's or Playes in Music have been used for above a Century amongst the *Italians;* most Cities in *Italy* have their Opera's, as also *Sicily* and *Savoy.* But *Venice* is the place where they are Triumphant. . . . They have there most Carnavals, Nine or Ten Opera's on seven several Stages, and each House striving to outdo the rest, the Music and Voices are always extraordinary. . . . They have little or no Machines there; their Decorations and Cloaths are but mean, and their Stages but ill Illuminated, but their Music makes amends for the rest: Yet tho strangers cannot but admire it, they find, as Mr. *Dryden* ingeniously observes upon another subject, that it is not pleasant to be tickled too long, and wish for the conclusion usually before the *Opera* be half done. Some other time I will perhaps give a larger account of them; and since we begin to rellish those entertainments in *England,* I do not doubt but they will make the practice and love of Music more general amongst us.

That was Motteux's opening salvo. He *seems* to concur with the present English taste (preached by John Dryden, practiced by Thomas Betterton, and upheld by the usual audience) for spoken drama embellished by incidental music, song, and dance having little to do with the action of the play. But even as he is agreeing that "the *English* Gentlemen, when their Ear is satisfy'd, are desirous to have their mind pleas'd," he is extolling the Italian all-sung opera, tantalizing the reader with the foreign delicacies of Venice.

The *Gentleman's Journal* is a running diary of Motteux's theatrical and musical activities from January 1692 through October–November 1694. Henry Purcell and Samuel Akeroyde each set music to verses by Motteux, which were printed in the first issue. Three of Motteux's songs set by Robert King, Giovanni Battista Draghi, and Nicola Matteis were included in the February number. Alexander Damascene set Motteux's "March," which followed Motteux's poem, "On His Majesty's Going for Holland," in the March issue. In the same number, his *Rondeau,* set by Ralph Courteville, appeared. In the April issue he published his own Pindaric Ode, "On His Majesty's Successes," some verses, and another song by Robert King. And so it went month after month. In the May 1693 issue, he modestly records, "We have had lately a Consort of Music, which pleased the most nice and judicious Lovers of that Art. . . . I only speak of the Notes which were by Mr. *Franck:* As for the words, I made 'em in Haste." He includes three excerpts in the same issue, labeling the first "Complaint in Recitative. . . . Sung with accompaniments of Instruments by Mrs. Ayliff." The concert with four characters and chorus was a form of all-sung masque complete with recitative and aria and a sustaining orchestra instead of the usual continuo of harpsichord and viola da gamba. The *London Gazette* recorded the date and place: 17 June 1693 at York Buildings. It was Motteux's first major appearance in the entertainment world.

It is perhaps significant that, of the six musicians who set the songs that appeared in the *Gentleman's Journal* during 1692 and 1693, four had gained some prominence on the Continent before coming to England. Nicola Matteis was an Italian violinist admired by John Evelyn. John Baptist (Giovanni Battista Draghi) was an Italian organist to Queen Catherine of Braganza and music tutor to the future Queen Mary and Queen Anne. In 1667 Pepys commended him for the way he sang and accompanied himself on a harpsichord in one of the acts of an Italian opera he composed but never produced. Alexander Damascene, of Italian origin but French birth, was the countertenor who took Henry Purcell's place in the Royal Chapel in 1695. Johann Wolfgang Franck had produced fourteen operas on classical subjects in Hamburg before coming to England, where he joined Robert King in a series of concerts extending over several years. English-born Robert King was a member of the Royal Band, taking John Bannister's place in 1680. And Raphael Courteville, first a chorister of the Royal Chapel, was organist of St. James, Westminster, in 1691.

By the end of 1693, Motteux must have known theatrical and literary London well, for he commented upon and commended new plays, concerts, and foreign and domestic books, and insinuated himself into all corners of entertainment and public life. His usual output of light verse and song was augmented by major efforts for special occasions, such as the sixty-line poem in extravagant praise of William and Mary which opened the January–February number, from which six lines set by John Blow were extracted and sung before their majesties, and another six lines set by Henry Purcell were performed at court before their majesties on New Year's Day, 1694. In the same issue, there is a "Song set by Mr. *Henry Purcell*, the Words by the Authour of this *Journal*, Sung at an Entertainment for Prince *Lewis* of *Baden*" at York Buildings.

Motteux had the ability to write verse for any occasion. At first he wrote pieces to be set by the lesser musicians from the court and working performers around London, but gradually he advanced to such prestigious artists as Sir John Blow and Henry Purcell, and eventually he was working in full collaboration with John Eccles, Purcell's successor. The progress was rapid from Courteville, Damascene, and King to Blow, Purcell, and Eccles—less than three years to the top rank and the best outlet to fleeting fame and doubtful fortune, the theatre.

Many changes, theatrical, political, and literary, came at the end of 1694. Thomas Betterton and eleven of the major players in London broke away from Christopher Rich's domination at Drury Lane early in December and petitioned for a license to open a new theatre. Queen Mary died on 28 December 1694, and all entertainment was curtailed for three months, until 25 March 1695, after which Betterton opened Lincoln's Inn Fields with William Congreve's *Love for Love*. These events coincided with or were perhaps decisive factors in Motteux's decision to give up the *Gentleman's Journal* with the October–November 1694 issue. Motteux had complained that the periodical took time from more important activities, such as his interest in seeing Sir Thomas Urquhart's 1653 translation of the *Works of Rabelais* republished; Motteux had supplied the preface, a long explanatory introduction, and a key to "the longest and finest Enigma that ever was writ." Motteux translated the remaining two books of Rabelais's *Gargantua and Pantagruel* by May 1694, and he found himself an accepted literary celebrity. With two theatres now in London, he was finally ready to embark upon a full theatrical career.

Henry Purcell had been the most important theatrical composer working with the United Company since 1680. At first he contributed single songs, but as time went on, he gradually came to supply all the music for plays, including the act tunes. His nearest approach to the operatic form came with his short *Dido and Aeneas* (December 1689) with verse by Nahum Tate, performed at Josias Priest's Boarding School in Chelsea. Purcell's three full-length "operas" in the accepted English manner were *The Prophetess* (by Massinger and Fletcher as revised by Betterton in 1690), *King Arthur* (by Dryden, 1691) and *The Fairy-Queen* (1692). When Purcell died in November 1695, he vacated not only the position of Master of his Majesty's Music but also the acknowledged role of the realm's leading purveyor of theatrical music. The double mantle fell to John Eccles, who had supplied incidental vocal music for revivals of the United Company before the actors' rebellion of 1695; among these revivals were plays by Shadwell, Dryden, Otway, Shakespeare, and Fletcher. Fletcher's play, *Valentinian*, revised by the earl of Rochester in 1684 and revived in February 1694, brought Eccles and Motteux into collaboration.

It is surprising how many plays written by Fletcher, or Fletcher in joint authorship with one or another of his contemporaries, were revised with important musical additions in the last ten years of the seventeenth century. To name only those which bear a close relationship to the present subject, there are *The Prophetess* (June 1690), with music and a masque by Purcell; *The Knights of Malta* (1691), with music by Purcell; *Valentinian* (1694), with music by Eccles, and the masque, *The Rape of Europa by Jupiter*, with music by Eccles (librettist not named); *Bonduca* (September 1695), with music by Purcell; *The Island Princess* (February 1699), "All the Musical Entertainments and the greatest Part of the Play new, and written by Mr. Motteux," with music by Daniel Purcell, Jeremiah Clarke, and Richard Leveridge; *The Pilgrim* (April 1700), altered by John Vanbrugh, with music by Daniel Purcell and prologue, epilogue, and secular masque by John Dryden; *The Mad Lover* (1700), with music by Eccles, and a masque, *Acis and Galatea*, by Eccles and Motteux.

There are several reasons for concentrating upon *Valentinian* and *The Mad Lover*. It has been proposed elsewhere[3] that Motteux wrote the libretto of *The Rape of Europa by Jupiter* for the 1694 revival of Rochester's free adaptation of the play, first produced by Betterton ten years before in

1684. It is easy to believe that this anonymous masque with its classical story was Motteux's first venture into the real theatre world. The unique copy bearing the date of 1694 is at the Henry E. Huntington Library with the unmistakable inked notation of Narcissus Luttrell on the title page that it was bought marked down from 6d to 3d on 2 October, obviously a remainder from the revival in January or February before Betterton left Drury Lane. There is also a two-line quotation from Ovid to introduce Jupiter, and the first two pages are devoted to the Argument in which the audience is instructed in details of the story. Motteux had been playing with classical stories since 1692. Each issue of the *Gentlemen's Journal* abounds in snippets from Ovid's *Metamorphoses:* stories and verses, among them a story about Acteon, a proclamation by Apollo, a burlesque of Orpheus, a whole series about Cupid, and an allegorical interpretation of the fable of Mars and Venus, a subject to be used later in one of Motteux's best works.

The third book of *Thesaurus Musicus* (licensed March 1694)[4] contains twelve pages of "Songs from the New Masque call'd *The Rape of Europa by Jupiter,* set by Mr. Eccles," but the author of the libretto is not named. The cast and the text of the libretto match the songs: John Bowman as Jupiter, Mr. Magnus as Mercury, Anne Bracegirdle as Europa, Mrs. Hodgson and Mrs. Cibber as Herse and Aglaura, and Thomas Doggett as Coridon.

Fletcher's *Valentinian* was primarily an examination of a subject's loyalty to his sovereign, but Rochester, by concentrating upon the violence done by that sovereign to the virtuous matron Lucina, changes the play into a Restoration female tragedy. The Emperour succeeds in luring Lucina to his palace by convincing her that her husband has sent for her. When he cannot seduce her with jewels, incense, music, and flattery, he seems to accept her refusal as he sends her to another room, supposedly to see her husband. When she has gone, he turns to his sycophant, Lycinius:

EMPEROUR: Where are the Masquers that should dance to night?
LYCINIUS: In the old Hall, Sir, going now to practise.
EMPEROUR: About it strait. 'Twill serve to draw away
          Those listning Fools, who trace it in the Gallery;
          And if by Chance odd noises should be heard,
          As Womens Shreiks, or so, say, 'tis a Play
          Is practising within.
LYCINIUS: The Rape of *Lucrece*
          Or some such merry Prank—it shall be done, Sir.

The next scene opens with dancers gossiping, practicing, and finally dancing before Lycinius returns, remarking,

          Bless me, the loud Shrieks and horrid Outcries
          Of the poor Lady! Ravishing d'ye call it?
          She roars as if she were upon the Rack.
          . . . .

These tumbling Rogues, I fear, have overheard 'em;
But their Ears with their Brains are in their Heels.[5]

After another dance, Lycinius's fellow panderers report that the rape has been accomplished. Lucina resolves to die for honor betrayed, and Valentinian is finally murdered by his own soldiers.

In the 1684 performance of *Valentinian,* the masque by Sir Francis Fane depicted a distressing dream by Lucina which foreshadowed events to come, but the actual rape took place offstage during the dance sequence. When Betterton decided to revive *Valentinian* in 1694, someone saw the possibilities in the cynical remark by Lycinius, "The Rape of *Lucrece*/ Or some such merry Prank." Betterton therefore devised a new masque, not to illustrate a dream but to be substituted for the dance and used to represent in classical symbolism the rape that was taking place offstage. Thus the masque became an integral part of the plot.

The masque, *The Rape of Europa by Jupiter,*[6] opens with Mercury descending in a chariot drawn by ravens, followed by Jupiter on an eagle singing his godlike intentions toward Europa and instructing Mercury as his pander. As they reascend, shepherds and shepherdesses join in singing and dancing. Europa voices her discontent in an aria and is comforted by Herse and Aglaura in aria and duet. A comic interlude serves as the antimasque, when to a "Symphony of Musick, the scene draws and discovers Europa on a Bull's back in the Sea." Following that, "the Scene changes to a Bower, and discovers Europa, her Hair loose about her, as just ravish'd." Europa thereupon laments in a mad song, after which she swoons, attendants place her in a chariot, and Jupiter, joining her in the celestial machine, promises that she shall shine in the heavens. The shepherds and shepherdesses join in chorus and dance for the grand finale as Jupiter and the new star ascend. The all-sung masque must have lasted about twenty-five minutes.

Motteux's activity in the theatre increased rapidly after 1694. Prologues, epilogues, and songs by Motteux abounded at Lincoln's Inn Fields until 1699 and then at Drury Lane as well. Motteux's first acknowledged classical masque was the delightful *The Loves of Mars and Venus* in November 1696, with music by John Eccles and Godfrey Finger. The three acts of this miniature opera alternated with the three acts of *The Anatomist,* a farce by Edward Ravenscroft. Motteux significantly called his work "A Play set to Music," and in the prologue spoken by Betterton he harkened back to his first discussion of opera in the *Gentleman's Journal* of January 1692:

> Yet is our Entertainment odd and new;
> . . . .
> And what we call a Masque some will allow
> To be an Opera, as the World goes now.

If there is a connection between the plots of the farce and the masque, it is the similarity between (and utter absurdity of) love on earth and love on Olympus. The importance of the long masque in 1696 was that the audience sat entranced for long periods, unconscious of the fact that they had listened to an all-sung entertainment with comprehension and delight, something that Dryden and Betterton had claimed was not possible.

In June 1697 *The Novelty,* a five-act divertissement planned by Motteux and three-fifths written by him, contained *Hercules,* an all-sung story, and music by Eccles, about whom Motteux wrote in his preface, "Mr. Eccles set it with his usual Success, and yet more masterly than my Mars and Venus, if possible."

In February 1699, Motteux, by this time the author of several plays and whole evenings' entertainments, supplied Drury Lane with his free adaptation of Fletcher's *The Island Princess,* which was still running when Betterton, at Lincoln's Inn Fields in the last months of 1700, decided to revive Fletcher's *The Mad Lover,* one of Betterton's own early successes. Scholars have long debated the relationship between an "Opera," *The Mad Lover,* and some songs in numbers of the *Mercurius Musicus, Or the Monthly Collection of New Teaching Songs,*[7] published in 1701. The January–February issue contained eight separate pieces giving the name of the singer and the source as either *The Mad Lover* or *Acis and Galatea;* the March–April issue contained two songs; and in the May–June number there were two more. Scholars long conjectured either that there was originally a complete opera manuscript, presumably lost, entitled *The Mad Lover,* or that *Acis and Galatea* was the second title of *The Mad Lover* (or vice versa).[8] Enough of the music with both titles (sometimes associated and sometimes separately noted) was printed in 1701 and thereafter to mystify but not enlighten the theatre historian. Eventually, careful reading of Fletcher's play and the music together, along with examination of the dates of the revival and the dates of the printed music (noting the singers mentioned in *Mercurius Musicus,* as well as applying Motteux's known technique with librettos and songs in connection with other revivals), solved the puzzle. The later "discovery" of the unique copy of the libretto of *Acis and Galatea* with the name of Peter Motteux on the title page confirmed the connection between the play and the masque.[9]

Eccles and Motteux were responsible for all the new instrumental music and songs indicated in the 1679 second folio (*The Mad Lover* has never been printed separately), as well as for extra songs pertinent to the recent military activities of William III.[10] The most important portion of the musical additions to *The Mad Lover* was the long, completely sung *Acis and Galatea,* which did not demand celestial chariots but substituted boisterous comedy and spectacular dance numbers for stage machinery, which was scarce at Lincoln's Inn Fields.

In *The Mad Lover,* Memnon, a great general and national hero, is rejected in jest by Princess Calis, sister of the king. He then goes mad for love, threatens to the consternation of everyone to commit suicide, but finally comes to his senses after five acts of tragifarcical action in which Polydore, his brother, wins the princess and receives the blessing of the restored Memnon. The king and court sit down to see the masque, *Acis and Galatea,* about forty-five minutes in length, at the happy conclusion of the plot. Motteux followed the same pattern that had been used for the revival of *Valentinian* and other plays, suiting the theme of the masque to the dramatic problem that it was to illustrate and illumine, in this instance, sudden infatuation, seeming repudiation of a loved person, temporary madness in the rejected lover, and a happy conclusion.

The principals of the speaking cast were Betterton in his original part of Memnon, Elizabeth Barry as Princess Calis, John Verbruggen as Polydore, and Anne Bracegirdle as Venus, a character she had played before in *The Loves of Mars and Venus* and would resume in the same season in the all-sung Congreve-Eccles *The Judgment of Paris.* Mrs. Bracegirdle joined the professional singers in the play's songs as well as in the main attraction of the evening as the principal singer in *Acis and Galatea.* The tremendous amount of music in what was primarily a spoken play has resulted in the erroneous designation of *The Mad Lover* as an opera.

In the interpolated masque, *Acis and Galatea,* Mrs. Bracegirdle sang the breeches role of *Acis* as the lover who goes mad because he is rejected in jest by Galatea, the nymph, sung by Elizabeth Bowman. The giant Polyphemus was sung by Mr. Cook; Roger, a country swain, by Thomas Doggett; Joan, his bride, by Elizabeth Willis, who flirts with Acis while he is mad but is finally won back by Roger. The Acis, Joan, and Roger section of *Acis and Galatea,* under the title of "The Country Wedding," was the longest-lived portion of the entire complex, actually being performed until 1739 when the Handel-Gay oratorio restored the tragic ending and superseded the Eccles-Motteux version.

After comparing the librettos of the masques in the two Fletcher plays (one in 1694 and the other in 1700), one can have little doubt that Motteux wrote both. *Acis and Galatea* is as appropriate a masque for the tragicomic action of *The Mad Lover* as the earlier *The Rape of Europa by Jupiter*[11] was for *Valentinian,* covering that play's offstage violence. Both were set to music by John Eccles; both used the same pattern of classical story to illustrate the main plot; both used the comic interlude as antimasque within the masque.

The Mad Lover was closely followed by the celebrated contest in which four composers set music to a full-length libretto for *The Judgment of Paris* by William Congreve, an ardent supporter of opera. The contestants were John Eccles, Godfrey Finger, Daniel Purcell, and James Weldon. It is significant, perhaps, that the little-known young Weldon won first prize because his setting was more in the Italian style than the others. The Eccles version of *The Judgment of Paris* was the most popular, however, with the same group of singers from Lincoln's Inn Fields for whom *The Rape of*

Europa by Jupiter, The Loves of Mars and Venus, and *Acis and Galatea* had been written.

Awareness of Motteux's knowledge of Italian opera, and his commitment to it as early as 1692, makes it possible to watch his maneuvers to place all-sung, easily understood, classical pieces before his audiences: the first collaboration with Eccles in *The Rape of Europa by Jupiter* (1694); the delightful comedy of *The Loves of Mars and Venus* (1696); the separate, sensational masque of *Hercules* (1697); the moving love story and high comedy of *Acis and Galatea* (1700). By gradual degrees, Motteux and Eccles built up an audience for the all-sung evening's entertainment. I have given special attention to the interpolated masques of *Valentinian* and *The Mad Lover* because they had not been "discovered" before as being, first, an important part of the 1690s revivals and, second, a clear indication that all-sung opera was rapidly approaching. Between them, the French Motteux and the English Eccles produced a mixture that exactly suited the growing demand for a theatrical form that went beyond the spoken word. They satisfied both the English audience's innate love of drama and its developing passion for a more international music.

The first acknowledged opera in the Italian style in England is *Arsinoe, Queen of Cyprus* (January 1705), with libretto translated and adapted by the ubiquitous Peter Motteux from an obscure Italian work, and with music supplied by Thomas Clayton, Nicolino Haym, and Charles Dieupart. The short preface, although signed by Thomas Clayton, could be the concluding paragraph to Motteux's first pronouncement on opera in the January 1692 issue of the *Gentleman's Journal:*

> The Design of this Entertainment is to introduce the Italian manner of Musick on the English Stage. . . . The Stile to express the Passions, which is the Soul of Musick. . . . The Musick being Recitative, may not at first meet that General Acceptation, as is to be hop'd from the Audience's being better acquainted with it: But if this Attempt shall, by pleasing the Nobility and Gentry, be a Means of bringing this manner of Musick to be us'd in this Country, I shall think all my Study and Pains very well employ'd.[12]

Notes

1. John Dennis, "An Essay on the Operas after the Italian Manner" (1706); rpt. in Dennis, 1:382–83.

2. John Eccles and Godfrey Finger, *The Music in Macbeth* [1696], British Library *Add. MS.* 12,219. Pointed out by Dr. Stoddard Lincoln, whose willingness to share his knowledge of Restoration music is reflected in this paper.

3. *On Stage and Off,* a collection of essays in honor of Emmett L. Avery, edited by John W. Ehrstine, John R. Elwood, and Robert C. McLean (Seattle: University of Washington, 1968), pp. 56–62.

4. *Thesaurus Musicus . . . The Third Book* (London, 1695), Folger Shakespeare Library, T 873.

5. John Fletcher, *Valentinian*, altered by the earl of Rochester (London: 1685), pp. 46–47.

6. [Peter Anthony Motteux], *The Rape of Europa by Jupiter, a Masque; As it is Sung at the Queens Theatre, in Dorset Garden* . . . (London: M. Bennett, 1694), Henry E. Huntington Library, K-D 46. Unique.

7. *Mercurius Musicus, Or, The Monthly Collection of New Teaching Songs . . . in the New Opera, call'd The Mad Lover. . . . Compos'd by Mr. John Eccles* . . . (London: W. Pearson for B. Brown, 1701), British Library, G 92.

8. Robert Newton Cunningham, *Peter Anthony Motteux, 1663–1718: A Biographical and Critical Study* (Oxford: Blackwell, 1933), p. 154. Also Arthur Colby Sprague, *Beaumont and Fletcher on the Restoration Stage* (Cambridge, Mass.: Harvard University Press, 1926), p. 272.

9. Peter Anthony Motteux, *The Masque of Acis and Galatea, With the rest of the Musical Entertainments, In the New Opera Call'd The Mad Lover, The Musick by Mr. John Eccles* . . . (London: W. Pearson for Henry Playford, 1701), Cambridge University Library, Syn. 6.68.594. Unique.

10. *Harmonia Anglicana Or the Musick of the English Stage, containing Six sets of Ayers and Tunes in 4 Parts, made for the Operas Tragedys and Comedyes of the Theatres. The Second Collection . . . In four part-books: First Treble; Second Treble; Tenor; Bass* (London: [1701]), Durham Cathedral Library, C37 (ii). Unique.

Also a manuscript book of *Theatre Tunes* containing the Overture and nine act tunes from *The Mad Lover.* Library of Congress, M15 15. All Case.

11. *The Rape of Europa by Jupiter* and *Acis and Galatea*, with all extant music for both masques and an introduction by Lucyle Hook, was published by the Augustan Reprint Society, William Andrews Clark Memorial Library, University of California, Los Angeles, California, in November, 1981. Publication number 208.

12. Peter Anthony Motteux and Thomas Clayton, *Arsinoe, Queen of Cyprus, An Opera, After the Italian Manner* . . . (London: Tonson, 1705), preface [A3].

6

The Librettos and Lyrics of William Congreve

STODDARD LINCOLN

Throughout his career, William Congreve wrote song lyrics and librettos for the finest composers of his day. Besides creating lyrics for his own four comedies, he supplied almost an equal number to be sung in the plays of other authors, as well as many single lyrics that first appeared as songs. Sometime during the three years between *The Mourning Bride* (1697) and *The Way of the World* (1700), he wrote a masque, *The Judgment of Paris*, which was followed in 1701 by an ode for St. Cecelia's Day, "Oh Harmony, to Thee We Sing," and an opera libretto, *Semele*, probably completed by 1706.

It is important to remember that Congreve wrote these works not with the hope that they would be set to music, but will full knowledge that they would be. John Eccles, one of the most popular theatre composers of the day, set most of Congreve's lyrics, including those for the last two comedies, *The Judgment of Paris*, the ode, and *Semele*. Besides settings by Eccles, there are also settings by Henry and Daniel Purcell, Godfrey Finger, John Weldon, and John Galliard.

Despite his preoccupation with the musical stage, Congreve's dramatic output has been the primary focus of critical commentary on his work; his lyrics have been either ignored or misunderstood.[1] The reason for this is simple: the achievement of a lyricist and librettist can only be judged in the context of its musical setting; in order to write for music, a poet must necessarily take into consideration the musical style of his time and make appropriate adjustments in his poetic style. It is therefore as futile to study the poetry without the music as it is to study the music of a song without its text. Unfortunately, Congreve's musical texts have usually been studied without the music, and the resulting critical commentary has been as harsh as it has been unfair.

116

When Congreve's lyrics and libretti are studied in their musical context and given the proper assessment due them, the judgment is quite different. One realizes that Congreve at first ignored the requirements of music but that, when he finally did recognize them, he was equally skilled in writing for both late Restoration and early eighteenth-century musical styles.

In seeking the poetic necessities of Restoration song, one can do no better than turn to John Dryden. Not only did he set a good example with his own work, but, typically, he spelled it out succinctly for others. In the preface to his opera *Albion and Albanius* (1685), Dryden writes that a song lyric "must abound in the Softness and Variety of Numbers; its principal Intention being to please the Hearing rather than to gratify the Understanding."

Dryden fully realized that the listener's attention would be primarily riveted to the music, not to the text. A good lyricist, he believed, should concentrate on ordering smooth, singable sounds into a variety of metrical patterns. The auditor could not be expected to follow involved conceits or detailed imagery even if they were set clearly. What was left out in meaning was to be made up for in the beauty of the music. When the composer did not fulfill this role, Dryden was unhappy. Such was the case when he was working with Louis Grabut, an extraordinarily untalented French composer, on the opera *Albion and Albanius*. Toward the end of his preface to this work, Dryden cavils:

> 'Tis True, I have not often been put to this Drudgery; but where I have, the Words will Sufficiently shew, that I was then a Slave to the Composition, which I will never be again. 'Tis my Art to invent, and the Musician's to humor that Invention. I may be counsell'd . . . but will never part with the Power of the Militia.

On the other hand, when he was working with a talented composer such as Henry Purcell, the relationship was felicitous. Dryden wrote in the preface to *Amphytrion* (1690) concerning that relationship:

> What has been wanting on my Part has been abundantly supplied by the excellent Composition of Mr. Purcell; in whose Person we have at length found an Englishman, equal with the best abroad.

A fine example of Dryden as master of the militia and Purcell humoring the invention is found in Venus's song from the fifth act of *King Arthur* (1691):

> Fairest Isle, all Isles Excelling,
>   Seat of Pleasures, and of Loves;
> Venus, here, will choose her Dwelling,
>   And forsake her Cyprian Groves.

The conceit, a simple one, is easily grasped by the listener. In the subse-

quent three stanzas, Dryden avoids contrast and sustains the initial mood
by the use of imagery which develops the single conceit. He also employs
consistently smooth and open sounds and casts them in a regularly paced
metrical pattern that is enhanced by the use of feminine endings.

Purcell, perfectly understanding the poet's intent, sets the text to one of
his most supple melodies: a flowing minuet cast in even phrases. Like
Dryden, he offers no musical contrast, sets his text syllabically with no word
repetition, and uses a simple strophic form that parallels the stanzaic structure of the poetry.

In contrast to this purely melodic style, Restoration composers also wrote
in a highly dramatic style. They used sudden changes of meter and tempo
to contrast moods. They enjoyed shifting from the broad gestures of a
declamatory delivery to the ordered world of measured melody. They
reveled in seizing on a meaningful word and uttering it again and again, or
coloring it with brilliant melismas and figuration. In this style, the composer could and often did do violence to the understanding of a text by
excessive coloration, fragmentation, and motivic development—in other
words, by overusing the very musical devices that are the essence of dramatic song. A musically knowledgeable poet, however, could write verses
with this style in mind and produce a lyric that not only invited dramatic
musical treatment but also gave the composer opportunity for contrast,
word coloration, and fragmentation. Such a poem is found in the third act
of Dryden's last play, *Love Triumphant: or, Nature will Prevail* (1694):

> What State of Life can be so blesst
> As Love, that warms a Lover's Breast?
> Two Souls in one, the same Desire,
> To grant the Bliss, and to require!
> But if in Heav'n a Hell we find,
>   'Tis all from thee,
>   Oh Jealousy!
>   'Tis all from thee,
>   Oh Jealousy,
> Thou Tyrant, Tyrant Jealousy,
> Thou Tyrant of the Mind!

Contrast is offered by the juxtaposition of the states of love and jealousy.
The former is described in the opening quatrain of iambic tetrameter.
Maintaining the same metrical scheme, Dryden changes the image from
heaven to hell and then tightens the rhyme scheme and repeats the two
short verses. Thinking like a composer, Dryden now offers repetition of
the harshest word in the poem, "tyrant," and then ties the stanza together
by its final rhyme word.

When John Eccles set this song at the beginning of his career, he found
that Dryden had already solved the problem of word repetitions and rests.
The first stanza is set syllabically to a serene melody, while the second

stanza changes its mood by means of word repetition and dramatic pauses. The song is not only musically satisfying, but also a perfect declamation of a text designed for just such a musical setting.

The Songs in the Comedies

On *reading* a comedy by Congreve, one is acutely aware of the wit, sparkle, and elegance of the language. On *hearing* a Congreve comedy, one becomes aware that a great deal of the sparkle and elegance is a result of the playwright's manipulation of sound. Listen to Lady Wishfort's wanton toying with the sounds of *ai* and l as she contemplates how best to make the first impression on Sir Rowland:

I'll lye—ay, I'll lye down—I'll receive him in my little Dressing-Room, there's a Couch—yes, yes, I'll give the first Impression on a Couch—I won't lye neither, but loll and lean upon one elbow.

But little of this delightful play on sound is found in the song lyrics Congreve wrote for his four comedies. He offers us neither Dryden's softness of sound nor his variety of numbers. The diction is terse, the meter, regular, and the stanzaic structure, rigid. The lyrics present complex conceits, involved imagery, and double meanings. In *Love for Love* (1695), for example, Sailor Ben winds up his saucy ballad with the punch line:

> And then he let fly at her,
> A Shot 'twixt Wind and Water,
> That won the fair Maid's Heart.

Even an exceptionally quick-witted Restoration rake would require more time to figure this out than any musical setting could possibly allow him.

Typical is the song written for the third act of *The Way of the World* (1700):

> Love's but the Frailty of the Mind,
> When 'tis not with Ambition joined;
> A sickly Flame, which if not fed expires;
> And feeding, wastes in Self-consuming Fires.
>
> 'Tis not to wound a wanton Boy
> Or am'rous Youth, that gives the Joy;
> But 'tis the Glory to have pierc'd a Swain,
> For whom inferior Beauties sigh'd in Vain.
>
> Then I alone the Conquest prize,
> When I insult a Rival's Eyes:
> If there's Delight in Love, 'tis when I see
> That Heart which others bleed for, bleed for me.

The conceit is so complex that it takes several readings to grasp it; the imagery is rich, varied, and full of contrast; and finally, the poem is cast in a rigid pattern of rhyme, meter, and stanzaic structure that makes no attempt to reflect its meaning and emotion in sound or rhythm. Congreve's intention, in fact, seems to be the opposite of Dryden's: he strives to "gratify the understanding" rather than to "please the hearing."

Eccles faced many problems in setting this text. If he was to transmit Congreve's meaning to an audience, he would have to set it syllabically, closely observing the word rhythms and line lengths. This would lead to a monotony of rhythms and phrase length. Also, if he followed the strophic structure in his music, he would have difficulty finding a single melody that would express the cynicism of the first stanza, the many images of the second stanza, and the triumph of the final one. Eccles, therefore, chose to ignore the structure entirely and to convey the meaning by musical devices in a declamatory song.

The first stanza is broken up into three short sections. The first portrays "frailty" by some fussy coloratura. The second quickens the tempo and stresses "ambition." The next two lines employ a sinuous motif suggesting "sickly." The second stanza is treated as a florid recitative with appropriate coloratura underlining such words as "wanton," "am'rous," "glory," and "sigh'd." The first three verses of the final stanza are contained in a well-developed single section that portrays its triumph by shifting from the minor to the major and making use of militant dotted rhythms. Particularly revealing of Eccles's complete understanding of Congreve's meaning is the striking way he transforms the opening motive of the song into a victorious motive for this section. It not only ties the piece together musically but also portrays the difference between love as a sickly flame and love as an object of conquest. The final verse returns to the minor and is treated as a dramatic coda.

This treatment admittedly does violence to Congreve's poetics, but it reveals a situation in which a composer, denied a structure compatible to the meaning of the text, had to forge one of his own. Eccles's setting is a virtuoso piece that creates a strong image of its own. By omitting it from revivals of *The Way of the World* today, we miss the whole point of the argument that rages between Millamant and Marwood.

The Judgment of Paris

On turning to the masque *The Judgment of Paris*, one is struck by Congreve's complete stylistic change. By choosing a well-known subject and a simple plot, Congreve could concentrate on working out Dryden's concept of "softness and variety of Numbers," and "pleasing the Ear rather than gratifying the Understanding." Avoiding the temptation to complicate the story with a counterplot or enliven it with the addition of rustic or comic elements, Congreve, undoubtedly with the advice of Eccles, cast the story into a structure obviously planned for musical development and expansion.

The masque falls into three natural sections, the first two equal in length to the last. The first section outlines the contest in a dialogue between Paris and Mercury, ushers in the goddesses, and shows us Paris's decision to act as judge. In the second section, each of the goddesses petitions for the prize. At this point Congreve could easily have concluded the work by moving directly to the final judgment. Instead, he offers the composer ample time to expand his portrayal of the goddesses by having Paris request a reshowing. Thus, in the third part, each goddess is granted additional stanzas and reinforces her pleas with symphonies and choruses. Only then is the prize offered in a sort of coda with a final choral celebration. Dramatically, perhaps, this structure is repetitious; seen from the composer's point of view, however, the structure is ideal and offers room and freedom for musical expansion.

Another aid Congreve offers the composer is the placement of the airs, ensembles, choruses, and symphonies so that they offer variety and lead to a single musical climax halfway through the third part.

In the opening section, the exchanges between Mercury and Paris are interrupted by a symphony for the descent of the goddesses; the symphony is followed by a duet between the two men. The second section consists of three airs for the goddesses and a concluding trio. The first appearance of the chorus is reserved until the third part, where it is used to reinforce the several arguments of the various goddesses. Juno's presentation terminates with a choral repetition of her first stanza. Pallas' format is slightly different in that it includes a symphony halfway through and then concludes with a chorus summing up her militant thoughts. The placement of symphony and chorus are completely different for Venus's plea. An opening symphony dispels Pallas's bombast, and the chorus is placed at midpoint in her seductive air. Thus, unlike her peers, she addresses her final words to Paris herself rather than through the impersonal medium of a chorus. Paris's passionate response, then, is to her directly. This simple device adroitly puts the focus irrevocably on Venus, neatly dismissing the personifications of war and power in favor of love.

Turning to the poetry itself, one no longer finds the metrical and stanzaic rigidity that characterized the songs in the comedies. Modeling his metrics and rhyme scheme on Cowley's "Pindaric" style (recommended by Dryden for song lyrics in his preface to *Albion and Albanius*), Congreve presents a free sequence of verses ranging from trimeter to pentameter. This "variety of Numbers" is seen in the opening airs for Mercury and Paris:

MERCURY:
From high Olympus, and the Realms above,
Behold I come the Messenger of Jove;
His dread Commands I bear:
Shepherd, arise and hear;
Arise, and leave a while thy rural care:
Forbear thy wooly Flock to feed,
And lay aside thy tuneful Reed;
For thou to greater Honors art decreed.

PARIS:
O Hermes, I thy Godhead know,
By thy winged Heels and Head,
By thy Rod that wakes the Dead,
And guides the Shades below.
Say wherefore dost thou seek this humble Plain
To greet a lowly Swain?
What does the mighty Thunderer ordain?

The length of each line is clearly defined by grammatical structure, rhythm, and the use of rhyme. An undulating counterpoint is created by the juxtaposition of a free rhyme scheme that is independent of the metrical scheme. The verse lengths of Paris's speech, for example, run *5 5 3 3 5 4 4 5*. Rather than paralleling it with the rhyme scheme *a a b b a c c a*, Congreve imposes a different scheme:

Meter: *5 5 3 3 5 4 4 5*
Rhyme: *a a b b b c c c*

Although the scheme of verse length is free, the various lengths are not arbitrarily chosen but are generally governed by meaning. The most common length found in the masque is tetrameter, which is used for neutral expression. Pentameter is used for more exalted thoughts and for references to the high-ranking gods. Trimeter is used for lower ranks, such as the mortal Paris, and all that is related to him as a shepherd. Thus Mercury states his Olympian credentials in two opening verses of pentameter. The third and fourth lines, referring to and commanding Paris, employ trimeter. In the fifth line, Paris is asked in pentameter to leave his rural cares, and the next two lines of tetrameter suggest how this may be accomplished. The final line of pentameter exalts Paris to greater honors.

Respecting Mercury's rank and his own lowly situation as a shepherd, Paris opens with three lines of neutral tetrameter and moves into trimeter when referring to the shades below. Their two ranks are the most contrasted in the pentameter (possibly hexameter, depending on the scansion) of the fifth verse and the trimeter of the sixth. The final verse, with its reference to Jove, uses the exalted pentameter.

"Variety of Numbers" is also used in the individual poetic feet. The basic foot is iambic, as is seen above in the speeches of Mercury and Paris. Attention is demanded by trochaic feet, as in the fourth line of Mercury's opening air. Pallas' militant nature is also shown by the use of trochees:

> This way, Mortal, bend thy Eyes.

Later, when she is chastising Paris for his Arcadian dallying, she abandons her masculine endings for deliberately weak feminine endings:

> Pipeing, toying,
> Nymphs, decoying.

Anapests and dactyls are rare, but when they are used their effect is telling. At the end of the second part, after the goddesses have each had their first airs, all cast in iambs or trochees, Paris reveals his rustic nature in a series of giddy, dancelike anapests:

> Distracted I turn, but I cannot decide;
> So equal a Title sure never was try'd.
> United your Beauties so dazzle the Sight,
>   That lost in a Maze,
>   I giddily gaze,
> Confused and o'erwhelmed with a Torrent of Light.

Nor did Congreve overlook Dryden's dictum that the poetry "must abound in Softness." The verses read smoothly and use many open sounds and voiced consonants that are ideal to sing. Coupling his use of metrics with the meaning of the verse, he uses the sound of the words to characterize his three goddesses in much the same way that a composer will associate a particular timbre or motive with a thought or character. Juno displays her superior position by rich diphthongs and hard consonants. Venus emphasizes her seductive charms by the use of closed vowels and soft consonants. Pallas falls somewhere between the two, serving as a sort of pivot. This technique is seen in even such a small detail as the names the goddesses use for themselves. Juno prefers the more imposing "Saturnia"; Athena discards the soft lilt of her name for the terse sound of "Pallas"; and even Venus, in her last plea, chooses the mellifluous "Cytherea" to evoke her last thoughts.

Congreve's most subtle control of characteristic sounds is found in the goddesses' three airs and trio in the second part of the masque.

> JUNO:
> Saturnia, wife of thund'ring Jove am I,
> Beloved by him and Empress of the Sky;
> Shepherd, fix on me thy wond'ring Sight,
> Beware and view me well, and judge aright.

PALLAS:
This way, Mortal, bend thy eyes,
Pallas claims the golden Prize;
A virgin Goddess free from Stain,
And Queen of Arts and Arms I reign.

VENUS:
Hither, turn Thee, gentle Swain,
Let not Venus sue in vain;
Venus rules the Gods above,
Love rules them and she rules Love.

The use of diphthongs is carefully controlled: Juno's air contains twelve, Pallas's eight, and Venus's only three. Thus the three quatrains begin in the sonorous diphthongs associated with prestige and gradually move to the more seductive effect of Venus's hushed and covert sounds.

The most clearly heard sounds of these three stanzas are the rhyme words, and therefore Congreve uses them to make his transition, or, to use a musical term, modulation, from Juno's characteristic sounds to those of Venus. The rhyme words of the three quatrains quoted above are:

Juno: *I; sky; sight; aright.*
Pallas: *eyes; prize; stain; reign.*
Venus: *swain; vain; above; love.*

An examination of these rhyme words reveals the use of the diphthong *ai* in the first six lines. This is the broadest diphthong in the language, running from the open central *a* to the closed front *i*. Congreve uses it to depict the queen of the gods. Pallas, as a pivotal figure, retains this sound for the rhymes of her first two lines. In her second two, she starts the modulation by changing the *a* to the midfront *e*, thus narrowing the diphthong *ai* to *ei*.

Venus picks up the *ei* for her first two lines, then drops all diphthongs in her last two lines and uses the midcentral ʌ for her final two rhymes. The numerical relationships also strengthen the gradual shift in sound; the *ai* is repeated six times, the *ei* four, and the ʌ only twice, which creates a virtual diminuendo from the broad *ai* to the neutral ʌ.

This vowel modulation is made even smoother by the final consonants. Juno's first *ai* has full resonance, being left open. She then stops it with a hard *t*. Pallas uses the same vowel sound but softens the effect by using a voiced *z* instead of the hard unvoiced *t*. Her next consonant, the nasal *n*, is even softer-sounding. Venus retains both the consonant and the vowel shift, using one of the softest consonants in the language: a labiodental voiced fricative, *v*.

In the trio that follows, Congreve treats the first three lines as a sort of mirror coda to the preceding three stanzas.

VENUS:
Hither turn thee gentle Swain,

PALLAS:
Hither turn to me again.

JUNO:
Turn to me for I am she.

The most obvious mirror device is the reversal of the order in which the goddesses enter the ensemble. Each retains the essence of the sounds she used in her solo air so that the three verses move from soft sounds to hard shrill ones. Furthermore, each goddess picks up characteristic words from the line of the goddess she follows but surrounds them with new sounds typical of her own character. Venus's line is soft, with its initial aspirate and voiced dental sound of *hither* and the triphthong of *swain*. Pallas retains the *hither* but adds more force with *to me* and hardens Venus's *swain* to *again*. Juno employs Pallas's *to me*, followed by the full diphthong *ai*, which was characteristic of her previous air, and then repeats the shrill *i* of *she*. Only after these carefully controlled entries of the goddesses does Congreve allow the composers to mingle the voices at the whim of his countrapuntal gifts.

Although Congreve's control of sounds is at its most brilliant in the stanzas discussed above, the same technique abounds throughout the masque. In the third section, for example, when the goddesses expand their claims to the prize, Venus sees fit to denigrate the rewards of empire and the glory of battle offered by her fellow contestants. She even stoops to downright mimicry as she incorporates some of Juno's and Pallas's sound palette in her song by referring to "racking thoughts that vex the great" and "fickle is the warrior's fate."

It is likely that Congreve originally conceived *The Judgment of Paris* with Eccles for Thomas Betterton's Company at Lincoln Inn's Fields to display the singing and beauty of Ann Bracegirdle. (Mrs. Bracegirdle sang only Eccles's music, and Congreve's attachment to her has been the subject of many suppositions about the actress' unflinching claim to virginity.) The libretto, however, was used for a contest for the best musical setting. Scores were submitted by John Weldon, John Eccles, Daniel Purcell, and Godfrey Finger.[2] After individual hearings and a gala presentation of all of them on the same evening at Dorset Garden (March–April 1701), the prizes were given in the above order.

Given historical hindsight, Eccles's score should have been granted first prize. It is the mature work of a composer at the height of his powers and sums up the Restoration ideal of a perfect union between words and music. The vocal style is comparatively simple, and the text, for the most part, is set syllabically with a minimum of word repetition and coloratura, thus allowing Congreve's poetry to be heard clearly. As Congreve characterized his goddesses by sound, so Eccles does his by orchestral coloration: Juno sings to strings, Pallas is reinforced by trumpets, and recorders accompany Venus. Outstanding in Eccles's score is the overall tonal architecture. The first part moves from D major to B minor. Juno takes the tonality to E major and Pallas pulls it back to A major. Venus continues in A minor. The reshowing of the third section returns us to the tonic D, but minor not major, and Pallas, with her trumpets, conveniently states her second argument in D major. Venus then pulls us into the only subdominant key of the work, G minor. Paris awards the prize in G major, and the final victory is celebrated by a return to the tonic, D major.

In contrast to Eccles's simplicity, both Weldon and Purcell attempt to overwhelm the listener with brilliance. Both settings shatter the text with constant word repetition; both overlay much of the poetry with exaggerated and often grotesque coloratura. Congreve's careful placement of the symphonies is altered for the worse, the orchestral forces are used for immediate effect rather than for characterization, and the tonal architecture in both scores lacks any overall design. Weldon's victory in the contest is explainable on the basis of his being young and unknown. His score, despite its many failings, brought a new sound to the theatre and included a splendid tune that remained popular for the remainder of the century.[3]

Semele

Although Italian opera suffered severe injuries in its transalpine journey to England and arrived as a paste-up of mutilated arias, its effect on London audiences was stunning.[4] However inept the music and translation of *Arsinoe* (Drury Lane, 16 January 1705) may have been, London audiences were, for the first time, exposed to the Italian concept of an entirely sung drama consisting of an alternation of recitative and aria. Thomas Betterton, in an attempt to bring authentic Italian opera to London, responded by mounting *The Loves of Ergasto* (9 April 1705) as the first presentation in the new theatre in the Haymarket. London, however, was not yet ready for opera in its original language and continued to support the pastiches offered by Rich at Drury Lane. Congreve, as co-manager of the new theatre, immediately recognized the possibilities of the Italian operatic style and wrote his libretto *Semele* for John Eccles, who was also studying the Italian musical style very closely.

Italian opera libretti at the time consisted of a series of unlikely events caused by outrageous coincidences, disguises, and mistaken identities. While there were moments of great musical beauty, the plots were hopelessly confused, lacking in logic, and the characters were more frequently than not unconvincing and undeveloped.

Although the plot of *Semele* is based on the supernatural, includes transformations and disguises, and resorts to a *deus ex machina* ending, it is logical and well constructed, and it reveals Congreve's ability to develop his characters. Semele, for example, starts out as a confused and inexperienced young girl who longs to consummate her affair with Jupiter even though her father tries to force her into a marriage with Athamas. After describing Semele's first night with Jupiter, the second act dwells on her insecurity, and she finally concludes that only immortality will offer her a secure place with her beloved Jove. In the final act she is filled with rash ambition, and even Jupiter's warning will not deter her from a scheme that ultimately causes her destruction.

Jupiter is portrayed as the typical Restoration rake, who treats Semele as a desirable toy. When he fully comprehends her scheme to attain immortality, however, he realizes his folly and tries in vain to change the course of events. Broken by his failure, he bitterly repents his thoughtless actions.

Only Juno, the catalyst of these events, remains unchanged. She first appears with her messenger, Iris, and, enraged with jealousy, curses the affair. She is then seen wheedling Somnus to put Semele's sister, Ino, to sleep so that she may assume Ino's place and deal directly with Semele. In the ensuing scene, Juno, knowing full well that an attempt to obtain immortality will spell Semele's destruction, plays on the young girl's vanity and convinces her to demand it. Just before Semele's immolation, Juno puts in her final appearance in an aria of triumph.

Nor does Congreve neglect the development of the minor characters. Athamas, betrothed to and in love with Semele, is loved by Ino. When Ino is about to see Semele married to her beloved Athamas, the latter offers Ino brotherly comfort, which she interprets as love. Athamas's gradual realization of Ino's true feeling toward him is beautifully portrayed by Congreve in a moving duet. Congreve develops Somnus by transforming him from a grumpy god of sleep into a lecherous old man when Juno bribes him with a young nymph. Even Iris displays individuality as she describes to Juno the dwelling place of Jupiter and Semele and their blissful existence. The characters of *Semele* are certainly more fascinating than those of Italian composers.

As for musical structure, Congreve offers the composer far more than the usual Italianate alternation of recitatives and arias as he introduces duets, trios, even a quartet, and choruses. Congreve's understanding of stage spectacle is seen in the fact that each of the three acts terminates with a different type of finale. The first act concludes with an ode for the priests, the second ends with a ballet, and the third-act finale presents a dazzling extravaganza of machines as Juno descends in a peacock-drawn chariot, Semele is immolated by a flashing cloud of lightning, and Apollo descends in a glory as the scene changes to a prospect of Mount Cithaeron.

The most difficult problem that confronted Congreve was to develop a type of poetry that would serve the Italian musical techniques of recitative and aria construction. Recognizing the difference between poetry for recitative and poetry for aria, Congreve points out in the preface of his libretto,[5] that recitative poetry need not follow the strict observations of meter and rhyme because it is "only a more tuneable speaking, . . . a kind of prose in Musick." The arias, on the other hand, require a strict observation of meter and rhyme. Congreve observed these differences with great care, and in the printed libretto the arias are distinguished from the recitatives by the use of italics.

The essential characteristic of Italian recitative is that the meaning of the words is more important than the music. This is accomplished by setting the words to a syllabic line that reflects the spoken rhythm and, more or less, the natural inflection of the text. The accompaniment is cut down to the barest harmonic support of widely spaced chords played by the continuo instruments only. It is in the recitative that the details of the plot are usually found and that the poet, if he wishes, can indulge in complex imagery and conceits.

A fine example of Congreve's recitative style is found at the end of the first act of *Semele*. Cadmus describes how Jupiter abducted his daughter by assuming the form of an eagle.

> While this we saw with dread Surprize
> Swifter than Lightning downward tending
> An Eagle stoop't, of mighty Size.
>   On purple Wings descending;
> Like Gold his Beak, like Stars shone forth his eyes,
>   Sudden he snatch'd the trembling maid,
>   And soaring from our Sight convey'd
> Diffusing ever as he lessening flew
> Celestial Odours, and Ambrosial Dew.

The sensuous imagery—with its appeal to sight, touch, and smell—is truly Baroque, and we witness the same "Pindaric" techniques of independent patterns of meter and rhyme that we saw in much of *The Judgment of Paris*. Congreve's use of metrics and sound to describe the event enhances the dramatic effect.

In the second act when Semele takes issue with Jupiter for treating her as a frail toy, Jupiter justifies himself in free verse.

> Thy Sex of Jove's the master-piece,
> Thou, of thy Sex, art most excelling.
> Frailty in thee is an Ornament,
> Giv'n to agitate the Mind,
> And keep awake Men's Passions;
> To banish Indolence,
> And dull Repose,
> The Foes of Transport, and of Pleasure.

Realizing that the imagery and conceits of such passages would be lost in the arias, Congreve carefully reserved this type of writing for the recitative throughout the opera and resorted to a different style for the arias. If the librettist reigns supreme in the recitative, the composer is the undisputed lord of the aria. Congreve had certainly become aware of this in *The Judgment of Paris*, but in order to satisfy the stringent requirements of the Italian aria, he had to go a step further in his poetry.

The musical requirements of an early eighteenth-century Italian aria are vastly different from those of a Restoration song. English song can be cast into a strophic form, or it can be through-composed and set in a series of short, contrasting sections. The aria, on the other hand, employs the *da capo* form, in which the first verses are repeated at the end with intervening material. Besides this formal difference, Italian structure is at odds with the traditional English melodic style. While English songs favored long, flowing phrases, the Italian aria is built of short, motto-like motives. Unlike the English style, which uses a minimum of repetition, the Italian style is based on taking one motto and subjecting it to constant repetition by means of sequence and variation. Thus a line of Italian poetry is usually short and forms the basis of the motto. As the Italian composer develops his motto, so he repeats the text that goes with it. In order to avoid repetition ad nauseam, however, the Italian poet often fills out his stanzas with more short lines that match the first verse and may be set to the ubiquitous motto. Thus the Italian librettist developed a type of poetry consisting of short lines with closely spaced rhymes and frequently favoring feminine endings and double rhymes.

When Italianate opera came to London, the librettos were either translated into English or written in the Italian manner in order to fit the musical style. The Italian language lends itself to this type of poetry because of the rhymes naturally offered by its system of grammatical endings. English, however, makes use of fewer grammatical endings, and when it does, syntax is shown more by consonants than by vowels. The problem is seen most acutely in the work of Peter Anthony Motteux, who supplied many of the translations for the early London pastiches. In his translation of Stanziani's *Arsinoe*, set by Thomas Clayton, we encounter:

> Guide me,
> Lead me
> Where the nymph whom I adore,
>
> Sleeping,
> Dreaming,
> Thinks of love and me no more.

There is certainly no overdose of imagery or even a conceit to be lost in the music. Four of the lines are bisyllabic and offer the composer succinct

material and feminine endings for a short motto. But the *da capo* form is his
undoing. When the first three lines are repeated at the end, we are left
dangling with the ungrammatical

> Guide me,
> Lead me,
> Where the nymph whom I adore. . . .

While *Arsinoe* admittedly stunned London with its new-fangled Italianate
music, its poetry left much to be desired. Small wonder that Italian opera
soon reverted to its native tongue.

These problems are deftly solved by Congreve. A brilliant example of his
technique is found in the second act of *Semele:*

> With my Frailty don't upbraid me,
> I am Woman as you made me.
>
> Causeless doubting, or despairing,
> Rashly trusting, idly fearing,
> If obtaining,
> Still complaining,
> If consenting,
> Still repenting,
> Most complying,
> When denying,
> And to be followed only flying.

As in the Motteux aria, the meaning is simple, but it is developed by
more verses, giving the composer new words rather than constant word
repetition for the working of his motto. Admittedly Congreve has relied
heavily on -ing for his feminine endings, but even so the piling up of
double rhymes is almost dizzying, as is Semele's complaint. This rush of
thought is emphasized by the shortening of the lines that bring the rhyme
words closer together. As far as satisfying the *da capo* form, the final repetition of the first couplet makes perfect sense.

Not only has Congreve supplied the composer with enough lines so that
he will not have to repeat the text excessively for motivic development; he
has also constructed the opening lines in such a way that the composer can
repeat single words that will emphasize the meaning rather than destroy it.
Eccles was fully aware of this in his setting; and as sung, the first two lines
are heard:

> With my frailty don't upbraid me,
> With my frailty don't upbraid me,
> Don't, don't, don't upbraid me,
> I am woman, woman, woman,

> I am woman as you made me,
> As you made me.

The secret of Congreve's success is that each line contains a complete image and that fragmentation will emphasize the meaning of the entire aria text. The repetition of *don't* is a natural emphasis on the negative. The repetition of *woman* strengthens the association with *frailty*. The repetition of *as you made me* strongly places the fault of Semele's frailty on her creator, Jupiter, to whom the aria is addressed.

While the text of this aria is incompatible with the English musical style of *The Judgment of Paris*, it is perfect for the motto style of the Italian aria *da capo*. Congreve has, in fact, raised the level of English poetry usually associated with this form and style and has also aided the composer considerably in his use of a motto and its development through repetition.

As Congreve absorbed and adapted the Italian operatic style, so did John Eccles in his setting. He created a truly English *secco* recitative, mastered the Italian-style aria, and combined it with the English tradition he knew so well. As in *The Judgment of Paris*, he created an overall tonal architecture for the work that also reflected the drama. Of all the composers and librettists trying to adapt opera after the Italian style to Augustan audiences, certainly the achievement of Congreve and Eccles in *Semele* is the most outstanding because of its true synthesis of the Italian and English traditions and because of its artistic worth.[6]

The fate of *Semele* is ironic. It was probably planned for the opening of the new theatre in the Haymarket in 1705. Eccles, however, did not finish his score until 1707, by which time Congreve had severed his connections with the Haymarket and Italian opera was rapidly becoming a foreign enterprise on English soil. As more genuine Italian music was being introduced along with Italian singers who insisted on performing in Italian, the last thing producers of this genre were looking for was an English score by two men already known for their work in the by now old-fashioned English musical theatrical tradition. Thus *Semele*, the first full-length English opera in the Italian manner, was never produced. The libretto, slightly modified, is known through Handel's setting and is totally ignored in Congreve criticism. Because of a few missing outer leaves, Eccles's score remained unidentified until recently.[7] *Semele*, a work that should be considered a landmark in English operatic history because of the high quality of both its music and its libretto, has not even had the dubious honor of becoming a historical curiosity in textbooks.

Although both Congreve and Eccles lived several decades after the composition of *Semele*, their association with the theatre terminated after their failure to mount it. Together they had brought the English tradition to a state of perfection in *The Judgment of Paris* and had created a synthesis of

Italian and English styles in *Semele*. It is impossible to assess either of these works as music or literature alone, as their worth is the result of a perfect marriage between poetry and music. Although this essay has necessarily concentrated on Congreve, the fact is that his growth and that of Eccles must be seen as a single achievement. In this light, we now realize that Congreve's development as a lyricist and librettist is as great as his development as a dramatist.

Notes

1. The treatment of *The Judgment of Paris* during the nineteenth and twentieth centuries is typical. John Hodges in *William Congreve the Man* (New York: Modern Language Association of America, 1941, and London: Oxford University Press, 1941), pp. 70–73, related the circumstances of the contest that revolved around the production of this masque, but offered no critical comment at all. Edmund Gosse, in his *Life of William Congreve* (London: Kennikat Press, 1888), p. 144, sums up his attack on the work by calling it "poor threadbare stuff." Charles Wilson, writing the year after Congreve's death in his *Memoirs of the Life, Writings and Amours of William Congreve, Esq.* (London, 1730), p. 14, understood the masque in its musical context and said that "every word in this masque is music."

2. The scores by John Eccles and Daniel Purcell were published by John Walsh, London, 1702. John Weldon's score survives in a manuscript copy in the Folger Shakespeare Library, Wahington, D.C. (MS. 1479). Godfrey Finger took his score with him when he left London shortly after the contest. It has not been found.

3. Thomas Arne, for example, included Weldon's setting of Juno's air, "Let Ambition Fire Thy Mind," in his music for Bickerstaffe's *Love in a Village* (1762).

4. For a more detailed discussion of the advent of Italian opera in London, see J. Merrill Knapp, "Eighteenth-century Opera in London Before Handel, 1705–1710," above, and my article, "J. E. Galliard and a Critical Discourse," in *The Musical Quarterly* 53 (1967): 347–64.

5. William Congreve, *The Works* (London: Tonson, 1710).

6. For a more detailed musical anaylsis of *Semele,* see my article "The First Setting of Congreve's 'Semele,'" in *Music and Letters* 34 (1963): 103–17.

7. Eccles's manuscript resides in the library of The Royal College of Music, London (MS. Add. 15318).

7

The Children of Terpsichore

EDWARD A. LANGHANS

Dancers came in all shapes, sizes, and colors in Restoration and eighteenth-century England, and the great variety and increasing popularity of dance activity during the period tells us much about the taste of the times. There were hundreds of serious dancers and choreographers active in the theatres, at court, in dance academies, at the circuses and fairs, and in private homes, but we should also include among the Children of Terpsichore the rope and wire dancers, acrobats, posture makers, folk dancers, harlequins, and other popular entertainers. Most dancers were specialists, but many were skilled in other ways: as actors, actresses, singers, intrumentalists, composers, equestrians, managers, authors, puppeteers. Some won extravagant praise, others caused riots; some behaved scandalously, others were models of decorum; some brought laughter, others drew tears. Through contemporary accounts, I hope here to capture some of the feeling of the dance world of the Restoration and eighteenth century—the conditions under which performers labored, the kinds of dancers who flourished, how they were received, and how dance grew into one of England's most popular forms of entertainment.[1]

A Dancer's Life

Though a few performers at the top of the theatrical profession earned handsome sums and could work as little or as much as they pleased, most settled for moderate or meager salaries and busied themselves in a variety of ways, hoping to survive and prosper. Even established performers could not always count on work. At the Folger Shakespeare Library, among the uncatalogued manuscripts, is a letter in fractured English from Peter D'Egville, an important member of a large family of French dancers. He wrote on 7 May 1776 to the Drury Lane proprietor Willoughby Lacy:

> Mr Dagville Compliment to Mr Lacy and wille be Glad to know if it is anny Room in your house next Saison for me as a ballet master principal Dancer and to act in the pantomine a principall charactere if is Wanted— at the Sallery of 160 pounds for the Saison an a benefitte in aprile 20 as j huse to have before. Mr Lacy will oblige mr Dagville of an ansWhere j am Sir your most obedient Servante.

The salary D'Egville requested was not unreasonable. The Drury Lane accounts at the Folger show the top dancers receiving about £400 for the 1776–77 season and the leading actors about £100 more. D'Egville had been dancing leading parts in London since 1768. But Drury Lane did not need him, and in 1776–77 he evidently had no regular London engagement.

Benefits were an important part of a performer's income, though they sometimes failed. Cape Everard in his *Memoirs of an Unfortunate Son of Thespis* told a funny-sad story about the summer benefits at Bristol of the hardworking dancer Vascours. In 1774 Vascours's benefit lost him money, but when he returned to London after the summer of 1775 he was happy: "Oh, grand!—capital benefice!—L'Eté passé, last somere, I lose at Bristol ten pounds by my benefit, and now dis time, I only lose two pounds six!"[2]

Many dancers augmented their income by teaching and composing dances. One of the famous masters of the Restoration period was Josias Priest. He began his career dancing at the Lincoln's Inn Fields Theatre in the 1660s, then worked in the 1670s as a dancing master. He choreographed with Luke Channel the dances for the operatic *Macbeth* at the Dorset Garden Theatre in 1673, and he provided the dances for the last great court masque, *Calisto*, in 1675. He kept a boarding school for gentlewomen in Leicester Fields and then in Chelsea, where in 1689 Purcell's *Dido and Aeneas*, an opera for which Priest composed seventeen dances, was presented.

Other dancers survived through fortunate (or clever) connections with the nobility. One was Monsieur St. André, who was active in London in the 1680s. The author of *A Comparison Between the Two Stages* in 1702 noted his lack of success:

> . . . The late Duke of Monmouth was a good judge of dancing, and a good Dancer himself; when he returned from France, he brought with him St. *Andre,* then the best Master in France: The *Duke* presented him to the Stage, the Stage to gratifie the *Duke* admitted him, and the *Duke* himself thought he wou'd prove a mighty advantage to 'em, tho' he had no body else of his Opinion: A Day was publish'd in the Bills for him to dance, but not one more, besides the *Duke* and his Friends came to see him; the reason was, the Plays were then so good, and *Hart* and *Mohun*

acted 'em so well, that the Audience wou'd not be interrupted for so short a time tho' 'twas to see the best Master in *Europe*. [Pp. 48–49]

Monsieur Isaac was also attached to the court, creating dances for Queen Anne's birthdays and teaching members of the court circle. Isaac also composed dances for the public theatres with considerable success in the early eighteenth century, when dance had grown in public favor. Anne Jacqueline Coulon was said by Peter Pindar (John Wolcot) in "Ode upon Ode" (in his *Works,* 1794) to have had a useful liaison with Lord Brudenwell:

> So much by dancing is his Lordship won,
> Behind the Op'ra scenes he constant goes,
> To kiss the little finger of COULON,
> To mark her knees, and many-twinkling toes.
>
> [1:386]

A dancer who had other talents was in a better position to succeed. Giovanni Andrea Battista Gallini was intimately involved with the destiny of the King's Theatre in the last half of the eighteenth century; and though he labored chiefly as an opera impresario, he was a dancer, dancing master, and choreographer. Arthur Murphy wrote in the *London Chronicle* of 18–21 November 1758 that

> Signor Galini is universally allowed to be one of the finest dancers in Europe; but at the King's Theatre, where he at present performs, he not only gives us the strongest proofs of his executive powers, but also of his skill in designing, by having composed three of the prettiest ballets I ever saw; and for plot, movement, humour, and, if I may make use of the expression, gesticulated wit, they are equal I believe, to any of those which Lewis the Fourteenth himself was so fond of.

Gallini also found time to teach private students and write *A Treatise on the Art of Dancing* (1762). Many dancers were expected to handle other chores—or, conversely, many actors and singers were expected to dance. Cape Everard described one of his typical days in the 1770s at Drury Lane:

> The porter, or call-man, used to come to my lodging of a morning, and, knocking at my door, this little dialogue use to pass:—"Mr. Everard. . . . At ten o'clock, if you please, to As You Like It. . . . At eleven in the Green Room, to the reading of the New Play. . . . At twelve, to Much ado about Nothing, Mr. Garrick will be there. . . . At one in the practicing room below, Mr. Grimaldi's dances in the Tempest. . . . At two, on the stage, Mr. Slingsby's dance, the Savage Hunters. . . . At half-past two, Signior Dagueville's Double Festival. . . . At three o'clock, Mr. Atkins's Sailor Revels. . . . At half-past three, Signior Galli's practice." . . . from ten till four in the afternoon, and having perhaps to dress and begin the play, from five to nearly twelve.[3]

Inevitably, some dancers who succeeded let fame go to their heads. Monsieur Dangeville, according to the *Daily Courant* of 2 May 1720, failed to appear on 29 April: "he refused to Dance, being puft up by the Applause he had the good Fortune to meet with; fancying he hath a Right to do so whenever he pleases." Anne and Janneton Auretti, two young French dancers at Drury Lane in midcentury, so exasperated the actor-manager David Garrick that in a letter to his brother George on 28 August 1752 he said, "Miss Auretti, Mon^sr Pitro. Mad^me Janeton, ye Father, Mother & all their Generation may kiss my A——se; I am so sick of their no Meaning Messages & Compliments, that every time I see her Name in a Letter, my Stomach falls a heaving." But such complaints were not very common, and it would appear that most dancers behaved themselves. They survived—and some prospered—by dint of long hours and hard work.

The Serious Dancers

The best of the serious dancers and choreographers dazzled their audiences, but one is hard put today to find vivid critical descriptions of their work. Dance, like music, does not make use of words on a printed page and thus is not easily described by them. The author of a review in the *Morning Chronicle* tried to tell us what happened at the King's Theatre on 2 June 1796:

> The most bewitching dance ever witnessed, for novelty of idea, charm of fancy, and delicacy of passion was performed last night. Not content with the common praise, the audience called forward the author, Didelot, and paid him the tribute due to original, and inventive talents. The ballet was entitled L'AMOUR VANGÉ. The invention, which was perfectly new, was that of bands of Cupids floating in air—suspended on their own wings, without the intervention of any grosser medium.

One is left with only a vague understanding of what the audience actually saw. Sometimes reporters simply wrote gobbledegook. A critic in the *Public Advertiser* of 18 March 1783 said of Charles Lepicq and Madame Rossi in a dance made from *Macbeth:* "The whole of the material questions of the scene were agitated with all the disadvantages of contrast with comparative inefficience."

Yet some helpful descriptions of dancers have come down to us. Samuel Phillips captured Mrs. Du Ruel's dancing in verse in the *Diverting Post* on 17 March 1705:

> Gods, how she steps! see how the blushing Fair,
> With nimble Feet, divides the yielding Air,
> As tho' she'd throw the common Method by,
> And teach us not to Walk, but how to Fly!

Look with what Art the Nymph displays her Charms;
Observe the curling Motions of her Arms!
See in what Folds her flowing Garments stream;
At once they cool and kindle up a Flame
In e'ery Breast, but her's!—she's still the same.

We also have fairly vivid descriptions of Marie Sallé. Her *Pygmalion*, which she choreographed and danced at Covent Garden on 14 January 1734, was remarkably innovative. The London correspondent to the *Mercure de France* wrote on 15 or 16 March:

> You can understand what all the passages of this action become, executed and danced with the fine and delicate grace of Mdlle. Sallé. She ventures to appear without basket [*panier*, presumably] with a dress, in her natural hair, and with no ornament on her head. She wore nothing in addition to her bodice and under petticoat but a simple robe of muslin, arranged in drapery after the model of a Greek statue. You cannot doubt, sir of the success this ingenious ballet, so well executed, obtained.

The success was largely due to Sallé's exquisite dancing (for her innovations in dress brought criticism from some), as a *Mercure* writer in April made clear:

> [T]he statue, little by little, becomes conscious, showing wonder at her changed existence and all around her. Amazed and entranced, Pigmalion takes her hand, leading her down from the pedestal. Step by step she feels her way, gradually assuming the most graceful poses a sculptor could possibly desire, with steps ranging from the simplest to the most complex. . . .[4]

Jean Georges Noverre, who benefited much from Sallé's development of the *ballet d'action*, wrote in his *Lettres sur la Danse:*

> She was possessed of neither the brilliancy nor the technique common to dancing nowadays, but she replaced that showiness by simple and touching graces; free from affectation, her features were refined, expressive, and intelligent. Her voluptuous dancing displayed both delicacy and lightness; she did not stir the heart by leaps and bounds.[5]

Charles Lepicq was overshadowed in the last quarter of the eighteenth century by Noverre and the older and younger Vestris, yet he was highly praised by critics. Baron Grimm saw Lepicq in *Caprices of Galathee* in September 1776 and wrote to Frederick of Prussia that Lepicq

> as the shepherd, left nothing to be desired. A charming face, the slenderest of waists, the easiest and lightest of movements, the purest and most vivacious and yet most natural style, such are the qualities which mark the talents of this new mime. . . . [H]e dances like the King of the Sylphs. If he has not all the nobility, all the expression of Vestris, all the strength

and balance of Gardel, he has perhaps in his execution something softer and yet more Brilliant. His grace and lightness triumph above all in demi-caractere dancing and that is the *genre* of the new ballet.[6]

We must thank Grimm, too, for a vivid description of Marie Guimard. He saw her in *La Chercheuse d'esprit* in the late 1770s:

> All her *pas,* all her movements, were distinguished by their softness and harmony, a sure and picturesque combination. Her simplicity is artless without being foolish. . . . How animated she becomes under the soft rays of feeling! She resembles a rose-bud which is seen to open, escape from the fettering tendrils, tremble, and flower. We have seen nothing so delightful and so perfect in this style of mime.[7]

Gennaro Magri in his *Trattato teorico-prattico di ballo* in 1779 was detailed in his description of the elder Vestris, Gaëtan; Vestris "during the same turn changes foot two or three times, which really deserves eternal admiration; but the most surprising thing is that while he is turning at the highest possible speed he stops in a-plomb, with such perfection that he remains perfectly immobile in that balancing position."[8] The vain Vestris had adoring patrons who would shush anyone in the audience who chanced to applaud him in middance, "lest the graceful movements *du dieu de la dance,*" as Dr. Burney noted, "or the attention of his votaries, should be disturbed by audible approbation."[9]

Just as popular and perhaps an even better dancer was Auguste Vestris. A letter, now among the Dixon Extracts at the Folger (MS. Ma52), was lavish in his praise:

> It is indeed impossible not to be transported at the ease, the ability & harmony of all his motions: they are so exquisite, that he scarcely appears a mortal but rather a sylph, formed of etherial mould, and destined to skim aloft in higher regions. . . .
> Vestris' figure is slender & elegant, his countenance is not handsome, but possesses a je ne sçai quoi extremely interesting and fascinating. The simplicity & modesty of his manners, form a striking contrast with the self conceited & supercilious manners of his father, who during the time of Voltaire's last stay at Paris, said, in a public company, "There are only three great men, now existing in the world, Vestris, Voltaire, & the King of Prussia." [3:69–71]

Auguste, unlike Gaëtan, did not mind the noisy response of an audience. Horace Walpole wrote to the Countess of Upper Ossory on 17 December 1780 after seeing Vestris at the opera house:

> The theatre was brimful in expectation of Vestris. At the end of the second act [of the opera *Ricimero*] he appeared; but with so much grace, agility, and strength, that the whole audience fell into convulsions of applause; the men thundered; the ladies, forgetting their delicacy and

weakness, clapped with such vehemence, that seventeen broke their arms, sixty-nine sprained their wrists, and three cried bravo! bravissimo! so rashly, that they have not been able to utter so much as *no* since, any more than both Houses of Parliament.[10]

The Popular Dancers

The popular entertainers of the Restoration and eighteenth century, although not so important to history as the serious Children of Terpsichore, are amusing to read about, and descriptions of their work are often quite detailed. These humbler but no less skilled performers appeared at the late summer fairs, in taverns, and on street corners, but many were often found providing entr'acte entertainment at the theatres. Their turns were usually comic or exotic or, in the case of the acrobatic rope dancers, displays of sheer skill. Their aim was merely to entertain, and they made little pretense to art. But they had a wider appeal than the serious dancers.

At the Restoration, dance did not hold nearly so strong an attraction for audiences as it did in later years. There were occasional dances within plays, and such performers as Nell Gwyn and Mary Davis sometimes offered dances at the end of a performance. But in the beginning the intent was less to entertain through dance than to titillate audiences by showing off an actress' legs. Samuel Pepys went to see *The English Princess* on 7 March 1667 and told his diary that

> little Mis Davis did dance a jig after the end of the play, and there telling the next day's play, so that it come in by force only to please the company to see her dance in boy's clothes; and, the truth is, there is no comparison between Nell's dancing the other day at the King's house [the Bridges Street Theatre] in boy's clothes and this, this being infinitely beyond the other.

Some accounts of popular entertainments may contain no small amount of fiction, so that one must be wary. Ned Ward in *The London Spy* at the end of the seventeenth century recorded his impressions of a visit to the Barnes-Appleby booth at Bartholomew Fair. He was quite taken with

> the German maid, as they style her in their bill, who does wonderful pretty things upon the rope, and has fine proportion to her limbs and much modesty in her countenance. She as much out-danced the rest as a greyhound will outrun a hedgehog, having something of a method in her steps, and air in her carriage, moving with an observancy of time and play with her feet, as if assisted with the wings of Mercury.
> . . . Then up steps the negress to the top of the booth, and began to play at swing-swang with a rope, as if the devil were in her, hanging sometimes by a hand, sometimes by a leg, and sometimes by her toes, so

that I found, let her do what she would, Providence or Destiny would by no means suffer the rope to part with her.[11]

Newspapers provided useful but possibly exaggerated advertisements. The *Post Man* issue of 5–8 September 1696 carried a puff about the Barnes-Appleby show, saying that Barnes would dance on the rope "with a Child standing on his shoulders, and with 2 children on his Feet, in Jackboots with Spurs, and [he] cuts Capers a yard and a half high, and dances a Jig on the Rope with that variety of steps, that few, or no Dancing Masters can do the like on the ground. . . ." Appleby, according to the same bill, would "fling himself over 16 mens heads, through 12 hoops, over 14 Halbards, over a Man on Horseback, and a Boy standing upright on his Shoulders. . . ." An unusual performance, according to a bill quoted in Henry Morley's *Memoirs of Bartholomew Fair,* was presented in July 1700, when "The Black Prince" and his "*Little Woman,* NOT 3 foot high, and 30 years of Age, straight and proportionable as any woman in the Land, which is commonly called the Fairy Queen, she gives a general satisfaction to all that sees her, by Diverting them with Dancing, being big with child."[12] Another popular import around the turn of the century was Sieur Allard, who appeared at Drury Lane to great applause. The author of *A Comparison Between the Two Stages* described Allard's antics:

Ay, the *Sieur* with a pox to him—and the two *Monsieurs* his Sons—Rogues that show at *Paris* for a Groat a piece, and here they were an entertainment for the Court and his late Majesty. . . . What a rout here was with a Night piece of *Harlequin* and *Scaramouch?* With the Guittar and the Bladder! What jumping over Tables and Joint-Stools! What ridiculous Postures and Grimaces! and what an exquisite Trick 'twas to straddle before the Audience, making a thousand damn'd *French* Faces, and seeming in labour with a monstrous Birth, at last my counterfeit Male Lady is delivered of her two Puppies *Harlequin* and *Scaramouch.* [P. 47]

Peg Fryer, a Restoration performer, returned to the stage at the Lincoln's Inn Fields playhouse on 11 January 1720 at the age of eighty-five to appear as Widow Rich in *The Half-Pay Officers* and dance a "Bashful Maid and Irish Trot." Whincop described her performance in his *English Dramatic Poets:*

Her character in the Farce was that of a very old woman; she went through it very well, but when, the Farce being done, she was brought upon the stage again to dance a jig, which had been promised in the bills, she came tottering in, as if ready to fall and made two or three pretended offers to go out again, but all on a sudden, the music striking up the Irish Trot, she danced and footed it away as nimbly as any wench of 25 could have done.[13]

About 29 December 1721, we learn from a clipping in the Burney Collection at the British Library, John Riner performed "his new and diverting Entertainments in Metamorphosis, in changing his Body into divers Shapes. First, a Pigmy Dance, he appearing to be two Foot and a half high . . . and a pleasant Entertainment of an Italian Scaramouch, with two Heads and four Legs." Another odd performer was Grimaldo Francolino, who appeared at the King's Theatre on 2 March 1727 in "a Dance call'd the King of Morocco's Diversions." The bill (transcribed in *The London Stage*) boasted of "surprizing Activity and Strength in a Dance on his Knees with a wonderful heavy Machine upon his Head, never yet attempted by any one before." The advertisement for 6 April 1727 stated that "Signor Grimaldo Francolino of Malta, Operator for the Teeth, being on his Departure, will perform for this Time only some of his wonderful Dances; particularly one within a Dark Lanthorn." Mr. Brunn, a puppeteer by trade, at the Great Room in Panton Street in March 1778 did a Spanish castanet dance blindfolded through a pattern of eggs laid on the floor with no mishap.[14] And what are we to make of the statement in the Bristol papers on 2 March 1782 about Mrs. Richards (previously Signora Mariana of Sadler's Wells in London)? She was to "perform on the Tight Rope without touching it with her Feet," a trick "never yet attempted by any but herself."

Audiences found plenty of variety. At the Royal Circus in 1793, according to the bills, Master Ackerill gave "Chironomical Performances" on the high wire and played "a Tune on the violin, the wire in full swing, and he standing on his head." At Sadler's Wells in 1795 two American Indian chiefs gave an exhibition of war dances.[15] And at a benefit for Mr. and Mrs. Adams on 24 September 1800 at the Royal Circus their daughter danced "a Grand MINUET and GAVOTTE (in Character)," Mr. Adams entertained patrons with bird imitations, and Miss Adams danced a "favourite Strathspey and Reel" in a pantomimic ballet.

Some entertainers were animals. At the Huntington Library is a bill for Astley's Amphitheatre, hand-dated 28 May 1785, claiming that "GENERAL JACKOO, the celebrated Monkey from Paris will, for the first time this season, change the whole of his dress in a surprising manner, and perform his war manoeuvres, dance on the Tight Rope with fetters on his feet, &c." Trained dogs were Signor Scaglioni's specialty. They appeared at Sadler's Wells in London, bringing £7,000 profit in May 1784.[16]

Spectators were sometimes treated to witting or unwitting risqué performances. An incident involving the dancer Miss Poitier must surely have been intentional. The *Theatrical Review* on 1 January 1763 described her scandalous behavior at Covent Garden Theatre the previous 30 December:

> Would any person suppose she could have the confidence to appear with her bosom so scandalously bare, that to use the expression of a public writer, who took some moderate notice of the circumstance, the breast hung flabbing over a pair of stays cut remarkably low, like a couple of empty bladders in an oil-shop. One thing the author of that letter has

omitted, which, if possible, is still more gross; and that is, in the course of Miss Poitier's hornpipe, one of her shoes happening to slipt down at the heel, she lifted up her leg, and danced upon the other till she had drawn it up. This had she worn drawers, would have been the more excusable; but unhappily . . . she was not provided with so much as a fig-leaf. The Court turned instantly from the stage—The Pit was astonished!

A similar, but unwitting, incident involving Monsieur La Croix at Penzance, probably in the 1750s, was recorded by Michael Kelly in his *Reminiscences:*

> He made his appearance in a fine pas seul; but, unluckily, in one of his most graceful pirouettes, a very important part of his drapery, either from its age or slightness, or from the wonderful exertion of its wearer, bcame suddenly rent in a most unmendable manner. Shouts of laughter and applause followed, which Monsieur La Croix imagined were given for his jumping; nor was the supposition at all unjustifiable, for the higher he jumped, the more he was applauded. At last some one behind the scenes called him off the stage; and he was so shocked at the mishap which had befallen him, that he could never be induced to appear again.[17]

Hazards of the Trade

The risk of embarrassment was nothing compared with the risk to life and limb, for theatres can be dangerous places, both behind and in front of the curtain line. As the audience's thirst for stage spectacle grew, the chances for accidents multiplied. At Covent Garden Theatre on 1 October 1736, according to the *Daily Post and General Advertiser,*

> in the Entertainment of Dr. Faustus [the pantomime *The Necromancer*] . . .when the Machine wherein Harlequin, the Miller's Wife, the Miller and his Man, was got up to the full Extent of its flying, one of the Wires which held up the hind part of the Car broke first, and then the other broke, and the Machine, and all the People in it fell down upon the Stage; by which unhappy Accident the young Woman who personated the Miller's Wife had her Thigh broke, and her Kneepan shatter'd, and was otherways very much bruised, the Harlequin had his Head bruised, and his Wrist strained; the Miller broke his Arm; and the Miller's Man had his Scull so fractured that his Life is despaired of.

The four who were in the accident were "Servants belonging to the Theatre, and only Representatives in the different Characters of [the dancers] Mr Lun, Mr Nivelon, Mr Salway, and Mrs Moreau," according to the *Daily Advertiser* of 4 October.

"Lady Isabella" was a posture maker and rope dancer who, according to W. R. Chetwood in his *General History of the Stage* (1749), risked performing in 1745 while pregnant:

The last, fatal, Time of her Performance, she was eight Months gone with Child; but the covetous Husband loved Money so well (as it is reported), that he would not allow her the necessary Repose required in her Condition; so that, in one of her Dances on a slack Rope, she fell on the Stage, where the Mother and Infant, newly born with the Force of the Fall, expired in a Moment, fatal Catastrophe! in the Twenty-first Year of her Age. This was the running Account of the poor Lady Isabella, after her Death, whose End was much lamented: For, notwithstanding her disreputable Employment, she was esteemed as a Woman of strict Virtue. [pp. 62–63n]

A clipping in the Daly Collection at the Huntington, hand-dated 1789 but probably belonging to 1788, details an accident that befell Auguste Vestris:

Vestris, the dancer, has had a very narrow escape for his life: this charming dancer, on Sunday [*sic*], the 11th instant, while performing [rehearsing?] at the opera, experienced a fatal disaster; on his alighting after a surprizing vault, one of the traps gave way, and he fell seventeen feet and a half: fortunately a board, which accidentally lay across the machinery, stopped the further progress of the trap, or the fall would have been at least fifty [*sic*] feet. We are happy to add, he has received no other hurt than what may [be] supposed from the shock.

Another hazard of the trade was violent audience reaction at a performance, and theatrical riots in London as often as not involved dancers. Many dancers who appeared in London were French; if they weren't, blockheaded Englishmen often took them to be French anyway. Since Franco-English relations were sometimes strained, dancers and managers in Continental troupes often found themselves in a pickle not of their own making. Typical was the engagement of Francisque Moylin and his French performers, who appeared in London in October 1738. The company was allowed to perform at the Haymarket Theatre, which had been closed to English troupes by the Licensing Act of 1737. Benjamin Victor described the opening night on 9 October in the first volume of his *History of the Theatres* (1761). When the curtain rose, two files of guards, with bayonets fixed, protected the players. The audience protested, and the guards were removed. Then catcalls prevented the actors from being heard, so they retired and let the dancers take over: "[T]hey opened with a grand dance of twelve Men and twelve Women; but even that was prepared for; and they were directly saluted with a Bushel or two of Peas, which made their Capering very unsafe" (pp. 57–58). The players again attempted to perform, but they were shouted down, and the show did not go on. No foreign troupes visited London again until 1745.

Audiences sometimes rioted over the behavior of favorite performers. The *Daily Advertiser* on 25 January 1740 carried a description of one such disaster:

On Wednesday night last a Disturbance happen'd at Drury-Lane Play-house, occasion'd by one of the principal Dancers [Mlle. Chateauneuf] not being there to dance at the end of the Entertainment, and after most of the People in the Pit and Galleries were gone, several Gentlemen in the Boxes pull'd up the Seats and Flooring of the same, tore down the Hangings, broke down the Partitions, all the Glasses [mirrors] and Sconces, the King's Arms over the middle front Box was pull'd down and broke to Pieces; they also destroy'd the Harpsichord, Bass Viol, and other Instruments of the Orchestra; the Curtain they cut to pieces with their Swords. . . .

The worst riot affecting dancers was occasioned by the importation by David Garrick of the eminent Jean Georges Noverre's *Chinese Festival* in the fall of 1755. With war between France and England threatening, Garrick prudently announced in the *Public Advertiser* of 8 November 1755 (the day of the first performance at Drury Lane) that few of the members of the troupe were French:

. . . The insinuation that at this Time, an extraordinary number of French Dancers are engaged, is groundless, there being at Drury Lane at present as few of that Nation, as any other Theatre now has, or perhaps ever had. Mr. Noverre and his Brothers are Swiss, of a Protestant family in the Canton of Berne, his Wife and her Sisters Germans: there are above sixty performers concerned in the Entertainment; more than forty of which are English, assisted only by a few French, (five Men and four Women) to complete the Ballet as usual.

That did not stop the English audiences from ruining the opening performance of Noverre's work. An anonymous correspondent in the *Journal Etranger* on 25 November gave a detailed description of the elegance of the scenery and costumes, the great size of the cast (ninety people were involved in one procession), and the presence of the king and his court. As soon as the ballet began,

the applause started immediately and was continued until the end but was however broken by three or four piercing calls and as many voices from the gallery echoing the cry, 'No French Dancers!' The Nobility and all honest folk shouted to throw them into the Pit and applauded the louder to drown the sound of the catcalls. The King left, well pleased with the Ballet and very ill pleased with the lack of respect of his people.

At the second performance the disturbance was much worse:

All the My Lords leaped into the Pit, some with staves, others with sword in hand, and descended upon a group of demonstrators whom they covered with blows. The English Ladies, far from being affrighted by the horrible scuffle, gave a hand to the gallants that they might leap into the Pit and pointed out to them the people to be knocked out. . . . The outraged Nobility struck right and left regardless, breaking arms and heads, and blood was running everywhere; the ballet ceased until finally the Nobility turned out the mutilated rioters.

And so the disturbances continued through the eighteenth of November, after which Garrick, according to the prompter Richard Cross (in his diary, now at the Folger), "was oblig'd to give up the Dancers." It was true, as Dr. Johnson said in the prologue that opened the 1747–48 season at Drury Lane, that those "who live to please, must please to live."[18]

Vain, humble, extravagant, exquisite, bawdy, decorous, serious, silly, diligent, lazy, vigorous, graceful, daring—the Children of Terpsichore in the Restoration and eighteenth century were all of these things and more. One is struck by the growing vitality and variety of dances and dancers, the increasing importance of dance—from serious *ballets d'action* to circus acrobatics—in the world of the theatre, the fanatic devotion of balletomanes to their favorites, the dazzling skill of the best performers. Theatrical dancing became an integral part of the whole world of entertainment, contributing to it much of the color and excitement—and the claptrap—that we associate with the theatre of the time.

Notes

1. The introductions to the five parts of *The London Stage* contain much useful information on dance and dancers in London from 1660 to 1800, and I especially commend to the reader those by Emmett L. Avery and George Winchester Stone. I have tried here to avoid duplicating what they set forth.

2. Cape Everard, *Memoirs of an Unfortunate Son of Thespis* (Edinburgh: James Ballantyne, 1818), pp. 41–42.

3. Everard, p. 40.

4. Quoted in Stanley W. E. Fince, "Marie Sallé, 1707–56," *Theatre Notebook* 12 (1958): 12–13.

5. Quoted in Cyril Beaumont, *Three French Dancers* (London: C. W. Beaumont, 1934), p. 25.

6. Quoted in Deryck Lynham, *The Chevalier Noverre* (London: Sylvan Press, 1950), pp. 89–90.

7. Beaumont, p. 28.

8. Quoted in Marian Hannah Winter, *The Pre-Romantic Ballet* (London: Pitman, 1974), p. 151.

9. *A General History of Music*, ed. Frank Mercer (London: G. T. Foulis, 1935), 2:893.

10. *The Letters of Horace Walpole*, ed. Mrs. Paget Toynbee (Oxford: Clarendon Press, 1904), 11:340–41.

11. *The London Spy*, ed. Arthur Hayward (London: Cassell, 1927), p. 181.

12. Henry Morley, *Memoirs of Bartholomew Fair* (London: Chatto and Windus, 1880), p. 252.

13. Quoted in Montague Summers, *The Playhouse of Pepys* (London: Kegan Paul, Trench, Trubner, 1935), p. 17.

14. William J. Lawrence scrapbook, MS. 4296, at the National Library of Ireland in Dublin.

15. Dennis Arundell, *The Story of Sadler's Wells* (London: H. Hamilton, 1965), p. 55.

16. Arundell, p. 37.

17. Michael Kelly, *Reminiscences*, ed. Roger Fiske (London: Oxford University Press, 1975), p. 234.

18. Samuel Johnson, *Poems*, ed. E. L. McAdam, Jr., with George Milne, (New Haven: Yale University Press, 1964), p. 89.

Theatre and the Visual Arts

8

Stage Drama as a Source for Pictorial and Plastic Arts

ROBERT HALSBAND

Although the eighteenth century in England cannot boast of great drama, it is indisputably the period when English visual arts flowered for the first time. From Hogarth to Gainsborough, Reynolds, and Romney (with Constable about to emerge), English artists, as never before, rivaled those on the Continent. Some of the vitality, strength, and variety in this efflorescence of the visual arts came from the stage and drama. In my rapid survey I am dividing the topic into five branches: book illustration, painting, portraiture, caricature, and ceramics. These categories may occasionally overlap—book illustration and caricature, for example, or painting and portraiture—but they can be conveniently separated.

Book Illustration

For book illustration of eighteenth-century drama Shakespeare is the logical dramatist to start with. Just as his plays were more frequently staged than any other playwright's—once out of every six performances[1]—so they were the most frequently reprinted and illustrated. In that sense he was an eighteenth-century dramatist by adoption.

In the previous century, as we all know, four editions of his collected plays were published, all in folio and none illustrated. The first popular edition came in 1709, Jacob Tonson's octavo in six volumes, the text edited (for the first time) by Nicholas Rowe, and each play illustrated with an engraved plate. None of the plates is signed; apparently they were drawn by a French artist, François Boitard, and engraved by an Englishman, Elisha Walker. For *The Tempest* the artist chose the opening storm scene,

Plate 1. Boitard, *frontispiece for* The Tempest *by Shakespeare.*

Plate 2. Du Guernier, *frontispiece for* Macbeth *by Shakespeare.*

based on the stage presentation of the current Dryden-Davenant version (plate 1). It has a gawky clumsiness, almost medieval in feeling. His plate for *Macbeth* is more realistic: the three witches address a foppish Macbeth dressed as though attending the court of Queen Anne. Charles Lamb's objection to Shakespeare illustrations is well known; yet he made an exception to this edition because (in his words) the plates, "being so execrably bad, serve as maps or modest remembrances to the text; . . . without pretending to any supposable emulation with it."[2]

Lamb's perverse compliment applied as well to Tonson's next edition, a duodecimo, five years later. For this the publisher engaged another French artist, Louis Du Guernier, to revise or replace the 1709 plates. In *The Tempest* Du Guernier replaced the violent opening scene with a peaceful one from act 5, where Prospero "discovers Ferdinand and Miranda playing at chess." Perhaps reflecting the rise of sentimentalism, the grotesque spectacle of the tempest has been replaced by a sentimentalized tableau. But for the *Macbeth* plate Du Guernier simply revised Boitard's design, intensifying its spooky intention by scattering some skeleton remains, and he dressed Macbeth in nondescript classical costume (plate 2).

If these editions of 1709 and 1714 did not advance the art of book illustration, they nevertheless enabled the reading public to visualize the plays as acted on the stage or as embodied in the artist's imagination. Stage historians have scrutinized these illustrations, and those in later editions as well, to determine their relation (if any) to stage design, scenery, costumes, and acting; but as engraved designs they are inferior to the illustrations being published on the other side of the Channel. More than any other English publisher at this time, Tonson, keenly aware of book illustrations and publications in Paris, tried to emulate Continental practices in his own country; but there were very few English artists whom he could have hired.

In 1725 Tonson published Pope's quarto edition of Shakespeare; though handsomely printed, it had no illustrations, nor did the octavo edition that followed. But the fourth edition, in duodecimo, reprinted the 1714 plates revised by still another French artist. This practice of adding illustrations to later editions of a publication, presumably to stimulate new sales, was not uncommon. In similar fashion, not the first but the second edition of Theobald's text added plates by Gravelot, an accomplished French artist. In all these plates the atmosphere is inescapably French rococo. In the illustration for *The Tempest*, Miranda offers to help Ferdinand with his task of piling the logs while Prospero looks on. For *Macbeth* the illustrator was assigned the banquet scene: the ghost of Banquo, not looking very ghostly, confronts Macbeth in a setting closer to Versailles than to a castle in Scotland.

Only a few years later, in 1744, Sir Thomas Hanmer hired Francis Hayman to supply the plates for a stately quarto edition printed at the University Press in Oxford. Hayman, an Englishman, designed most of the plates,

Plate 3. Hayman, frontispiece for The Tempest *by Shakespeare.*

which were engraved by Gravelot. For *The Tempest*Hanmer assigned the
scene near the end of the first act, when Ferdinand approaching hears
Ariel's song (plate 3). It is a carefully constructed composition, the figures
beautifully modeled and balanced against each other. If Hayman in this
plate for *The Tempest* illustrated the printed text, in his plate for *Macbeth* he
seems to have copied the stage setting for Lady Macbeth's sleepwalking
scene. It has a simplicity and directness that conforms to the spirit of the
dramatic situation. In his maturity Hayman designed theatre scenery and
decorations as well as theatrical conversation pieces. In this early work he
raised the level of Shakespearean illustration from hackwork to art. He had
the advantage of designing the plates not for an ordinary publisher, whose
fees would have been low, but for a wealthy patron-editor.

The next illustrated edition of Shakespeare was the inexpensive
duodecimo published by John Bell in 1773 and republished in the 1780s, in
twenty handy volumes of elegant design. The artists Bell chose to illustrate
the plays were not the most eminent, in fact not more than competent
craftsmen. The one who designed the plate for *Macbeth,* Edward Edwards,

adapted the 1714 illustration without improving it much. He chose the second apparition, "a bloody child," seen by Macbeth in the act 4 witch scene, but the figure looks more like a misplaced Cupid than a horrifying apparition. When Bell reprinted the edition ten years later, his artists presented more sentimental versions—as in the illustration for *The Tempest* by John Sherwin. Here the height of absurdity is reached in the artist's topping the picture with the Prince of Wales's three feathers—his boast that he had been appointed Engraver to His Royal Highness!

The next set of Shakespeare illustrations was that of Alderman Boydell. In his three-pronged enterprise, begun in 1786, he commissioned large paintings from all the leading artists of the time; and after the canvases were exhibited in his Shakespeare Gallery on Pall Mall, they were engraved to be sold as a collection of prints, and finally (along with newly commissioned designs) engraved in smaller format as illustrations for the 1802 edition of the plays.

This method of producing book illustrations differed radically from previous practice. Designs for book illustration had been drawn only for that purpose; hence were usually the same small size as the plate, and in black and white with gray wash to make easier the engraver's work of transferring the design to the copper plate. But following the establishment of the Royal Academy in 1768 with its annual exhibition, artists could paint large, brilliantly colored canvases to be exhibited; and after these were copied by the engraver (in greatly reduced size, of course), the original picture could be sold. Such work was more prestigious and more profitable. It was an inducement for ambitious, successful artists to turn their attention to literary illustration, particularly of Shakespeare, because it did not confine them to the limited and poorly paid work for book publishers.

What kind of illustrations were made for non-Shakespearean drama? Early in the century French artists and engravers were used, but with the rise of a native school they were replaced by English ones. It is curious that Tonson provided no plates for Congreve's *Collected Works* in 1710, though for a sumptuous edition of Racine in 1723 he used an able French artist (Chéron), resident in London. For his edition of Congreve's works in 1753, however, he engaged Hayman to design a set of elegant plates, and these were also used by Baskerville, the century's finest English printer, for his 1761 edition of Congreve. It was John Bell, though, who, as in his Shakespeare edition, lavishly added plates to his collection of British Theatre—100 plays in twenty-one volumes. Sometimes scenes from plays, the illustrations are more often portraits of leading actors and actresses in their roles. For Vanbrugh's *The Relapse* James Roberts drew a portrait of Mrs. Yates as Berinthia, and for Rowe's *Tamerlane* a double portrait of Mr. and Mrs. Barry as Bajazet and Selima.

I have spoken so far of collections of plays, Shakespeare's and others'.

Plate 4. Hogarth, frontispiece for The Tragedy of Tragedies *by Fielding.*

Single contemporary plays, whose texts were cheaply printed as small pamphlets, were often illustrated. Addison's *Cato* is one example. Produced in 1713, it was spectacularly successful, but not until the seventh edition, that same year, did Tonson add the frontispiece by Du Guernier (whom he used the next year for the Rowe Shakespeare).

A different kind of frontispiece introduced Fielding's burlesque *The Tragedy of Tragedies, or the Life and Death of Tom Thumb the Great* in 1731. Designed by Hogarth, it can also be classified as caricature—as I said, the categories sometimes overlap—because it has been suggested that the shorter woman, Princess Huncamunca in the play, portrays George the Second's eldest daughter, a notably well-fed young woman (plate 4).

About thirty years later Hogarth again drew a frontispiece—this time for his friend Garrick's *The Farmer's Return from London*. In his preface to this "interlude," Garrick wrote that he "would not have printed it, had not his Friend, Mr. *Hogarth*, flattered him most agreeably, by thinking *The Farmer and his Family* not unworthy of a Sketch of his Pencil." Here, then, the play was printed for the sake of the frontispiece. When Garrick published *A Christmas Tale* in 1774, its title page advertised: "Embellished with an Etching, by Mr. *Loutherbourg*," as a compliment no doubt to Loutherbourg, who had designed the scenery.

Not until the last decade of the century did English illustrators of books, including drama, match those on the Continent. But the earlier ones at least drew on the stage and the drama to enlarge the scope of visual invention and imagination not only for themselves but also for an increasing number of readers.

Painting

When we turn to painting we find that the drama had a decisive effect on one of the richest eighteenth-century genres, the "conversation piece"—a label first used in a *Spectator* paper. It is a painting, small-scaled in size and informal in mood, that shows two or more persons in a state of dramatic or psychological relation to each other. Hogarth, who painted many conversation pieces early in his career, wrote: "I wished to compose pictures on canvas, similar to representations on the stage. . . . I have endeavoured to treat my subjects as a dramatic writer: my picture is my stage, and men and women my players, who by means of certain actions and gestures, are to exhibit *a dumb show*."[3]

In fact, Hogarth's first oil painting is simultaneously a stage scene and a conversation piece, based on *The Beggar's Opera*, the ballad-opera that conquered London in 1728. His preliminary study in chalk outlines the scene in act 3 where Macheath, in chains and condemned to die, stands between his two wives, whose fathers spurn their pleas for mercy. The five actors are firmly set in their symmetrical triangle design, centered on Macheath, a bold and virile figure. The audience surrounding the actors is accurately if faintly suggested; and the modest proportions of the stage are those of the theatre in Lincoln's Inn Fields. If this first sketch can be called reportage, in his final version—the sixth—Hogarth achieved a masterpiece of art.

It is a masterpiece of stunning brilliance (plate 5). The stage has been greatly magnified: it is deeper, wider, and higher, the audience in the back has been replaced by extras carrying pikes, and the proscenium draperies and Latin mottoes, as well as the satyrs on either side, have been invented and added. The satyr on our right points down to the front figure, the true-life character involved with the actress facing him. It is the duke of Bolton, facing his mistress Lavinia Fenton, who abandoned the stage at the end of the season to become his full-time "companion" and (after his wife's death) his duchess. Beginning with a simple stage scene, Hogarth has created a theatrical conversation piece that comments on the stage and on the society that patronized it.

Plate 5. Hogarth, painting of The Beggar's Opera *by Gay.* (By permission of the Yale Center for British Art)

Plate 6. Zoffany, painting of Love in a Village *by Bickerstaffe.* (By permission of the Detroit Institute of Arts)

It is no mere coincidence that John Zoffany, the other eighteenth-century painter as famous as Hogarth for conversation pieces, should also be eminent for his "theatrical conversations." An example is a scene from Isaac Bickerstaffe's popular comic opera *Love in a Village* (plate 6). It captures the moment when Hawthorne expounds his philosophy of life: "Health, good humour and competence is my motto: and if my executors have a mind, they are welcome to make it my epitaph." Using a different scene in the same comic opera Rowlandson painted a watercolor of the romantic Young Meadows declaring his love for Rossetta in the garden. The stage scene is a garden, to be sure, but Rowlandson seems to have removed it from the stage to outdoor nature.

The drama thus offered the artist stage scenes for theatrical conversations, which in turn animated his social conversation pieces. Later in the century, the drama played an important part in still another genre: history painting, whose previous subject matter had been sacred and ancient history. The Royal Academy expounded history painting in its schools and encouraged in exhibitions what it regarded as the noblest form of pictorial art, defined as "certainly the most elevated species, a mode of epic." Painters turned to Shakespeare, finding in his plays inspiration for flights of imagination on immense canvasses. They were assisted by progress in Shakespearean scholarship and criticism as well as by bardolatry.

Francis Hayman, who had illustrated Hanmer's 1744 edition, executed four scenes from Shakespeare for Vauxhall Gardens in the mode of history painting; each canvas was eight feet wide. But the impresario of Shakespeare illustration, as I have mentioned, was Alderman Boydell. The painters he engaged were permitted to give their own interpretations; and while some of them occasionally reflected stage practice, most of them treated their subjects in the convention of history painting. Boydell himself had announced in the preface to his catalogue: "To advance the Art towards maturity, and establish an *English School of Historical Painting,* was the great object of the present design."

As an example, George Romney's *Prospero and Miranda,* the play's opening scene, was done in a manner grandly temptestuous (plate 7). Romney took infinite pains with the picture, drawing many preliminary sketches; he regarded it as one of his most important works, a history painting in the grand style.It is a contrast to Henry Fuseli's famous *Titania and Bottom in the Woods* or *Titania's Awakening,* which was so lavishly admired that one newspaper reviewer wrote: "If Shakespeare had been a painter, he would perhaps have given somewhat of a similar picture."

Artists found subject matter beyond the London stage or printed plays. Strolling companies toured the provinces; and Hogarth—whose connection with the drama and stage is endless—recorded the bizarre activities of one such company in *Strolling Actresses Dressing in a Barn.* It is, in a way, a conversation piece, with its large cast of characters, intimate action, and elaborate decor (much of it emblematic).

Plate 7. Romney, illustration of The Tempest *by Shakespeare.*

Plate 8. [attrib. Mortimer], Portrait Group. (By permission of the Yale Center for British Art)

In the theatre, there is generally dramatic action on both sides of the footlights, and both were observed by eighteenth-century artists. In the watercolor *Box at the Opera,* Rowlandson departs from his customary style of caricature, capturing a group of spectators engrossed by the performance. Another example of the theatre as subject matter for the artist is a conversation piece, both striking and subtle, attributed to John Hamilton Mortimer (plate 8). The playbill held by the young woman tells us that a performance of *King Lear* is being played on stage, but the spectators seem too preoccupied with their personal concerns to be moved by Shakespeare's tragedy.

Portraiture

When we turn to portraiture and its connection with the stage, we are confronted with so many portraits of Garrick[4] and of Mrs. Siddons that we wonder when—if they sat so often—they found time to stand and act! These stars, and their images, shone after the mid-century.

One of the earliest portraits of an actor in a dramatic role is by Godfrey Kneller in 1689, that of Anthony Leigh playing the part of Dominic in Dryden's *The Spanish Friar* (plate 9). Through Colley Cibber's description of Leigh we can judge how successfully Kneller caught his psychological likeness. "In the canting, grave Hypocrisy of the *Spanish Friar,*" writes Cibber, "[Leigh] stretcht the Veil of Piety so thinly over him, that in every Look, Word, and Motion, you saw a palpable, wicked Slyness shine through it."[5] It would seem uncharacteristic in this pre-Garrick era for an actor to commission a full-length portrait, and, to be sure, this was painted for the earl of Dorset, poet and rake, described by Cibber as "equally an admirer, and a Judge of Theatrical Merit."

About one hundred years later Thomas Lawrence painted a comparable though contrasting portrait of an actor that graphically projects his role— John Philip Kemble as Coriolanus (plate 10). Here the actor is larger than life—in both senses, for the canvas is nine and a half feet high and six feet wide. His image is projected forcefully and arrogantly as he strides toward us from out of the frame, while we see in the background the flaming town he has just conquered. This portrait has recently been called by an art historian a landmark "in the history of English romanticism;"[6] and a share of that significance must be attributed to the actor who served as model.

Portrait painting was the bread and butter of English artists, and those who aspired to a more elevated genre—history painting, particularly— complained of this economic vassalage. But its popularity with the growing middle class and with gentry and peers, all of whom conspicuously consumed portraiture, kept it a booming industry. Joshua Reynolds, its most successful practitioner, managed in his career to paint over 4,000 portraits

Plate 9. Kneller, Anthony Leigh in The Spanish Friar *by Dryden.*

(helped, of course, by studio assistants). In 1771 he painted a portrait of the comic actress Frances Abington playing the part of Miss Prue in Congreve's *Love for Love* (plate 11). Although the portrait is full of informal charm—as she leans on the back of the Chippendale chair while her lap dog looks through—I wonder whether it shows her in character. Congreve's Miss Prue is identified in the cast of characters as "a silly awkward country girl." Perhaps her gesture of finger held to lips is meant to characterize her silliness, but everything else in the picture marks her as an elegant lady of the beau monde. Reynolds seems to have been bewitched by the woman herself and to have forgotten the part she is playing. Other theatrical painters, especially Zoffany and De Wilde, were more faithful to the theatrical roles of their sitters, generally portraying them in action on stage.

Reynolds frequently posed his women subjects full-length as allegorical or mythological figures, thus satisfying his craving for the grand style. *Lady Sarah Bunbury Sacrificing to the Graces* he called one picture, in a pose adapted from a classical relief. The noble subject—actually a duke's daugh-

Plate 10. Lawrence, John Philip Kemble in Coriolanus *by Shakespeare.*

Plate 11. Reynolds, Frances Abington in Love for Love *by Congreve.*

ter—seems to be play-acting; it is a theatrical tableau yet not of the theatre. In contrast, when Reynolds painted Mrs. Abington as the comic muse there is no sense of the theatre; it is *she* who could be a duke's daughter in her insouciant pose. Only the mask dangling from her hand suggests her allegorical identity.

Unlike the comic muse, the tragic muse, with its solemn rhetorical reverberations of history painting and the grand style, inspired Reynolds to one of his great paintings. George Romney had already painted Mrs. Yates in that role, but Reynolds's Mrs. Siddons as the tragic muse was a greater tragedienne and a greater portrait (plate 12). It borrows the pose and gesture from Michelangelo's prophet Isaiah on the ceiling of the Sistine Chapel. As an essay in sublimity through portraiture, it is justly famous; and its emblematic figures of Aristotelian Pity and Terror on either side of the Muse add grandeur. Only a great actress could have inspired this virtuoso performance in paint.

Offstage Mrs. Siddons could still inspire painters. In the portrait by Gainsborough she is a patrician lady, dressed in the highest fashion, fairly quivering with elegance (plate 13). And as modestly set down in informal dress by Thomas Lawrence, she is somewhat plain, without glamour but with soulful eyes, like a character in a Jane Austen novel.

Except for Garrick (inevitably) and Mrs. Siddons, sculptured portraits of stage figures are relatively rare. Colley Cibber, in the bust by Roubiliac, is one (plate 14). The portrait shows him as the nimble comedian of his earlier career in a moment of relaxation. A very different kind of portrait is the one of the comic actress Eliza Farren (plate 15) by the Honorable Mrs. Damer, Horace Walpole's talented cousin. As Thalia, the title of this marble, Miss Farren hardly conveys any sense of the muse of comedy. Instead, she looks down with neoclassical calm, as though contemplating her retirement from the stage to become the countess of Derby.

Caricature

One flourishing eighteenth-century art form—the caricature—found in the stage a plentiful source of material, which is not surprising since the stage often presents analagous comic drama. We have already seen examples of such caricature in Hogarth's frontispiece to Fielding's burlesque *Tragedy of Tragedies;* and perhaps Hogarth's *Strolling Actresses* can be regarded as caricature.

A view of the other side of the footlights is caricatured in a print by Hogarth entitled *The Laughing Audience* (plate 16). This encompasses the dour orchestra players, the spectators in the pit laughing (except for one disapproving man in the third row—a critic probably), and in the box two

Plate 12. Reynolds, Mrs. Siddons as The Tragic Muse. (By permission of the Huntington Library and Art Gallery)

Plate 13. Gainsborough, Mrs. Siddons.

Plate 14. Roubiliac, Colley Cibber.

Plate 15. Damer, Elizabeth Farren as Thalia.

rakes so busy flirting that they are deaf to the comedy being played on stage.

As a pioneer in the copyright and sale of satiric prints, Hogarth prepared the way for the two leading caricaturists of the later eighteenth century— Rowlandson and Gillray. Both these masters found material in the theatre. We have seen Mrs. Siddons in her sublime aspect; Rowlandson takes us behind the scenes to show her at her grubby task of rehearsing. His caricature of the theatre audience during an intermission—*Box Lobby Loungers*— is a merry and bustling microcosm of London high life (plate 17). Posted on the wall is a Covent Garden playbill, and the titles can easily be applied to the loungers: *Way of the World* and *Who's the Dupe*, an afterpiece by Hannah Cowley. Curiously enough, these two plays were in the repertoire of Drury Lane and not Covent Garden.[7]

James Gillray was a more savage artist, attacking political issues with astonishing brutality—and not sparing either the politicians themselves or the royal family. He occasionally turned to the stage and its practitioners. The great success of Sheridan's *Pizarro*, a tragedy adapted from Kotzebue, aroused Gillray to caricature; and the fact that Sheridan was embroiled in politics intensified the attack. In a lighter vein Gillray could ridicule the social pretensions of an actress offstage—as in the print of 1797, whose title comes from a famous classical group: *The Marriage of Cupid and Psyche* (plate 18). Psyche is the comic actress Eliza Farren, and Cupid is the earl of Derby, who elevated her from mistress to wife.

Ceramics

About midcentury the manufacture of porcelain—already flourishing in France and the German States—began its brilliant development in England. It produced a wide range of products—from individually modeled and hand-painted porcelain figures, at one extreme, to mass-produced, transfer-printed tiles at the other—thus dispersing its products through the entire scale of social classes. The affluent bought fine porcelains such as Bow, Chelsea, and Derby; the middling, Staffordshire pottery, including Wedgwood; and the humble bought the utilitarian Liverpool-delft tiles.

It is a tribute to the popularity of the English drama and the London stage that porcelain and pottery makers chose to model many of their figures on characters from plays, especially Shakespeare's, as well as on living actors and actresses. In ceramic popularity Garrick, James Quin, and dramatic characters competed with general types such as shepherds and shepherdesses, musicians, gardeners, and figures from the commedia dell'arte, often copied from the famous set modeled by Kändler for the Meissen porcelain factory. (Kändler's character of Pantaloon is sometimes mistaken in England for Shylock as portrayed by Macklin.) Identifiable

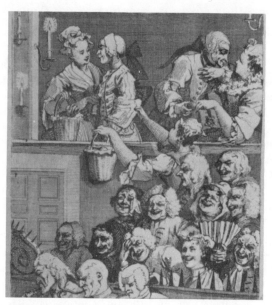

Plate 16. Hogarth, The Laughing Audience.

Plate 17. Rowlandson, Box Lobby Loungers.

103 The Marriage of Cupid and Psyche Gillray

Plate 18. Gillray, The Marriage of Cupid and Psyche.

individuals of equal ceramic status with stage characters include the royal family, conspicuous military heroes (Frederick the Great, Field Marshall Conway), and political leaders (Pitt the Elder, Wilkes). The most distinguished potter of the century, Josiah Wedgwood, also used actors and actress as models for busts, statuettes, plaques, and medallions: Garrick, Mrs. Siddons, and John Kemble were the most frequent models.

Both the Chelsea and Bow porcelain factories produced for the luxury trade a pair of figures, Kitty Clive and Henry Woodward as the "Fine Lady" and the "Fine Gentleman," characters in Garrick's first dramatic effort, *Lethe,* staged in 1740. Kitty Clive in white porcelain was made by Bow in 1750, a beautifully modeled figure; and Woodward is a virtuoso piece, the sword visible behind his legs (plate 19). But the most popular stage subject was Falstaff as portrayed by Quin. This figure was made in Bow, Derby, and Staffordshire factories. The figure was so popular, in fact, that Derby factories turned it out in six different sizes, to fit consumers' varying decors and purses.

The stage and its actors were also made visible on more utilitarian objects for the luxury trade. The Chelsea porcelain factory turned out a cane handle in the likeness of Peg Woffington. (Could it be because she was so well known for the britches part of Sir Harry Wildair?) Play scenes and characters appeared on dinner plates and tea services, snuff boxes, patch

Plate 19. Clive and Woodward in Lethe *by Garrick.*

Plate 20. Garrick in The Alchemist *by Jonson.*

boxes, and fans, on tea caddies and even on pulls for cabinet drawers. The decorative arts thus borrowed plentifully from the dramatic arts.

For those of more modest taste and pocket the Staffordshire factories turned out coarse copies or variants of the fine porcelain figures of actors and theatrical characters. These were cast from molds instead of being individually modeled. Cheaper still, and more easily cast, were portrait plaques, showing an actor in profile. Recently I saw, indeed handled, a fascinating example: a large plaque of Mrs. Siddons, not in any theatrical role, but as pure and ethereal as a Greek goddess, surrounded by small allegorical figures. It may have hung on the wall of a cottage as a memento of a performance once seen or simply as a mute tribute to an actress of glamorous reputation. Alas, I saw it not in a humble cottage but in a New York Fifty-seventh Street shop with a price tag of 2,500 dollars.

Images of stage actors were also used to decorate tiles used as wall ornaments and as lining for stoves and fireplaces. Called Liverpool-delft—from its place of manufacture and its composition (tin-glazed earthenware)—the tiles were decorated by a process called "transfer printing" with portraits, taken from published prints, of prominent actors and actresses in dramatic roles. Each tile was five inches square, and printed in black or red or puce. One showed Garrick as Abel Drugger, its source a print based on Zoffany's painting of a scene from *The Alchemist* (plate 20). Altogether, at least thirty-two designs were used.

Thus eighteenth-century decorative arts drew on the drama and stage for images, ideas, and motifs to satisfy as wide a segment of the population as attended the theatre—in a word, everybody.

If I may sum up these random observations and illustrations, eighteenth-century drama in England had a widespread effect on the visual arts. As a rapidly growing literate public consumed popular editions of Shakespeare and other playwrights, enterprising publishers added illustrations to the text. The drama and stage affected some major forms of painting—the conversation piece, history painting, and portraiture. The rise of stage luminaries such as Garrick and Mrs. Siddons brought the development of what we call "publicity"—with portraits that depicted them, caricatures that satirized them, and ceramics that deified them. The stage and its actors have made this contribution to the visual and plastic arts. The debt has been paid back, for thanks to these same arts, the actors—called by Hamlet "the abstracts and brief chronicles of the time"—whose artistry is so ephemeral and transitory, have been permanently and visibly immortalized.

Notes

1. Charles Beecher Hogan, *Shakespeare in the Theatre 1701–1800* (Oxford: Clarendon Press, 1952, 1957), 2:715.

2. Charles Lamb, "Detached Thoughts on Books and Reading," in "The Last Essays of Elia," *Life, Letters, and Writings,* ed.P. Fitzgerald (London: Gibbings & Co., 1897), 3:402.

3. Quoted in Ellis Waterhouse, *Painting in Britain 1530 to 1790* (London: Penguin, 1954), p. 120; R. B. Beckett, *Hogarth* (London: Routledge and Kegan Paul, 1949), p. 11.

4. Since David Garrick's portraits are the subject of Kalman Burnim's essay, I have excluded him from my discussion.

5. Cibber, pp. 85–86.

6. Joseph Burke, *English Art 1714–1800* (Oxford: Clarendon Press, 1976), p. 307.

7. In Rowlandson's drawing, on which this engraving is based, the playbill on the wall in the upper right is blank, but in the print he misremembered the name of the theatre.

9

The Anti-Evolutionary Development of the London Theatres

ARTHUR H. SCOUTEN

A survey, casual or sustained, of books about the theatre will quickly reveal the concept of unbroken continuity in the physical shape of English play-houses over the centuries. Whether we look at a book intended for the general reader, such as the handsomely illustrated *Theater Pictorial* of George Altman,[1] a scholarly study such as Allardyce Nicoll's *The Development of the Theatre,*[2] or a reference work designed for the specialist, such as E. K. Chambers's *The Elizabethan Stage,*[3] we will find that they all chart a sequential development of the London theatres. To be sure, some of the charts offer different origins and varying lines of progress. Some trace a route from Greece and Italy: some stay on native ground. Others incorporate all of the origins and all of the routes. Victor Albright, in his *The Shaksperian Stage,*[4] followed by numerous stage historians, finds a steady continuity from the nave, choir, and sanctuary of a medieval church to the stage for *The Castle of Perseverance* and the Cornish Theatre at Perranzabulo to the guild plays in the marketplace, the inn yards, and then the Bankside playhouses of the Elizabethan era. To E. K. Chambers, however, the development comes from the Italian Renaissance theatres. He speaks of the "houses" on the stage for plays by Plautus and Terence at private showings in the homes of Tudor grandees, or plays at court for Queen Elizabeth in the 1570s, and states that this practice was carried over into the construction of the professional playhouses.[5] Early in Nicoll's *The Development of the Theatre,* we are given the full sweep: "The forms and conventions of the classic playhouses set an indelible seal upon the theatres of Renaissance Italy, and thence were carried over, through the Elizabethan and Restoration periods in England, to modern times."[6] However, later in the book we learn that Burbage's structure called "The Theatre" and the Globe both

171

attempt to reproduce in London the forms of a Roman playhouse.[7] So, too, Cécile de Banke, in *Shakespearean Stage Productions: Then and Now,* when she says, "The ground plan of the modern theatre . . . is derived from the Greek and Roman amphitheatre by way of the public theatres of Elizabethan London."[8]

A foreign influence is also postulated by George R. Kernodle, in *From Art to Theatre.* He says, "The Elizabethan Stage was not an isolated invention but was, on the contrary, a logical result of the patterns and conventions of the visual arts of the Renaissance,"[9] and he is echoed by George Altman, who states that the Continental Renaissance theatre "came to Elizabethan England." The production of *The Castle of Perseverance* and the Cornish theatre at Perranzabulo suggest a different configuration to Leslie Hotson, for Hotson sees theatre in the round. In his *Shakespeare's Wooden O,* he says that since "pageant production was in the round," the Elizabethan theatres were built to allow the audience to surround "an oblong stage" with a "tiring house . . . underneath, inside the hollow stage."[10] Evidence to support Hotson's views is difficult to find. I recall, some fifty years ago, asking my professor, John Earle Uhler, about problems in diagrams of the first Globe playhouse. He laughed and replied that no one knew what the inside of either Globe Theatre looked like.

This statement was not private information, unknown to the scholarly world. In 1909, Victor Albright was aware of this lacuna, and he attempted to resolve the problem by projecting the concept of unbroken continuity of English playhouses. He looked at the copy of De Witt's famous drawing of the Swan Theatre and rejected it, because, he said, "it creates a stage entirely out of harmony with any European or succeeding English stage."[11] (This verdict is ironical to us today, as the statement is quite correct.) He announced that he would show a "typical Elizabethan stage" by examining "the form of the Restoration stage—the successor and perhaps the direct outgrowth of the Elizabethan."[12] Albright then reproduced, in his plate 6, an engraving from Elkanah Settle's extravaganza of 1673, *The Empress of Morocco,* a play that was produced at the new Dorset Garden Theatre (completed in November 1671 and reputedly designed by Sir Christopher Wren). Of the acting space in this playhouse, he asked, "Is it not more reasonable to suppose that it is simply a modified form of the Old Elizabethan stage?"[13] Having answered this question to his own satisfaction, he proceeded to demonstrate that there was an inner stage in the Elizabethan Bankside playhouses:

> Since both the Shaksperian and the Dryden theaters had outer-inner stages, the exploration of a scene on the later stage affords some assistance in proving the method of producing the same kind of scene on the earlier.[14]

Let me summarize his method. On page 81 he described the staging in a

New York theatre in 1907 of a current melodrama that alternated scenes from the Wild West and Alaska with scenes in the interior of a house in New York City. Next, he reproduced a drawing of the London Covent Garden Theatre in 1763. Then he commenced a survey of plays to provide his proof. He chose Henry Fielding's *The Historical Register, for the Year 1736,* a dramatic satire that had its premiere on 21 March 1736 at the Little Theatre in the Haymarket.[15] Albright accurately quoted a stage direction from the text of this play to show that a curtain was drawn to reveal the rear stage. Unfortunately, Albright got into several difficulties here. First, the only curtain an early eighteenth-century theatre had was the great curtain at the proscenium pillars. Next, the Restoration and eighteenth-century theatres had one to three grooves in the floor, through which the two halves or parts of a flat or flat scene could be pulled by the stagehands.[16] Some picture or "prospect" was painted on the canvas; that is why it was termed a "flat scene." After 1660, the term "scene draws" meant only that the stagehands had pulled the two parts of the flat off the stage to reveal a space further back. When an audience entered the playhouse, they saw a green curtain hanging at the back of the forestage. It was rolled up after the prologue and back down again after the epilogue, sometimes at the end of the play. There are only a few examples to indicate that the great curtain was used during the performance of the play. What is amusing is that Albright has pounced on the one person whom modern theatre experts believe did experiment by using the curtain during the action of the play— Henry Fielding. Consequently, these theatre historians would not be likely to accept an example from Fielding's *Historical Register* as evidence for use of the curtain at Drury Lane or Covent Garden within the same year, much less as the practice of the theatres for the seventy-five years prior to this production. Fielding was an experimenter, an innovator.

Albright's next example comes from the duke of Buckingham's *The Rehearsal,* produced in December 1671 at the Theatre-Royal in Brydges Street. It is followed by a citation from Otway's comedy *The Soldier's Fortune,* produced at Dorset Garden in June 1680, where the term "scene draws" again means the drawing of flats from the stage. Next, he cites what he calls "The Virgin Prophetess," really Betterton's adaptation of Massinger and Fletcher's *The Prophetess, or the History of Dioclesian,* acted at Dorset Garden in June 1690.[17] Oddly enough, the great curtain was used in act 4 of this opera, an experiment noted by Montague Summers in 1934.[18] This line of testimony is certainly based upon the construct that there was an unbroken development of the theatre from Elizabethan times down through the years.

At this point, readers may feel that I am being too severe on a book published in 1909. However, what I want to do is pursue Professor T. J. King's important point that for many years a number of stage historians followed Albright instead of going back and examining the surviving primary documents.[19] If we turn to Ashley Thorndike's *Shakespeare's Theater*, we will find a continuation of Albright's thesis of unbroken continuity, for Thorndike writes, "The theaters of the Restoration period were manifestly modeled on the Elizabethan."[20] On page 90, Thorndike accepts Albright's reconstruction of the Globe stage, reproducing it and endorsing it.

In 1923, E. K. Chambers followed Albright's position by saying that "there was no sudden breach of continuity with the earlier period." He also follows Albright in saying that the Elizabethan managers used stage sets. Elsewhere, Chambers provides a drawing entitled "Square theatre (Proportions of Fortune)."[21] This drawing is almost identical with Thorndike's drawing entitled "Ground Plan of the Fortune Theater."[22] In W. J. Lawrence's *The Physical Conditions of the Elizabethan Public Playhouse*, he includes a sketch drawn by William Archer called "Conjectural Elizabethan Stage."[23] Professor King calls it remarkably similar to the sketches by Albright, Thorndike, and Chambers; he also says that the frontispiece to Lawrence's *Those Nut-Cracking Elizabethans*, entitled "A Typical Public Theatre," is remarkably close to Albright's drawing.[24]

At this point, I can stop quoting from Professor King and offer an observation of my own: that the frontispiece to J. Cranford Adams's *The Globe Playhouse* resembles Albright's sketch.[25] One does not instantly see the similarity because of the striking appearance of the three "houses" at the top of Adams's picture; besides, the front of the platform or scaffolding in Albright's sketch is more wedge-shaped than is Adams's. Otherwise, in both illustrations we see a wide curtain between two doors, set at forty-five degrees, closing off the "inner stage," and a curtained upper stage between "window stages" set above the entrance doors. Adams was followed by Irwin Smith, who (with Adams, I understand) designed and made the model now exhibited at the Folger Library. The detailed plans in Smith's *Shakespeare's Globe Playhouse* follow those of Cranford Adams and are also quite similar to those of Albright.[26]

In Irwin Smith's next book, *Shakespeare's Blackfriars Playhouse*, he assumes an unbroken continuity between playhouses of the sixteenth and seventeenth centuries. In seeking to demonstrate "a curtained rear stage" at Blackfriars, he quotes from Thomas Killigrew's comedy, *The Parson's Wedding:* "the stage curtains are drawn, and discover a chamber, as it were, with two beds."[27] Killigrew's play was first performed at the new Brydges Street Theatre in Drury Lane by the King's Company, of which Killigrew was the proprietor. One would presume that stage directions in the first printing of this play, in 1663, would refer to the theatre in which it was performed. In his index, Smith enters twenty references to this play and to Davenant's *News from Plymouth* (1673). Adams also quotes frequently from *The Parson's Wedding* to document his theories about Elizabethan theatres.[28]

I have grave doubts about the value of stage directions as evidence about the physical structure of a theatre. For example, let us look at the variant readings from the two surviving early texts of John Fletcher's play *The Woman's Prize* (ca. 1611). The 1647 folio has a stage direction reading, "Enter Livia discovered abed, and Moroso beside her" (5.1). At this point in the manuscript of *The Woman's Prize* in the Folger Library we find, "Enter Livia sick carryed in a chair by servants: Moroso by her." The best explanation of the discrepancy between these two stage directions is that Elizabethan actors adjusted to the physical area in which they had to perform. This fact, well known to those who have had practical experience in the theatre, should not be forgotten by historians attempting to make reconstructions of older theatres. If John Barton's Royal Shakespeare Company were given enough inducement to produce a play in the Folger Library, they would do it. Ian Richardson, Richard Pasco, and the rest would put on a play wherever they were told. They could perform it at the end of the reading room on the main floor, using the mezzanine as a balcony. If they were required to stage the play in the exhibition gallery, the players could hang a blanket over the rear door.

A former director of the Folger Library, Louis B. Wright, refused to permit performances in the Folger Theatre, alleging Washington fire department and insurance company regulations as his reason for the ban. I suspect that Wright, an eminent scholar himself, knew that reconstructions of Elizabethan theatres were not taken seriously by scholars, nor did he want to hear the distinguished stage historian George Reynolds ask his devastating and unanswerable question: "Where did the actors at the Globe hang the curtain of the inner stage?" D. C. Mullin calls the models of the Globe made by Adams, Smith, and others (with their half-timbers, plaster, and thatch) "Merrie Olde England."[29]

At this point I want to recount an episode in the controversy over the so-called inner stage. Stage historians are familiar with the numerous articles by Professor Richard Hosley rejecting the notion of an inner stage, as well as the "multiple stage" and other portions of the Smith-Adams model of the Globe playhouse. Hosley has repeatedly stated his belief that Adams and other stage historians of his persuasion took, "whether consciously or unconsciously, most of these elements of the so-called Elizabethan stage" from theatres built after 1660—in fact, chiefly from nineteenth-century theatres.[30] At the 1966 meeting of the American Society for Theatre Research in New York, Professor Hosley showed slides of Victorian theatres and of modern renderings of Elizabethan theatres to demonstrate the similarity between them. After his presentation, a heated controversy ensued in which no one mentioned any of the illustrations that Professor Hosley had shown, and one scholar asked how Othello could have strangled Desdemona if the Globe had lacked an inner stage.

At this unfortunate spectacle, where the participants in the debate clung tenaciously to their previous views unaffected by facts, I realized that the argument was not going to be resolved by documentary evidence and that this bizarre notion of unbroken continuity must rest upon some philosophical concept or theory. Later, I learned from O. B. Hardison that this concept of unbroken continuity arose from an effort to apply Darwinism to literary history. E. K. Chambers, a serious scholar, undoubtedly wanted to elicit some respect for his work. In his time, the road to respect and recognition came through scientific methodology, and Darwinism was in vogue. Also, Hardison explained, the great mass of dramatic works in the Middle Ages from short tropes to a complete Corpus Christi cycle, was itself susceptible to the evolutionary construct.[31] If one examines early twentieth-century histories of the Elizabethan stage, he will find plenty of evidence in support of Hardison's critique. That indefatigable researcher Charles W. Wallace cites the Farrant lease, some letters of the earl of Leicester, and various records pertaining to the first Blackfriars theatre, and says that "they furnish the missing links in the evolution of the English drama into artistic form."[32] Another example is provided by W. J. Lawrence, a highly esteemed stage historian. In his chapter "The Evolution and Influence of the Elizabethan Playhouse," he writes: "The private theatre formed the connecting link between the platform stage of Shakespeare's day and the picture stage of Dryden's."[33]

The notion of the existence of an "inner stage" appeared long before 1859. Richard Hosley quotes John Payne Collier, writing in 1831: "The curtains at the back of the stage . . . served, when drawn, to make another and an inner apartment, when such was required by the business of the play."[34] Then in 1836, Ludwig Tieck coined the term *Hinterbühne*. The expression does not appear in the works of the major nineteenth-century British specialists in the drama—Alexander Dyce, William Giffard, Francis Cunningham, or A. H. Bullen—but it was picked up and used heavily by Brodmeier and other German scholars. Scholars connected with universities seemed to depend on this notion more than did those historians who were primarily connected with the professional theatre. There were some exceptions, such as William Archer, who uses the term "rear stage," and Harley Granville-Barker, who appears reluctantly to accept the idea.[35] But no mention of the term appears in Percy Fitzgerald's several histories. In his *Shakespearean Representation* of 1908, Fitzgerald berates current producers for using elaborate sets when the plays should be acted on a bare stage; at the death of Desdemona, he says that the bed was brought forward.[36] Sydney Lee alludes to the bare boards of the Elizabethan theatres and in one passage speaks of the actors coming through loose curtains at the back of the stage "and passing to the forepart of the stage."[37] It is pretty certain, in this context, that Lee was either unaware of the term "inner stage" or was ignoring it. Nevertheless, if the university professors were the ones who exploited this notion, it was a university professor who expelled it; all students of the Elizabethan stage should be grateful to Richard Hosley for his trenchant work in repudiating this erroneous idea.

With this albatross removed, let us go back to the time of James Burbage and his "Theatre" of 1576 to see what we can see. The unroofed Bankside playhouses were apparently round, except for the Fortune, which was square. Inside these round structures, carpenters erected Richard Southern's booth stage. Until recently, stage historians believed that these buildings were built on the model of inn yards. If so, there was some evolutionary development from an innyard with galleries for a residential structure into a building used solely for playacting. The dominant view now, however, as set forth by Glynne Wickham, is that the playhouses in Southwark were modeled on bear gardens.[38] If so, since there is no relation between a bear garden and a theatre, Burbage's structure would have been an innovation as a theatre.

At the close of the interregnum, Sir William Davenant secured permission to offer concerts in his home. His "home" had previously been the abode of the countess of Rutland, who had lost her property because she was a Catholic. Davenant's "First Dayes Entertainment" took place then, in the great hall of a Tudor mansion, which most certainly had not evolved from any known theatre. In 1660, Charles II licensed two companies, and acting was resumed. The Puritans had methodically demolished all of the London playhouses except the Red Bull. As there were no other existing theatres, the actors needed a large structure that had capacity for customers. They turned to two tennis courts. They were rectangles, thirty-one feet eight inches by one hundred and ten feet. Gibbons's tennis court was thus converted into the Vere Street Theatre, with dimensions of twenty-three feet by sixty-four feet. Lisle's tennis court was also remodeled into the theatre in Lincoln's Inn Fields with dimensions of thirty feet by seventy-five feet.[39] It is plausible to suppose that some changes were made after the patterns of the Jacobean and Caroline indoor theatres. If so, there would have been continuity in the staging area but not in the shape of the building itself.

Next, we find the fan-shaped auditorium. In the 1670s, entirely new playhouses were built. Instead of buildings remodeled from a structure originally intended for some other use, such as a monastery or a tennis court, the new playhouses were designed by an architect. We have now reached the period called "Neoclassic" and hence should not be surprised to find the Roman amphitheatre used as the model. All curves on the plan are struck from a single center.[40] The pit benches and the front of the jutting apron are both oval. The side walls of the theatre splay outward so that the auditorium increases in width as one moves away from the stage, the side boxes growing correspondingly narrower until, about thirty-six feet into the auditorium, they curve around to meet the outer walls of the theatre. The pit or auditorium is raked, sloping up toward the rear. The side walls of the auditorium reduce in height as they near the scenic area, designed for perspective. That is, the Corinthian order that decorates the side walls decreases in size as it nears the stage, providing an illusion of perspective.Meanwhile the walls slope inward toward a vanishing point. This is baroque architecture, of course. What the architect has created (whether it was Wren or not) is a fan-shaped auditorium, an ideal form, because the sound spreads out and the audience's vision narrows in. The majority of the audience is in an advantageous position to see and hear the players; testimony from contemporary commentators on this point is unanimous. Finally, the audience is enclosed in an architectural environment that makes them fully conscious of participating in the perspective scene. (It is of interest to note that modern architects are returning to this form today; the new Olivier in Southwark is an example.)

Today, the best account of the Restoration and eighteenth-century theatres is that of Richard Leacroft, in his *The Development of the English Theatre*. Leacroft is an architect (rather than an academic stage historian), and he makes his drawings to scale, very helpful to simple readers like me. I know that other reputable books about theatres provide dimensions for illustrations, but reading these figures is one thing and studying scale drawings is another. In Leacroft's book, a scale drawing of the first Theatre Royal in Drury Lane occupies about one-third of a page, whereas Holland's Drury Lane of 1794 occupies two pages. The most casual observer can see that the latter is a larger building than the former. Because of Leacroft's discovery of Sheppard's drawings of 1778, all stage historians who wish to mention this Drury Lane Theatre or who wish to print reproductions of it should consult Leacroft's book.

This excellent architectural pattern, used in all of the newly erected playhouses in the Restoration period, was abandoned by Sir John Vanbrugh in his construction of the first Haymarket theatre. It was a large, rectangular structure, about one hundred thirty feet by sixty. Of it, D. C. Mullin writes, "The structure was unlike that of any previous English theatre, or of any continental one, for that matter."[41] Leacroft concurs, quoting the *London Survey* as saying, "very different from any Other House in being." (Darwinians should be forced to copy these statements a hundred times in their notebooks.) The example is not unique. Seventeenth-century Parisian theatres did not derive from the Hotel de Bourgogne, the oldest known public playhouse in Paris, dated about 1548. Of it, Mullin writes, "The Bourgogne was a building with no classical antecedents, and was practically unrelated to the development of theatre architecture elsewhere."[42]

The remaining London theatres, newly erected in the first half of the eighteenth century, were built with a fan-shaped auditorium. The architect was Edward Shepherd, who designed and build both the first Covent Garden playhouse and the second Goodman's Fields theatre in 1732. Leacroft prints Dumont's contemporary sketches of Covent Garden (which I did not know when *The London Stage* was being compiled), and from them we can see that the side walls flare out, so that the distance at the back of the pit is much greater than the width of the stage.[43] The stage front is curved, as are the rows of benches in the pit. The Folger Library has James Winston's copies of Capon's drawings of Giffard's Theatre in Goodman's Fields, and they show a fan-shaped auditorium. The benches and box fronts follow the same curve as the orchestra rail. The side walls flare out, widening toward the rear of the building. Before remodeling, old Drury Lane held about 800 to 900 people; Covent Garden had a capacity of about 1,300; and Goodman's Fields held about 750, as can be seen from my calculations in *The London Stage.*[44]

From all this information we can draw some conclusions. Modern stage historians who specialize in the Augustan period often display something of an inferiority complex, which should now be discarded. That is, we have lived in the shadow of the Globe where Burbage, Arnim, Lowin, and Shakespeare performed in daylight, in the intimacy of a crowded circular shell, with great numbers of people standing in the pit, nearly surrounding the stage scaffolding. The Globe, so conceived, has held the mystique of an ideal theatre. With the Augustan theatre, with every aspect integrated in the fan-shaped auditorium, a deep stage showing perspective scenes, and an audience close enough and well-placed enough to see every facial movement and hear every word uttered as Betterton, Barry, and Bracegirdle appeared on that stage, we can now claim a Gestalt of our own.

When new theatres were built at the end of the eighteenth century, the architectural design had entirely changed. With Henry Holland's Covent Garden Theatre, opened on 17 September 1792, an entirely different structure could be seen: the horseshoe shape of the Italian theatres, as imported to London from Paris. When gunpowder was introduced and armor rendered obsolete, the Italian aristocracy immediately made the medieval tournament into the dominant Renaissance mode. For these tournaments, a horseshoe structure was built. It had high galleries, and the knights entered at the open end, in their horse-drawn chariots, as if waiting for Cecil B. De Mille. When Italian opera emerged, the carpenters built opera houses on the model of the tournament arenas. For example, see reproductions of the opera house in Milan, the San Carlo of Naples, and the Teatro Farnese at Parma. (By way of contrast, the great Imperial Theatre in Vienna [1668] was square.)

The plans for Holland's Covent Garden show a tremendous structure, seating over 3,000 spectators in a horseshoe arrangement, in which the acoustics were poor for those near the back wall, and a high percentage of the audience needed to turn their heads and shoulders to view any action on the stage. There was no longer any apron stage; tiers of boxes had replaced the old proscenium arrangement. Numerous contemporary complaints by established actors indicate that they experienced great difficulty in attempting to adjust to the new stage. Holland's new Drury Lane house of 1794, with four tiers, followed the same horseshoe design, as did the Pantheon in 1795. Both Covent Garden and Drury Lane burned down within a few years, but most of the new theatres that succeeded them were again in the horseshoe or egg shape of the Italian and Parisian theatres. In speaking of the early nineteenth-century London theatres, Mullin says: "The playhouses were changed almost beyond recognition. One cannot even compare the playhouses and production techniques of the Restoration with those of the 1820's."[45] In the last half of the nineteenth century, newly built theatres were square or rectangular, deserting the horseshoe pattern of the previous period. The architecture was eclectic, but every theatre of which I have seen a diagram or reproduction had a picture-frame stage. The front of the stage had been cut back for the orchestra, thereby providing more space for the stalls as well.

To recapitulate, instead of an evolutionary development in the London theatres, being perfected in adjustment to the environment, we first find round bear-baiting or bull-baiting game houses used as a model for the Elizabethan Bankside playhouses. These were followed by theatres made in rectangular rooms or in areas within a larger building used for some other purpose, such as a monastery or a palace. Next, we find a theatre consisting of the long, narrow hall in Rutland House. Then we see rectangular tennis courts being remodeled into playhouses. At the relatively late date of the 1670s, the classical Roman amphitheatre was drawn upon to create the fan-shaped auditorium of Restoration theatres, which were designed by architects. This style was replaced in the 1790s by a completely different design: the horseshoe auditorium on the model of Parisian and Italian theatres. The changes in this sequence, it seems to me, entirely repudiate the concept of an evolutionary progress in the development of English playhouses.

Notes

1. George Altman, *Theater Pictorial* (Berkeley, Calif.: University of California Press, 1953).

2. Allardyce Nicoll, *The Development of the Theatre*, 4th ed. (1927; rpt. New York: Harcourt, Brace, 1958).

3. E. K. Chambers, *The Elizabethan Stage*, 4 vols. (Oxford: Clarendon Press, 1923).

4. Victor Albright, *The Shaksperian Stage* (New York: Columbia University Press, 1909).

5. Chambers, 4:359–62; 3:41–45, 60.

6. Nicoll, p. 17.

7. Ibid., p. 123.

8. Cécile de Banke, *Shakespearean Stage Productions: Then and Now* (London: Hutchinson, 1954), p. 29.

9. George R. Kernodle, *From Art to Theatre* (Chicago: University of Chicago Press, 1944), p. 2.

10. Leslie Hotson, *Shakespeare's Wooden O* (New York: Macmillan, 1960), p. 281.

11. Albright, p. 39.

12. Ibid., p. 38, and again on p. 103.

13. Ibid., p. 48, and also p. 80.

14. Ibid., p. 80.

15. All dates of performance for this period are taken from *The London Stage*.

16. For a fuller account of Restoration staging practices, see Richard Southern's section of vol. 5 of *The Revels History of Drama in English* by John Loftis, Richard Southern, Marion Jones, and A. H. Scouten (London: Methuen, 1976), pp. 83–118.

17. Albright, p. 89–91.

18. Summers, *The Restoration Stage*, p. 101.

19. T. J. King, "The Stage in the Time of Shakespeare," *Renaissance Drama* 4 (1972): 199–235.

20. Thorndike, p. 77.

21. Chambers, 3:48, 69–71.

22. Thorndike, p. 75.

23. W. J. Lawrence, *The Physical Conditions of the Elizabethan Public Playhouse* (Cambridge, Mass.: Harvard University Press, 1927), p. 22.

24. W. J. Lawrence, *Those Nut-Cracking Elizabethans* (London: The Argonaut Press, 1935), p. 215.

25. J. Cranford Adams, *The Globe Playhouse* (Cambridge, Mass.: Harvard University Press, 1942; rpt. New York: Barnes & Noble, 1964).

26. Irwin Smith, *Shakespeare's Globe Playhouse* (New York: Scribners, 1956).

27. Thomas Killigrew, *The Parson's Wedding* (New York: New York University Press, 1964), p. 345.

28. J. C. Adams, pp. 262, 265, 276, 278.

29. *The Development of the Playhouse* (Berkeley, Calif.: University of California Press, 1970), pp. 34, 38.

30. "The Origins of the So-called Elizabethan Multiple Stage," *Tulane Drama Review* 12 (1968): 29.

31. O. B. Hardison, *Christian Rite and Christian Drama in the Middle Ages* (Baltimore: Johns Hopkins Press, 1965), pp. 6–14.

32. Charles W. Wallace, *The Evolution of the English Drama up to Shakespeare, with a History of the First Blackfriars Theatre* (Berlin: Georg Reimer, 1912), p. 3.

33. W. J. Lawrence, *The Elizabethan Playhouse and Other Studies* (Philadelphia: Lippincott, 1912), p. 16.

34. Quoted by Richard Hosley in his Introduction to the revised edition of C. Walter Hodges, *The Globe Restored* (New York: W. W. Norton, 1973), pp. 1–3.

35. William Archer, "The Elizabethan Stage," *Quarterly Review* 208 (1908): 442–71; Harley Granville-Barker, "A Note upon Chapters XX and XXI of *The Elizabethan Stage*," *Review of English Studies* 1 (1925): 60–71.

36. Percy Fitzgerald, *Shakesperean Representation* (London: Elliot Stock, 1908), p. 102.

37. Sydney Lee, *Shakespeare and the Modern Stage* (New York: Scribners, 1906), p. 40.

38. Glynne Wickham, *Early English Stages*, 2 vols. (London: Routledge and Kegan Paul, 1959–1963).

39. Abstracted from part 1 of *The London Stage*.

40. This account is taken from Richard Leacroft, *The Development of the English Playhouse* (Ithaca, N.Y.: Cornell University Press, 1973), pp. 89–99.

41. D. C. Mullin, p. 71; Leacroft, p. 99.

42. Ibid., p. 17.

43. Leacroft, pp. 106–7.

44. *The London Stage*, part 1, pp. xxiii–xxvi.

45. Mullin, p. 86.

10

Looking upon His Like Again: Garrick and the Artist

KALMAN A. BURNIM

On 20 January 1779 Eva Maria Garrick entered in her journal, "At a quarter before eight, my Husband sighed, and Died without one uneasy moment, the Lord be Praised." It is comforting to hear that Davy had died as well as he had lived. His life had been blessed with happiness, acclaim, and wealth; and except for the frustrations that plague the daily business of a theatre master, it had been, to an extraordinary degree, free from uneasy moments. David Garrick's death, in the famous words of Samuel Johnson, head "eclipsed the gaiety of nations, and impoverished the public stock of harmless pleasure," an epitaph that Mrs. Garrick had incised on her husband's monument at Lichfield, the city of his youth.

Davy's death also set off a flood of public grief without parallel in English literature, the arts, or the stage. In a splendid funeral procession stretching the entire length of the Strand and down Whitehall to the Abbey, the cortege and the fifty coaches and the hundreds of friends and admirers passed by thousands of mourners. The dukes, viscounts, earls, and right honorables, all Garrick's friends, who served as his pallbearers, could not

Except for several deletions, the text of this essay is printed essentially as it was read at the conference. The projection of color slides of the original portraits was important to the presentation. In this publication it has not been possible to reproduce the portraits in color, and thus in some instances engravings of the originals have been substituted.

The author acknowledges a heavy debt to Messrs. Iain Mackintosh and Geoffrey Ashton, the devisers of *The Georgian Playhouse* exhibition at the Hayward Gallery, London, from 21 August to 12 October 1975. Professor J. H. Plumb's essay in *The Pursuit of Happiness*, the catalogue of the inaugural exhibition at the Yale Center for British Art, New Haven, in 1977, has also been especially suggestive.

Since this paper was delivered, an extensive annotated list of the portraits of David Garrick has been published in volume 6 of *A Biographical Dictionary of Actors, Actresses, Musicians, Dancers, Managers, and Other Stage Personnel in London, 1660–1800*, edited by Philip H. Highfill, Jr., Kalman A. Burnim, and Edward A. Langhans.

Plate 1. Apotheosis of Garrick, *engraving by Caldwell and Smith, after Carter.*
(Photo courtesy of the Folger Shakespeare Library)

themselves have hoped for such a tribute at their demise. No Englishman, save a monarch or two, had ever been buried in grander style than was this Caesar of Drury Lane. And no human being, I suspect, has ever been wafted to his reward in a sillier manner and wearing a more satisfied expression than is little Davy in the canvas by George Carter (plate 1), which now hangs in the Art Gallery of the Royal Shakespeare Theatre. Here seventeen well-known actors, dressed in the costumes of their most popular Shakespearean roles, wish him bon voyage to Parnassus, where he is to be welcomed by the muses of tragedy and comedy and the god of his idolatry, Shakespeare. The picture was exhibited at the Royal Academy in 1784, when Horace Walpole summed it up as "ridiculous and bad."

During his lifetime Garrick had assured his immortality by the genius of his own artistry on the stage and by the pains he had taken to project his public image. While he yet lived, he had seen himself made into a national icon by an impressive array of artists: Hogarth, Gainsborough, Reynolds, Zoffany, Dance, Kaufmann, Hayman, Wilson, Vandergucht, Batoni, Liotard, Roberts, De Loutherbourg, and many others—and by the sculptors Roubiliac, Nollekens, and Van Nost, not to mention numerous estimable engravers.

In the preface to the catalogue of the inaugural exhibition of the splendid paintings that Mr. and Mrs. Paul Mellon have bestowed upon Yale and country, Edmund Pillsbury, then the director of the Yale Center for British Art, has written:

> In establishing the pursuit of happiness as a natural right equal to that of life and liberty, Thomas Jefferson affirmed in the Declaration of Independence one of the cornerstones of English life in the eighteenth century. Beginning with the Glorious Revolution of 1688, England witnessed a popularization of culture which during the course of the succeeding century brought many of the things that had enriched the life of the small aristocracy into the hands of the middle class. Private ownership of land, the development of parks and gardens, travel both within Britain and abroad, sporting activities, literature, theatre, music, art, and science—all flourished during the eighteenth century in England. Happiness became the goal to which every citizen had the right to strive.

The Yale exhibition was appropriately entitled "The Pursuit of Happiness," and in his essay in the exhibition catalogue J. H. Plumb reminds us that many thousands, who now had abundant food and modest harpsichords, for the first time in centuries could enjoy "the civilities, the culture, the arts—indeed the leisured happiness."[1] As never before, music was written, bought, and performed; musical-instrument makers flourished. As never before, plays, novels, and other forms of literature were published. During the middle third of the century, Drury Lane under Garrick and Lacy and Covent Garden under Rich flourished and profited as no theatres ever had since the Restoration. From the establishment of the Bath Playhouse in 1705, the provincial theatre expanded throughout the three kingdoms by the century's end, and the theatres at Bristol, York, Edinburgh, Dublin, and some lesser places were fine enough and yielded box-office receipts enough to attract the great performers of the period, such as Macklin, Woodward, Siddons, the Kembles, the Edwins, the Barrys, and the Kings—though very seldom the high mogul himself, who after a few excursions in the 1740s preferred to pass his summers in the pursuit of happiness at the country houses of the wealthy and influential and at his own serene retreat on the banks of the Thames at Hampton.

As with literature, music, and theatre, so it was with the visual arts, which also responded to affluence. By 1800 Britain was "alive with painters, engravers, watercolorists, satirists, and drawing masters." The new English happiness "found full recognition" in the art of the period—prints, panoramas, illustrated books, drawings, watercolors, and especially paintings, particularly portrait paintings.

Fortunately the growth of affluence in the middle and upper classes made possible this "cultural revolution," this quest for leisure well spent to exercise the mind, the body, and the heart. It was a world, Plumb reminds us, made for the dilettante and the collector. The market in culture was exploited, expanded, and innovated by men who knew there were profits to be had. The "entrepreneurial spirit" of painters such as Hogarth, Hayman, Lambert, and most conspicuously Zoffany, Gainsborough, Reynolds, and Romney, made considerable fortunes. Between 1750 and 1790, Reynolds, Gainsborough, and Romney produced about 5,000 portraits among them, and in 1757 alone Reynolds had 183 sitters. Art achieved a mass market, galleries and museums were established, societies formed, exhibitions given. Although the middle class was unable to afford the works of major or even minor artists, they could adorn their walls with engravings of all kinds, or they could have them as illustrations to their books. The demand for prints was a phenomenon previously unknown and, as Hogarth knew, the print trade offered a market as profitable as the canvas trade.[2]

English portrait painting and David Garrick came to their zenith together. Garrick's position was central in the arts of mid-Georgian England. No other actor in the history of the English theatre prior to the development of the camera has been the subject of so many portraits, original or engraved, in private or stage character, as was David Garrick. It is likely, indeed, that Garrick was the subject of more original paintings than any figure in English history. His listing in the *British Museum Catalogue of Engraved British Portraits* is exceeded only by that for Queen Victoria. The *Catalogue of Engraved Dramatic Portraits in the Harvard Theatre Collection* lists almost twice as many portraits for Garrick as for any other performer, including Kemble, Siddons, Kean, and Irving. In the Garrick iconography compiled for the sixth volume of the *Biographical Dictionary of Actors, Actresses, Musicians, Dancers, Managers, and Other Stage Personnel in London, 1660–1800,* we find at least 90 original portraits of him in 29 stage characters. Engravings of these portraits, plus engravings for which no originals are known to exist, amount to 235 different versions. The sum of original and engraved portraits, in various stages of oil, watercolor, pencil, ink, mezzotint, etching, and the like, comes to a grand total of more than 450 items—and these do not include at least 30 sculptures, woodcarvings, porcelains, and medallions in plaster. Moreover, I make no claim for completeness. Certainly, somewhere in some galleries, libraries, and museums, and in the hands of private collectors in the United Kingdom, the United States, and Europe, there are items still unknown to us.

During Garrick's lifetime theatrical painting developed into a specialized genre, as had landscape, history, and portrait painting. Garrick took care to project his image in many ways: by puffs in the newspapers (some of which he owned interest in), by the Jubilee of 1769, and by the spreading of his likeness around the town, the country, and the Continent. Engravers limned him in many of the roles he played, and prints were readily available for a shilling or two. "If one preferred Garrick as a chimney ornament, statuettes of him were available, either in fashionable Bow or plain Staffordshire."[3]

As *The Georgian Playhouse* exhibition arranged by Iain Mackintosh and Geoffrey Ashton at the Hayward Gallery in 1975 made quite clear, in Garrick's time "the fine and theatre arts were then more closely intertwined than ever before or since."[4] The tradition begins with William Hogarth, who gave a visual unity to the age.[5] The interplay of theatre and subject picture permeated almost all the works of Hogarth, who affirmed: "I have endeavored to treat my subjects as a dramatic writer; my picture is my stage, and men and women my players, who by means of certain actions and gestures exhibit dumb show." "I wished to compose pictures on canvas, similar to representations on the stage; and further hope that they will be tried by the same test and criticized by the same criterion."[6]

Hogarth's earlier works include the famous scene from *The Beggar's Opera,* the paintings and engravings of *The Rake's Progress* and *Marriage-a-la-Mode,* and the Shakespearean pictures at Vauxhall—all descriptive in movement and action. Hogarth provides us with one of the first theatrical portraits of Garrick, perhaps the most famous of all theatrical scenes, Richard III starting from his dream in the tent (plate 2), painted in 1745. Garrick's legendary "debut" in that role at Goodman's Fields Theatre on 19 October 1741 was his catapult into instant fame, and next morning at his writing table twenty-four-year-old Davy confronted his brother Peter with the irreversible fact that he was giving up the wine business—"I hope when You shall find that I may have ye genius of an Actor without ye Vices, You will think Less Severe of Me & not be asham'd to own me for a Brother."[7] The roadways to the East End were jammed by crowds eager to see the new sensation at Henry Giffard's little outlaw theatre. London was captivated by Garrick's exciting acting style, by which "he threw new light on elocution and action; he banished ranting, bombast, and grimace; and restored nature, ease, simplicity, and genuine humour."[8] The former Lichfield wine merchant was proclaimed by William Pitt as "yᵉ best Actor yᵉ English Stage had produc'd."[9]

When Hogarth painted this scene of Garrick as Richard III, he took as his inspiration, in part, Charles Le Brun's painting of the *Tent of Darius* and his illustration of *Fear.* At Paris in 1669 Le Brun had delivered an illustrated lecture on the expression of the passions; after his death (in 1690), Le Brun's lecture was published as *Méthode pour apprendre à dessiner les passions* (1698), a study of a physical expression of moral and emotional states, analyzing the manifestation of such expressions as "Anger," "Esteem," and "Veneration." Hogarth's work shows an expert knowledge of the expression of the passions as considered by Le Brun and others; he concentrates wholly on what Merchant terms Garrick's "realistic horror," without bringing on the apparitions that had usually been seen in previous

Plate 2. Garrick as Richard III, by Hogarth. (Photo courtesy of the Walker Art Gallery, Liverpool)

renditions. A careful analysis of how the physical expression of emotion has developed hand in hand with the history of art, and especially theatrical painting, lies outside the scope intended for this essay, but it would, I believe, offer some fascinating and very fruitful observations.

Hogarth's painting of Garrick as Richard III brough him £200 from a Mr. Duncombe of Duncombe Hall in 1746. The payment, Hogarth himself recorded, "was more than any portrait painter was ever known to receive for a portrait."[10] The painting descended through the family line of Thomas Duncombe, whose grandson became the first earl of Faversham in the nineteenth century, and remained with the earls of Faversham until it was acquired by the Walker Art Gallery at Liverpool in 1956. At least fourteen engraved versions were issued, the earliest of which was by Hogarth and Grignion in 1746.

Garrick was painted, drawn, or engraved as Richard III by at least twenty different artists. The earliest portrait of him in that character seems to be that painted by Thomas Bardwell in 1742; it is now in the Russell-Cotes Art Gallery, Bournemouth.

Francis Hayman's portrait (plate 3) shows Garrick in his middle years, at

Plate 3. Garrick as Richard III, by Hayman. (Photo courtesy of the National Theatre, London)

the age of about forty-three. After Garrick had been a guest speaker at a dinner held by members of the new Society of Artists in June 1759, he was placed on a committee with over thirty persons, including Ramsey, Reynolds, and Hayman, to plan the society's first exhibition. The exhibition opened in April 1760, when Hayman's portrait of Garrick as Richard III became the first of him to be exhibited in public. Hayman had been a scene painter at Goodman's Fields and Drury Lane in the 1740s, and he subsequently became one of the most influential artists of his day. His work is essentially theatrical in nature. He was, as Merchant points out, "a major figure in the transmission of traditional values into the age of Garrick, perpetuating the precise observation of Hogarth and, in his close examination of gesture unobliterated by conventional mannerisms, he carried over into painting the revolution in acting and gesture of which Garrick was the main instrument."[11] For some generations the portrait was owned by descendants of Lord Howe; in 1918 it came into the hands of Somerset Maugham, who subsequently bequeathed it to the National Theatre, where it now hangs.

Yet another portrait of Garrick as Richard III at Bosworth Field is engraved on the subconscious of any Folger reader who makes the daily midafternoon pilgrimage down the steps to the respite of tea and talk—the painting (plate 4) by Nathaniel Dance, a pupil of Hayman. Done about 1769 and exhibited at the Royal Academy in 1771, it shows the mature Garrick, then about fifty-two. The version hanging in the Folger stairway is not the original. The original had been intended for Garrick, but Dance sold it to Sir Watkin Williams-Wynn, who offered the more substantial price of £150. For many years it hung at the Williams-Wynn family residence, No. 20, St. James's Square, in a frame made especially by the brothers Adam. It was sold at Sotheby's in 1947 to the Stratford Corporation for the nominal sum of £55 to replace the Gainsborough of Garrick lost in the fire of December 1946. It still hangs in the Stratford Town Hall council chamber. Three smaller versions or copies are known. The Folger one, presumably, is by Dance; in the Garrick Club is a copy by Henry Morland; and in the National Theatre is a late copy by an inferior artist. There are six different engravings of the original.[12]

Most of the theatrical portraits of Garrick, by Hogarth, Dance, Hayman, and especially Zoffany, are characterized by "their greater fidelity to natural gestures."[13] Consequently, the settings reflect a greater realism: not an absolute fidelity to historical fact and setting—that would come later—but a sweeping away of theatricality in the way that Garrick's new style had swept away Quin's old style when they confronted each other on the stage of Covent Garden in a performance of *The Fair Penitent* one night in the season of 1746–47. "Heavens, what a transition," exclaimed Richard Cumberland in his *Memoirs;* "it seemed as if a whole century had been stept over in the transition of a single scene; old things were done away, and a new

Plate 4. Garrick as Richard III, by Dance. (Photo courtesy of the Folger Shakespeare Library)

order at once brought forward, bright and luminous, and clearly destined to dispel the barbarisms and bigotry of a tasteless age."

Bright and luminous indeed! Witness Hayman's painting of Garrick as Ranger and Mrs. Pritchard as Clarinda in *The Suspicious Husband* (plate 5). It was painted soon after the premiere of Benjamin Hoadly's comedy at Covent Garden on 12 February 1747, during the season in which Cumberland had witnessed the heavenly transition. There were two versions, both by Hayman and both claimed by their present owners to be the original. The one reproduced here is at the Museum of London. The other, slightly larger, is evidently the one painted for Benjamin Hoadly, the play's author; it had been acquired in 1835 by the Garrick Club, where it resided for 135 years until it was sold in 1970 to Paul Mellon; and it now hangs in the Yale Center for British Art. Depicted is the moment in act 4 when Clarinda, who has been flirtatiously accepting the advances of her cousin, unmasks, to the comic dismay of Ranger, who declares in an aside to the audience, "I must brazen it out." Plumb (p. 42) points to this canvas as an early example of a type of theatrical conversation piece that became increasingly popular. The focus is upon a given moment in a specific play, with the figures arranged and deported in about the same poses and expressions as would have been seen in an actual performance on the stage.

Three paintings by Benjamin Wilson bear the stamp of stage authenticity. In 1753, Wilson painted Garrick and Mrs. Bellamy as Romeo and Juliet in the tomb (plate 6). Little is known of the provenance of this canvas except that it was sold to Henry Hoare in November 1757 and recently was owned by the American Shakespeare Festival Theatre at Stratford, Connecticut; it is now owned by Paul Mellon. Two other versions of the *Romeo and Juliet* painting by Wilson exist. One is at Stourhead, Wiltshire (see *Art Bulletin* 47 [1965]: 83–116); the other, sold at Christie's on 3 August 1978 (lot 34), is in a private collection in London. There are three engraved versions, the best being the impressions by S. F. Ravenet in 1753 and 1765. The painting came soon after the victory of Garrick and Mrs. Bellamy at Drury Lane over Barry and Mrs. Cibber at Covent Garden in the famous *Romeo and Juliet* war. That competition lasted twelve consecutive nights and provoked the irritation of the town, as witnessed in a brief poem in the *Daily Advertiser:*

> "Well, what's today," says angry Ned,
>   As up from bed he rouses.
> "Romeo again!" and shakes his head,
>   "Ah, pox on both your houses."

Among Garrick's "improvements" to this play were some sixty-five lines of his own, during which Juliet awakens to take leave of her lover before the poison finally kills him. (Otway had wrought the same change in his *Caius Marius,* but Garrick felt that Otway's lines possessed insufficient "Na-

Plate 5. Garrick as Ranger and Mrs. Pritchard as Clarinda in The Suspicious Husband, *by Hayman.* (Photo courtesy of The Museum of London)

Plate 6. Garrick as Romeo and Mrs. Bellamy as Juliet, engraving by Ravenet, after Wilson. (Photo courtesy of the Folger Shakespeare Library)

ture, Terror, and Distress.") Soon after Juliet awakens, a love duet follows, during which Romeo "brings her from the tomb" out to the graveyard, closer to the audience for Garrick's impressive but prolonged death agonies. From the various accounts of this scene and from Wilson's painting of it, we can deduce the precise manner of staging. As I have written in detail elsewhere, Wilson's painting should be considered a valid rendition of the stage picture, in many ways as useful as a photograph.[14]

About 1760, Wilson painted Garrick as King Lear in the storm, with Astley Bransby as Kent and William Havard as Edgar. The painting is now lost, but its image survives in four prints by different engravers published in 1761 (plate 7). The impact of Garrick's rendering of Lear on the verge of madness was described by Thomas Wilkes:

> I never see him coming down from one corner, with his old grey hair standing, as it were, erect on his head, his face filled with horror and attention, his hands expanded, and his whole frame actuated by a dreadful solemnity, but I am astounded. . . . Methinks I share in his calamities, I feel the dark drifting rain, and the sharp tempest.[15]

Garrick was remarkable in the delicate and gradual revelation of the madness, developing it like the brushing on of a color that flowed from the highest to the darkest tint without delineating shades. For Joseph Pittard the insanity was the portrayal of "Royalty in Lunacy."[16]

Between the years in which Wilson did the *Romeo and Juliet* and *King Lear* canvases, he painted Garrick as Hamlet. The painting is lost, but the engraving by J. McArdell was published by the artist in 1754 (plate 8). Though he had infused his Hamlet with more delicacy and sentimentality than had Betterton, Garrick's Dane was still a man of action. As no writer ever penned a ghost as did Shakespeare, so no actor ever saw a ghost as did Garrick. There are many descriptions of Garrick's first encounter with the specter, including that of a German visitor named Friedrich Gunderode, who saw Garrick, at the age of fifty-seven, play the scene and pronounced him "the greatest and most excellent actor of the century."[17] Fielding's Partridge, you recall, was so startled by the whole ghost business, especially Garrick's reaction, that his knees were set to knocking—"if that little man there upon the stage is not frightened, I never saw any man frightened in my life." Perhaps Garrick did overplay his famous moment. Johnson gibed that such a reaction would surely frighten the ghost. But from the account given by another German traveler, Georg Lichtenberg, it is evident that for all the careful plotting and calculated postures, it must have been a supreme moment:

> Hamlet appears in a black dress, the only one in the whole court. . . . Horatio and Marcellus, in uniform, are with him and they are awaiting the ghost; Hamlet has folded his arms under his cloak and pulled his hat

Plate 7. Garrick as King Lear, engraving by McArdell, after Wilson. (Photo courtesy of the Folger Shakespeare Library)

Plate 8. Garrick as Hamlet, engraving by McArdell, after Wilson. (Photo courtesy of the Folger Shakespeare Library)

down over his eyes; it is a cold night and just twelve o'clock; the theatre is darkened, and the whole audience of some thousands are as quiet, and their faces as motionless, as though they were painted on the walls of the theatre; even from the farthest end of the playhouse one could hear a pin drop. Suddenly, as Hamlet moves toward the back of the stage slightly to the left and turns his back on the audience, Horatio starts, and saying, "Look my lord, it comes," points to the right, where the ghost has already appeared and stands motionless, before anyone is aware of him.

Garrick moved to the left and away from the audience in order to draw attention away from the rising of the ghost.

At these words Garrick turns sharply and at the same moment staggers back two or three paces with his knees giving way under him; his hat falls to the ground and both his arms, especially the left, are stretched out nearly to their full length, with the hands as high as his head, the right arm more bent and the hand lower, and the fingers apart; his mouth is open; thus he stands rooted to the spot, with his legs apart, but no less of dignity, supported by his friends, who are better acquainted with the apparition and fear lest he should collapse. His whole demeanour is so expressive of terror that it made my flesh creep even before he began to speak. The almost terror-struck silence of the audience, which preceded this appearance and filled one with a sense of insecurity, probably did much to enhance this effect. At last he speaks, not at the beginning, but at the end of a breath, with a trembling voice: "Angels and ministers of grace defend us!" words which supply anything this scene may lack and make it one of the greatest and most terrible which will ever be played on any stage.[18]

A painting by Johan Zoffany captures the same moment. In addition to Garrick as Hamlet, it depicts Bransby as the Ghost, Ackman as Marcellus, and either Havard or Packer as Horatio. The painting once belonged to Henry Irving; it is now at the Folger Shakespeare Library (plate 9).

Zoffany, of course, did a series of "theatre conversation pieces" during the period of his life when he made his reputation in England as the principal theatrical painter. Those with Garrick as centerpiece all reveal the great actor's lively personality, on and off the stage. German by birth, Zoffany was in England by 1758 and soon became the assistant of Benjamin Wilson, in whose studio Garrick met him in 1761. Garrick, finding great promise in Zoffany, commissioned him to paint his first theatrical painting in 1762, a scene from *The Farmer's Return,* a comic interlude by Garrick that was first produced at Drury Lane on 20 March 1762 (plate 10). As we see, Garrick's instinct was right again, for Zoffany would record his image for posterity with a skill far greater than that manifested in the paintings by Wilson, who became so jealous, it seems, that Zoffany had to take refuge at Garrick's Hampton villa. In this painting we see Garrick as the farmer, Mary Bradshaw as his wife, and Edward Cape Everard and Ann Heath as the children. After being exhibited at the Society of Artists in May 1762

Plate 9. Garrick as Hamlet, by Zoffany. (Photo courtesy of the Folger Shake-speare Library)

Plate 10. Ann Heath, Edward Cape Everard, David Garrick, and Mary Bradshaw in The Farmer's Return, *engraving by Haid, after Zoffany.* (Photo courtesy of the Enthoven Collection, Victoria and Albert Museum)

(only a few months after the premiere of this play), it was owned by Garrick and hung in the dining room of his house at the Adelphi. The painting was bought for £33 12s. by the earl of Durham at the Garrick sale on 23 June 1823 (lot 43); it is now in the superb collection of Zoffanys owned by Lord Lambton. Replicas are owned by Paul Mellon and Lord Leigh. An engraving by J. G. Haid was published by Boydell in 1766. A contemporary newspaper report described Zoffany's work as "a most accurate representation on canvas of that scene as performed at Drury Lane. The painter absolutely transports us in imagination back again to the theatre. We see our favorite Garrick in the act of [relating a story about the Cock Lane ghost]. . . . And we see the wife and children—and we saw them on the stage—in terror and amazement; such strong likenesses has the painter exhibited of the several performers that played the characters."[19] (A drawing of this same scene rendered by Hogarth is in a private collection; an engraving by J. Basire was published as frontispiece to an edition of Garrick's interlude in 1762.)

Zoffany's portraits of Garrick made the artist's reputation and led to more fashionable commissions. His second theatrical painting, that of Garrick as Jaffeir and Mrs. Cibber as Belvidera in *Venice Preserv'd,* was exhibited at the Society of Artists in 1763 (plate 11). The original version hung alongside *The Farmer's Return* in Garrick's Adelphi dining room and also was purchased, for 25 guineas, for the earl of Durham at the Garrick sale in 1823. It is now in the possession of Lord Lambton. A second version, once owned by Henry Irving, found its way to Somerset Maugham and thence to the National Theatre. Other versions are in the Garrick Club and in the Budapest Museum of Fine Arts.[20] An engraving by McArdell was published in 1764.

Zoffany's painting of the nightwatch scene in *The Provok'd Wife* was commissioned by Garrick and depicts a performance of 18 April 1763, showing Garrick as Sir John Brute, with other Drury Lane actors as the watchmen (plate 12). After having been exhibited at the Society of Artists in 1765, it was issued in a superb engraving by Finlayson in 1768; the engraving was fine enough to be exhibited at the Society of Artists in 1769. The painting hung in the dining parlor of Garrick's villa at Hampton, and was left by him to his trusty brother George. It remained in the family for many years until it was sold in 1929 at Sotheby's by Henry Garrick Trevor, a descendant. Recently it was sold by a dealer to the Wolverhampton Art Gallery. A second version was still in Zoffany's effects in 1811, but it was bought after 1834 by the marquis of Normansby, with whose family it remains.

Although Garrick was not universally acclaimed in the role of Sir John Brute, he had brilliant moments. Many critics preferred Quin's coarse, drink-sodden boor, but Garrick added a dimension to the part that would not have been within the scope of Quin's powers, that of the more subtle and delightfully debauched rakish gentleman. In Vanbrugh's original text the clothes that Sir John steals from the tailor and then puts on as a disguise were those of a clergyman, but in a subsequent version the author converted them to those of a woman of quality, no doubt in deference to Collier. Garrick added the ridiculous headdress inspired by the female fashion of the time. The extent to which the picture reflects in detail what was actually seen on the stage is difficult to assert, but it must be acknowledged that the pictorial composition is excellent for the stage. A single figure of Garrick done by Zoffany as a study for the larger canvas was also owned by Garrick. Eventually it passed from Somerset Maugham to the National Theatre.

In 1766 Zoffany did two splendid paintings of scenes from Garrick's *Lethe.* One of the paintings depicts Astley Bransby as Aesop, William Parsons as the Old Man, and Watkins as John the Servant. It was engraved by John Young in 1788. The other painting, which was not engraved, shows Garrick as Lord Chalkstone, Ellis Ackman as Bowman, and Astley Bransby as Aesop (plate 13).[21] Both canvases were owned by Sir George Beaumont;

Plate 11. Garrick and Mrs. Cibber in Venice Preserv'd, *engraving by McArdell, after Zoffany.* (Photo courtesy of the Harvard Theatre Collection)

Plate 12. Garrick in The Provok'd Wife, *by Zoffany.* (Photo courtesy of the Wolverhampton Art Gallery)

they were exhibited for the first time in 1814, at the British Institution. They remained with the Beaumont Trustees at Coleorton Hall, Leicester, until their sale at Sotheby's on 30 June 1948 to A. Tooth & Sons, from whom in that year they were acquired by the Birmingham City Art Gallery, for £1,850 (with the aid of a grant of £950 from the National Art Collections Fund).

A painting by Zoffany of Garrick and Mrs. Pritchard as the Macbeths, done about 1768, was acquired by the Garrick Club with the Charles Mathews Collection in 1835. Another version, differing in some details and probably the original, was owned by George Keate when an engraving of it by Valentine Green was published in 1776 (plate 14); it is now in the Baroda Museum, India. The painting, probably the most familiar of the artist's theatrical paintings, is not one of Zoffany's better efforts, for it fails to capture the mood of tremulous horror that the two masterful performers created. Tom Davies, who used to play Ross in the Drury Lane production of *Macbeth,* described the awesome moments surrounding the murder of Duncan:

> The beginning of the scene . . . was conducted in terrifying stage whispers. Their looks and actions supplied the place of words. You heard what they spoke, but you learned more from the agitation of the mind displayed in their action and deportment. . . . The dark colouring given by the actor to these abrupt speeches, makes the scene awful and tremendous to the auditors. The wonderful expression of heartful terror, which Garrick felt when he shewed his bloody hands, can only be conceived and described by those who saw him![22]

Zoffany shows Garrick in a frozen but studied posture of fear, with his feet set in ballet-like position and his expressive hands thrown out in front of his body. He is costumed in the traditional Windsor uniform, a scarlet coat, a waistcoat laced with silver, a wig and breeches of contemporary cut. Zoffany makes no attempt to disguise Garrick's small stature. (Garrick wore built-up shoes onstage to make himself taller.) Mrs. Pritchard, also in contemporary dress, points to the double-paneled door, which, open, allows light to be shed into an otherwise darkened hall. The scene bears theatrical validity.[23] Mary Webster points out that the background represents Zoffany's only known attempt "at the Gothick and the sublime," and probably copies the original stage setting, which itself may have been influenced by the publication in 1765 of Walpole's *Castle of Otranto.*[24]

At the Royal Academy in 1770, Zoffany exhibited his scene of *The Alchymist,* which presents Garrick as Abel Drugger, John Palmer (center) as Face, and Edmund Burton as Subtle. Walpole called this excellent canvas "one of the best pictures ever done by this genius." The painting was purchased by Sir Joshua Reynolds for 100 guineas. Lord Carlisle half an hour later offered Reynolds 120 guineas, which he accepted, passing along the profit

Plate 13. Garrick, Ackman, and Bransby in Lethe, *by Zoffany.* (Photo courtesy of the City of Birmingham Art Gallery)

Plate 14. Garrick and Mrs. Pritchard in Macbeth, *engraving by Green, after Zoffany.* (Photo courtesy of the Folger Shakespeare Library)

of 20 guineas to Zoffany. The painting is now at Castle Howard. An engraving by James Dixon was published in 1771. Zoffany (or his studio) also did four portraits of Garrick solo as Abel Drugger (plate 15). Two at the Ashmolean Museum are thought to be studies for the larger picture. A single figure of Garrick is at the Garrick Club, and another is at the Players Club in New York.

Garrick's Abel Drugger was a rich, broad portrayal of extraordinary humor. To comedy he brought a body and limbs of surprising flexibility and elasticity, wonderfully marked features, remarkably expressive eyes, and a mind as quick as his genius. He played with the "exactest Precision, without Buffoonery or Grimace," reported the *London Chronicle* of 5–8 March 1757. "There is no Twisting of Features, no Squinting, but all is as correct as if a real Tobacco Boy were before us. It is really surprising how he . . . can present us such a Face of Inanity." Hannah More, who saw him act both Hamlet and Drugger in the last weeks of his career, exalted, "Had I not seen him in both, I should have thought it as possible for Milton to have written 'Hubidras' and Butler 'Paradise Lost,' as for one man to have played *Hamlet* and *Drugger* with such excellence." In the painting Garrick is shown in act 2, scene 6, holding the pipe of tobacco he has brought to Subtle. His stature is more diminished than in previous renditions by Zoffany. Comic acting is a mercurial and transitory thing, more easily appreciated when seen than when talked about. Zoffany has helped us, I believe, to gain some understanding of the contagious effect of David Garrick's devilish grin.

In May of 1751 Garrick and his wife left for a two-month excursion to Paris, where, like most tourists, they plunged into a round of sightseeing and theatregoing, visiting fifteen palaces and seventeen churches and attending the theatre or opera thirteen times. While in Paris, when not on the run, Garrick sat for his portrait by Jean Liotard. The painting at one time was reported to be at the Burghley Estate, Stamford, Lincolnshire, but it is not there now. A copy, after Liotard, is in Drury Lane Theatre. A pastel of him also done by Liotard in 1751, once at Chiswick House, the home of the Burlingtons, is now at Chatsworth, the home of the Devonshires.

The Garricks returned to the Continent in 1763 for a two-year grand tour. At Rome in March 1764, Garrick sat for a bust by the eccentric English artist Joseph Nollekens, for which the actor paid twelve guineas; he presented it to the Reverend William Arden, whose widow later gave it to Lord Spencer. The bust remains at the Spencer estate, Althorp, Northampton. While abroad, Garrick was also painted at Paris by De Carmontelle, at Rome by Angelica Kaufmann, at Florence by Thomas Patch, and at Venice by Alessandro Longhi. The last painting shows Garrick in a salon at Venice; it has been regularly and erroneously attributed to Hogarth and called *Garrick in the Green Room.*[25] The best work of Garrick done abroad was the portrait painted at Rome in 1764 by Pompeo Batoni (plate 16),

Plate 15. Garrick as Abel Drugger in The Alchemist, *engraving by Dixon, after Zoffany.* (Photo courtesy of the Folger Shakespeare Library)

Plate 16. Garrick, 1764, by Batoni. (Photo courtesy of the Ashmolean Museum, Oxford)

which shows him holding a Vatican edition of Terence's comedies. The portrait is now in the Ashmolean Museum; a copy by an unknown artist is in the Garrick Club.

The great actor also sat for a number of portraits in private character. In the lovely painting by Hogarth in 1757 (plate 17), we see him wearing a somewhat noble smile—quite unlike that of Abel Drugger—as he sits thoughtful over a prologue he is writing for Foote's *Taste,* a satire which had its premiere on 11 January 1752 at Drury Lane.[26] Behind him stands Mrs. Garrick, who is archly attempting to pluck away his pen. Hogarth's theatrical virility saves the painting, as John Hoadly wrote to Joseph Warton on 21 April 1757, from "so much fancy as to be affected or ridiculous and yet enough to raise it from the formal inanity of a mere portrait." Garrick seems not to have liked the painting, and he never paid for it. The canvas remained in Hogarth's studio until after both Hogarth and Garrick had died; then it was given by one widow to the other. It came into the royal collection about 1826 and now is at Windsor Castle.[27]

Garrick's good friend and club colleague Joshua Reynolds did a number of portraits of him—or at least a number are attributed to him and called Garrick. One of the suspect portraits presumes to show Garrick standing, leaning on the shoulder of Mrs. Garrick, who, according to one description, "holds their sleeping daughter on her lap." This painting at one time was in the possession of Mr. T. Grissell, but its present location in unknown; photographs of it are in the Enthoven Collection and the British Museum. The identification of the sitters must be questioned: they do not look much like the Garricks; and the Garricks had no children, a circumstance that Reynolds certainly knew. A sketch of Garrick by Reynolds is in the Harvard Theatre Collection. A painting, the details and provenance of which are unknown to me, is in the collection of Lord Laurence Olivier. A suspect painting by Reynolds, called *Garrick and His Wife,* is at the Victoria and Albert Museum. And a painting attributed to Reynolds, supposedly of Garrick and once owned by Augustin Daly, was bought by Henry Clay Folger in 1924 and hangs in the office of the Friends of the Folger Library.

Four portraits of Garrick can be attributed to Reynolds with certainty. The earliest and among the silliest, the one showing him between Comedy and Tragedy (plate 18), was exhibited at the Society of Artists in 1762. As Walpole described it, "Tragedy exhorts him to follow her exalted vocation, but Comedy drags him away and he seems to yield willingly, though endeavoring to excuse himself and pleading that he is forced." This picture was bought from Reynolds by Garrick's neighbor, the second earl of Halifax. It is now owned by Lord Rothschild. Smaller copies after Reynolds, by unknown artists, are at the National Theatre and the Garrick Club, and several others float around. Numerous engravings were done, at least ten different versions. In 1766 George Colman wrote from Paris to tell Garrick that "There hangs out here, in every street, pirated prints of

Plate 17. David and Eva Maria Garrick, 1757, by Hogarth. (By gracious permission of Her Majesty Queen Elizabeth II)

Plate 18. Garrick between Comedy and Tragedy, engraving by Corbutt, after Reynolds. (Photo courtesy of the Harvard Theatre Collection)

Reynolds's picture of you, which are underwritten 'L'Homme entre le Vice et le Virtu.'"

In 1768 Reynolds painted Garrick as Kitely in *Every Man in His Humour* (plate 19). As fine as it is, this rendering cannot be regarded as a character portrait in the theatrical tradition of Hogarth, Hayman, Wilson, or Zoffany. The portrait is now in the collection of Her Majesty, at Windsor. A copy, after Reynolds, is in the National Portrait Gallery.

Reynolds's portrait of Garrick reading to his wife, on a garden seat, was exhibited at the Royal Academy in 1773. It is now owned, I understand, by Major General E. H. Goulburn.[28]

Reynolds's portrait of Garrick seated at a table, hands clasped and resting on a paper inscribed "Prologue" (plate 20), was commissioned by Mrs. Thrale and exhibited at the Royal Academy in 1776. I do not know the location of the original, but in 1865 it was in the possession of the descendants of Dr. Burney, who had bought it in the Piozzi sale for 175 guineas. There are two other versions by Reynolds, one at Knole and the other at the Folger, and at least six copies after Reynolds exist, including examples at the Folger, the Garrick Club, and the National Portrait Gallery. Some nineteen engraved versions are known.

At least four portraits by the other great master of English portraiture in

Plate 19. Garrick as Kitely in Every Man in His Humour, *by Reynolds.* (By gracious permission of Her Majesty Queen Elizabeth II)

Plate 20. Garrick, 1776, by Reynolds. (Photo courtesy of the Folger Shake-speare Library)

the eighteenth century, Thomas Gainsborough, are known, but I can deal now, and briefly, with only two.[29]

In 1767, Stratford began to erect a new town hall. When the burgesses requested Garrick to send "some statue, bust or picture" of Shakespeare along with a portrait of himself to be placed in the new building, "that the memory of both may be perpetually together," little did they know what would result: the Jubilee of 1769, which was almost wholly the invention of David Garrick. Nor could they have imagined in their wildest nightmares that they were planting a seed that 200 years later would rise on their meadow in the shape of a Hilton hotel. The statue of Shakespeare done by John Cheere was presented by Garrick to the town. Gainsborough was commissioned to paint the portrait of Garrick. The artist reworked a picture which he had exhibited at the Royal Academy in 1766, and was paid £63 by the Corporation. That portrait, which Mrs. Garrick thought was the best likeness of her husband, hung in Stratford Town Hall until it was destroyed by the fire of 5 December 1946. The statue of Shakespeare, made of sturdier stuff, endured and still is there. But a version of Gainsborough's portrait survives in Valentine Green's engraving (plate 21) and in a terrible copy painted by John Hoppner that is at the Folger.

In 1770, a truly fine portrait of Garrick by Gainsborough was exhibited at the Royal Academy and was bought by the sitter (plate 22). Subsequently it was owned by Albany Wallis, Garrick's executor, and then in the early twentieth century became the property of Lady Swinton at Swinton Park. In 1975, it came into the collection of the National Portrait Gallery. An autographed copy was painted by Gainsborough for James Clutterbuck and eventually found its way through the family to Tockenham Manor. A second autographed copy was painted for Dr. Ralph Schomberg, Garrick's physician, and after several sales over the years settled in the Mellon Collection.

By 1752, having enjoyed five very rewarding seasons of management at Drury Lane, Garrick became ambitious to acquire a country seat, quite natural in a gentleman of refined tastes and expanding income and social horizons, living in a golden age of power and privilege. He wrote to his brother Peter, "I love a good Situation prodigiously, & I think the four great Requisites to make one are, Wood, Water, Extent, & inequality of ground"—and, he added, he "must have a River." So in January 1754 he rented a large yellow-brick house on several acres of ground at Hampton, thirteen miles from Drury Lane. In August of that year he bought the property and began making improvements that eventually included a new white Palladian front by Robert Adam, tasteful gardens in the new style by Capability Brown, and the classical riverside temple to Shakespeare (plate 23). It was to be his retreat for the next twenty-five years and to provoke Samuel Johnson to sigh when he saw it: "Ah, David! It is the leaving of such a place that makes a death-bed terrible."

Plate 21. Garrick with the Bust of Shakespeare, 1769 (the Stratford picture), engraving by Green, after Gainsborough. (Photo courtesy of the Folger Shakespeare Library)

Plate 22. Garrick, 1770, by Gainsborough. (Photo courtesy of the National Portrait Gallery, London)

Plate 23. Garrick's estate at Hampton, engraving by Stradler, after Farington.
(Photo courtesy of the Harvard Theatre Collection)

At Hampton, recalled Letitia Hawkins, "Mr. and Mrs. Garrick took the rank of *noblesse;*—his highly-finished manners, and his lady's elegance of taste, making their house and themselves very attractive" to an incessant stream of visitors. On 7 September 1770 the *Gazetteer* reported that "Mr. Garrick has given two Silver Cups, to be played for at Cricket, between Chertsey and Hampton—on Moulsey Hurst." Up and down the river he was entertained by such folks as General Conway and Lady Hilesbury, at Park Place, near Henley. The Garricks, in return, entertained frequently at Hampton. On 20 August 1774 they gave a splendid *fête champêtre* in celebration of their twenty-fifth wedding anniversary. The eminent pyrotechnist Morel Torré conducted "a most brilliant fire-work," there was an "elegant concert of music," then the "Temple of Shakespeare, and gardens, were illuminated with 6000 lamps, and the forge of Vulcan made a splendid appearance,"[30] to the utmost satisfaction of a great number of nobility and gentry.

In two splendid paintings, Zoffany shows the Garricks at Hampton in more subdued leisure. Both paintings were owned by Garrick and then by his widow. The were purchased in the 1823 Garrick sale at Christie's for a total of £77 14s. for the earl of Durham and have been passed down to the present owner, Lord Lambton.

The first (plate 24), painted about 1762, shows Garrick with his wife on the steps of the Shakespeare Temple, with two dogs, a boy (probably his nephew Carrington Garrick, brother George's eldest son), a servant coming on with tea, and a view of the reach of the river.[31] The painter has carried over the manner of his stage groupings into the "private" repertoire. This technique of freezing characters into a tableau at a particular "moment of animation" is beautifully seen in the painting by Zoffany, done about 1765, of the Garricks taking tea on their lawn (plate 25). The clergyman is identified as George Bodens, the angler is George Garrick, the faithful but lackluster brother, and the standing figure is Charles Hart, the family butler. Simon Schama's description of the scene (conjured up in his *TLS* review on 14 January 1977 of the Zoffany exhibition at Carlton House that year) is appropriately picturesque and languid:

> The great man is surrounded by the visible emblems of worldly success. His immaculately dressed actress wife sits beside him at the elegant table; brother George fishes . . . and is being beckoned by Garrick to take a dish of tea, King Charles spaniels loll; the willow droops, a puffball cloud hangs in the sky. Nature is ordered, domesticated and benign. Yet a moment's lingering produces a more curious and disconcerting impression. The figures are grouped with studied carefulness in the midground, rather as though Zoffany had mustered them behind the footlights. . . . The painting has a remarkable tableau-like quality in which figures and objects have been frozen at one particular moment of animation and have been transformed by the artist into an aesthetic arrangement.

Something of a masterpiece, this work is especially evocative. It is the epitome of the conversation piece—that fusion of Arcadian metaphor with naturalness, tinged with a glow of sensibility—that made the stage an extension of real life. It is the visual statement of the mental framework through which, according to Wylie Sypher, each era explains and orders its experience, the key modality of the age, the order and balance of Newtonian physics, the concerto, or the landscape gardening of Capability Brown. It is the image of contemporary enthusiasm for the good life, a sort of unnatural naturalness, an aesthetic existence, handsome, tranquil, free of sordidness or conflict. If the ascension painting by George Carter, with which I began these remarks, is a manifestation of the kind of apotheosis that Garrick might have dreamed was his due *after* his death, then surely Zoffany's canvas is a representation of Garrick's heavenly existence on earth. Painted a decade before Jefferson's Declaration established the pursuit of happiness as a natural right, and thus began the American Dream, this scene of Garrick taking tea by his peaceful river, surrounded by "the visible emblems of worldly success," declares to Georgian Britain that he had achieved the English dream.

Plate 24. The Garricks on the Steps of the Shakespeare Temple at Hampton, ca. 1762, by Zoffany. (Photo courtesy of Lord Lambton)

Plate 25. The Garricks taking tea upon their lawn at Hampton, ca. 1765, by Zoffany. (Photo courtesy of Lord Lambton)

Notes

1. J. H. Plumb, *The Pursuit of Happiness. A View of Life in Georgian Britain* (New Haven, Conn.: Yale Center for British Art, 1977), p. 28.

2. Ibid., pp. 14–23.

3. Ibid., p. 15.

4. Iain Mackintosh, introduction, *The Georgian Playhouse.*

5. W. Moelwyn Merchant, *Shakespeare and the Artist* (London: Oxford University Press, 1959), pp. 44–45.

6. William Hogarth, "Autobiographical Notes," in *The Analysis of Beauty* ed. Joseph Burke (Oxford: Clarendon Press, 1955), pp. 209–11.

7. *The Letters of David Garrick*, ed. David M. Little and George M. Kahrl, 3 vols. (Cambridge, Mass.: Harvard University Press, 1963),1:28.

8. Thomas Davies, *Memoirs of the Life of David Garrick*, 2 vols, (London: Longman, Hurst, Rees, and Orme, 1808), 1:44.

9. *The Letters of David Garrick*, 1:31.

10. Hogarth, p. 213. See also Ronald Paulson, *Hogarth: His Life, Art, and Times* (New Haven, Conn.: Yale University Press, 1971), 2:22–31.

11. Merchant, p. 46.

12. For a discussion of the several versions, see Raymond Mander and Joseph Mitchenson, *The Artist and the Theatre* (London: William Hinnemann Ltd., 1955), pp. 181–85.

13. Merchant, pp. 59–65, treats the congruity of settings with the new attitude toward character that was stimulated by Garrick.

14. K. A. Burnim, *David Garrick Director* (1961; rpt. Carbondale, Ill.: Southern Illinois University Press, 1973), pp. 137–38. The influence of Wilson's *Romeo and Juliet* painting on the work of Joseph Wright of Derby is treated by Lance Bertelsen in "David Garrick and English Painting," *Eighteenth Century Studies* 11 (1978): 308–24.

15. Thomas Wilkes, *A General View of the Stage* (London: J. Coote, 1759), pp. 234–35.

16. Joseph Pittard, *Observations on Mr. Garrick's Acting* (London: J. Cooke and J. Coote, 1758), pp. 14–18.

17. Cited by John Alexander Kelly, *German Visitors to English Theatres in the Eighteenth Century* (Princeton N.J.: Princeton University Press, 1936), p. 61.

18. *Lichtenberg's Visits to England,* as described in his letters and diaries translated by Margaret L. Mare and W. H. Quarrell (Oxford: Clarendon Press, 1938), p. 9.

19. Cited by Mary Webster in *Johann Zoffany,* the catalogue of the exhibition held by the National Portrait Gallery at Carlton House, 14 January–27 March 1977. In her introduction, Webster discusses the "conversation" or "family piece."

20. For a discussion of the several versions see Mander and Mitchenson, pp. 5–11.

21. An inferior version, probably by a copyist, of the painting that shows Garrick was given by Somerset Maugham to the National Theatre. Zoffany also painted two versions of Garrick solo as Lord Chalkstone as studies for the larger group. The original, exhibited at the Society of Artists in 1766, belonged to Garrick and now is owned by W. R. Hearst; the other is at the Garrick Club.

22. Thomas Davies, *Dramatic Miscellanies*, 3 vols. (London: printed for the author, 1784), 2:93–94.

23. See Burnim, *David Garrick Director*, p. 114.

24. Webster, p. 45.

25. The painting's present curator at the Lady Lever Art Gallery, Port Sunlight, questions the identification of the main subject as Garrick. An engraving by W. J. Ward, with the title *Garrick in the Green Room* and with a key plate by G. Daniels that erroneously identifies the English actors presumed to be present, was published in 1829.

26. In his prompter's diary on that night Richard Cross wrote, "Mr. Garrick spoke y^c

Prologue in the Character of an Auctioneer, with surprising Applause" (Manuscript in Folger Shakespeare Library).

27. Bertelsen (pp. 312–16) points out the relationship of this portrait to the principles Hogarth set forth in *The Analysis of Beauty* (1753), calling it "a positive as well as negative aesthetic statement."

28. The portrait is reproduced in *The Letters of David Garrick*, 3:1104.

29. The two not discussed here are: one engraved by W. Boucher for a plate to Knight's *Life of Garrick* (1894), the present location of the original unknown; and the sketch offered in the Burdett Coutts sale at Sotheby's, 16–17 May 1922, present owner unknown.

30. *London Chronicle*, 18–20 August 1774.

31. Another version, owned by the Dowager Lady Mickelham of Strawberry Hill, was sold at Scott and Fowler's, New York, on 28 May 1923; it was offered for sale at Sotheby's on 21 March 1979.

11

Theatre and the Art of Caricature

LEO HUGHES

> Daumier was but one of several men recruited by
> Philipon from among the talented but impecuni-
> ous. . . . Of necessity the squad took over the inherited
> stock-in-trade of their profession—the symbolic type-
> character whose antics embody the moral or political
> behavior of a whole class, the *portrait-charge* whose
> irregularities of feature were cleverly overstressed.
> OLIVER W. LARKIN, *Daumier: Man of His Time*[1]

Any reversion to the practice, so popular in the eighteenth century, of
celebrating "The Union of the Three Sister Arts"[2] must necessarily begin
with some theoretical considerations. I propose to confine my theorizing to
the problem of definition, in the most literal sense of drawing some rigid
limitations. If I allow myself the broad definition of *caricature* (*portrait-
charge*) that Professor Larkin uses, quite correctly, in treating the great
nineteenth-century French graphic satirist, I shall require at least a sizable
tome, which is not at my disposal. The "symbolic type-character" *is* the
dominant figure in much of English comedy in any age. Recall the observations of Abbé le Blanc, made, ironically enough, in the very year I shall
single out as the high point of English stage caricature, 1737: "The English,
if you'll permit me to use a term of painting which can only express my
idea, love caricaturas: they are more struck with a large face and great nose
designed by Callot than with a noble and graceful countenance trac'd by
Corregio's pencil. For this reason their comic characters are more over-
strain'd than ours."[3] The French observer was attending the Little Haymarket, among other places, at the height—and the unforeseen end—of Henry
Fielding's theatrical activities, but what he says might apply as well to Ben

Jonson or Thomas Shadwell or, for most of their plays, to William Congreve or R. B. Sheridan.

To find a more manageable range of observation I return for a moment to the useful French term *portrait chargé* or to the Italian term *caricatura*. In the work of the almost legendary Pier-Leone Ghezzi, for example, the picture is of an *individual* whose features may be overdrawn, to be sure, but not beyond recognition.[4] It is a *portrait* even though it is a *loaded* one, to keep the meaning of the Italian root or the French attributive. In *Art and Illusion* Gombrich says, in his brief remarks on a Swiss caricaturist, "Rambling at a leisurely pace through the fields of aesthetics, Töpffer comes to insist increasingly on the conventional character of all artistic signs and concludes that the essence of art is not imitation but expression."[5] This dictum applies with special weight to dramatic art, particularly in that form of play which most nearly resembles graphic caricature. The admittedly brief list of playwrights I treat here have something to *say*, often violent, almost always disapproving, about particular persons who in their view represent a clear and present danger to society. The picture may be so *expressive* as to defy recognition, especially in the judgment of the victim, but it must provide some semblance of a likeness if it is to have any effect.

Limiting the scope of my treatment in a sharply different way, I propose to concentrate on the decades of the mid-eighteenth century, beginning with the banner year of English satire, 1728. It would be unconscionable, however, for me to ignore entirely the years leading up to that point. So vigorous a period, both in and out of the theatre, could hardly miss doing burlesque and caricature, as several plays witness. Robert Howard treats in crude mockery in *The Committee* (1662) the Puritans who had been in charge of English affairs before 1660. John Wilson's *Cheats* (1663) was acted briefly and then suppressed by royal order. Thomas Shadwell's first play, *The Sullen Lovers* (1668), was allowed to run even though it caricatured Robert Howard as Sir Positive At-all in highly amusing fashion; evidently no person in power felt that any injustice was done the knight. Shadwell did encounter trouble later in such heavily satirical plays as *The Lancashire Witches* (1681). But an anti-Whig play such as Crowne's *City Politiques,* attacking Shaftesbury, seemed perfectly wholesome to the Stuarts.

The one play that must not be passed over in silence has nothing to do with politics but is devoted to burlesquing the new venture into heroic drama led by Dryden, Robert Howard, Davenant, and others—*The Rehearsal* (1671). It seems unlikely that the group who produced the play had any idea of what they were achieving, which was nothing short of a paradigm for generations to follow. The rehearsal form allowed them to put extra distance between audience and play, with the two critical commentators and the author in the center foreground. Unlike the rest, who have tag names, the commentators in *The Rehearsal* have generic names, Smith and Johnson, so that audience identification with them is virtually guaranteed.

The contents of the play do follow the *portrait chargé* tradition. The bombastic speeches, the pretentious manners, the swagger—all sound, if somewhat remotely, like the heroic drama being imitated. The frenetic search after the "new"—a word frequently repeated—caricatures an attitude that all conservative spectators see in what we today call "experimental" drama. And, finally, there is the addition of material that really has no share in a likeness but is piled on with the merest intent to ridicule: the slapstick, the use of local place names guaranteed to raise laughter in such a context, Brentford, Acton, Twick'nam, Piccadillé.

By the time the play was ready for its first performance the principal target, Bayes, had undergone at least two shifts in identity, so that knowledgeable spectators could recognize under the guise of the current laureate, John Dryden, some features of both Robert Howard and William Davenant. By the time it had reached a third edition, in 1674, it had undergone considerable expansion. In its long run through much of the next century—Hogan gives a performance as late as 1792—it underwent numerous topical additions and deletions.

It would be difficult to find a year more nearly approaching a satirical millenium than 1728, or so it must have seemed to the Scriblerus group. Swift had already set a fast pace for his confederates two years earlier in his masterful mock utopia. Pope was to issue his poetic attack on the dunces—whose name was legion—in May of 1728. By then the third member of the triumvirate had scored his great triumph, by means of the stage: on Monday, 29 January *The Beggar's Opera* began its record shattering run at Lincoln's Inn Fields. Fortunately the story of this triumph is so well documented that I need do little more than call attention to a few salient features of the play as a work of burlesque or stage caricature. John Gay's great inspiration was in his design: the highly clever double reversal of norms by which he seems at first glance to be indulging in a simple travesty in which underworld characters ape the "quality," but which on closer inspection reveals the quality stripped of their masks, behaving like the underworld or even worse. "What business hath [Macheath] to keep company with lords and gentlemen? He should leave them to prey upon one another." "Why, thou foolish jade, thou wilt be as ill used, and as much neglected, as if thou hadst married a lord!" And so on and on for three rich and full acts, with songs of the same ironic sort, fresh in their tenor but set to familiar tunes.

I do need to revert to one story, the well-documented account of the audience's behavior on the first night, as Pope told it to Spence, for in the theatre uniquely the perceptiveness, growing even into participation, of the audience is of utmost importance. On this night the novel offering proved baffling at the start, but before the first act was over the spectators began to get the drift of things. By the end—at least before the end of the long first run—they were quite possibly seeing meanings beyond those Gay had intended. For, though the basic design was to present *generalized* social satire, there was satire of particular persons[6] here, too, and of persons of the highest social and political rank. The first note is sounded in the third scene, where Peachum studies "a register of the gang," winding up with "Robin of Bagshot, alias Gorgon, alias Bob Bluff, alias Carbuncle, alias Bob Booty." Given the obvious double and triple meanings scattered throughout, the audience could hardly have helped gathering from this litany of aliases that a very high-placed Bob, indeed their prime minister, was the target. And when, in the second act, Peachum and Lockit, scoundrels both, quarrel over their misdeeds, the audience would have ventured another step and managed to see a parallel with the notorious quarrel between Walpole and Townshend. They would have been prompted even further at this juncture by Lockit's song:

> When you censure the age
> Be cautious and sage,
> Lest the courtiers offended should be.
> If you mention vice or bribe,
> 'Tis so pat to all the tribe;
> Each cries—That was levell'd at me.

In the long run, perhaps the device that proved most useful was the "great man" theme, which was to appear repeatedly in later dramatic and graphic satire. The play begins with a solo by Peachum—fence, informer, thief taker—stressing man's wolfish behavior toward his fellows, a song closing with two lines setting the moral tone of the play:

> And the statesman, because he's so great,
> Thinks his trade as honest as mine.

A few brief scenes later Mrs. Peachum—it will soon be disclosed that her title as wife to the exemplary Peachum is as bogus as nearly everything else in the play—gives some motherly advice to the boy Filch, already an accomplished pickpocket: "If an unlucky session does not cut the rope of thy life, I pronounce, boy, thou wilt be a great man in history." And so "greatness" is sounded over and over until the label by a form of prescription has become the exclusive property of Walpole. Plate 25 in the first volume of M. Dorothy George's *English Political Caricature* shows an engraving by George Bickham dated 1740 entitled *The Stature of a Great Man or the English Colossus.* Beneath the figure of a gigantic English gentleman in full wig, wearing the insignia of knighthood, appears in small but quite distinct type "Sir R. Walpole," and, under the title, lines 135–41 of Cassius's speech in *Julius Caesar,* 1. 2.

> Why, man, he doth bestride the narrow world like a Colossus,
> And we petty men walk under his huge legs and peep about

To find ourselves dishonourable graves. Men at some time are
Masters of their fates: the fault, dear Brutus, is not in our
Stars, but in ourselves, that we are underlings.[7]

In the triumph of Gay's piece we must not overlook the quiet arrival on
the London scene in January 1728 of a figure who was to prove in time
more important in stage caricature than Gay. According to W. L. Cross,[8]
young Henry Fielding came up at this time from the West Country to
arrange for the publication of his first poem, *The Masquerade,* and to see
about his first play, *Love in Several Masques,* which had been accepted by
Drury Lane but was forced to wait for a break in the successful first run of
Cibber's *Provok'd Husband.* Neither the poem nor the play requires any
extensive treatment here; I wish merely to call attention to the pseudonym
on the title page of the former, "Lemuel Gulliver, Poet Laureat to the King
of Lilliput," and to stress the point that this first work of a professed
follower of the Scriblerians is aimed at a particular person, the inscription,
also on the title page, being to a certain "C——T H——D——G——R,"
which Fielding could confidently expect the public to recognize as Count
Heidegger, Swiss impresario currently in charge of the masquerades alter-
nating with operas at the King's Theatre in the Haymarket.

Neither Fielding's first play nor his second, *The Temple Beau,* performed
almost two years later at the newly opened Goodman's Fields, has any
interest for us in the present context. His third, *The Author's Farce,* performed 30 April 1730 at still another house, the Little Haymarket, is quite
another matter. By using a variant pseudonym, Scriblerus Secundus, the
playwright declared his intention of following in the path opened by Gay.
Like *The Beggar's Opera, The Author's Farce* is a ballad opera, in part at least,
employing old tunes to new—and topical—words. Also like *The Beggar's
Opera,* it uses burlesque, chiefly in the "puppet play," which provided the
subtitle, *The Pleasures of the Town.* Like Gay, Fielding combines general
satire with satire on recognizable individuals, although in this early version
the likenesses are shadowy, as indeed they were in Gay's opera. All are
connected to the London world of entertainment, chiefly theatrical. Two of
the Drury Lane triumvirate appear: Cibber as Marplay, Wilks as Sparkish.
Casting Wilks as Sparkish is not really satirical but is only meant to identify
him with a comedy-of-manners role.

But even Cibber is only mildly satirized. There is a hint of his noted
arrogance in the choice, and rejection, of plays. His name, Marplay, is not
to be misconstrued by us; Cibber has not yet ventured into his more ambitious revision of Shakespeare in *King John,* although his recent disaster in
imitating Shakespeare, *Caesar in Egypt,* is mentioned. The marring has to
do with what the young author considers the inept revisions forced upon
plays submitted for performance. There are even murkier references to
publishers. Bookweight, who appears in act 1 presiding over his crew of

wretched hack writers, could be almost anyone, but Curry, the bookseller in act 3, is usually thought to be the notorious Curll. Monsieur Pantomime is almost certain to be John Rich, recently prospering from *The Beggar's Opera* and, more important for Fielding's purposes, such pantomimic successes as *Perseus and Andromeda,* the newest hit, which had for weeks been the chief attraction although serving as afterpiece to such farcical bits as *The Anatomist, The Country House,* or *The Cheats of Scapin.*

In its earliest phase, *The Author's Farce* is important only in that it revealed to the young Fielding what his proper métier was. After a few seasons of successful practice with similar pieces, especially *Tom Thumb,*[9] he revamped his first burlesque, greatly expanding and pointing up the satire on individuals. Marplay is still there, but he has been transformed into Marplay senior, now poet laureate and therefore composer of odes. There is, of course, a Marplay junior (Theophilus Cibber) who, because of his recent activities as a leader of the actors' revolt at Drury Lane, gets more attention than his father. He replaces Sparkish, Wilks now being dead, in the scene of revising and then rejecting poor Luckless's play, and he shares a brand-new scene, easily the best in the play, with his father, in which the elder Marplay teaches the younger some of the arcana of success. One exchange will serve as a sample. After the father has scornfully refused to consider the wishes of the audience and threatens to cram plays rejected by them down their throats—

> MAR. JUN.: I wish, Father, you wou'd leave me that for a Legacy, since I am afraid I am like to have no other from you.
> MAR. SEN.: 'Tis Buff, Child, 'tis Buff—True Corinthian Brass: And Heav'n be prais'd tho' I have giv'n thee no gold, I have giv'n thee enough of that, which is the better inheritance of the two.

No London theatregoer of the least sophistication could fail to recognize the heavily charged likeness here, particularly in the light of recent events involving the Cibbers and in view of the full treatment accorded both father and son in satire of all forms, literary, theatrical, and graphic. *The Author's Farce* at its first appearance had been too early in the year 1730 to capitalize on the amazing choice of a new poet laureate, that event coming toward the end of the year. But other satirists had responded at once. On 30 November 1730 the Little Haymarket offered a bill composed of two plays by Fielding, *The Coffee-House Politician* and *Tom Thumb,* "also *The Battle of the Poets; or, The Contention for the Laurel.*" Although this short-lived piece professes on its title page to be the work of Scriblerus Tertius (possibly Thomas Cooke), although it was attached to his plays, Fielding announced in the *Daily Journal* that he had no responsibility for it.[10]

By the time Fielding saw fit to revise *The Author's Farce,* the younger Cibber had come into even greater notoriety than his father. The latter had sold his share in the Drury Lane patent to a wealthy Mr. Highmore, but the purchaser was eventually obliged to use force to gain possession of his new property, at which point Theophilus instigated a revolt among the actors and drew a good part of the company into a proposed move to the Little Haymarket. Immediately there was a great war in the newspapers, some commentators siding with the rebels, the more violent ones opposing them, or rather young Cibber, for, as one correspondent to *The Craftsman* of 9 June puts it, "Picking a gentleman's pocket of six thousand pounds is [not] perfectly consistent with the principles of liberty."[11] Before Theophilus could get his troupe together, "a gentleman late of Trinity-College, Cambridge," usually identified as Edward Phillips, brought out at Covent Garden on 27 July a dramatic caricature entitled *The Stage-Mutineers; or, A Playhouse to be Let,* with this interesting observation in the prologue:

> Long to our sight the stage has partial shown
> Some fools of all professions—but their own;
> Long has she laugh'd at follies of the age—
> Laugh, in your turn, at follies of the stage.

The principal target here is the leader of the mutiny, a certain Pistol, who comes swaggering onstage spouting such heroic bits as "Bid pamper'd Jades of Asia, etc." If such rhetorical flourishes have a familiar ring to us, they were even more familiar to the audience of 1733, for by this time the role of Pistol in *Henry IV*, Part 2, had become something of a property of Theophilus Cibber. When the latter finally did get his recruits assembled it was late summer and time for the annual fairs. On Thursday, 23 August, Bartholomew Fair opened with no fewer than six theatrical booths, one of which was the "Cibber-Griffin-Bullock-Hallam Booth by Hosier Lane," all the listed proprietors being members of the mutiny. By 4 September they were playing *Tamerlane* plus *The Comical Humours of Sir John Falstaff, Justice Shallow, Ancient Pistol and Others,* with Cibber as Pistol, plus *The Riddoto al Fresco,* subtitle to Theophilus's new *Harlot's Progress.*

By this time the graphic satirists of the day had also begun to focus on young Cibber. In July, Rich's scene painter Laguerre published a caricature called *The Stage Mutiny,* in anticipation of the performance of Phillips's play. A scene of the confrontation of the two factions from rival theatres, the print gives prominence to both Cibbers: Theophilus swaggers in the foreground as Pistol; Colley sits down front, wearing the laurel wreath and clutching his money bags, as he smugly gestures toward the contestants.[12]

In the fall of 1733 Hogarth, doubtless amused by these petty theatrical wars, made use of Laguerre's caricature by copying it as the showcloth to be hung over a booth, labeled "Cibber and Bullock," in his famous *Southwark Fair.* The particular booth is just in the midst of collapsing, the players in all their gawdy finery headed for disaster. The topical comment is not hard to grasp: the playbill reads *The Fall of Bajazet,* the subtitle of *Tamerlane,* in which Theophilus had been playing Bajazet. To single out the proper targets, Hogarth adds a legend under the portrait of Theophilus, "Pistol[s] alive," and under Colley, "Quiet and Snug."

Fielding might well have continued his attack on his theatrical enemies or rivals with impunity for decades, for neither the Cibbers nor Rich had the power or the disposition to retaliate. He did in fact keep up his gibing, especially in 1736 and 1737 in *Pasquin, The Historical Register, Eurydice,* and *Tumble-down Dick,* this last being dedicated, ironically, to "John Lun, vulgarly called Esquire."[13] *Pasquin,* "a dramatic satire on the times: being the rehearsal of two plays, viz., a comedy called *The Election* and a tragedy called *The Life and Death of Common-Sense,*" first appearing at the Little Haymarket on 5 March 1736, still keeps up the banter at Rich, whose "entertainments" are designed, according to our playwright, to drive Queen Commonsense and her followers, such as Shakespeare and Ben Jonson, from the stage and install in their place Queen Ignorance and her followers, Harlequin and Squeekaronelly—that is, pantomime, represented by Rich, and opera, represented by the castrato Farinelli. Cibber appears in the most indirect fashion and in connection with the political part of the satire, the part that was to prove the great attraction of *Pasquin,* and Fielding's ultimate undoing. A scene in the second act shows us Lord Place and Colonel Promise bribing voters, one of whom would like a place at court, for he loves fine clothes and sack:

> LORD PLACE: Sack, say you? Odso, you shall be poet-laureat.
> 2 VOTER: Poet! No, my Lord, I am no poet, I can't make verses.
> LORD PLACE: No matter for that,—you'll be able to make odes.
> 2 VOTER: Odes, my Lord! What are those?
> LORD PLACE: Faith, sir, I can't tell well what they are; but I know you may be qualified for the place without being a poet.[14]

The play is heavily charged with precisely those traits to which the opposition, to which Fielding adhered, had been relentlessly calling attention: the use of state money to propagandize by the free distribution of the party journal, *The Daily Gazetteer;* the buying of offices by bribery; the corruption of the leaders; and the submissiveness of the followers, of whom Cibber would represent a prime example (for as early as 1717 the future laureate had shown his loyalty to the establishment by writing *The Nonjuror*). Now he was reaping his reward, the laurel crown, the generous stipend, the annual butt of sack.

The triumph of *Pasquin,* which ran for weeks at the Haymarket and even appeared at the fairs, exhilarated Fielding to the danger point. By March 1737 he was ready with a new piece, *The Historical Register for the year 1736.* Although the title suggests a sprawling plot and Fielding's persona, Medley, professes scorn for the unities, this piece is far more concise than *Pasquin* and far more incisive. It proved in the event to be devastating, more devastating to the playwright and to English stage satire in general than to its target.

Just half the length of *Pasquin*, Fielding's new play makes every sentence count as it resumes its attack on several old enemies and adds some new ones. The Cibbers are back but under new names. The laureate, now named Ground-Ivy, appears before Apollo, who is casting parts for a revival of *King John*. Cibber objects to the choice of play: "No, sir. Shakespear was a pretty fellow, and said some things which only want a little of my licking to do well enough; King John, as now writ, will not do—But a word in your ear, I will make him do." He is equally arrogant about his ability as an actor but no more so than his son Pistol, who has now moved on to other business. He is leading a mob of associates again, but this time his project is to thrust his wife, Susanna, into the role of Polly in *The Beggar's Opera,* a role commonly thought to be the property of Kitty Clive.[15] Having allowed the younger Cibber to posture and orate for a long scene, Medley dismisses him in summary fashion: "My lord, Pistol is every insignificant fellow in town. . . . Come, go on."

The "every insignificant fellow"—taking us back to our epigraph on Philipon and his recruits—suggests some of the less individualized caricature early in the play. Again Fielding is using the rehearsal format, with Medley offering two critical friends a preview of his play, the friends also serving as satiric types: Sourwit, the pattern of critical surliness and faultfinding, and Lord Dapper, who represents the spoiled young aristocrat. Lord Dapper is unable to pay sustained attention to the play, insisting that "one does not go to see the play but the company." In the auction scene that follows, Fielding confuses the names of his characters by having the auctioneer knock down an "Interest at Court" to an otherwise unidentified "Beau," who turns out also to be called Mr. Littlewit—none other than Lord Dapper. Mention of an auction leads us to the auctioneer, Mr. Hen, whom Fielding could count on everyone's recognizing as Christopher Cock, proprietor of the fashionable auction room.[16] Both Fielding and Hogarth quite sensibly recognized Cock as not the cause but merely the symptom of certain social follies. The playwright is here using the device of an auction, within the even more established device of a rehearsal, to assure maximum exposure of frivolities. Mr. Hen's Lots 5 and 6 illustrate the range of targets: "All the wit belonging to Mr. Hugh Pantomime, composer of entertainments for the playhouses [presumably Theobald; Rich will appear at the very end of the play as 'the great Lun'], and Mr. William Goosequil, composer of political papers in defense of a ministry."

The allusion to *a* ministry brings us to the political leitmotiv of the play. *Pasquin* shows Fielding employing only casually Gay's "great-man" theme; *The Historical Register* rings the changes, although not with quite the vigor Fielding will employ in the next decade in *Jonathan Wild.* The very first scene of the play within a play is set in Corsica, where "the greatest men" are in charge of the state, "for you may be sure all well-regulated governments . . . will employ in their greatest posts men of the greatest capacities." Four of the five participants in the conclave are engaged in a scheme to fill the state's coffers, but the leader maintains a mysterious silence, which Medley is quick to explain: "Sir, my first and greatest politician never speaks at all, he is a very deep man, by which you will observe, that the chief art of a politician is to keep a secret." Fielding has already alerted his audience to fill any gaps in information: as the rehearsal is about to begin, two players discuss their parts, the first Player wishing the satire could be more plain-spoken.

> 2 PLAYER: Ay; prithee, what subject wouldst thou write on?
> 1 PLAYER: Why, no subject at all, sir; but I would have a humming deal of satire, and I would report in every page, that courtiers are cheats and don't pay their debts, that lawyers are rogues, physicians blockheads, soldiers cowards, and ministers—
> 2 PLAYER: What, what, sir?
> 1 PLAYER: Nay, I'll only name 'em, that's enough to set the audience a hooting.

Plainly there had developed in the theatre a form of participatory expressionism going beyond what our Swiss caricaturist Töpffer had assigned to the artist. In the decade presided over by Gay and Fielding the audience had become hypersensitive to political nuances, a point Fielding himself was to allude to when he came to publish his play, as we shall see in a moment.

Meanwhile, just as the "first and greatest politician" ruled his menials in silence in the opening scene, his counterpart, Quidam, presides much more genially over the Four Patriots in the closing one. And he does it by an even more flagrant bribing than Lord Place in *Pasquin*, pouring out before them a great purseful of guineas, which they greedily snatch up as Quidam tunes his fiddle to lead them in a grand dance. But, as Medley explains, this generosity is all show: "Sir, every one of these patriots have a hole in their pockets, as Mr. Quidam the fiddler there knows; so that he intends to make them dance till all the money is fallen through, which he will pick up again, and so not lose one halfpenny for his generosity."

The Historical Register enjoyed the same kind of success as *Pasquin*, and the author's euphoria was naturally increased as his dedication, quite appropriately "To the Public," shows. This curious mixture of playful exuberance and seriousness is worth fuller study than I have time for here. It is shot through with ironies: The author scorns the charge that he is opposing the government—"I am a ministerial writer"! He repeats part of the prologue, which takes the form of a silly "Ode to the New Year," more mockery of the laureate. He pretends to scorn the audience for assuming allusions where no satire was intended; he tells the story of how one clever fellow misleads his myopic companion by pointing to the ass's head hung before the inn and calling out, "Bob, Bob, look yonder, some impudent rascal has hung out your picture on a sign-post," whereupon the short-sighted man flies into a rage at the proprietor.[17] Yet Fielding ends on quite a different note—unless I read into his remarks more of a premonition than he felt. The last paragraph quite soberly thanks the public for "the very great indulgence you have shown my performances at the little theatre these last two years" and promises he will strain to the utmost to provide "cheaper and better" fare than they have been getting from the favored patent houses. "If nature hath given me any talents at ridiculing vice and imposture, I shall not be indolent, nor afraid of exerting them, while the liberty of the press and stage subsists, that is to say, while we have any liberty left among us."

The Historical Register was advertised for publication on 12 May.[18] Eight days later the House of Commons ordered the preparation of a bill amending the act of vagrancy as it applied to actors. In less than a month it had passed both houses and been signed by George II. Either of its two main provisions, restricting the acting of plays to the two patent theatres and requiring that every play be submitted to the Lord Chamberlain for a license before being acted, was enough to destroy Fielding's theatrical career. By 1 November 1737 he was enrolled as a law student at the Middle Temple, his career in the theatre effectively ended.

Before glancing ahead at the fortunes of dramatic caricature as the century progressed, I should like to make a few observations about the impact of the new law upon that particular form of drama and the position to which it reduced all playwrights. The Licensing Act of 1737 placed the writer for the stage in a quite distinct category: he, quite unlike his fellows in journalism, poetry, fiction, the graphic arts, or whatever, was in effect judged guilty unless and until he could persuade, not a court of law but a minion of the crown—actually of the prime minister—that he was innocent. In contrast, the journalist, the novelist, and the graphic artist carried on with virtual impunity. Mrs. George expresses surprise over the freedom, even the violence of scurrility, with which the attack on Bute was carried on in the early 1760s. "It is also remarkable, if perhaps natural, that print-sellers as such were not prosecuted for seditious libel. Doubtless the worst prints were too scurrilously obscene to be *brought into court* [emphasis supplied] or given publicity, but they may have had their influence on Press prosecutions, even on the famous proceedings against No. 45 of the *North Briton*."[19] She gives a rough count of 400 prints attacking Bute, who was assailed for his supposed Jacobitism, his favoritism toward his fellow Scots, his alleged secret alliance with the French, his aversion to liberty, and his scandalous affair with the young king's mother.[20] "Bute quailed before the storm of abuse and resigned on 8 April [1763], in spite of his unshaken majority."[21]

Returning to the stage and to the fateful year of 1737, I should now like to survey more briefly what remained for the dramatic caricaturist. Dramatic caricature in its wider sense of "symbolic type-character" was still allowed, to be sure. Even caricature of particular individuals was possible, but on a far more limited scale and with diminished social importance. After all, the work of "the English Aristophanes, the theatrical caricaturist of his age"—it would require no great search to find a whole florilegium of such exalted and exalting terms applied to Samuel Foote—was still to come.[22]

Foote's first appearance on the London stage, 6 February 1744, was at the theatre with which he became almost completely identified in time, the Haymarket, but in a role totally alien to his fame, Othello. His first venture into dramatic caricature came a full ten years after the passage of the Licensing Act and in defiance of that statute. *The Diversions of the Morning; or, a Dish of Chocolate,* performed at the Haymarket beginning 22 April 1747,[23] was evidently never submitted to licenser or publisher, never reduced actually to a fixed text, so that it is impossible to know except in very general terms what it was like. Still there are notices in contemporary newspapers submitted by some of the objects of Foote's satire—or just possibly submitted by Foote posing as his victims—from which we learn of the public ridicule of "Orator" Henley, a favorite butt of numerous satirists.[24] The following season he served *Tea* at Covent Garden, earning Rich a rebuke from Fielding for his protecting this attacker of "private characters."[25]

It was only in January 1752, when he began to perform his *Taste* at Drury Lane, that Foote began to face the scrutiny of the licenser of plays. Since he was merely gibing at Hogarth's old enemies, the connoisseurs of art, he evidently ran no great risk of having his play banned. His *Author,* too, first performed at Drury Lane on 5 February 1757, seemed innocent enough and was readily licensed. True, there were rumors that Foote was mocking not only a particular person but a friend in Cadwallader, but he issued a public statement that "all the persons in that piece are fictitious and general." When, however, he tried to revive the play on 18 December 1758, his Welsh friend, now victim, secured an order from the Lord Chamberlain stopping the play.

A similar fate threatened his *Minor,* some part of which he began delivering as a "Comic Lecture" at the Haymarket in 1759 and later in Dublin. It first appeared as a play on 28 June 1760 at the Haymarket, carefully billed as being done "By authority," despite the absence of any sign of an application for a license. He also rushed the play into print; by early fall the third edition had appeared. Such success had the predictable result of calling the attention of Whitefield and his disciples to the play, for *The Minor* has as its primary purpose an attack on the "itinerant field orators" then infesting England, to echo Foote's induction to the play. The disciple of highest station was Lady Huntington, who sought the ear of the duke of Devonshire, the then Lord Chamberlain, and, unable to move him, the archbishop of Canterbury, Thomas Secker, a foe to enthusiasm but a friend of tolerance. Meanwhile Garrick had scheduled the play for 25 October but was unable to perform it because of the death of George II, an event that closed the theatres for three weeks. On the same day the duke of Devonshire wrote the Drury Lane manager a friendly note telling of the pressures being put on him but assuring Garrick—"this to yourself"—that "very little alteration" would satisfy the archbishop's objections. Garrick hastily secured a copy of the third edition, found out what changes were deemed indispensable, and submitted *The Minor* for licensing on 20 November, two days before its actual premiere at Drury Lane.

The central figure in *The Minor* who actually appears *on stage* is a disagreeable bawd named Mrs. Cole, played by Foote, whose mixture of sanctimonious cant and bawdry—she is a procuress and a member of the new evangelical revival—was bound to please the many enemies of the movement. Hovering over the scenes like a malign presence but never actually appearing is a certain Dr. Squintum, whom all could recognize by the allusion to his physical defect as Whitefield. It was doubtless this comparatively remote attack on the actual evangelical leader rather than the stage caricature of the fictitious but representative disciple that prompted the petitions to the Lord Chamberlain.

Compare with this less than heroic attack on Whitefield, less than heroic or even admirable in the eyes of the powerful, a sharply contrasting event in the world of graphic satire. Aroused by Reynolds's recommendation of enthusiasm in art in *Idler* No. 79, the aging Hogarth prepared a picture, accurately styled "Dantesque" by Paulson, called *Enthusiasm Delineated*, sometime in 1760. This very busy scene, ironically dedicated to the archbishop of Canterbury, is aimed at a whole range of ecclesiastical enthusiasms, liturgical, oratorical, and so on, bearing down most heavily on Catholics but by no means sparing Anglicans and sketching in "Whitefield" as a howling dog. Dissuaded by friends or having had second thoughts, Hogarth did not have his picture engraved in its original form, but with the furor in early 1762 over the Cock Lane ghost (said to have been exploited by some of the Methodists), he redrew the *Enthusiasm* piece and, abandoning the attack on religious art and liturgy and concentrating his satire on Whitefield and his followers, retitled the new version *Credulity, Superstition, and Fanaticism.*[26] Note that the decision to suppress and the later one to revise were based on the artist's own decision and not on any intervention by legal authorities.

Foote's last play—I follow his own lead in treating *A Trip to Calais* and *The Capuchin* as versions of the same piece—met a far harsher fate, and in its brief history revealed a far more insidious application of the Lord Chamberlain's power. This time Foote made a grave, not to say fatal, error in choosing his target. Lady Kitty Crocodile, pretending abject sorrow over the loss of her husband, was instantly recognizable as the notorious duchess of Kingston, recently bereft of the titled husband she had married while still legally married to a gentleman of lower rank and fortune. When Foote applied for a license, he was refused by the then Lord Chamberlain, Lord Hertford, who had been approached on the duchess's behalf by the duke of Newcastle.[27] In the voluminous correspondence which followed, much of it in the press and now available in Miss Belden's book,[28] there are two notable references to Foote in the role of Aristophanes, a sarcastic one by Horace Walpole to "Aristophanes's Grecian virtue"—alluding to what seemed an attempt at blackmail by the playwright—and an implied one by the author himself in his protest to the Lord Chamberlain: "Upon all occasions I have exerted my little powers (as indeed I thought it my duty) in exposing follies." Even it we could treat this claim seriously, we would have to point out how ill-timed it was. Though something faintly like the Old Comedy of Greece might have been possible in England before 1737, no hint of such all-licensed expression was possible afterward.

The plain fact is that no stage caricaturist of Fielding's ability, courage, and character—most certainly Foote was no match for his predecessor—appeared on the scene in the latter half of the century, or, less sweepingly, no one who matched Fielding in ability was allowed to put those abilities to their proper use. There were men of some ability and considerable courage, such as Joseph Reed, or men of considerable ability but no special zeal for significant reform or social criticism like Garrick or the elder Colman who produced their quota of Fribbles and Lord Chalkstones and Polly Honeycombes, but none of these could approach the graphic caricaturists who set their still-visible mark on the last quarter of the century.

Let R. B. Sheridan serve as a prime example for my final point. His last comic play, and the last play showing any of his great abilities, *The Critic*,[29] appeared in the fall of 1779. The following year he plunged into a busy life of politics and henceforward became not a producer of caricature but a target for Rowlandson and Gillray and others who practiced their often abusive art with something nearly approaching anarchy. The art that gave Aristophanes an enduring reputation, banned from the stage, found the outlet for its expression in the hands of the painter and printmaker.

Notes

1. Oliver W. Larkin, *Daumier: Man of His Time* (New York: McGraw-Hill, 1966), p. 17. Charles Philipon was founder and editor of two famous French periodicals, *La Caricature* and *Charivari*. I should say here at the start that whereas Larkin uses the hyphenated compound of two nouns, *portrait-charge*, I shall be using what I take to be the favored French form of noun plus attributive, *portrait chargé*.

2. I deliberately choose a title from a production by John Rich, first performed in November 1723. For an attempt to justify the combination of drama, music, and spectacle, see the dedication of *The Rape of Proserpine* (1727) signed by Rich.

3. I quote from the English translation, *Letters on the English and French Nations* (London: J. Brindley et al., 1747), 2:42. If Le Blanc had used the Italian term, he would have spelled it *caricature*. What he actually uses is the French equivalent, having both *charge* and *chargé* on the corresponding page. *Caricature* had not become domesticated in English as yet. Writers such as Fielding and Hogarth used the Italian form, in good part to express their rejection of the practice they thought it represented. Actually both were at times caricaturists but rejected the label in much the same way, and with the same justification, that they rejected *low*, a scornful term applied to them by the school of decorum.

4. I call Ghezzi legendary not because he was fictitious but because he is more talked about than seen. Of the few reproductions readily available, I cite two: (1) a not very flattering drawing of "Le castrat Farinelli en femme" reproduced in *La Caricature: Art et Manifeste* (Paris: Skira, 1974), p. 42; (2) what Gombrich and Kris call a "clever but unaggressive portrait-caricature" reproduced as Fig. 8 in their splendid little *Caricature* published by Penguin (1940). In his *Laocoon*, early in chapter 2, Lessing refers disapprovingly to early Greek caricaturists as "the Greek Ghezzis," and Hogarth copies a caricature by "Chezze" at the foot of his *Characters and Caricaturas* (1743). Both adopt similar attitudes but for quite different reasons.

5. E. M. Gombrich, *Art and Illusion* (New York: Pantheon, 1960), p. 356.

6. Gay disclaimed any intention of attacking "particular great persons" in his preface to *Polly* (1729), a traditional disclaimer that the reader accepts at his peril. Fielding, in his rebuttal to Foote, *Jacobite's Journal* No. 10, alters the phrase to "private characters," implying somewhat disingenuously that his own persona John Trott-Plaid was not a *public* character and therefore not fair game.

7. M. Dorothy George, *English Political Caricature* (Oxford: Clarendon Press, 1959).

8. W. L. Cross, *The History of Henry Fielding*, 3 vols. (New Haven: Yale University Press, 1918), 1:53.

9. When, a year later, Fielding revamped this mock-heroic play chiefly by parodying pedantic scholarship in the published *Tragedy of Tragedies*, he was, of course, engaging in a form of burlesque or caricature, but the main object of his satire belongs rather to the study than to the stage.

10. The disclaimer appeared in the *Daily Journal* on 30 November also, thus adding to the suspicion with which one justifiably greets such statements.

11. *The London Stage* for June gives quite enough detail from current press stories to enable anyone to follow these "mighty contests."

12. See Paulson, 1:318–24, for a detailed account and reproductions of both prints.

13. It seems almost supererogatory to recite Pope's apotheosis:

> Immortal Rich! how calm he sits at ease
> 'Mid snows of paper, and fierce hail of pease;
> And proud his Mistress' orders to perform,
> Rides in the whirlwind, and directs the storm.
>
> [*Dunciad*, 3. 261–64]

14. Fielding with almost malicious ingenuity managed in the first two weeks to hire Cibber's daugher Charlotte away from her father's company to play Lord Place.

15. *The London Stage* gives us some idea of the heat generated by the quarrel, especially in the account for 31 December 1736.

16. See Paulson, passim, for Hogarth's relations with Cock, "friend and neighbor."

17. That others may have seen "Bob" where there really was none is suggested by an entry in the earl of Egmont's diary—it is reproduced in *The London Stage* for 18 April 1737—which

tells of his attending a performance of *The Historical Register* and *Eurydice Hiss'd* in a mood to find more in the afterpiece than Fielding must have intended, at least more than a modern reader can find.

18. Cross, 1:222.

19. George, 1:122.

20. See Mrs. George's plate 33, or, for even bolder caricatures, plates 5–7 in John Wardroper, *Kings, Lords, and Wicked Libellers* (London: John Murray, 1973).

21. George, 1:125.

22. For a full and sound treatment of Foote's plays, see Mary Megie Belden, *The Dramatic Work of Samuel Foote* (New Haven, Conn.: Yale University Press, 1929).

23. The entry in *The London Stage* for this date seems to point to an evening performance in spite of the title; the next one, three days later, specifies noon.

24. For Hogarth's treatment of Henley see Paulson, 1:226, and plate 85.

25. *The Jacobite's Journal* 10.

26. See Paulson, plates 284 and 295 and the accompanying exposition.

27. Contrast with this raw display of power to protect a reputation hardly salvageable the history in caricatures of the Prince of Wales and his numerous affairs beginning with Perdita Robinson. See, in addition to Mrs. George and John Wardroper, *Social Caricature in the Eighteenth Century* (1905; rpt. New York: Arno Press, 1968) by George Paston (Emily Morse Symonds), and *The Cartoon History of Britain* (New York: Macmillan, 1971) by M. W. Jones.

28. Miss Belden chooses to give her detailed account of the fortunes of this last play not in regular sequence with the other plays, but earlier as the almost final episode in Foote's life—a sound decision, for the event proved fatal to the playwright.

29. Among the last memorable stage caricatures in the century—if not the very last one—is the sketch of Richard Cumberland as Sir Fretful Plagiary.

Theatre and Fiction

12

An Early Eighteenth-Century Prose Version of *The Tempest*

CHARLES C. MISH

The body of English short fiction before the mid-eighteenth century contains prose paraphrases of three of Shakespeare's plays. Two of these narratives have engendered a small collection of commentary; the third, found only in a unique copy in the British Library, seems to have entirely escaped attention.[1] The relation of the narrative text to the Shakespeare play whose story it tells is different in each case and, in each case also, puzzling.

Shakespeare's *Pericles,* a retelling of the story of Apollonius of Tyre and the latest in a series of versions of the tale in Western literature since its first appearance as a Greek romance in the second or third century, was published in 1609 in an unsatisfactory quarto, which, as Bullough says, is "at times . . . almost unintelligible."[2] A year earlier, however, in 1608, the year in which *Pericles* was entered in the *Stationers' Register,* there appeared a prose romance by George Wilkins called *The Painfull Adventures of Pericles Prince of Tyre. Being the True History of the Play of Pericles, as it was lately presented.* It is not at all certain that the play referred to as "lately presented" was Shakespeare's, though, of course, it may have been.[3]

Titus Andronicus is represented as prose fiction by a chapbook printed in the mid-eighteenth century, which exists in a unique copy at the Folger Shakespeare Library. Entitled *The Tragical History of Titus Andronicus,* it is sometimes considered to be a reprint of a possible sixteenth-century original, and, to quote Bullough again, "may well represent a major source of the play."[4] There is again an outside possibility that the prose version is a retelling of Shakespeare's play, though this relationship is not generally accepted and has been categorically denied in the most recent article on the subject, that by G. Harold Metz.[5]

The third case before us, however, seems to be a clear-cut one of a prose tale being based directly on a play, though again complicating factors cloud the picture somewhat. In 1720 there appeared a prose version of *The Tempest*, under the title of *The Force of Nature: Or the Loves of Hippollito and Dorinda. A Romance.* The title page goes on to claim that the book was "Translated from the French Original, and never before printed in English," a claim it seems safe to ignore. The complication arises from the fact that this story was not based directly on Shakespeare's play, but upon the operatic reworking of the Dryden-Davenant version. Since the prose follows the dramatic text fairly closely, reproducing a great many phrases and turns of speech verbatim, as well as rearranging and reorganizing material, some comment on the two preceding texts may be helpful in approaching the narrative.

The Dryden-Davenant version of Shakespeare's play, called *The Tempest, or, The Enchanted Island,* was produced for the first time on 7 November 1667. The quarto was published in 1670, with a preface by Dryden in which he modestly ascribes the major role in the adaptation to his collaborator, no longer alive, but the editor of this play in the California *Dryden,* Maximillian Novak, thinks the fact that *The Tempest* was always printed in lists of Dryden's plays while being excluded from the folio collection of Davenant's writings published in 1673 may be an indication that Dryden "regarded his own contribution as the major part in the revision."[6] The alterations in the original were profound. Gone are the symbolism, the magic, and the themes of forgiveness and redemption; instead, we have a number of comic scenes involving two pairs of lovers (Miranda is given a sister, Dorinda, for whom a suitable lover is provided) and low comic scenes with Trinculo (now called Trincalo) and his group, including Caliban, who is conveniently also given a sister, Sicorax, whom Trincalo may marry. The serious action is hence much reduced in importance. What Dryden and Davenant did was to change *The Tempest* from whatever it was into a Restoration comedy, and once one has got over his feeling of sacrilege, he must admit that the changes produce a play that is amusing and entertaining. In the words of Novak, Dryden and Davenant turned Shakespeare's *Tempest* "into a viable play for Restoration audiences at a time when the original would have been regarded as old-fashioned and unentertaining."[7]

The operatic version of *The Tempest*, which bears the same title as the Dryden-Davenant version, was made for the Dorset Garden stage and produced in 1674, the quarto appearing the same year.[8] The work is usually ascribed to Shadwell.[9] The reviser, whoever he was, made many small changes in his original, cutting speeches and parts of speeches, rearranging scenes, and adding songs and two masques. He also added, or rather strengthened, a part: Ariel is provided with a female counterpart, an aerial spirit named Milcha.[10] In spite of rearrangements and other changes, the opera seems very much the same play as the Dryden-Davenant version with the simple addition of music. It is not at all the sort of thing we are accustomed to call opera today; the actors presented the spoken lines as usual, and the singers and dancers added the musical part at the proper moments. Still, in the final masque something impressively "operatic" must have been seen on the stage, with the music, the dancing, Aeolus descending from above, and Ariel flying about the stage.

In 1720, for reasons that must remain mysterious, an unknown hand turned the dramatic text into a prose narrative.[11] Though he put his material through considerable reworking, the prose writer based his story not on Shakespeare's own play or on the Dryden-Davenant version but on the operatic text, as one may see from the wording of the lines of the masque in act 2 scene 3, and the final speeches of Ariel and Prospero. With these exceptions, the narrative presents material common to both stage versions, and with which it takes the liberty of rearranging scenes, cutting speeches by omitting lines, and, of course, changing dialogue to narration.

The most remarkable change in going from drama to narrative is the presentation of all antecedent material—the arrival of Prospero and his two daughters,[12] Ariel's history (how he was released from the cloven pine), Caliban's birth and relationship with Prospero—at the very beginning of the story, in true "once upon a time" style. (Indeed, the prose begins with Prospero actually ruling in Milan as duke before proceeding at once to recount his ouster by his brother and his subsequent abandonment to the mercy of the sea.) Then, before the tempest and shipwreck are mentioned, we are told why Antonio, Ferdinand, Alonzo (now called the duke of Savoy), and the others were on their voyage: as in the two dramatic texts, their purpose had been to aid the king of Portugal in his struggle with the Moors. Ariel then reports on how he managed the tempest and how those on the ship had come ashore.

With a typical narrative phrase for transition, "But let us leave them a while, and return to Prospero," the story proper begins.[13] As in the two dramatic versions, but perhaps more noticeably here, the main story line concerns the romantic tale of the two pairs of lovers. The comic action of the doings of Trincalo and his group is also present, this material again somewhat shortened and less emphasized than in the dramas.

The central idea governing the lovers' dialogue and behavior is the fact that Miranda, Dorinda, and Hippolito (Dorinda's lover) have never seen a member of the opposite sex. The resultant naiveté displayed on both sides leads to some risqué comments and to misunderstandings that forward the plot (indeed, constitute the plot), the chief incident of which is the fight between Ferdinand and Hippolito ending in the apparent death of the latter. Prospero's anger over the supposed murder and the consequent ruin of his plans to marry Miranda to Ferdinand ("No Marriages can prosper which are with Murderers made," he comments) brings about the climax of the action: confrontation with Antonio and the others, the sudden and unlooked-for revival of Hippolito, forgiveness all around, and the inevitable pairings off. After that, all prepare to leave the island and Ariel is freed from further servitude; he sings "Where the Bee sucks" and makes Prospero a farewell speech, to which Prospero responds formally, announcing that henceforth that island will be a place of refuge for the afflicted.

Whatever his purpose, the author has succeeded in producing a genuine piece of short fiction, the transference from one medium to another having been quite handily managed. The story as it stands seems a little old-fashioned both in style and taste; if it was designed for any particular readership, it was undoubtedly one at some distance from the cultural forefront of 1720. The fact that the book was produced by provincial printers probably means that it was intended to be carried about by chapmen[14] and hence that its readers would probably be people who had never been in a theatre or in London and were probably innocent of any knowledge of Shakespeare's or anybody else's *Tempest*. For such readers the story must have been a satisfactory mixture of magic, wonder, and romance, with just enough suspense to spice it up a bit. But there was no second edition, perhaps because taste was changing too fast, perhaps because the story failed to please for other reasons. As it is, it attests, along with the frequent performances of *The Tempest* recorded in theatrical history, to the staying power of Shakespeare's imagination.

Notes

1. In view of the fact that the running title of the book, *The History of Prospero, / Duke of Milan,* might well have alerted Shakespeareans to the nature of the text, its neglect is surprising. Arundell Esdaile's bibliography of early fiction, where the main entry is under the catch title *Hippolito and Dorinda,* also divulges the same running title (*English Tales and Romances . . .* [London, 1912], p. 246).

2. Geoffrey Bullough, *Narrative and Dramatic Sources of Shakespeare,* (London: Routledge and Kegan Paul, 1966), 6:349.

3. This possibility, though remote, seems implicit in Kenneth Muir's remark in the introduction to his edition of Wilkins's tale (Liverpool: University Press, 1953), p. v. He says: "The novel was based on a play, though not necessarily on *Pericles* as we now have it."

4. Bullough, 6:7.

5. G. Harold Metz, "The History of Titus Andronicus and Shakespeare's Play," *Notes and Queries* 22 (1975): 163–66.

6. Dryden, *Works,* 10:322.

7. Dryden, *Works,* 10:339.

8. The text of the operatic version of 1674 has frequently been confused with the rather different Dryden-Davenant text of 1670. The Furness Variorum edition of *The Tempest,* for instance, reprints in an appendix the 1674 text under the assumption that it is the same as the 1670 text.

9. Charles E. Ward in his article "*The Tempest:* A Restoration Opera Problem," *ELH* 13 (1946): 119–30, offers what seems to be convincing evidence that Shadwell could not have

done the adaptation but that Betterton probably did. Recent writers on Shadwell, however, do not accept his conclusions. See Michael W. Alssid, *Thomas Shadwell* (New York: Twayne, 1967), and Don R. Kunz, *The Drama of Thomas Shadwell* (Salzburg: Institut für englische Sprache und Literatur, 1972).

10. Although her name is not listed among the Dramatis Personae, Milcha does make a belated and solitary appearance in the Dryden-Davenant version. At the end of the play, Ariel, freed at last, calls for her, and she duly appears and speaks her one-word part, "Here!" Then the two spirits dance a saraband.

11. The titlepage gives little hint as to the source of the story, but one hesitates to accuse the anonymous author of deliberate concealment since both the caption title at the head of the text and the running-titles throughout read "The History of Prospero, Duke of Milan." The appearance of *The Force of Nature* in 1720 may owe something to the ongoing popularity of *Robinson Crusoe,* published the year before. John Robert Moore claimed *The Tempest* as a source for an episode in *Crusoe* ("*The Tempest* and *Robinson Crusoe,*" *RES,* 21 [1945], 52–56; see also Maximillian E. Novak, *Defoe and the Nature of Man* [London: Oxford University Press, 1963], p. 62), and perhaps Raikes and Dicey thought the basic situation in both stories close enough to attract the public to their book.

12. Surprisingly, the prose specifies that Prospero has been on the island for twelve years, rejecting the fifteen years of the Dryden-Davenant opera and thereby returning to Shakespeare's own figure.

13. A number of similar narrative tags appear throughout the prose, such as "but with what Reluctance, I leave the amorous Reader to judge," "What will be, will be," "For he, as many an Honest Fellow had been before him, was quite tir'd of his Bargain."

14. Henry R. Plomer says that "Dicey published at Northampton a number of chap-books; the first of these to be advertised . . . was *The Force of Nature*" (*A Dictionary of the Printers and Booksellers . . . from 1668 to 1725.* [London: Bibliographical Society, 1922], p. 103).

THE
Force of Nature;
OR THE
LOVES
of
HIPPOLLITO *and* DORINDA
A
ROMANCE.

Translated from the FRENCH Original,
and
never before printed in ENGLISH.

NORTHAMPTON:
Printed by R. RAIKES and W. DICEY,
over against *All Saints Church,* 1720.
(Price Three Pence.)

The most Renowned
HISTORY
OF
PROSPERO,
DUKE of MILAN.

In the Dukedom of *Milan,* there sometime reigned a most noble Duke called *Prospero,* who had a Brother named *Antonio,* to whom he trusted the Manage of his State: he himself being for the most part wrapt up in secret Studies; not in the least surmising, that his Brother would ever throw off the NAME, and chuse that of an Usurper, for the sake of his Dominions. But the false *Antonio* having obtained the Craft of granting Suits, and of denying them, of advancing and deposing; and being prompted on by wild Ambition; wak'd in his Soul an evil Nature, and began to suppose himself the Duke, because he executed the outward Face of Sovereignty; and at last made that traiterous Thought so natural to him, that he resolv'd it should be real: And to this End confederated with the Duke of *Savoy*, (who was an inveterate Enemy to *Prospero*) promising him Tribute, and to do him Homage; if he would constitute him Duke of *Milan*, in the room of his Brother. To which *Savoy* consenting, *Antonio,* in the dead of the Night, (as they had secretly agreed) open'd to him the Gates of *Milan*; and hurry'd the lawful Duke to *Savoy*, and with him two young Princesses his Daughters, the Eldest named *Miranda,* and the Youngest *Dorinda,* who were the dear Pledges of their Father's former Love, and the pretty Remembrancers to him, of a Lady, who in her Life-time was all Vertue. As also an Infant call'd *Hippolito,* the Right Heir, to the Dukedom of *Mantua*, whose Father dying, bequeath'd him (but three Years old) to the Care of *Prospero*, and who, by *Antonio*'s Cruelty, was expo'ed to the same Fate as that much wronged Duke. When they arriv'd at *Savoy*, they were put aboard a Vessel at *Nissa*, of which *Gonzalo,* a Nobleman of *Savoy*, was appointed Master, who bore them out some Leagues to Sea, where there was a rotten Carcase of a Boat prepared for their Reception, without either Rigging, Tackle, Sail, or Mast. However, *Gonzalo* knowing the Duke was an entire Lover of his Books, was so generous as to furnish him (but from his own Library) with some Books which he set a Value on, as also some rich Garments, which afterwards stood these Royal Exiles in good stead: They had also a small Quantity of Food, and some fresh Water. And thus they were left to the Mercy of the Waves, which proving greater than that of his unnatural Brother, they were at length thrown on an Island uninhabited, save only by two Brats, which *Sicorax,* a most damn'd Witch, who had been banish'd from *Argier* to that desolate Place, for manifold Mischiefs, and Sorceries too terrible for human Hearing, had litter'd there. These two freckled Hag-born Wretches were named, the Male *Caliban,* and the Female *Sicorax.* On this Island was the noble Duke, and his innocent Companions thrown: What shall *Prospero* do now? He knows he is upon enchanted Ground, and has no Hopes of any Succour, from the two confounded and poisonous Brats of this old deceased Hag: He had Magick sufficient, however, to defend himself from their Insults, and even to punish them for whatever Affronts they should offer; for he was a Man of most occult Study, and had penetrated into the very Pith of Sorcery: Yet he thought it more advisable to endeavour to bring that accurs'd Slave over to his Service, by fair and courteous Means: So having lodg'd his two Infant Daughters in a Cave, which he himself had accommodated for them; and hous'd *Hippolito* in a Rock at some Distance from their Cell, for a Reason which you will hear in the Sequel; he left them, and went in search of the Monster, whom, having found, he us'd all gentle Means to bring to his Lure; he strok'd and made much of him, gave him to taste of some rich Cordials, which he had brought with him; taught him to name the Sun and the Moon: And by these Means excited in that wretched Creature a Love towards him; so that he shew'd him all the Qualities of the Isle, as the fresh Springs, fertile Places, &c. And *Prospero,* to requite this Gratitude of the Slave, took Pains to make him speak; for before this he was savage, and could only gabble; and to defend him from the Inclemency of the Weather, lodg'd him in his own Cell; 'till, on a Time, this filthy Slave, *Prospero* being absent, attempted to dishonour his two fair Daughters, who were now grown to Maturity, having been twelve Years upon this desart Isle: But the Duke returning before the brutal Villain could accomplish his accurs'd Intent; and being inform'd of what *Caliban* had attempted; he, by the strong Power of his Art, pent him up in a Rock, afflicting him with Cramps and Side-stitches; causing the Urchins to suck his Blood, and the Bees to sting him; and fill'd his Bones with such Aches, that he would often roar so hideously, that the very Beasts trembled at the Noise he made: Besides this, he deservedly made him his Slave, to fetch Wood, make Fires, and serve in the most drudging Offices; still punishing him in the abovesaid Manner, whenever he neglected the least Tittle of what he had commanded. Thus the Monster, not being contented with the Happiness that he might have enjoy'd in a quiet Subordination, was oblig'd to put up with a Slavery which he could not avoid, as a Punishment he had justly deserv'd.

The Hag *Sicorax* (his Dam) had once under her Command, when she was banish'd to this Island, a Spirit call'd *Ariel,* whom by the mighty Power of her Sorceries, she had oblig'd to follow her in her Exile: But he being a Spirit too delicate to act her abhorr'd Injunctions; she, for his refusing to obey her detestable Orders, in her unmitigable Rage, imprison'd him in a cloven Pine, where he vented Groans, as fast as Mill-Wheels strike, and which even made Wolves to howl, and penetrated the Breasts of angry Bears. In this Pine had he been confin'd for the Space of twelve Years, and would have wearied out twelve Winters more, had not *Prospero,* as he was one Day musing in a Place near to the Prison of this unfortunate and miserable Spirit, heard his Complaints, and by the potent Virtue of his Magick, made the Pine to gape and let him out: After which he took him into his Service, employing him in Affairs that tended to restoring him again to his Hereditary Right; which not long after happen'd, in the Manner following:

About this Time it fell out, that the *Moors,* who were become very formidable, began to infest the Kingdom of *Portugal,* daily committing all Manner of Hostilities; nor could they be reducd (so great was their Strength, and so resolute their Undertakings) without an united Force. In this Plunge, for what Reasons I shall not here determine, *Antonio,* Duke *Prospero*'s false Brother, accompany'd with *Alonzo* the Duke of *Savoy,* who had usurp'd the Dukedom of *Mantua* from the Infant *Hippolito*, whom we have just before spoken of; and *Ferdinand* his Son, as also *Gonzalo*, the Nobleman of *Savoy*, who had been Pilot to the depos'd Duke, as is above taken Notice of; went with a sufficient Force to assist the Crown of *Portugal* against the Barbarians: And being bless'd by Heaven in their Design, after having reduc'd those Pagans, were returning to their own Country. But *Prospero*, whose Art reach'd even to the Knowledge of what was acted in Places remote, knowing they were upon the Return, gave Orders to *Ariel* to raise a Tempest on the Sea, whereby they might be separated; but with this Caution, that they should all be thrown (tho' in different Places) on the Inchanted Island, and that not a Hair of them should perish.

Ariel having receiv'd the Duke's Commands, immediately boarded the Ship wherein the aforesaid Noblemen were, and there began his Pranks. Sometimes he would be upon the Beak of the Ship, then in the Waste, and Deck; never a Cabin was left unmolested: Sometimes he seem'd to burn on the Top-Mast, presently after on the Yards and Boltsprit; where he flam'd distinctly and even rain'd a Shower of Fire upon them. This gave every Soul a Fever in his Mind, and urg'd them to play Tricks of Desperation: As for *Ferdinand*, he (with Hair up-staring, more like Reeds than Hair) was the first Man that plung'd into the foaming Brine, crying out, *Hell's empty and all the Devils are here:* Upon which he was immediately follow'd by *Antonio*, *Alonzo*, and *Gonzalo*; every one of them lustily beating the Billows, and riding on their Backs: The Mariners indeed did not care to quit their Ships, and so were at last drove ashore dry-shod on the Island, where also all the rest were arriv'd, but as far from each other, as their Thoughts were, of ever meeting again.

But let us leave them a while, and return to *Prospero*, who, as I have already told you, kept his little Family separate; for he had found by Calculation of *Hippolito*'s Birth, that Death threaten'd that Youth, if, 'till some Time were past, he should behold the Face of any Woman: He therefore went to pay him a Visit one Day, and assur'd him that it did not proceed from any Unkindness, that he restrain'd him in that Rock; *For* (says the Duke) *Heaven knows, and you your self can bear me Witness how much I have loved you from your Infancy: But, my gentle Youth,* (continued he,) *a black Star threatens thee*; *if, 'till some Time be past, you chance to set Eyes on a dangerous Creature that haunts this Island, call'd* Woman. *Hippolito*, who knew not what a Woman was, from the Time he was first cast on that Island, (when he was but three Years old) made Answer, that *Prospero* had taught him, that Man was Sovereign over all other Creatures, and that therefore he had no need to fear; *Besides,* (my dear Lord, says he,) *I had rather meet Death than be a Prisoner. But,* (says *Prospero*) *these are Creatures that share Man's Sovereignty by Nature's Laws, and oft depose him for* [sic] *it.* "Pray what are they like, my Lord?" *Oh* Hippolito, (returns the Duke) *imagine something more beautiful than Man, with killing Eyes*; *and Voices like Nightingales*; *Creatures that are made up of Enchantment; and for ever enslave all that behold them; when once you have seen them, they'll haunt you in your Sleep; while you will be without all Possibility of Revenge; for they are so beautiful, that you can never attempt to hurt them.* This Discourse set his Soul on Fire, and he made use of all his Eloquence to persuade *Prospero* to let him have a View of them; he told him, he had seen the Plumes of Swans, the Peacock's Feathers, the Gloss upon the Necks of Doves, and the various Beauties of the Rainbow; and had without Danger wonder'd at them; "Can they be more beautiful than these? And has Nature made nothing but Woman dangerous and fair? If they meddle with me, I'll shut my Eyes, and fight with 'em." To this *Prospero* reply'd, that they were the most dangerous Creatures in the World; but that in a short Time he would give him leave to have a Sight of them: But charg'd him to forbear desiring to see them, 'till 'twas his Pleasure. This *Hippolito* at last unwillingly complied with; but when *Prospero* was taking his Leave; *Sir,* (says the young Duke of *Mantua*) *I will keep out of their Way, as much as I can; but if they come to me, and provoke me, I'm sure I sha'n't forbear 'em.*

Prospero had, before this, forbidden his two Daughters, ever coming that Way, for fear they should meet the Man whom he had represented to them, (for they likewise had never had seen one but their Father) as a dreadful and poisonous Creature; and that if a Woman came near him, she would feel a Pain full nine Months[.] That tho' he himself was a Man, he was tame; but that there were young Men who were wild. To this they made Answer; (for they long'd to see one of these wild young Men;) "Father, if we see one, we will stroke him, and make him gentle; and then sure he won't hurt us. And if he should catch us, we'll down on our Knees and ask Pardon, as we do to you, when we have done a Fault. Then pray Sir, let us see him; for my Sister and I too, had rather feel a Pain nine Months, than lose our Longing." But the Duke at that Time strictly enjoin'd them never to ask him any more on that Affair; for he would never grant them Leave.

But he might better have given them Permission, for his sole Interdict made them resolve to disobey; and they were got near to his Cell, with a Design to see this terrible Creature; where at last they espy'd *Hippolito*; whereupon *Dorinda* says to her Sister; "See! yonder it is; and it walks about like one of us; and it talks too; nay, if you observe, 'tis the very Picture of us: I'm not half so much afraid of it, as I was. I'll go nearer to it. I'll warrant you this is a tame Man, and will not hurt me." But *Miranda,* who was equally smitten with the Charms of this beautiful Object, would have dissuaded her Sister from being too venturesome, that she might be the more: And therefore, (being the eldest) took upon her to reprimand *Dorinda,* telling her; 'Twas a dangerous Thing; that she herself would go nearer, and take a full View of it; and afterwards come and tell her. "For (says *Miranda*) I would not for the World you shou'd venture. My Father charg'd me (if ever we should happen to see it) to secure you from it." But *Dorinda* would not be persuaded; saying "You chide me for that Disobedience you your self want to commit; if I die for't, I'll go nearer."

At this Instant, *Prospero,* who was passing by them, in an adjacent Meadow, in his way to his Cell, overheard their Talk, and thereupon immediately call'd out for *Miranda.* They both heard his Voice, and *Miranda* (tho' she knew that she was call'd) would have sent *Dorinda* to her Father: But the other would not consent to go, arguing that every one should answer to their Name; and was so obstinate in her Refusal, that *Miranda* was oblig'd to retire, (the Duke continuing to call), but at parting, told her Sister, she would repent it.

As soon as she was gone, *Dorinda,* not a whit terrify'd by her Father's former Injunctions, or her Sister's Threats, boldly advances up to him. But when they came within Sight of each other, what Pen can describe the sudden Admiration, Emotion, and Pleasure of Soul, that they felt. He (*Hippolito,* I mean) thinking she was dropt from the Sun, went to her in a most submissive Manner, and desird to know what she was? She, on the other Hand, full of Wonder at his Comeliness, which yet was not without a Fear of what had been told her concerning his cruel Disposition, made Answer, That she was a Woman, as she thought, and desir'd him not to hurt her: "For (says she) I never knew what 'twas to be an Enemy, nor never can to one that looks like you: And tho' I am charg'd to shun your Presence (if you are a Man) I'd rather die than lose it." "I am indeed a Man, (replied *Hippolito*) but be not frighten'd; for I'd sooner tear my Eyes out, than consent to do you any Harm: Besides, I am told that I must fear you." "I wish we are not Poison to each other; (says the innocent Maid) can't we meet, but we must die?" He told her, there was no Death but in their parting; and desir'd she would let him but touch her Hand; which she consenting to do; they both soon found the Effects of it; for *Dorinda* confess'd, that while she held his Hand, something (she knew not what) made her sigh; *and yet* (says she) *I could grasp it for ever.* He answer'd, That her Touch went thro' him; and that he felt both a Pleasure and a Pain at his Heart. By this Time *Miranda* had told her Tale to the Duke, who now calling for *Dorinda,* the two Lovers were oblig'd to part (not without Promises of meeting;) but with what Reluctance, I leave the amorous Reader to judge.

Alonzo, the Duke of *Savoy, Antonio,* the Duke of *Milan,* and *Gonzalo,* had now found out each other; but instead of being mutual Comforts, they only serv'd to aggravate their respective Miseries: The two Dukes appear'd like Men distracted; and good *Gonzalo's* Tears run down his Beard, like Winter-Drops from Eves of Houses: *Alonzo* was brimful of Grief, for the Loss of his Son *Ferdinand,* whom he suppos'd to be drown'd; and reproach'd *Antonio* with his being the Cause of all their Sorrows; which he indeed could not deny; but laid the Crime at *Alonzo's* Door. And to compleat their Terror and Amazement, *Alonzo* pulling a Tree, Blood issued out of it; and *Antonio* was disturb'd with the swift Voices and Groans of lamenting Ghosts. The Earth began to gape, as if it would swallow them; and on a sudden a horrid Masque of Spirits appear'd, who in a dismal Consort sung as follows:

1. Spir.:   *Where does the black Fiend Ambition reside,*
             With the mischievous Devil of Pride?
2. Spir.:   *In the lowest and darkest Caverns of Hell*
             Both Pride and Ambition does dwell.
3. Spir.:   *And such who their Brothers to Death have betray'd,*
             In Hell upon burning Thrones shall be set.
                          All sing together.
             —In Hell, in Hell with flames they shall reign,
             And for ever, for ever shall suffer the Pain.
1. Spir.:   *—His Cruelty does tread*
             On Orphans tender Breasts, and Brothers dead!
2. Spir.:   *Can Heaven permit such Crimes should be*
                          Attended with Felicity?
                          All sing together.
    Care their Minds when they wake unquiet will keep,
    And we with dire Visions disturb all their Sleep.
1. Spir.:   *Say, say, shall we bear these bold Mortals from hence?*
2. Spir.:   *No, no, let us show their degrees of Offence.*
3. Spir.:   *Let's muster their Crimes up on every Side,*
             And first let's discover their Pride.
             Lo here is Pride who first led them astray,
             And did to Ambition their minds then betray.
             And Fraud does next appear,
             Their wandring Steps who led,
             When they from Vertue fled,
    They in my crooked Paths their Course did steer.
             From Fraud to Force they soon arrive,
             Where Rapine did their Actions drive.
             There long they could not stay;
             Down the steep Hill they run,
    And to perfect the Mischief which they had begun,
             To Murder they bent all their way.
                          All sing together.
             Around, around we pace,
             About this cursed Place;
             While thus we compass in
             These Mortals and their sin.

After this, they vanish'd, and left them all in the utmost Consternation; but especially *Alonzo*; who was quite unmann'd; a cold Sweat trilling down all all [*sic*] o'er his Limbs, as if he were dissolving into Water: And in this Condition, he would ever and anon cry out; *Oh!* Prospero, *my Crimes against thee sit heavy on my Heart!* Which was seconded by *Antonio*, who reproach'd himself with his inhuman Barbarity to his Brother; and the Wrong he had done to young *Hippolito*.

They had not gone much further before a terrible Storm of Thunder, Lightning, Wind, Hail, and Rain arose; which was accompanied with a most frightful Voice which seem'd to issue from the deep Caverns of the Earth; distinctly pronouncing what follows:

> *Arise, arise! ye subterranean Winds*
> *More to disturb their guilty Minds.*
> *And all ye filthy Damps and Vapours rise,*
> *Which use t'infect the Earth, and trouble all the Skies;*
> *Rise you, from whom devouring Plagues have Birth:*
> *You that i'th'vast and hollow Womb of Earth,*
> *Engender Earthquakes, make whole Countries shake,*
> *And stately Cities into Desarts turn;*
> *And you who feed the flames by which Earths Entrails burn.*
> *Ye raging Winds, whose rapid Force can make*
> *All but the fix'd and solid Centre shake:*
> *Come drive these Wretches to that part o'th'Isle,*
> *   Where Nature never yet did smile:*
> *Cause Fogs and Storms, Whirlwinds and Earthquakes there:*
> *There let 'em houl and languish in Despair,*
> *Rise and obey the pow'rful Prince o'th'Air.*

All this while was *Alonzo*'s Son *Ferdinand* wandring about this desert Island, in quest of something that might alleviate his Griefs, if perchance he might meet with any of their Fleet that had been fortuitously driven on that Island: But his Search was vain; for he could find out no Companions; no Mortal, to tell his lamentable Tale to. The invisible *Ariel*, however, (by *Prospero*'s Command) attended him; not that he was directly to give him any Comfort, nor yet to drive him to Despair, but to keep him in Suspence. And this he did, by sometimes affording him the Delight of most sweet aerial Musick; and sometimes by melancholy and afflicting Cadences, which seem'd to intimate his Father's Death. In this Plight, let us now leave him; to see how some of the common Mariners far'd; for there was not one Soul lost, only dispers'd from each other.

And we shall find the best Part of the Boatswain's Crew, gotten into one Corner of the Island, with a Runlet of Brandy before them, as merry as so many *Greeks*, laughing at the Dangers they had past, and without fear of those that were to come, at least as long as their Brandy lasted.

They now began to be pretty well wetted within, as well as without; and their Cold Tea began to have as great an Influence on them as our Hot has upon the Drinkers of it; for it set their Tongues a running plentifully: One was talking of the Danger they had escap'd, which he said was owing to a

Fellow that was aboard, who had a hanging Look; *and*, says he, *If he had not been born to be hang'd, we had certainly been drowned:* Another was swearing that he look'd back as he was swimming to shore, and saw the Runlet of Brandy that was then before them, swimming after him, as it were out of pure Pity. *Fill apace,* says a third, *we can't live long on this barren Island; and why mayn't we take a Soop before Death, as well as others drink at our Funerals? Hang Losses,* says another, *as long as we have Brandy left:* A Fifth was maudlin and weeping at the Thoughts of the Sorrow that his Wife would be fill'd with, if he should perish on the Island, *She's a good Old Jade,* says he, *and has but one Eye left, which she'll weep out too, when she hears of my Misfortunes:* His next Man was brimful of Grief for the Loss of a gilt Nutmeg his Sweetheart had given him: *But come,* says he, *Sorrow's Dry, so here's to ye.*

And now their Cagg began to empty apace, and they had scarce any Brandy left to think on; so they bent their Notions another way. A Politician that was amongst them was for erecting a Government on that Island: This was agreed to; but who should be King was the Question: So to it they went Helter Skelter about it; for the Brandy had made them all Princes; and every one thought himself the Sovereign; and there were bloody Noses in the Case.

But all this while they ne'er thought of *Trincalo,* who was their Boatswain, and who being cast on another distant part of the Island, by chance met with the Monster *Caliban,* who having recommended his Sister *Sicorax,* as the greatest Beauty in that Island, and also as the Queen thereof; prevail'd upon the Sailor (See what Ambition will do!) to marry her, that he might be a King. And now who so great as *Trincalo?* He had got 2 Subjects, his Wife and her Brother: And with these two he was making his Progress over his new Kingdom; when he came at last, where the rest of the Crew were in the abovemention'd Dispute: When he knew the Reason of their Quarrel, he gave them to understand that he would be only Supreme Monarch there, for says he, *I have married the Lawful Inheritrix of this Island, Queen Blouze the 1st, and by her I hold my Title: Therefore either take this Cagg, sit down, and drink my Health, by the Name of Duke* Trincalo; *or be sober, ill-natur'd, and hang'd; which you please: For I've married a Witch, and we have a thousand Devils of our Party.* At that Word, they all cry'd out, *Peace and the Runlet; long Live Duke* Trincalo! And at last came to these Terms, That he should allow them part of his Brandy, and they would acknowledge him sole Ruler of that Island. And ever since his Reign, this has been found an effectual Means of procuring Votes for those that want 'em more than they deserve 'em.

All this while *Ferdinand* was wandering about the Island; and at last came to a Place where *Prospero* was in Discourse with his Daughter *Miranda;* who espying him, bid her look at him. At first she was struck with Amazement, thinking it had been a Spirit, and told her Father as much: But he assured her that it was a Man; who (but that his Beauty was stain'd with the Griefs he underwent) was indeed a goodly Person.

By this time he came up close to them, and being entirely captivated by her Charms, he thus address'd her; *Fair Excellence, if, as your Form declares, you are Divine, be pleas'd to instruct me how you will be worshipp'd; so bright a Beauty cannot sure belong to human kind.* To this she modestly and innocently reply'd, that she was a Mortal like him, if he was so. He hearing her speak Italian, broke forth into the following Exclamation; *My Language too! O Heavens! I am the best of them who speak this Speech when I'm in my own Country.* At this *Prospero* took him up sharply, saying, *What wert thou if the Duke of Savoy heard thee? Ferdinand* said he himself was *Savoy;* and that if that bright Angel (meaning *Miranda*) were a Virgin, and her Affections not gone forth, he would make her Mistress thereof; *for* (says he) *these Eyes not many Hours since, saw the Duke of Savoy, my Father, shipwreck'd.* But *Prospero*, who was resolv'd to let him know the Power he had over him, retorted, That he usurp'd a Name that was not due to him, and came as a Spy on the Island, to get the Government from him: *And therefore as a Traitor,* (continues Duke *Prospero) I imprison thee; and thou shalt be in Bonds. Thy Drink shall be Sea Water, and thy Food wither'd Roots, and Husks of Acorns.* But *Miranda* intreated her Father in his Behalf, saying, She was sure there could be no Harm in him; and that she would be his Surety: But the Duke chid her; commanding *Ferdinand* to follow him; which he refusing, and offering to draw, was charm'd from moving; whereupon he immediately own'd the Power of *Prospero*; but begg'd tho' he was a Prisoner, he might have the Happiness to see that Charming Maid once a Day; But this was deny'd him: And when *Miranda* endeavour'd to Comfort him, by saying her Father was of a better Nature than he appear'd by his Speech; the Duke immediately commanded him into a Cave which he had prepar'd for him, and there left him.

I told you above that the Duke mistrusted some Ill Chance would befal *Hippolito*, if he should see a Woman before such a Time; nor was his Mistrust vain: For *Hippolito* one Day meeting with *Ferdinand*, who was walking within the Narrow Bounds of his Prison, which was Contiguous to that of *Hippolito*'s, after having ask'd him concerning his Fate, began to make his Complaints to him, that he was kept Confin'd only for fear he should behold a Woman: Upon which *Ferdinand* told him they were indeed Dangerous; for he had seen one since he came on the Island, whose Beauty had pierc'd his Heart. *I believe,* says *Hippolito, you are like me; for I have been unquiet ever since I saw Woman, and am always wishing for I know not what. But,* (says *Ferdinand) in that you and I differ; for I know too well what I wish for; I can have no Happiness without her; If I have not her, I cannot live.* At this *Hippolito* was angry, and told him that none but himself must have her. *Ferdinand* told him that perhaps 'twas not the same Woman that he lov'd. *What,* says *Hippolito, are there more Women, You shall not, must not pretend to claim one, for if there were a hundred of them, I must love 'em all.* Ferdinand admiring at his Simplicity, told him, that he labour'd under a very great Mistake, if he suppos'd that he might indifferently love, and be belov'd of all the Women he should see; for that he must fix his Affections to one only: *And Sweet Youth* (added he) *perhaps when you behold the Woman I admire, you will find that you cannot fancy her.* But *Hippolito* protested he would have as many as he could; and told *Ferdinand* that he must either promise him that he would love no Woman, or vindicate his Pretensions by Force. *Ferdinand* fearing that if they talk'd longer on the Subject, *Hippolito* would urge him beyond what he could bear; thought it most advisable to break off the Discourse; and therefore excus'd himself, that he was indispos'd with Weariness and Grief; and was willing to retire awhile; adding, that some other Time he would confer with him further on that Affair. *Hippolito* told him he might love him, and as many Men as he pleas'd; *for,* says he, *that is Friendship*; Prospero *has taught me how to be a Friend; and next to Women I could love you; but all that Angelical Sex must be mine.* He desir'd *Ferdinand* to consider of it; and so they parted for that time.

In the meantime *Miranda* had not fail'd incessantly to importune her Father that she might once more see the Stranger, who was his Prisoner: And at last prevail'd upon him to grant her Leave. He said she might go, but chargd her to behave her self with a prudent Reservedness, and to let her Visit be but short: Told her she must insinuate into his Mind a Kindness for *Hippolito,* for *Prospero* was earnest to unite their Souls, thinking, such an Union might secure *Hippolito* from the Dark Danger which his Art foreboded: But this Care of the Duke brought that very Fate on the Youth which he was striving to avert. What will be, will be.

Away she goes as fast as Love cou'd hurry her; and being come to the Prison of her Lover, she gave him such a Call as would have wak'd the Dead. *Ferdinand* soon knew her Voice; and presently appear'd. As soon as she saw him, she kindly enquir'd of him how he bore his Misfortunes. He made Answer, that her Presence made his Prison a Palace, *Ah!* says the Innocent Maid, *You talk as if you lov'd me; but how shall I be certain of it? Look to it, for I will die if you are false, and then I will haunt you; for I have heard my Father tell of Maids who died, and afterwards haunted their False Lovers.* Quite confounded with her Innocency, he call'd Heaven and Earth to witness his Constancy. The Joy that she conceiv'd thereupon is not to be express'd. She now thought of her Father's Injunction concerning *Hippolito,* and resolv'd to try his Love (so ignorant was she of that burning Passion *Jealousy*) by enjoyning him to love *Hippolito* for her sake, in the manner following. *I have a suit to you, and that, Sir, shall be now the only Tryal of your Love: 'Tis to love one for my sake, who for his own deserves all the Respect which you can ever pay him: Such a one, who, for his Sweetness, and his goodly Shape, (if I, who am unskill'd in Forms, may judge) I think can scarce be equall'd. Pray, Sir, do not scruple to grant the first Request I ever made? He's wholly unacquainted with the World, and wants your Conversation. If you saw him as I have done, so full of Youth and Beauty, you would certainly love him.*

This put *Ferdinand* upon the Rack, and quite poison'd all his Hopes. He then began to think of what *Hippolito*had said, when he mention'd *Miranda* to him, who told him then, that he would have her. He concluded therefore she was like the rest of her Sex, fair and false; but wonder'd she had not Art to hide it. Therefore he thus accosted her: *Had it been your Father, his Usage of me could not make me hate him, because he gave you Being, which cancell'd all the Wrongs he could offer me. But if there is another whom I ought to love for your sake; to oblige me to't you should discommend him, not praise him: If you bid me love him I must hate him.* *Miranda* fear'd she had offended him, and hearing a Noise, for that time left him, for fear of being surpriz'd by her Sister, who was in an adjacent Meadow, in a deep Conference with *Hippolito*, who, as we have taken Notice before, having heard of more Women besides her self, told her he would have them all.

Dorinda upon this angrily told him, that she did not mind what he said, (tho' indeed it went to her Heart). *I don't care what becomes of me: But I had better have taken my Father's Counsel, and kept you at your due Distance. Besides,* says she, *I never saw any Woman but my Sister here.* Upon that he told her he would go where they were; for this was but a poor World: And in the mean time desir'd that she would introduce him into the Company of her Sister. Upon which in a Passion she told him, that he could not love both of them; and that if he lov'd her, she would not value him; *besides,* (says she) *my Sister has seen another Man, and likes him best.* At this Word she left him, without ever giving him her Hand, or affording him the least Hopes of enjoying her Person if he lov'd any other Woman.

As he was by himself, blaming of the Stranger for coming to take his Women from him; and exclaiming against *Prospero* for endeavouring to fright him from the Conversation of Women-kind, that he might have them to himself: *Ferdinand* came into his Walk; and as they were both seiz'd with the same Passion; they both thought themselves wrong'd; both were resolv'd to redress themselves. *Ferdinand* look'd upon him as a Rival, on Account of what *Miranda* had said; *Hippolito* look'd on him as a Robber that came to plunder him of all that was dear to him in the World; so few Words brought them to the Point of the Sword; in which the latter was dangerously wounded, and fell: *Prospero* happening to come that Way at that unhappy Instant, was struck with a deep Amazement and fell to rubbing him, but all to no purpose: He then cry'd out, *How much in vain doth feeble Art Endeavour to resist the Will of Heaven!* And turning to *Ferdinand* said, *O thou cruel Son of an Inhuman Father! all my Designs are ruin'd and unravell'd by this blow; no Pleasure now is left me but Revenge.* Upon which *Ferdinand* pleaded his Innocence: But *Prospero* immediately call'd *Ariel*, to know why he did not prevent this fatal Action? The Spirit thus reply'd, *Pardon, great Sir, I meant to do it, but I was forbidden by the ill Genius of* Hippolito, *who came and threaten'd me, if I disclos'd it, to bind me in the bottom of the Sea, far from the lightsome Regions of the Air, (my Native Fields) above a hundred Years.* Upon which *Prospero* said to him, *I'll chain thee in the North for thy neglect; within the burning Bowels of Mount* Heila; *I'll singe thy airy Wings with sulph'rous Flames, and choak thy tender Nostrils with blew Smoak, at every Hick-up of the belching Mountain thou shalt be lifted up to taste fresh Air, and then fall down again.* Ariel thereupon humbly begg'd Pardon; which *Prospero* seem'd to consent to; but the Conditions were, that he should immediately bring *Alonzo* and his Company, who were wandering in a remote Part of the Island, to be Witnesses of *Ferdinand*'s Death. He had no sooner spoke, but into his Presence they came, panting and weary, like Beasts that were hunted into Toils. *Alonzo* presently knew his Son *Ferdinand*; and *Antonio,* after some small time, remember'd his Brother *Prospero*; upon which they were all struck with Amazement, and *Gonzalo* shed Tears for Joy: But this Joy was presently quash'd; when *Prospero* after having given his Brother *Antonio* a severe Reproof, thus address'd *Alonzo*; *Usurping Prince, know, by my Art, you were shipwreck'd on this Isle, where, after I a while had punish'd you, my Vengeance would have ended, I design'd to match that Son of yours, with this my Daughter* (pointing to *Miranda*). *Alonzo* told him he was most willing to it, and desired him to proceed in the Match: But the Duke made him this Reply; *No Marriages can prosper which are with Murderers made; look on that Corps, this, whilst he liv'd, was young* Hippolito, (pointing to *Hippolito*) *that Infant Duke of* Mantua, *Sir, whom you expos'd with me; and here I bred him up, 'till that Bloodthirsty Man, that* Ferdinand—*but why do I exclaim on him, when Justice calls to unsheath her Sword against his Guilt.* Alonzo ask'd his Meaning. To which the Duke made him this Reply, *To execute Heaven's Laws, here I am plac'd by Heaven, here I am Prince, though you have dispossess'd me of my* Milan; *Blood calls for Blood; your* Ferdinand *shall die, and I, in bitterness, have sent for you, to have the sudden Joy of seeing him alive, and then the greater Grief to see him die.* Alonzo then drew his Sword to resist the Execution, but *Prospero* soon stopt his Revenge, by quite unmanning him, so that he had not power to move. He then in bitter Grief cry'd out, *Have I for this found thee, my Son, so soon again to lose thee!* And addressing himself to *Prospero*, he said, *Ah* Prospero *hear me speak! You are a Father! Look on my Age, and look upon his Youth.* He was seconded by *Miranda*, who could hold no longer, but on her bended Knees thus intreated her Father, *Dear Sir, be not so cruel to the Man I love, or be so kind to let me suffer with him: Oh that we cou'd change our Fates! Then he might grieve for me, and I with Joy wou'd die for him.* But all these melting Expressions could not move *Prospero*, who was inexorable; and taking *Dorinda* by the Hand, led her to *Hippolito*'s Corps, saying, *Behold your Lover, murder'd by the Man who lov'd your Sister. Now both of you may see what tis to break a Father's Precept; you would needs see Men, and by that sight are made for ever wretched.* Hippolito *is dead, and* Ferdinand *must die for murdering him.* And he then immediately order'd *Ferdinand* to prepare for the fatal Stroke; and *Caliban* was sent for, to do the Execution. Mean while the two Sisters upbraided each other of their Disobedience; and *Dorinda* seem'd to rejoice at *Fer-*

dinand's Death, for that he had slain *Hippolito*; which so incens'd *Miranda*, that she declar'd she'd never love *Dorinda* more.

Caliban was now come, and *Ferdinand*'s Neck was bare; when on a sudden *Hippolito*, after having fetch'd a heavy Sigh, reviv'd; for his extream Loss of Blood, had only (as it were) entranc'd him. He presently ask'd what was become of *Ferdinand*; who being shewn to him, prepar'd to die for the suppos'd Murder of him; He presently desir'd he might not die; for says he, *It was my Fault he hurt me, I urg'd him to it first.* His Request was easily granted, and there immediately follow'd a general Reconciliation: *Antonio*, with a thousand Intreaties for Pardon, resign'd the Dutchy of *Milan* to his Brother *Prospero*. *Alonzo* would not be behind *Antonio* in Justice, so he render'd back the Dukedom of *Mantua* to *Hippolito*. The Wonder that seiz'd that Young Prince is inexpressible, when they told him he should be Lord of a great People, that were all Men and Women; and what were his Thoughts when they told him he should have *Dorinda* for his Bedfellow, I leave the Amorous Reader to judge. In fine, all Matters were adjusted to the mutual Satisfaction of each Party [;] *Ferdinand* was betrothed to *Miranda*, *Hippolito* to *Dorinda*; their Ships were in readiness to carry them to their Native Country; nothing was wanting now, but the Crew; when on a sudden in comes *Trincalo*, the Boatswain, his fair Fuss *Sicorax*, *Caliban* her Brother, and the rest of the Sailors. They then found that in all this Wreck they had not lost one of their Company: Yet the Boatswain was in Danger; for he threaten'd to hang himself, because his Dear Friend the BUTT was empty. However they soon comforted him, when they gave him hopes of seeing his own Country again, and losing his new Spouse: For he, as many an Honest Fellow has been before him, was quite tir'd of his Bargain. So to content all Parties, The Sailors were restor'd to their respective Posts, *Caliban* and *Sicorax* were left sole Rulers of the Island, *Ariel* was set at Liberty, and made once more a free Spirit, to range the Air, which you may perceive by the following Song, which he sung as well out of Gratitude to *Prospero*, as to give the Company a Taste of the Aierial Musick. It was thus.

> *Where the Bee sucks, there suck I,*
> *In a Cowslips Bed I lie;*
> *There I couch when Owls do cry.*
> *On the Swallows Wings I fly*
> *After Summer merrily.*
> *Merrily, merrily shall I live now,*
> *Under the Blossom that hangs on the Bow.*

After which he congratulated *Prospero*, and the Company, as follows:

> *My Noble Master!—*
> *May theirs and your blest Joys never impair,*
> *And for the Freedom I enjoy in Air,*

I will be still your Ariel, *and Wait*
On Aiery Accidents that work for Fate.
Whatever shall your Happiness concern,
From your still faithful Ariel *you shall learn.*

And then *Prospero* thus took his leave:

Thou hast been always diligent and kind.
Farewel, my long lov'd Ariel: *Thou shalt find*
I will preserve thee ever in my Mind.
Henceforth this Isle to the Afflicted be
A Place of Refuge, as it was to me:
The Promises of blooming Spring appear,
And all the Blessings of the ripening Year:
On my Retreat let Heaven and Nature smile,
And ever flourish the Enchanted Isle.

FINIS.

13

Congreve, Fielding, and the Rise of Some Novels

BRIAN CORMAN

In eighteenth-century studies formal realism, like the middle class, is ever on the rise, most frequently in discussions of the novel. Ian Watt's *The Rise of the Novel,* the source of most critical commonplaces on the topic for the past generation, links formal realism to the new middle class in a chronicle of their simultaneous triumph.[1] Standard procedure is to define the end result—the modern novel—and show how the eighteenth-century aspect or author in question contributes to the great tradition. For example, a recent study of Richardson begins by declaring: "By the modern English novel I mean those prose works that create for the reader an illusion of the real world by presenting human personality portrayed in a psychologically real-istic manner, involved in probable situations, and dramatically depicted in a physically and temporally conceived universe." Predictably, the author contends that "the modern novel began with Richardson" and proceeds to support this hypothesis.[2]

Such an approach has proven particularly felicitous for studies of Defoe and Richardson. The results have been less happy for writers of another mold. When asked for his "second thoughts" on *The Rise of the Novel,* Watt himself candidly pointed to one important consequence of his approach: "I have had to grow accustomed to figuring in some minds as a permanent picketer for the Union Novel (International President H. James), carrying a sign which reads 'Cervantes Go Home' on one side, and 'Fielding is a Fink' on the other."[3]

While this literary equivalent to the Whig interpretation of history has been most prevalent in the criticism of the novel, it has not failed to gain currency in discussions of other forms; invariably, the same dialectical polarizations result. Studies of late seventeenth-century drama have pointed (without the same unmixed tone of celebration) to the increased realism of the turn-of-the-century playwrights: "an aristocratic Tory drama" is giving "way to one which is increasingly bourgeois and Whig."[4] Rose Zimbardo attempts to explain the change in the drama by looking at changing concepts of imitation from 1660 to 1730. Her stimulating discussion concludes with this speculative link between the drama and the rise of the novel:

> In *The World Upside Down: Comedy from Jonson to Fielding,* Ian Donaldson says, almost as an aside, "The work which seems the natural successor to *The Way of the World* is . . . *Tom Jones.*" I would go a giant step further and say that so great is the change in the fundamental aesthetic conception "imitation of nature" from the last decades of the seventeenth century to the first decades of the eighteenth that the *necessary* successor to the drama is the novel. The novel answers the needs of the new conception well for a number of reasons. We can "enter into" the characters in a novel much more easily and fully than we can those in a play. We can share their unspoken thoughts and feelings. The novel provides us with a wider range of adventures and puts us, the readers, into situations in which we can experience subtle changes of heart and consciousness with its characters. When drama is a serious form of art, it must always exhibit to some degree an awareness of its own illusory quality; it must always entail "play." The reader can open the door of a novel, enter, and quietly shut the door behind him.[5]

The Whig view of literary history continues to thrive. Zimbardo uses the verb *can,* but there is only one novel, as there is only one drama. Like most critics of the drama and the novel, she generalizes from a single tradition in each genre, thus multiplying the distortions. The exclusiveness of her sense of generic forms is especially curious when juxtaposed to her reference to Donaldson and his two examples, for no two authors resist more vigorously the application of the template of formal realism than Congreve and Fielding. The most successful practitioners of both the drama and the novel in their respective generations, Congreve and Fielding nonetheless both rejected the new "realism"; and, as Zimbardo suggests, nowhere can cause for their joint resistance be seen more clearly than in their concept of imitation.

Congreve's most explicit declaration of dramatic theory is found in his response to Collier, a context in which he finds it necessary to go back to first principles:

> Before I proceed, for method's sake, I must premise some few things to the reader, which if he thinks in his conscience are too much to be granted me, I desire he would proceed no further in his perusal of these animadversions, but return to Mr. Collier's Short view, &c.
>
> *First,* I desire that I may lay down Aristotle's definition of comedy; which has been the compass by which all the comic poets, since his time, have steered their course. . . . Comedy (says Aristotle) is an imitation of the worst sort of people . . . in respect to their manners.[6]

Like Aristotle, then, Congreve insists upon the imitative nature of art, which, as Aubrey Williams has pointed out, was the fundamental issue in the Collier controversy. Collier quite simply refused to acknowledge any difference between life and art.[7] (In so doing, ironically, he contributed significantly to the later prevalence of the doctrine of formal realism.)

In the "uncommonly judicious" preface to *Incognita*,[8] Congreve makes clear that he applies the same Aristotelian principle of imitation to the novel that he finds operative in the drama. In fact, he takes special pride in claiming to be the first novelist to model his plot on the drama: "Since all Traditions must indisputably give place to the *Drama,* and since there is no possibility of giving that life to the Writing or Repetition of a Story which it has in the Action, I resolved in another beauty to imitate *Dramatick* Writing, namely, in the Design, Contexture and Result of the Plot."[9] Like Aristotle, Congreve found that the immediacy of viva voce presentation made the drama the most powerful and hence the highest of literary forms. But though his comparison here is not to the exalted epic but only to the humble novel, he nonetheless devotes considerable care to finding an appropriate structural equivalent:

> The design of the Novel is obvious, after the first meeting of *Aurelian* and *Hippolito* with *Incognita* and *Leonora,* and the difficulty is in bringing it to pass, maugre all apparent obstacles, within the compass of two days. How many probable Casualties intervene in opposition to the main Design, *viz.* of marrying two Couple so oddly engaged in an intricate Amour, I leave the Reader at his leisure to consider: As also whether every Obstacle does not in the progress of the Story act as subservient to that purpose, which at first it seems to oppose. In a Comedy this would be called the Unity of Action; here it may pretend to no more than an Unity of Contrivance.
>
> [A7]

Congreve's "unity of contrivance," as manifested in *Incognita,* is indeed the singularly inferior structure implicit in the Preface, particularly when compared to his subsequent realization of the "unity of action" in the four comedies. Nevertheless, the nonqualitative similarities are evident, especially with hindsight. "Whatever he has to say in a letter, in a dedication, in a prologue about his art is worth listening to with all our ears."[10]

For Congreve, then, novels belong to the same literary family as plays, a claim that does not apply to all forms of prose fiction. He carefully excludes romances because they operate on different principles:

> Romances are generally composed of the Constant Loves and invincible Courages of Hero's, Heroins, Kings and Queens, Mortals of the first Rank, and so forth; where lofty Language, miraculous Contingencies and impossible Performances, elevate and surprize the Reader into a giddy Delight, which leaves him flat upon the Ground whenever he gives of, and vexes him to think how he has suffer'd himself to be pleased and transported, concernd and afflicted at the several Passages which he has

Read, *viz.* these Knights Success to their Damosels Misfortunes, and such like, when he is forced to be very well convinced that 'tis all a lye. Novels are of a more familiar nature; Come near us, and represent to us Intrigues in practice, delight us with Accidents and odd Events, but not such as are wholly unusual or unpresidented, such which not being so distant from our Belief bring also the pleasure nearer us. Romances give more of Wonder, Novels more Delight.[A5ᵛ–A6ʳ]

In removing romances from the legitimate mainstream of literature because of the differences in their respective ends, Congreve anticipates Fielding's well-known position in the preface to *Joseph Andrews,* the document in which he, too, announces the invention of a "Species of writing . . . hitherto unattempted in our language."[11] Fielding is also concerned that his reader "may have a different Idea of Romance with the Author of these little Volumes," that is, that his "comic Romance" or "comic Epic-Poem in Prose" might be mistaken for one of "those voluminous Works commonly called *Romances.*" Writers of "history," such as Fielding or Cervantes or Scarron (Congreve's most likely model for prose fiction[12]), "are contented to copy Nature," unlike "the Authors of immense Romances, or the modern Novel and *Atlantis* writers; who without any Assistance from Nature or History, record Persons who never were, or will be, and facts which never did nor possibly can happen: Whose Heroes are of their own Creation, and their Brains the chaos whence all their Materials are collected" (*Joseph Andrews,* pp. 187–88). Fielding's "epic," like Congreve's "novel," is thus "the counterpart of the term *drama*," in "a systematic classification of poetic species from which [the older, unnatural romances] are conspicuously omitted."[13]

It is because Congreve and Fielding rely in part on the norm of nature to distinguish their works of prose fiction from those of the romance writers that subsequent critics have often considered them members of the movement toward formal realism, and as often have chastised them or apologized for their failure to realize its goals. But although both Congreve and Fielding look to the world of nature, they do so to find objects of imitation. Each may refer to his work as history (Fielding on his title pages); but neither attempts to pass his work off as genuine history in its twentieth-century sense. Like Aristotle, Congreve and Fielding prefer *fictional* history because it is not "confined to a particular Period of Time" but rather "is the History of the World in general" (*Joseph Andrews,* p. 188).

Nor did Congreve or Fielding share twentieth-century attitudes toward history. Just as Dryden required a translator to do more than reproduce literally what was in the original, Congreve and Fielding expected more from a historian; neither discipline had yet to be dominated by their respective equivalent doctrines of formal realism. "Some few embellishments," Fielding maintained, "must be allowed to every historian: for we are not to conceive that the speeches in Livy, Sallust, or Thucydides, were literally spoken in the very words in which we now read them. It is sufficient that every fact hath its foundation in truth."[14] Literal-minded demands for accuracy in transcription can only deny the audience that pleasure it has a right to expect from literature. "I believe," Congreve told Dennis, "if a Poet should steal a Dialogue of any length, from the *Extempore* Discourse of the two Wittiest Men upon Earth, he would find the Scene but coldly receiv'd by the Town."[15]

Congreve had no more interest than Fielding in pretending to factuality in his art. "The distance of the Stage requires the Figure represented, to be something larger than the life; and sure a Picture may have Features larger in Proportion, and yet be very like the Original."[16] Late seventeenth-century acting, of course, was not known for attempts at naturalism, and Congreve's statement would seem to come, at least in part, from his experience in writing for the theatre. Henry Knight Miller has argued that Congreve and Fielding both maintained an "aesthetic" theory of art against the newer and increasingly dominant "affective" theory of Otway or, later, Richardson.[17] (Otway's relationship with Elizabeth Barry and with the stage—as opposed to Congreve's with Anne Bracegirdle—would seem more to confuse life and art, that is, to be less "aesthetic" than his plays themselves.) But while few readers or viewers have ever been in danger of mistaking Restoration tragedy for cinéma vérité, the emphasis on part rather than whole in the design of affective literature contributed to the dominance of the kind of literature rejected by both Congreve and Fielding. It is as a result difficult to accept the following recent interpretation of Congreve's sense of the relationship between the drama and the novel as formulated in the Preface to *Incognita:*

> Congreve's homage to the drama is meaningful, since it suggests a hierarchical mimetic theory which established that art is best that comes closest to everyday reality. . . . Hence comes the relationship of the novella to comedy and the grounds for the argument of the aesthetic superiority of both forms to romance and tragedy, for the closer a work of art is to our experience, the more we are able to believe; the more we are able to believe, the greater our pleasure in the work of art.[18]

In terms of "the modest realism of the late seventeenth century, which appeared fitfully but increasingly and insistently in terms of probability of action, recognizable motivation, acceptable dialogue, psychology, and social setting,"[19] Congreve largely remained a literary conservative in the novel as he was in the drama. Aphra Behn, "whose technique of presentation is at times so like [Congreve's] as to make it seem likely that he had read her with some attention,"[20] provides an interesting contrast in her pursuit of the new realism in her prose fiction. Author of the first epistolary novel in English, Behn often maintained that her prose fiction was history and that she was merely serving as "editor" in conveying factual material (sometimes written, sometimes oral, sometimes observed) to the reading public. (It is worth recalling, too, that the first master of the realistic novel in England, Defoe, was Congreve's contemporary and ten years his *senior*.)

Congreve's conservatism in the drama is evident in his defense of *The Double-Dealer*, his first work to encounter significant hostile criticism. In the dedication to Charles Montague, Congreve feels compelled to point out that in spite of any particular errors, he has not "miscarried in the whole; for the Mechanical part of it is perfect" (*The Complete Plays*, p. 118). The first concrete objection he turns to is to his use of soliloquy, "an Objection [that] does not relate in particular to this Play, but to all or most that ever have been written" (p. 119). "I grant," Congreve begins, "that for a Man to Talk to himself, appears absurd and unnatural," but in some circumstances it is necessary to convey to an audience information that is inappropriate for another character to overhear. Congreve continues to lecture his recalcitrant critics in principles of drama by reminding them that when we see a character in soliloquy,

> we ought not to imagine that this Man either talks to us, or to himself; he is only thinking, and thinking such Matter, as were inexcusable Folly in him to speak. But because we are conceal'd Spectators of the Plot in agitation, and the Poet finds it necessary to let us know the whole Mystery of his Contrivance he is willing to inform us of this Person's Thoughts; and to that end is forced to make use of the expedient of Speech, no other better way being yet invented for the Communication of Thought. [P. 120]

Clearly Congreve was not prepared to accept his critics' demand for more "realism" as a "better way." Because Congreve takes more pride in the design of his art than in its realistic probability, he likens his artistic activity to that of a builder who has "built a House according to the Model laid down before him" or a gardener who has "set his Flowers in a knot of such or such a Figure" (p. 119). Fielding, too, found himself criticized for violating some notions of probability by insisting upon his right to maintain what Watt refers to as the "incongruous bedfellows" of "neoclassical theory," verisimilitude, and the marvelous. As a result, for Watt (and again I use him as a typical if prominent spokesman for formal realism), Fielding's concessions to "the doctrine of the marvellous . . . tend to compromise the narrative's general air of literal authenticity by suggesting the manipulated sequences of literature rather than the ordinary processes of life."[21] Watt, of course, assumes that what Fielding wished to do—or should have wished to do—was to reproduce "the ordinary processes of life." But Fielding's "wonderful long Chapter concerning the Marvellous" makes quite clear that he had no such desire:

For though every good Author will confine himself within the Bounds of Probability, it is by no means necessary that his Characters, or his Incidents, should be trite, common, or vulgar; such as happen in every Street, or in every House, or which may be met with in the home Articles of a News-paper. Nor must he be inhibited from shewing many Persons and Things, which may possibly have never fallen within the Knowledge of great Part of his Readers.[22]

As long as an author does not exceed the bounds of probability, and for Fielding "what is probable is what a given character is likely to do"[23] the author remains within the legitimate boundaries of good fiction.

Fielding followed Congreve's lead, too, in rejecting the lure of the epistolary novel: "I know not of any essential Difference," he argues, "between this, and any other way of writing Novels, save only, that by making use of Letters, the Writer is freed from the regular Beginnings and Conclusions of Stories, with some other Formalities, in which the Reader of Taste finds no less Ease and Advantage, than the Author himself." And no doubt with Richardson in mind, Fielding adds that "sure no one will contend, that the epistolary Style is in general the most proper to a Novelist, or that it hath been used by the best Writers of this kind."[24] Like Congreve, Fielding lectured his critics in the basic principles of his art, principles he was not prepared to give up in deference to the strictures of the new realism. Still more open is his contempt for critics who think we should identify with the characters and action represented, those of "so little Historic or Poetic Faith, that they believe nothing to be either possible or probable, the like to which hath not occurred to their own Observation" (*Tom Jones*, 1:396). Congreve has no such explicit statement on the need to identify with, but there is every reason to think he would have shared Fielding's prejudice.

Just as Congreve's first play, *The Old Batchelour*, is a derivative piece of apprentice work "furnished with comick characters by the perusal of other poets,"[25] Fielding's dramatic comedies have always seemed to most critics "to be exercises in the manner of Wycherley and Congreve, a mere pastiche."[26] But while *The Old Batchelour* was a great success, *Love in Several Masques* and *The Temple Beau* met with indifference, largely, according to Arthur Murphy, because Fielding chose to make "Congreve his model."[27] The success of newer forms of comedy, plays more in line with growing demands for formal realism, would, in part, expain why plays written on Congreve's model could no longer succeed. Fielding's great success as a dramatist, of course, came in his more purely satiric plays, including the burlesques and parodies. To distance the audience from the action Fielding repeatedly uses such devices as play within a play *(Pasquin, The Historical Register for the Year 1736)* or parody (*The Tragedy of Tragedies*, which also includes for the reader its self-conscious, Scriblerian apparatus). Fielding does not allow his audience to forget that they are in the theatre; he does everything possible to destroy the illusion other playwrights were working hard to achieve. So well does Fielding succeed (in all his works) that a recent critic has concluded: "I think that Fielding's novels, like his plays, are essentially undramatic and, as I have tried to show, that Fielding's interests were ultimately inimical to the dramatic mode."[28]

In his history of early epistolary fiction, Robert Adams Day observes:

> The drama, then, shared authors, readers, booksellers, and in a sense form and structure, with early letter fiction. If we agree that epistolary fiction comes very close to the dramatic method, we should be able to reverse the proposition and suggest that in an age when fiction was decidedly informal, writers who had had some experience as playwrights and who turned to fiction when the stage was denied them wrote fiction that departed as little as possible from the dramatic conventions they knew. In short, it seems likely that the earliest English epistolary novels may have evolved from the drama. This is a repetition—no less logical— of the statement that they were progressing toward it.[29]

Day's account may well be accurate for most of the writers of epistolary novels, perhaps even for most of the early English novelists. It does not, however, explain the case of Henry Fielding (the most prominent figure to fit the above specifications). Fielding's first published work of prose fiction was indeed in epistolary form, but no one has ever mistaken Fielding's Parson Tickletext for a realistic Richardsonian "editor." *Shamela* shares in common with Fielding's plays a largely parodic structure, and the use of Tickletext even tends to turn Shamela's story into an epistolary novel within an epistolary novel, thus achieving an effect antithetical to the formal realism of most epistolary novels. (Helga Drougge sees *Incognita* largely as a parody of the newer, more realistic French fiction, a prose equivalent to *The Rehearsal*. Since Congreve's treatment of other writers is far more indirect and gentle, it is difficult to think of *Incognita* as parody in any standard sense. Nonetheless, Drougge is surely right to see *Incognita* as very "literary" and very "artificial," not "because Congreve is careless or inept at creating a sense of reality; but rather because he is careful not to."[30]) Any critical view of the progress of the novel that assumes a single novel and a single drama cannot do justice to the wealth and variety of drama and prose fiction produced between 1660 and 1800. A parallel case for a very different tradition would have to be constructed to allow Congreve and Fielding to fit Day's pattern.

W. L. Renwick maintains that in Fielding's theory of the comic prose epic, it is the "in prose" part of the definition that "plants us firmly down, once and for all, in the ordinary world,"[31] a view to be expected from a critic who sees the novel as the novel of formal realism. But if epic is in fact the counterpart to drama, then it is the "comic" component of Fielding's definition that is responsible for its class of characters. Those characters in turn require the appropriate kind of language. The medium must be suitable for the matter, but the latter determines the nature of the former. Both Congreve and Fielding follow similar strategies for translating the demands of the drama to the demands of the novel. One would predict that a dramatist turning to prose fiction (or a young writer of prose fiction who uses the drama as his literary model) would depend heavily on dialogue to convey his plot, characters, meaning, etc. In fact, though both Congreve and Fielding have passages of sparkling dialogue in their novels, neither relies on dialogue as a significant ordering principle. Instead, to reproduce the artifice and unity of the drama, along with the necessary distance, each turns to a third-person, virtually omniscient narrator, the predominant and controlling presence in all of their novels.

There is in fact more wit in the narrator of *Incognita* than in any of the other characters. Congreve is perfectly well aware of this and seems to take his greatest pleasure in those passages in which he most thoroughly indulges his narrator's wit. Quite early in the narration, the story is interrupted for a declaration of rights by its teller:

> Now the Reader I suppose to be upon Thorns at this and the like impertinent Digressions, but let him alone and he'll come to himself; at which time I think fit to acquaint him, that when I degress, I am at that time writing to please my self, when I continue the Thread of the Story, I write to please him; supposing him a reasonable Man, I conclude him satisfied to allow me this liberty, and so I proceed [Pp. 11–12].

The somewhat disingenuous tone suggests that rather than talking down to his readers, Congreve is sharing his joke with them—or at least with the learned among them. And quite rightly, since much of the charm of *Incognita* lies in its narrator's digressions.

The centrality of the narrator to Fielding's novels is of course commonplace, and the reasons are again similar. Like Congreve's, his narrator never allows the reader to forget that his work is a created artifact, not reality itself. Digressions also provide Fielding with an important technique for maintaining the desired control of the reading process, as his famous defense makes clear:

> Reader, I think proper, before we proceed any farther together, to acquaint thee, that I intend to digress, through this whole History, as often as I see Occasion: Of which I am myself a better Judge than any pitiful Critic whatever; and here I must desire all those Critics to mind their own Business, and not to intermeddle with Affairs, or Works, which no ways concern them: For, till they produce the Authority by which they are constituted Judges, I shall plead to their Jurisdiction. [*Tom Jones*, 1:37]

The rhetorical stance and tone are somewhat different, but in structure, function, and effect, Fielding's digressions parallel Congreve's.

Robert Alter uses the umbrella term *stylization* to refer to Fielding's various distancing techniques. He rightly points to its significance: "Stylization is pervasive in Fielding's fiction and this is one of the reasons why it works so well: The whole world of his comic novels, though modeled on reality, is carefully stylized, not merely the language." His conclusion from this is a particularly interesting one: "In this respect, I am sure Fielding was not only following the bent of his native genius but applying in new ways techniques he had learned in his years of writing for the theater."[32] Clearly Fielding applied the same literary principles to his novels (except, perhaps, *Amelia*[33]) that he had applied to his theatrical work. And although by the time Fielding wrote his novels his views about literature were probably no longer in the mainstream, he nonetheless was part of another tradition of both the drama and the novel, a tradition that included such works as Congreve's *Incognita* in addition to a number of better-known Continental prose fiction antecedents and the line of drama that includes Fielding's own plays.

Few, if any, of Fielding's narrative techniques are unprecedented, even in English prose fiction. Another of his habitual distancing techniques that was anticipated by Congreve is capturing the reader's imagination through the use of rhetorically inflated passages which are then abruptly undercut by an interjection of the narrator. A good example is his description of Incognita first revealing her face to Aurelian:

> Why, she pull'd off her Mask, and appear'd to him at once in the Glory of Beauty. But who can tell the astonishment *Aurelian* felt? He was for a time senseless; Admiration had suppress'd his Speech, and his Eyes were entangled in Light. In short, to be made sensible of his condition, we must conceive some Idea of what he beheld, which is not to be imagined till seen, nor then to be express'd. Now see the impertinence and conceitedness of an Author, who will have a fling at a Description, which he has Prefaced with an impossibility. One might have seen something in her Composition resembling the Formation of *Epicurus* his World, as if every Atome of Beauty had concurr'd to unite an excellency. Had that curious Painter lived in her days, he might have avoided his painful search, when he collected from the choicest pieces the most choice Features, and by a due Disposition and Judicious Symmetry of those exquisite parts, made one whole and perfect *Venus*. [Pp. 40–41]

The passage continues for another page and a half, rivaling in length, if not quality, Fielding's introduction of Sophia in "A short Hint of what we can do in the Sublime, and a Description of Miss *Sophia Western*":

> Reader, perhaps thou hast seen the Statue of the *Venus de Medicis*. Perhaps too, thou hast seen the Gallery of Beauties at *Hampton-Court*. Thou may'st remember *each bright* Churchill *of the Gallaxy*, and all the Toasts of the *Kit-Cat*. Or if their Reign was before thy Times, at least thou hast seen their Daughters, the no less dazling Beauties of the present Age; whose Names, should we here insert, we apprehend they would fill the whole Volume. . . . Yet is it possible, my Friend, that thou mayest

have seen all these without being able to form an exact Idea of *Sophia:* for she did not exactly resemble any of them. [*Tom Jones*, 1 : 155–56].

Fielding, too, continues for some time, though by the time he has finished, his reader, unlike Congreve's, at least knows the color of his heroine's hair and skin.

Critics began calling attention to Congreve's influence on him early in Fielding's career, and have continued to do so to the present.[34] Fielding quotes frequently and extensively from Congreve's plays and criticism (see, e.g., the discussion of wit and humor in *The Covent Garden Journal* No. 55). A number of Fielding's characters exhibit remarkable similarities to Congreve's (e.g., Lady Booby and Mrs. Western[35] to Lady Wishfort, Squire Western to Sir Wilfull Witwoud[36]), and even particular lines are frequently echoed (e.g., Wilson shocks Adams with his account of impressing the ladies by writing letters to himself [*Joseph Andrews*, p. 203], just as Witwoud's account of Petulant's behavior astounds Mirabell [*The Way of the World.* 1.1.376–77]; Honour's rationale for betraying to Sophia Jones's confession on the grounds that the book she swore on was not the Bible [*Tom Jones*, 1:207] recalls Mincing's discovery of Fainall and Marwood's adulterous relationship [*The Way of the World*, 5.1.486–91]; the ogling contest between Jones and Mrs. Waters [*Tom Jones*, 1:511–13] is reminiscent of the sighing contest between Aurelian and Incognita[37] [*Incognita*, pp. 97–98]). It is difficult to overestimate the importance of Congreve as an influence on Fielding.

The most significant way in which Fielding follows Congreve's lead is in producing a kind of comedy which uses the artificial—the crafted—nature of its form to achieve effects as significant morally as those produced by the comedy of a Steele or a Richardson. Through the use of strong antagonists (Fainall and Marwood) and through the presentation of genuine suffering in characters less prudent and fortunate than Mirabell and Millamant (particularly Mrs. Fainall), Congreve was able to create a moral seriousness rarely found in comedy before *The Way of the World.*[38] Similarly, in *Joseph Andrews* the interpolated narratives, usually referred to as digressions, lend perspective to the success of Joseph, Fanny, and Adams. "Hence in the world of the novel's narrator Providence generally protects the good; in the 'real' world as portrayed in the novel's interpolations, Providence is not likely to be so active; and in the 'actual' world outside the novel, the contrast of life and benevolent comedy is still sharper."[39] It is thus possible for Fielding or Congreve to use their comedies to provide models for mankind in general—though clearly in a way radically different from that of Steele or Richardson. Again, in *Tom Jones* Fielding violates the standards of probability demanded by the doctrine of formal realism in order to emphasize that "what happens to Tom is neither impossible nor probable but merely possible."[40] As a result, "we are not disposed to feel, when we are done laughing at Tom, that all is right with the world or that we can count on Fortune always intervening, in the same gratifying way, on behalf of the good."[41] Even Congreve's witty dialogue and Fielding's stylized narrative, the most frequently admired techniques of their respective artifices, can thus be seen as alternative means to the moral seriousness so often celebrated in the novel—and its antecedent drama—of formal realism.

In a very helpful extended analysis of the scene in which Joseph pleads for his virtue to Lady Booby (*Joseph Andrews*, pp. 39–42), an analysis intended to demonstrate why it is Richardson and not Fielding who initiates a "central tradition in the novel," Alter points out that, while the scene contains two characters in dialogue, it remains essentially undramatic because "what Fielding does instead is to make the self-conscious activity of the narrator, who stands, as it were, between us and the stage of action, an integral part of the novelistic event." He then contrasts Fielding's way to that of "a writer of Richardsonian inclinations" who might have evoked the passage of that time by plunging us into the vortex of the thwarted lady's emotions."[42] Even critics sensitive to Fielding's relationship to the eighteenth-century novel of formal realism have failed to recognize that just as there are novels—even fine novels—which are not in a central tradition, there are great plays that elude attempts to define a central tradition in the drama. And although it is easy to see why Richardson's special brand of realism can encourage critics to label his novels dramatic, they are certainly not dramatic in any recognizable eighteenth-century sense.

A dramatic novel is captured with far greater historical accuracy in Maximillian Novak's apology for Aurelian's soliloquy on love and duty in *Incognita*:

> This kind of rhetoric was to vitiate prose fiction throughout the eighteenth century. One may find it in full flower in Smollett; there are elements of it in Fielding and Fanny Burney. It was a borrowing from the stage where soliloquies, though sometimes considered antithetical to verisimilitude, were regarded as vital for producing lyrical and emotional effects. Baneful as such rhetoric was for the novel with its illusion of reality, it is clearly an integral part of the texture of a novella like *Incognita*.[43]

Without defending the excessive rhetorical flourishes of many eighteenth-century novels, one can still claim that it is this very rhetorical tradition, particularly as embodied in the masterpieces of Congreve and Fielding, which made possible the rich alternatives to formal realism to be found throughout the eighteenth century. Novak's apology is based on a single novel just as Alter's analysis ignores much of the drama of Fielding's time, including his own. Even the best single-tradition approaches to the drama and the novel necessarily ignore—or condemn—some of the most important works in each genre. Further discussion of the complex relationship between the drama and the novel must be more inclusive in its conceptions of both. Perhaps "Fielding *or* Richardson" remains a useful classroom dialectic; its usefulness in more advanced discussion has been exhausted.

Notes

1. Ian Watt, *The Rise of the Novel* (Berkeley and Los Angeles: University of California Press, 1957).
2. Ira Konigsberg, *Samuel Richardson and the Dramatic Novel* (Lexington, Ky.: University of Kentucky Press, 1968), p. 1.
3. Ian Watt, "Serious Reflections on *The Rise of the Novel*," *Novel* 1 (1968): 207.
4. Hume, p. 494.
5. R. A. Zimbardo, "Imitation to Emulation: 'Imitation of Nature' from the Restoration to the Eighteenth Century," *Restoration* 2 (1978): 7–8.
6. William Congreve, *Amendments of Mr. Collier's False and Imperfect Citations, &c.,* in *The Dramatic Works of William Congreve, Esq.,* 2 vols. (London: S. Crowder, C. Ware, and T. Payne, 1773), 2:235–36.
7. Aubrey Williams, "No Cloistered Virtue: Or, Playwright versus Priest in 1698," *PMLA* 90 (1975): 235–39.
8. Samuel Johnson, *Life of Congreve,* in *Lives of the English Poets,* ed. George Birkbeck Hill, 3 vols. (Oxford: Clarendon Press, 1905), 2:214.
9. *Incognita: or, Love and Duty Reconciled* (London, 1692; rpt. Menston: Scolar Press, 1971), sig. A6^v. Subsequent quotations from *Incognita* are from this edition.
10. Virginia Woolf, "Congreve's Comedies," in *The Moment and Other Essays* (London: Hogarth Press, 1964), p. 30.
11. *Joseph Andrews,* ed. Martin C. Battestin (Oxford: Clarendon Press, 1967), p. 10. Subsequent quotations from *Joseph Andrews* are from this edition.
12. In *The Old Batchelour,* written roughly at the same time as *Incognita,* when Bellmour enters Fondlewife's house "in Fanatick Habit" to seduce Laetitia, rather than a "prayer-Book" he carries a volume of "trusty Scarron's Novels" (4.2.6). All quotations from Congreve's plays are from *The Complete Plays of William Congreve,* ed. Herbert Davis (Chicago and London: University of Chicago Press, 1967).
13. Homer Goldberg, "Comic Prose Epic or Comic Romance: The Argument of the Preface to *Joseph Andrews,*" *Philological Quarterly* 43 (1964): 199, 197. I am greatly indebted to Goldberg for my understanding of Fielding's preface.
14. Preface to *The Journal of a Voyage to Lisbon,* in *The Criticism of Henry Fielding,* ed Ioan Williams (London: Routledge and Kegan Paul, 1970), p. 144.
15. William Congreve, *Letters and Documents,* ed. John C. Hodges (New York: Harcourt, Brace and World, 1964), p. 181.
16. Congreve, *Letters and Documents,* pp. 180–81.
17. Henry Knight Miller, *Henry Fielding's "Tom Jones" and the Romance Tradition,* English Literary Studies, Monograph Series, No. 6 (Victoria, B.C.: University of Victoria, 1976), p. 27. Miller borrows the term *affective* from Eric Rothstein and equates it with *providential,* an equation I cannot accept.
18. Maximillian E. Novak, "Congreve's *Incognita* and the Art of the Novella," *Criticism* 11 (1969): 329–42.
19. Charles C. Mish, "English Short Fiction in the Seventeenth Century," *Studies in Short Fiction* 6 (1968–69): 329.
20. Ibid., p. 299.
21. Watt, pp. 252–53.
22. *The History of Tom Jones, A Foundling,* ed. Martin C. Battestin and Fredson Bowers, 2

vols. (Oxford: Clarendon Press, 1975), 1:406–7. Subsequent quotations from Tom Jones are from this edition.

23. Robert V. Wess, "The Probable and the Marvelous in *Tom Jones*," *Modern Philology* 68 (1970): 34. My discussion of Fielding on the probable relies heavily on Wess's excellent article.

24. Preface to *Familiar Letters on David Simple*, in Williams, *The Criticism*, pp. 132–33.

25. Johnson, 2:216.

26. F. W. Bateson, *English Comic Drama, 1700–1750* (Oxford, 1929; rpt. New York: Russell and Russell, 1963), p. 117.

27. Arthur Murphy, "An Essay on the Life and Genius of Henry Fielding, Esq.," in *The Works of Henry Fielding, Esq.* (London: W. Strahan et al., 1784), 1:43.

28. J. Paul Hunter, *Occasional Form: Henry Fielding and the Chains of Circumstance* (Baltimore and London: Johns Hopkins University Press, 1975), p. 235.

29. Robert Adams Day, *Told in Letters: Epistolary Fiction Before Richardson* (Ann Arbor, Mich.: University of Michigan Press, 1966), pp. 195–96.

30. Helga Drougge, *The Significance of Congreve's "Incognita,"* Studia Anglistica Upsaliensia, No. 28 (Uppsala: Acta Universitatis Upsaliensis, 1976), p. 39.

31. W. L. Renwick, "Comic Epic in Prose," *Essays and Studies* 32 (1946): 42.

32. Robert Alter, *Fielding and the Nature of the Novel* (Cambridge, Mass.: Harvard University Press, 1968), p. 50.

33. C. J. Rawson, for one, maintains that "Fielding's admiration for *Clarissa* doubtless helped him to see that a great masterpiece could be created from materials for which official literary theory, and his own gentlemanly and temperamental predilections, made no allow-ance: a minute rendering of fact and emotion unmediated by protective ironies and styliza-tions, an assumption of the human importance and interest of the smallest sensation, a total and intimate involvement of both narrator and reader in the drama." For Rawson, *Amelia* reveals Fielding moving toward a more Richardsonian novel (*Henry Fielding and the Augustan Ideal Under Stress* [London and Boston: Routledge and Kegan Paul, 1972], p. 96).

34. Ronald Paulson and Thomas Lockwood reproduce an explicit reference (though hardly favorable) from *The Grub-street Journal* (1732) in *Henry Fielding: The Critical Heritage* (London: Routledge and Kegan Paul; New York: Barnes and Noble, 1969), p. 64.

35. Miller, p. 95.

36. Brian Gibbons, ed., *The Way of the World*, by William Congreve, The New Mermaids (London: Ernest Benn, 1971), p. xxvii.

37. Novak, p. 339.

38. Brian Corman, "*The Way of the World* and Morally Serious Comedy," *University of Toronto Quarterly* 44 (1975): 199–212.

39. Howard D. Weinbrot, "Chastity and Interpolation: Two Aspects of *Joseph Andrews*," *Journal of English and Germanic Philology* 69 (1970): 30.

40. Wess, p. 44.

41. R. S. Crane, "The Concept of Plot and the Plot of *Tom Jones*," in *Critics and Criticism: Ancient and Modern* (Chicago: University of Chicago Press, 1952), p. 638. For a more extensive theoretical discussion of morally serious comedy, see Sheldon Sacks, "Golden Birds and Dying Generations," *Comparative Literature Studies* 6 (1969): 274–91.

42. Alter, pp. 191–94.

43. Novak, p. 338.

14

The World as Stage and Closet

J. PAUL HUNTER

The visible success of eighteenth-century English theatre has never al-together obscured the poverty within, and grand public occasions and spec-tacular performances only dramatize the limits of creative energy that characterize plays written for the eighteenth-century stage. If the trium-phant performances of Betterton, Booth, and Garrick were then among the most distinguished ornaments of English culture, the men and women who wrote for those talented actors were not, and it is something of an index to the level of writing talent available that scholarly efforts can seri-ously be made to elevate the likes of Lillo, Inchbald, and Foote to major literary status. Not that there are not moments of genuine literary significance in the eighteenth-century theatre (*The Beggar's Opera* and *She Stoops to Conquer*, for example), and the early accomplishments of Farquhar and the later ones of Sheridan merit comparison with better times. But it is hard to avoid a sense that whatever small promontories we find here and however pleasing the little prospects we discover, we are plainly in the foothills of the literary history of theatre, and no amount of historical digging into modes of production and acting techniques or contextual explanations of social impact can hide the fact that drama as a literary outlet was in a period of deep decline. Even before the middle of the century verbal energies had shifted so noticeably away from the stage that it was predictable that the next generation of major writers would, when they wrote plays at all, employ the genre without expectation of public performance, as pieces fit not for the stage but for the closet.

More or less concurrent with the decline of English drama is the so-called rise of the novel—the emergence into prominence and popularity of that distinctly new kind of prose fiction—and a connection between the decline of drama and the rise of the novel has long been assumed if not altogether

271

specified. John Loftis speaks authoritatively about "the deflection of creative energy,"[1] a phenomenon that has been widely assumed but never much explored. In this essay I want to consider some explanations for these two movements and their possible interrelationship, review some characteristics of the two literary modes, suggest the implications of some historical events, and speculate a bit about the meaning behind changing directions of taste during the eighteenth century.

I

Trying to date the demise of English drama is risky as well as thankless, and a plausible case could be made for almost any date after 1616. Blaming playwrights for lacking Shakespeare's genius or ages for not being Elizabethan—perennial pastimes still—came to be standard critical procedure long before the end of the seventeenth century, and, picking commentary and facts carefully, one could prophesy from almost any individual season the beginning of the end. It may well be, as one standard literary history has it, that drama had already declined so radically in the late 1630s that "on literary grounds there can be no complaint against the drastic act of the Puritan parliament" in closing London playhouses on 2 September 1642.[2] Certainly the eighteen-year darkness of London playhouses during the Civil War and Puritan interregnum provides an early suggestion of the drama's loss of prestige as a literary vehicle and of the theatre's loss of its broad constituency in English urban culture. And the eruption of the Collier controversy in 1698 and the enactment of the Licensing Act of 1737 provide other possible dates on which conveniently to hang the decline. Specific events, however, seem to me to be manifestations of deeper forces rather than actual causes of the decline, and I want to argue that the increasingly bad signs accumulate until the 1740s, when a meaningful change in the status of drama can be documented.

In one sense, the Restoration represents the peak of post-Renaissance English theatre, and (in another) even its brilliance and euphoria represent signs of ill health. Both the number of active Restoration playhouses and the narrowed audience are cautionary indicators. Instead of the half dozen playhouses that often flourished concurrently in Elizabethan and Jacobean times, London after 1660—although the city was now much enlarged— usually supported only two playhouses, and for fourteen years in the 1680s and 1690s only one had regular seasons. And as a far more respectable and court-connected institution, the theatre regularly had a far smaller "popular" audience. Colley Cibber's repeated plea, in his *Apology* of 1740, for a regulated single theatre in London so that all the human and financial resources could be centered there, involves tacit admission that eighteenth-century English culture would not support theatre so broadly or so enthusiastically as had once been the case.

But even if the reduced scale and legitimized social stature of the relighted playhouses indicates fundamental trouble ahead, the place that Restoration drama assumed in English literary circles became the measure for future times. The single most impressive fact about Restoration theatre—even more significant than the brilliance of individual plays and performances—is that it attracted almost without exception the most talented writers of the generation, a large and heterogeneous group of them that cut broadly across class lines, something that no other theatrical era had ever done. Drama had now taken on a firm literary prestige, as well as social acceptance, and although the broad cultural suspicion of theatre remained, the old disrespect that had allowed the stage to men such as Shakespeare and Jonson but denied it to men of letters such as Sidney and Spenser had altered drastically. Ambitious young writers now assumed that the theatre was the place, or at least a place, to try their hand; call the roll of major belletrists in the Restoration, and except for those who were already middle-aged by 1660, you name men (and one woman) who made at least part of their reputation as playwrights: Dryden, Etherege, Wycherley, Congreve, Rochester, Otway, Lee, Behn, Sedley, Shadwell, and Tate. The only exceptions I can think of are Oldham, that "ah too short, *Marcellus* of our tongue," and Traherne or (if one extends the definition of "major" broadly enough) possibly Sackville or Charles Cotton.

The force of that expectation carried well over into the eighteenth century, and one crucial measure of the decline of drama involves the time when that expectation ceased. In the early part of the century, the major talents almost all dabbled in plays even if drama was not their primary interest: Addison, Steele, Vanbrugh, Thomson, Gay, Fielding, and even Pope wrote hopefully and sometimes well for the stage, and those few who did not—Swift, for example, and Prior—consciously structured their writing careers in opposition to public expectation. Just as significant, perhaps, is the way dramatic expectations helps to structure nondramatic works. In *The Rape of the Lock*, for example, Pope is as dependent on dramatic precedent and expectation as Dryden was in setting the *Essay on Dramatic Poesy* as a dialogue on a Thames barge, and the pageantic and theatrical aspects of the *Dunciad* owe as much to dramatic tradition as any poem specifically designed for the page reasonably can. As late as the 1730s, young, aspiring men of letters such as Samuel Johnson and Tobias Smollett would pack off for London armed with a youthful would-be play, although the fate of *Irene* and *The Regicide* suggests that the temperaments of the young were more closely attuned to the directions of change than were their external hopes and expectations.

Another measuring device is the subject matter and scope of the drama that followed the turn of the century. Even in the Restoration the narrowed scope of drama is readily apparent, with comedies rarely expanding beyond the social bounds of drawing rooms and contemporary mores and "serious plays" shrilly reaching for resonance by trying settings and metaphors increasingly exotic and far away. It is hard to think of any play in the Restoration that represents the broad spirit of its age as *Tamburlaine* may be thought to do, or *The Alchemist,* or *Hamlet,* or *As You Like It,* and in the early eighteenth century it would hardly occur to writer or audience that any play could achieve such scope and magnitude. When new plays alluded to history to clarify a present moment, it was in a bald and heavy way, as in *Cato* or *Jane Shore,* and repeated attempts to create "relevant" theatrical moments try to disguise a rampant insecurity that the present moment is not important or interesting enough to warrant serious dramatic treatment. Attempts to modernize Shakespeare and his contemporaries and attempts to write new plays about contemporary politics share a sense that only the transitory matters, and the retreat from a sense of larger and more enduring issues results in thinner and more strictly occasional plays. Of the two ways to engage politics, drama largely chooses the ephemeral one while the best poetry tries for a larger perspective through which to see the moment, and it is no wonder that Pope and Swift and Gay remain readable while most of the plays of the Harley and Walpole years do not.

Attempts to spice up old plays parallel the search for new ways to entertain audiences beyond the limits of verbal possibility, and the gimmicks of stage machinery, the importation of operatic spectaculars, and the addition of songs, dances, pantomimes, and variety shows to evenings of drama all share a common fear that plays are not sufficient to hold an audience in eighteenth-century English theatre. No doubt the Augustan poets exaggerate the diminishing of the word in their time, but the stage offered them a sufficient example that gratification of the senses seemed increasingly to be desired, and it would be fair to say that drama was more and more a failure even when theatre continued to prosper.

Measuring the decline of drama by the number of playhouses, the size and breadth of audiences, the taste for extraverbal entertainments, the tendency to modernize old works, and the attempt to narrow dramatic focus onto the momentary cumulatively suggests the obvious: that, increasingly as the century went on, the drama had less of a central place in the minds of hopeful writers. By the 1740s, the finest creative energies were going into other modes. The lack of good new plays meant that for most of the first forty years in the eighteenth century, the best nights of theatre consisted, not surprisingly, of Restoration and (especially) Renaissance revivals. By the 1740s there were almost no new plays at all. "Very few new dramas appeared at either theatre," says *The London Stage* about the 1739–40 season. And about the 1745–46 season it says: "Covent Garden again went through a season without offering a single new play." Few new plays of any sort, and no memorable ones, appeared in the entire decade. Writing for the stage was not something that any longer inspired those who aspired to literary fame: the stage was not their world, nor was the world a stage in any sense except that of forgotten metaphor. Drama had achieved a revered place in literary history as it had not a century and a half earlier, but the bright young writers were again working outside the traditional literary forms.

II

Richardson and Fielding are no Shakespeare and Jonson, but their role in elevating the novel to literary respectability roughly parallels what had happened to drama a century and a half earlier. Whatever their motives and reasons—both circumstantial and substantive—for turning to prose fiction, their novels of the 1740s were both a sign and a cause of shifting sensibilities, and the so-called dramatic nature and theatricality of their novels only emphasizes how complete was their modal commitment to printed texts despite a fondness for the power of public performance. Wherever one turns in the literature of the 1740s, the dominance of the new fiction is apparent. The sheer number of fictional "histories"—many of them old-fashioned in their commitments to a world of romance and not really "novels" in any meaningful sense of the term, even more of them hardly artistic successes by any standard—suggests how ready was the reading public for this sort of popular art.[3] Richardson's venture into the "new species" of prose fiction suggests the coloration of moral respectability that began to touch prose fiction, and Fielding's self-conscious invocation of classical models hints at the stirrings of literary respectability. But both of their literary "careers" seemed to happen upon prose fiction rather than being the product of conscious design, and it is Smollett's new presence on the novelistic scene at the end of the 1740s that demonstrates the actual arrival of a new era. ·

Richardson, humble printer and modest purveyor of practical advice (even if an insatiable egomaniac behind the title pages he presented to the world), is almost a stereotype of the new kind of artist emerging in the late seventeenth and early eighteenth centuries. His sense of calling, his almost autistic confidence in his own subjectivity, and his pragmatically trained verbal ease in the vernacular quietly led him to a prominent role in letters that still seems so inappropriate and comic to critics that they habitually treat him as an unconscious puppet of some higher power he did not understand. His drift from the mechanics of print itself into the making of verbal models for print makes him an easy example of a milliner's Milton, a vessel of popular culture thrust against his will into the artistic and intellec-

tual currents of enlightened Europe, but he really is that complex concate-
nation of obsessions, prohibitions, and energies that comprise the new
writer: a prophet of modernity, driven by a compulsion he identifies with
old-fashioned values and traditional needs but finely attuned to the new
social and emotional possibilities of his time. Richardson is no historic
accident, and the accounts of the triumphs of his unconscious have been
greatly exaggerated. In many ways he is the paradigm of the career novelist
and the modern writer more generally; in prose fiction he found the vehicle to express the vision he wished to promulgate, and he found in the
flexibilities of the new mode a form appropriate to his personal inhibitions
and polemical zeal, just as did Austen, Dickens, Lawrence, Woolf, and
Joyce.

If Richardson gave up nothing but silence and privacy for his career as a
novelist, Fielding on the other hand left behind a successful career in the
theatre, and his midcareer switch of modes provided a convenient—and I
think accurate—symbol of the shift of energy from one mode to another.
Cibber's dismissal of him as "a broken Wit"[4] in the *Apology*—that epithet
couches a refusal even to mention his name—might not have seemed a bad
guess in 1740, for the Licensing Act did indeed take the stage away from
Fielding, intimidating the directions of his art even if it did not literally
drive him from the public arena. Fielding had always been extremely conscious of literary models and of the influence upon him of the career
patterns of others, traits that led him as a fledging writer to emulate Pope
and Swift, to try to follow Vergil, and to affect an Augustan tone and
vision.[5] And the same traits assert themselves in his new direction as novelist when he rationalizes Homer as a model and waffles on the novelty of his
own enterprise. Yet the turn to his "new province" of writing is in fact new,
and his repeated attempts to tie what he does to old traditions, old ways of
thinking and perceiving, and older literary modes is the mark of a writer
conscious of expanding radically a sense of what innovations the literary
tradition can tolerate without being destroyed. In another place, I have
argued that Fielding's natural bent was, in any case, for printed prose
narrative rather than theatrical performance, and here I only want to
suggest that the timing of Fielding's career change helps us to date the
moment when novelistic experience began to be more central to the English literary tradition than dramatic experience. Fielding's courage in
making a modal switch—even if prompted by legal constraint and led on by
serendipity more than by any single decision to become a novelist per se (by
1743, he more or less discovered that he already was a novelist rather than
that he wanted to be one)—suggests that he found it possible and perhaps
even necessary to take a career direction that ten years earlier would not
have seemed a possibility.

Smollett's career, because it does not represent any real change of direction, provides an even better index than Richardson's or Fielding's of how

fully the novel had subsumed literary power by the end of the 1740s. The simple fact that Smollett chose, at the age of twenty-seven, a career as novelist says a great deal about the expectations of young writers and about their perceptions of choices open to them. That Smollett could aspire to be a man of letters and regard prose fiction as the main cable of his aspiration marks a substantial change in the perception of literary possibility. At age twenty-seven, Swift could not have made that decision in 1694, or Pope in 1715, or Fielding in 1734.[6] Just as it had become possible by 1660 for dramatists such as Wycherley to conceive of a literary career chiefly fashioned in prose instead of verse, so by 1748 it had become possible to think of making a literary career in prose fiction, and Smollett is the first example of a major English literary talent to make a clear and conscious choice. His translations, histories, satires, and poems are, of course, crucial to his credentials, but his novels represent the main thrust of his literary reputation.

III

It was (to paraphrase Virginia Woolf but choose a much earlier date) on 7 April 1740 that the world changed. That was when *An Apology for the Life of Colley Cibber, Comedian* appeared in London, and the reactions of Fielding and Pope, while extravagant, may not have been excessive. Pope understood perhaps better than anyone in his time how significant trivialities could be, and it is to his refusal to discount minor (but cumulative) events in the interest of a larger perspective that we owe the profound and prophetic sense of cultural change that his poetry analyzes, from *The Rape of the Lock* to the *Dunciad* of 1743. Whether or not Lewis Theobald ultimately "works" as hero of the 1728–29 *Dunciad*, Cibber's appropriate heroism fuses perfectly with Pope's sense of how power may accrue and cling to people, places, and things that should, but cannot, be overlooked, transferring the moral imperative from its ideal position in action to its modern pragmatic one in satiric observation. Not allowing his contemporaries to overlook such matters was one of Pope's most annoying and most important characteristics, and if, in attacking Theobald, his personal feelings might be thought to be a primary cause, his elevation of Cibber involves concerns that transcend the personal. Cibber's yawning presence presides over the land of Dulness like a weathercock over a barnyard, and it is not so much his official place in his culture that makes him a perfect monarch for a poem about taste as his uncanny ability to read the taste of his contemporaries. By 1740 Cibber had been accurately gauging taste and angling among politicians for nearly a half century and had demonstrated that survival, promotion, and symbolic prominence depended on the satisfaction of the common taste and on careful insinuation of oneself among the powerful. His version of "a man of many parts" had many faces but no definable character, and in choosing the poet laureate whose literary career had been, until the last minute, entirely associated with the theatre, Pope characterized the century's first forty years and acknowledged a new moment when the prophecy was fulfilled. His point was not unlike that of Swift in *Tale of a Tub,* but Swift's brooding impersonation had caught the monster hatching, long before it slithered its way up to Drury Lane and thence west to Westminster.

In one sense there is nothing out of character at all in Cibber's writing his *Apology,* for he is there the same man of many faces and roles as he had been on the stage. But in a more important sense the *Apology* is an act of rebellion and a landmark of cultural change. The oddity of publishing one's autobiography in 1740 was much remarked upon immediately (and justly so), but his choice of mode in writing the *Apology* is all the more remarkable because of the extreme contrast between the public Colley Cibber and the fact that he chose such a private vehicle. It is not that the private Cibber is very much different from the public one—both are garrulous, vain, and extraordinarily fond of seeming practical and socially agile, and neither seems to hide much beyond what is obvious at first glance—but that the Cibber used to crowds of people and the observable responses of a communal audience now finds himself trying to talk to the "gentle reader," one consciousness at a time, alone in the private closet.

Cibber is very self-conscious about the radical differences between public and private life and between public and private modes of address, and he ties his values firmly to the power of public performance. Over and over he contrasts print and performance, always concluding that performance is far more powerful. "The Stage, and the Press," he says in one passage comparing performed and printed libels, ". . . are very different Weapons to wound with. If a great Man could be no more injured, by being personally ridicul'd, or made contemptible, in a Play, than by the same matter only printed, and read against him, in a Pamphlet, or the strongest Verse; then indeed the Stage, and the Press might pretend, to be upon an equal Foot of Liberty: But when the wide Difference between these two Liberties come to be explain'd, and consider'd, I dare say we shall find the Injuries from one, capable of being ten times more severe, and formidable, than from the other" (pp. 156–57). The tenfold estimate he repeats, in fact, several times; and without ridiculing the effect of communication to a private reader, he emphasizes the power of communal response. After arguing the force of an acted libel, for example, he contrasts the effect upon a reader. "But alas!" he says, "the *quiet* Reader of the same ingenious Matter, can only like for *himself;* and the Poison has a much slower Operation, upon the Body of a People, when it is so retail'd out, than when sold to a full Audience by wholesale" (p. 160). "Characters," he says in another place, "that would make the Reader yawn, in the Closet, have by the strength of . . . Action, been lifted into the lowdest Laughter, on the Stage" (p. 86). Cibber would have agreed with Defoe that "if my own watch goes wrong, it deceives no body but my self; but if the Town Clock strikes false, it imposes upon the whole Parish."[7]

At home with audiences of any sort, Cibber is noticeably uncomfortable with the "gentle reader" he addresses, and his uncertainties about how he will be interpreted lead him repeatedly to plead for a uniformity of response that he acknowledges is impossible when single readers contemplate his words in print in their solitary retreats. His nostalgia for communal response no doubt seemed ludicrous to traditionalists such as Fielding and Pope, for whom community implied more lasting relationships than the random ones involved in a playhouse audience, and Cibber's nostalgia for community is certainly based on a newer and narrower sense of what the dynamics of response are all about. The value that Cibber sets upon communal response seems to derive entirely from his experience in the theatre itself; it does not seem to have been derived from a larger philosophical commitment. For Cibber, the stage was his world, and there is little in his *Apology* or in his career that suggests anything but vestigial traces of the old metaphor that had given the theatre its resonance by suggesting it as a synecdoche for a world of interrelationships. For Cibber, the metaphor can be made to serve a literal comparison ("The *Government* of the Stage is but that of the World in Miniature," p. 234, italics mine) but has no resonance or symbolic significance.[8] For Sidney and Shakespeare and their contemporaries, the world as stage had still meant applicable correspondences and metaphors that validated reality, a sense that communal assent tested the truth of things and that community was more important than the perception of any one individual. In Cibber's time (how odd, but accurate, it is to think of the age as Cibber's and not as Pope's or Swift's), the fragmentation was far advanced, and while invocations of a *consensus gentium* still abounded and a fear of individualism was strident and often shrill, Cibber's devotion to the vehicle without responsibility to the tenor typifies the desire to hold on to the old ways without seeing the implications of new ones. And his surrender to the privacies of print—a matter he uncharacteristically wonders about repeatedly in the *Apology*—is a fair index of how fully the cultural conduits were shifting from public and communal ones to private and subjective ones.

IV

The garbled singular and plurals of Fielding's desire to "hold the glass to thousands in their closets" (*Joseph Andrews*, 3:i) fairly suggests both the clear intention and the uncertain methodology of novelists in the 1740s. In both of his first two novels, Fielding had been busy updating the world-as-stage metaphor, now pretending that its appropriate vehicle was a stagecoach in which writer and reader could confer amicably together and trace in harmony the larger outlines of the world's government through a study of particulars that could be illuminated by commentary, interpretation, and the observation of response. The slippery metaphor (Fielding's admission that cosmic metaphor has dwindled to verbal punning) is part of his larger rhetoric of communality, and in one way after another he pretends that his "rational" approach to consensus socializes a mode that, he is all too aware, is ultimately a lonely and subjective one. Whatever Fielding's personal feelings about Richardson's art, he understood as well as anyone in the 1740s that writing for readers involved greeting them in the privacy of their closets where they were responsible only to themselves for their responses to a world of print.

The phenomenology of the English closet is an interesting one, and its history suggests its central location in the changing focus of literature and culture more generally. The architectural history of the closet is in fact a social history of the age, and the most interesting parts are those about which we can at present only surmise some of the details. One can readily trace, as Mark Girouard has recently done,[9] the growing importance of the closet in country houses during the seventeenth and early eighteenth centuries, and from structural changes alone one can readily see that in stately homes private space was an increasingly important phenomenon. Most striking, perhaps, is the way that private space became increasingly available to young family members and to women. It may be that a grudging respect was beginning to develop for members of the family unit who had traditionally been relegated to inferior positions and who had been assumed to need less personal space than public figures or heads of families whose daily life would naturally be punctuated with obligatory conferences and a variety of social interactions that would make obvious the necessity of their having a place of retreat from company and social cares. Very likely the shape of English Protestantism and the growing urbanization of England were influential in the process; Puritanism's heavy emphasis upon the isolation of the individual, the need for private devotion, and the integrity of the will ultimately touched the habits, routines, and assumptions of people who would have nothing to do with its creed. And the urban crowding of strangers into cramped shared spaces heightened the urgency of the need to find a time and place to be alone.

The right of individuals to have a private space seems to be generally accepted by the early eighteenth century, and the existence of such a space—even for women, children, and servants—is assumed by the writers of domestic guidebooks and handbooks of family devotion, even those intended for use by the poorest economic classes and the lowliest social classes. No doubt that right was abrogated in many individual cases, but even in lowly and primitive circumstances it was also generally observed, if we are to believe the evidence of *Pamela*—evidence that Richardson's contemporaries clearly had no trouble accepting. Had it not been for Pamela's closet—and the nearly limitless supply of paper and ink that she managed to stash there—we could have no record of her perils or lucubrations, and Richardson goes to some length to convince us of the sacred integrity of her space.

In her vulnerable state, Pamela repeatedly retreats to her closet, confident or at least trusting of its security and integrity, and some of the power of Mr. B.'s insidious stratagems derives from his violation of her right of privacy, a right that to Richardson is nearly as significant as the sexual honor it represents. At the very beginning of *Pamela* we hear little about the heroine's closet, for her need for privacy is minimal. But as privacy and violation become increasingly important to the narrative, closets become both security and threat, and Pamela quickly shows herself aware of the psychological impact of space. The first closet mentioned is that of Pamela's late mistress; Mr. B. first takes Pamela there to give her some clothes, then sets up a meeting with her there to further his designs upon her person, so that to Pamela it soon becomes "a Room I once lov'd, but then as much hated."[10] Pamela's nostalgia for the humble "Loft" still preserved for her in her parents' cottage becomes the countertheme to "that sad Closet Affair" (p. 112) in which she discovers the limits of her privacy in Mr. B's house. Actually, there are two closet episodes that reflect each other as narrow escapes of Pamela's virtue. In the first (pp. 64–68), Pamela is attacked in bed by Mr. B., who has hid in "the wicked Closet" of Mrs. Jervis, and this is when Pamela manages a three-hour faint and finds Mr. B's hand in her bosom. In the second episode (pp. 78–81) she is rescued by sentiment and the natural power of her virtue, for Mr. B., who has hidden in a closet off the green room where she is sorting her clothes and mementos of the house, is moved by her remembrances of his mother and by her kind and pathetic remarks: he retreats from his wicked design in tears.

It is when Pamela is spirited away into the watchful care of Mrs. Jewkes that she learns to make use of her own closet, and for fully half the novel (the middle half) we see her primarily there, usually reading letters or writing letters or plotting her escape. Ultimately, at precisely the halfway point in the novel, Mr. B. invades her closet to search for her papers, a most suggestive and ominous violation, but the crisis is nearly past now, and soon she is able to restore her closet to the pristine purity of its traditional spiritual uses. When she gains a promise of marriage from Mr. B., Pamela goes straight "to my Closet, and threw myself on my Knees in Raptures of Joy" (p. 235); a paragraph later, Mr. B. joins her there to see her "with Pen and Ink before me in my Closet," thus uniting the closet themes of threat and salvation and sanctifying the place for its appropriate function as a bower of introspection and devotion in a context of family harmony and love. Later, Mr. B. fetches her physically from her closet in respect and love (p. 280), and after the wedding itself she immediately repairs there with pen and ink, then prays there, and then is joined there by Mr. B. before they consummate their marriage (pp. 291–95). From this three-quarter point to the end of the novel, Pamela spends time "in Prayer and Thanksgiving in my Closet" (p. 306), for her needs for a private place have shifted significantly.

Pamela tells us, in fact, a great deal more than Richardson might have been comfortable in telling us directly about the uses of the closet in the eighteenth century and of its significance in literary history. Richardson is sometimes said to be a seventeenth-century thinker or the holder of seventeenth-century religious beliefs and assumptions, and it is true that in some of his traditional loyalties he looks backwards, but his appearance of being born a half century late is more impressive than the reality that lies behind it. He liked to seem a fussy and prissy man much concerned for older proprieties, but the energy of his work is the energy of the 1740s, and his naked artistic power derives at least in part from his frank engagement with contemporary social realities, even if he sometimes had to invent a kind of neomedieval virginity cult in order to contain appropriately the energies he was quite openly probing. How he uses the closet in *Pamela* is a case in point, for his straddling of seventeenth- and eighteenth-century rhetoric is very revealing indeed.

Seventeenth-century guidebooks largely assume that closets are places for devotion, self-examination, prayer, and devout reading, but not long into the eighteenth century one observes a sharp tonal shift. Instead of the commendation of certain exercises and the recommendation of certain appropriate books, there are warnings about the misuses of private time and space. Assumptions that people come to their closets to pray now shift into assumptions that closeted individuals titillate themselves with novels and romances. Warnings about this misuse of privilege had, of course, begun before the turn of the century, but the insistence and shrillness grew noticeably during the first half of the eighteenth century. Before midcentury there were close associations in the public mind between secular reading—especially of fiction—and the private closet. Almost all of the familiar references to servants, women, or young people wasting their time in idle reading locate the seat of their worry in what had come to seem the pernicious misuses of the individual closet. Author after author and moralist after moralist report that books unfit for public rooms may be found in the closets of even the most devout families. And I am sorry to have to report that Richardson's first heroine is very much of her generation in retiring to her closet for other than prayer and meditation, even though her author is careful before the end of the novel to affirm the old values of the closet and allow Pamela the leisure again to say her proper prayers. But for the bulk of the novel—until Pamela has gotten a promise of matrimony from Mr. B.

and has become confident that he will keep his word rather than lurk again in a closet or bury himself in women's clothing—Richardson sends her to her closet primarily to record her plight. Even the broadest sense of self-examination would not justify, to the seventeenth-century moralists whom Richardson is supposed to resemble, so loose a use of the place that was, in Protestant iconology, a sacred as well as secret place, a place where the individual was alone with God and where the object of meditation was the soul—not the body that is always central to Pamela's thought.

No doubt Richardson felt that Pamela had spent her time in a worth-while cause: publicizing her plight and her strategems to preserve her public and private honor. And I am not one of those who thinks that Richardson was ignorant of what he did. In truth he was having it both ways: allowing her, early on, to use an established institution for purposes that seem to her own moral benefit and, later, allowing her to resanctify her closet, when she is Mrs. B., as the center of her religious life. Richardson the pragmatist would only have denied the iconographic significance of her earlier conduct and insisted on Pamela's practical good sense. Pamela is a good eighteenth-century pragmatist taking advantage of seventeenth-century traditions and beliefs that Richardson upheld as best he could in a changed world. In any case he was precisely right to locate the origins of novelistic energy in the forbidden place, the closet become secularized and solipsized with pen and ink.

V

According to one of literary history's most persistent legends, church bells were set ringing in English villages when the natives heard of Pamela's marriage to Mr. B. Charming though it is, the legend is misleading about the directions of English art and entertainment in midcentury. It may well be that bells really did ring in one or more of the places about which the legend is circulated, but even if some village blacksmith or other did gather the villagers together and read all of *Pamela* orally to them, the phenomenology of the experience was not typical of what was happening in 1740.[11] It may be that the illiterate, the infirm, the weak of sight, and those too poor or unfortunate to acquire their own copy of *Pamela* were eager listeners at many such public readings, as they have been on many occasions since, but *Pamela* is peculiarly ill-suited to public reading; and if dramatic adaptations of *Pamela* could readily capitalize on the sensation of the book, it was still the book itself that brought the news of a new era.

Pamela's epistolary form is one indication of its need to function as a printed document, to be contemplated by the private reader in solitude. The prurient sense—hard to define but impossible to ignore in Richardson—is crucial to the total effect, and the private satisfaction (and discomfort) we feel in casting our eyes upon someone else's mail is an effect that can be gained only by an individual act of will when we are invading with our eyes, snooping, prying. No cooperative eavesdropping, no passive act of listening to someone else invade a private communication and offer it to a communal group matches the active act of reading. Richardson may or may not have known that he was tapping into a vein that was then becoming vital to the consciousness of his age, and, of course, there is much more to his art and its triumph than the mere decision to join a number of lesser contemporaries in the epistolary mode, but the epistolary nature of his novels is one indication of privacy as a central issue, for the reader of novels as well as for the protagonists within. Whether or not the novel is *about* the individual and sponsored by the thematic concerns of individualism, it seems certain that its phenomenology is individualistic and is crucially aimed at the private, solitary response of one reader reading, usually alone. Many other characteristic features of the novel are also dependent on the assumption of the solitary reader—its length; its wealth of detail; its intricacies of plot and interrelationship; the complexities made possible by its multiple or shifting points of view;[12] its scope, in defiance of human memory; its subtleties of syntax and language, which sometimes require rereading. These are all features that sometimes require the rechecking of passages read earlier. Novels such as Richardson's would have been badly suited for those who lacked either the artifact itself or the eyes to pursue it. Communal hearing requires different skills; and no matter how dramatic or theatrical individual passages or scenes may be, the novel as a whole requires a different act of reception to enter the human consciousness appropriately. Diderot well understood Richardson's characteristic art when he wrote:

> Les details de Richardson déplaisent et doivent déplaire à un homme frivole et dissipé; mais ce n'est pas pour cet homme-là qu'il écrivait, c'est pour l'homme tranquille et solitaire, qui a connu la vanité du bruit et des amusements du monde et qui aime à habiter l'ombre d'une retraite et à s'attendrir utilement dans le silence.[13]

Fielding, Smollett, and other contemporary novelists may aim less obviously at the solitary reader in the private closet, but that is because these authors are so conscious of approaching a "dear reader" instead of an assembled group that they try to create the illusion of a social atmosphere—by pretending to talk directly with a putative reader, by imagining a family of responders or a group who are participating in the creation of the book or hearing its story together, or by creating situations in which stories are told and an audience within is created to pretend to mirror an external audience—trying to minimize the reality of a solitary reception of cold hard print.[14] But even the attempts to socialize reading experience—or to pretend that it can be socialized—amount to an open admission that the reading process is by nature solitary and at a distant remove from the idea of a theatre, with an audience sharing laughter and pathos and helping to create a communal response by, in effect, responding to each other. A thousand readers indeed stare, from their closets, into the single mirror of print, and each of them does it all alone.

In a very real sense the London reader of 1740 may have been more completely alone than any Englishman or Englishwoman had ever felt before. Partly it was a matter of urbanness and of that indefinable sense one gets from self-imposed shields in the midst of a crowd. But it was also a matter of the brooding sense that the things that hold human beings together—families, traditional interest groups, institutions such as the church—were breaking down. It was the sense that the solitary figure that the romantics would soon isolate so well was the person of the future. The flow in that direction had begun long before, encouraged by a great variety of philosophical, political, and social currents, and if Puritanism may be said to stand for most of those tendencies, it is not, in and of itself, a single, simple explanation. When, in 1728 for example, a particular moment could be marshaled to foster a nostalgic sense of communal togetherness, drama could still be a viable force, and *The Beggar's Opera* mines that lode as well as any eighteenth-century work of art could do. But increasingly it was only an opposition to something that could provoke what there was of consensus and togetherness, and Pope was largely right to assume in the early 1740s that what traces there had been in his time of a Roman sense of community had now become the most ironic sense that a word like *Augustan* could produce. He was never so acute as Swift in *Tale of a Tub* in isolating the subjective that sponsored the new world of the private closet, but he had a finer and more resonant sense of what was lost when one's world was no longer the stage and when the stage no longer could stand for or even shadow forth the world as it was.

If I am right that the reciprocity between drama and the novel as the central modes of English letters was less a matter of external events and more a matter of profound cultural changes that were at the heart of living habits and social expectations, then the shift of dominance is datable as a phenomenon of the 1740s, and the achieved energy of the novel by mid-century is interpretable as a logical outgrowth of fundamental cultural change. We need not be mystical to speak of the shift of artistic energy from dramatic to narrative modes in the mid-eighteenth century: The shift involves a rapidly changing perception of what medium is viable, and we can date fairly precisely the time that major writing talents arrived at that perception, even if the processes that brought it about date from at least a century before. In a real sense, the Puritan fear of theatre as a force of immoral infection, the growing cultural distrust of village festivals, the proscription of the telling of traditional tales, the court terror of nonconformist assemblies that led to laws such as the Conventical Act, and the political fears that produced the Licensing Act of 1737 were all part of the same sense that communality was now so thoroughly debased that group reactions could no longer be trusted in public occasions, and that the route to influence was a private and subjective one, to be found only in private converse between a fixed book and the response of an individual reader, deciding silently and alone. Repeatedly one finds in books a nostalgic sense of a world lost, a community remembered, a budding hope that the mind and spirit of individuals could be enough. Even communal visions of men such as Pope end up with detailed footnotes that interact with the text, double columns that need to be read against each other, and visual puns that depend upon the seeing of print. After 1740, Pamela's private closet could, and did, become an object on the public stage, but the stage then was borrowing from the mode that had superceded it. More typical of 1740 itself is the playwright, theatre manager, actor, and poet laureate alone in his closet writing affectionately about the theatre gone by for other readers alone in their closets, addressing his dear reader long after his last audience has gone home.

Notes

1. John Loftis, *Comedy and Society from Congreve to Fielding* (Stanford, Calif.: Stanford University Press, 1959), p. 136.

2. Tucker Brooke, "Caroline Drama, 1625–42," in *A Literary History of England*, ed Albert C. Baugh (New York: Appleton-Century-Crofts, 1948), p. 589.

3. No single attempt to count novels or works of prose fiction in the eighteenth century has become standard, largely because of the difficulties of definition and of distinguishing fiction from fact. But however one counts, the tremendous increase in the number of works of prose fiction in the 1740s is very striking indeed; in this all the checklists agree.

4. Cibber, p. 155. Future references to this edition are in the text.

5. I have discussed the directions and intentions of Fielding's career at some length in *Occasional Form: Henry Fielding and the Chains of Circumstance* (Baltimore: Johns Hopkins University Press, 1975).

6. Swift does seem to have been almost prescient, however, in his sense that something was in the air, and one way of regarding *Tale of a Tub* is as an attack upon the authorial and audience sensibility that came to sponsor the novel.

7. Daniel Defoe, *Review* 3, no. 66 (10 August 1706).

8. Cibber uses the metaphor similarly elsewhere. "I have," he says near the end of the *Apology*, "so often had occasion to compare the state of the stage to the stage of a nation, that I yet feel a reluctance to drop the comparison" (p. 283). All Cibber's comparisons are, however, involved with the *state* of the stage and nation.

9. Mark Girouard, *Life in the English Country House* (New Haven and London: Yale University Press, 1978).

10. Riverside Edition, ed. T. C. Duncan Eaves and Ben D. Kimpel (Boston: Houghton Mifflin, 1971), p. 43. Future references to *Pamela* are in the text. For a good discussion of Richardson's consciousness of place, see Robert Folkenflik, "A Room of Pamela's Own," *ELH* 39 (1972): 585–96.

11. For a discussion of the varieties of the story about *Pamela's* being read to villagers, see Alan Dugald McKillop, "Wedding Bells for Pamela," *Philological Quarterly* 28 (1949): 323–25.

12. See Robert Scholes and Robert Kellogg, *The Nature of Narrative* (New York: Oxford University Press, 1966), pp. 51 ff.

13. Denis Diderot, *Eloge de Richardson*, in *Oeuvres Complètes* (Le Club Français, 1970), 5:132.

14. I have discussed this matter and some related ones in "The Loneliness of the Long-Distance Reader," *Genre* 10 (1977): 455–84. For an excellent discussion of the shift away from works written to be read before an audience, see William Nelson, "From 'Listen, Lordings' to 'Dear Reader,'" *University of Toronto Quarterly* 16 (1976–77): 110–24.

15

Richardson's Dramatic Art in *Clarissa*

JOHN J. RICHETTI

Samuel Richardson gave *Clarissa* a completely conventional subtitle, *The History of a Young Lady,* thereby linking his narrative for contemporary readers with any number of books that used the term *history* on their title pages to advertise the more or less domestic and contemporary events within. From the first, however, Richardson had unconventional aims, and he warned readers in his preface that his book was designed for more than amusement and would "probably be . . . tedious to all such as dip into it, expecting a light novel, or transitory romance" (1:xv).[1] In due course, he claimed an overarching dramatic conception for his work, and in his "Postscript" in defense of the book against those who wished it happier or shorter than it was, he described it as a sort of revisionist Christian tragedy. There, he invoked Aristotle (by way of Addison) and Rapin to justify *Clarissa*'s unhappy ending as an occasion for morally improving pathos and the book itself as a divine comedy in which pathos is crowned by a "consideration of the doctrine of future rewards; which is everywhere strongly enforced in the history of Clarissa" (4:556).[2] The serious and thoughtful reader Richardson wished for encounters a drama in which his own involvement is transformed from the pleasures of pity and terror into moral-religious satisfaction that is intended as far superior to the poetic justice some of his readers demanded for his heroine. The book remains a "history," since there was no literary classification available to do justice to it, but Richardson groped toward a more exact label when he referred to himself as the "author of the history (or rather dramatic narrative) of Clarissa" (4:554). Much of the most discerning praise of *Clarissa* since then has focused on that parenthesis, and Richardson's achievement as pioneer and perfecter of the psychological novel can perhaps be accounted for by his merging of drama and prose narrative.

Such hybridization seems to come naturally to prose fiction, and many of the novels we identify with the beginnings of modern narrative are inter-twinings of different and sometimes conflicting literary modes. *Don Quixote* is an ironic blending of picaresque, pastoral, and romance, and this Cer-vantic mixture is what animates *Joseph Andrews* and *Tom Jones*. Defoe's novels work by combining the secular energies of picaresque and criminal biography with a moral introspection and devotional pattern that make them strangely profound. At first glance, the literary lineage of *Clarissa* is much simpler than these other narrative hybrids. Richardson's story is the staple of numerous popular amatory narratives of the first forty years of the century, and in common with them it has a tendency to a theatricality of theme and style. The amatory novella as practiced expertly by Eliza Hay-wood, for example, tends toward erotic and pathetic moments featuring broad rhetorical flourishes and equally broadly rendered themes of love and honor, innocence, and betrayal. So, too, *Clarissa* is a dramatic narrative because on one rather obvious level it tends toward those large theatrical moments and allows some of its characters an occasional operatic grandeur of speech and gesture.[3] *Clarissa* is dramatic, moreover, because these theatrics support a simple and intense set of conflicts. As the story unfolds, the main characters come to occupy clearly defined and radically opposing moral-cultural positions, and *Clarissa* turns into a dramatic spectacle in which it is easy for the reader to become, as it were, a spectator.

To be sure, Richardson is much better at this sort of importation of theatrical themes and styles than were hard-pressed hacks such as Mrs. Haywood. Modern literary history has shown in detail how *Clarissa* is specifically an integration of those themes and styles into Richardson's narrative, and how behind "each of Richardson's main protagonists there lies a stage tradition," as Mark Kinkead-Weekes has put it.[4] But what every critic who has explored the dramatic and theatrical matrix of *Clarissa* neces-sarily adds is that Richardson transforms his materials and uses them for his own purposes, that is, for a moral and psychological realism beyond the capacities of his dramatic models.[5]

The catalyst in that transformation was, of course, the epistolary conven-tion as hugely expanded and intensified by Richardson. Such a convention provides opportunity for soliloquy and dialogue in which character and theme can aspire to that independence and objectivity of presentation as-sociated with the dramatic mode. But again, these are merely external features of drama, and soliloquy and dialogue in themselves hardly guarantee dramatic achievement. It is, rather, Richardson's enormous powers of concentration and identification with his characters that validate these dramatic externalities. Richardson did not simply manage to efface himself in *Clarissa*. By virtue of an involvement in his correspondents prob-ably without parallel in narrative literature, he disappeared from the text in more than the literal sense enforced by the letter convention. As he boasted to Lady Bradshaigh, his immersion in his characters was much more than ventriloquial animation: "Here I sit down to form characters. One I intend to be all Goodness; All Goodness he is; Another I intend to be all Gravity; All Gravity he is. Another Lady G——ish; all Lady G——ish is she. I am all the while absorbed in the character. It is not fair to say—I, identically I, am any-where, while I keep within the character."[6] Richardson's claims involve a psychological participation in character that is an implicit revision of eighteenth-century theatrical practice, focused as that was on matters of external rhetorical effectiveness (or he aspires to the achievement of an old theatrical ideal of total identification with character).[7]

Richardson's description of his method (or rather the effect on himself of an antimethod) leads to an internalizing revision of any literary means for imagining and presenting character. What matters is not really the validity of his claim, since we cannot know "where" he stood as he spoke for Clarissa or Lovelace. It is, rather, the effect of Richardson's example as author for his characters that is of interest. Just as he claims to be doing much more than speaking lines and reproducing the convincing externalities of dramatis personae, his characters seem to be doing something more than speaking lines or writing letters. Lovelace and Clarissa, in different ways, are observed by the reader in acts of self-presentation and even of highly self-conscious dramatization, and those acts derive in many cases from the dramatic repertory and the theatrical conventions of the time. Ultimately, what makes that process supremely absorbing is that *Clarissa* produces an awareness of the imposed or invented theatricality of such acts, of their arbitrary and inessential nature. To put the case at its formalist extreme, the epistolary convention as Richardson enlarged it creates a situation in which the reader is made conscious of the fundamental instrumentality of the text as it is manipulated by the main correspondents. Viewed this way, *Clarissa* implies a self somewhere within or beyond the text, a self exploiting the text to express itself but somehow not wholly contained by the text, even though it has nothing to assert itself with except the text.

Now to some extent, any letter writer or any text is open to such charges and is full of these instabilities and paradoxes. The presumed spontaneity of experience and the authenticity of the self are, moreover, naturally compromised by their insertion in so formalized a convention as eighteenth-century correspondence. What Richardson narrates in *Clarissa* is the inevitability of self-dramatization, and what the book may be said to seek for its main characters is a way out of that circularity and implicit inauthenticity. Thus, what John Traugott acutely describes as Richardson's manipulation of theatricality is only the beginning of a description of his achievement. Traugott calls him "a master of realism who has a sense of how and why human beings need to be theatrical, need to put themselves on stage to voice their fantasies. Clarissa's 'she-tragedy' histrionics are what Lovelace wants to match his 'smart cock' charades."[8] Richardson's realism involves the elaboration of a situation in which his protagonists try to develop ways to control or understand or even to discard what Traugott calls their theatrical needs. The nature or the location of the self that has these needs of which Traugott speaks so confidently is precisely what is at stake, since its reality and independence are compromised by those needs. The moral and psychological realism for which Richardson is justly praised is inseparable from his exploration of his characters' attempts to locate that self and to establish a stable relationship between the self and the stylistic and generic means by which it dramatizes or externalizes itself. The effort, in short, is to dramatize the limits of dramatization, to call a halt to self-presentation and present a self.

Such reflexive literary activity is an occasional possibility on stage, even in so manifestly artificial a location as the Restoration heroic play. Eric Rothstein has argued that heroic rant may sometimes be seen in the context of a play as being expressive of a character's failure with language or with himself. Rothstein says that a character such as Lee's Massinissa both identifies and undermines himself with his explosive rant; the character's language thus expresses an impossibly unstable personality.[9] In *Clarissa* that failure is a constant possibility, as the continuous rush of language the novel requires from its two protagonists forces them and us to scrutinize their language for impropriety, that is, for uncontrolled significances where characterization passes out of the hands of the writer and the audience interprets and completes what is being said.

All the characters in *Clarissa* constitute themselves as characters, first and obviously by identifying themselves in the imagined world of the narrative, and secondly by expressing a self through a particular way of speaking, a style. But style is here much more than a decoration of language or an apt choice of forceful figures for emotional moments. For Lovelace and Clarissa, who are granted the large stretches of expression necessary for such things, style is a cumulative manner of self-presentation and a way of understanding self and others. Both of them are from the first preoccupied with asserting a particular self and establishing a particular kind of world; both of them make themselves present by an insistent literary revision of the normal and ordinary discourse all around them. Their development of appropriate styles is a matter of resisting in opposing ways the limitations and compulsions that language and literary occasion contain. Neither of them wishes to be like Lee's Massinissa, and each develops a distinct strategy for handling language so that it does not betray the self that lies (in some difficult sense) behind it.

This wary attitude to language may be what constitutes the special narrative discourse associated with the novel. It may be that this self-conscious withdrawal from language (or a bracketing of its formulations) is especially visible in *Clarissa* because of the dramatic matrix of the book. That is to say, Richardson's protagonists take their opposing stances by developing different relationships between themselves and readily available dramatic modes of action and understanding; and insofar as both of them achieve self-consciousness about their projects, they are presenting different novelistic alternatives to those simpler dramatic modes.

Some thirty letters are exchanged before Lovelace's first letter is printed, and twenty-four of these are from Clarissa to Anna Howe. In these letters Clarissa is consistently aware of the necessity of self-control, and what she outlines to her friend is a delicate balance between resistance and submission to the demands of her family. Her asides during her narration of negotiations with her family show her to be clearly aware of the need to maintain an appearance of submission rather than to challenge her family's plans overtly. At the same time, she manages by suggestion and analysis (a sort of literalness and accuracy of observation and memory) to project in their presence a version of herself that refuses to compromise and that defends her resolution not to marry Solmes. Clarissa establishes herself as a character whose self-presentation insists upon a complexity that is very difficult to dramatize and even to articulate very clearly. Indeed, her prolixity and that of the novel itself are obvious effects of the complexity of character Richardson seems to be after.

Anna Howe functions as a moral and stylistic variation on Clarissa. In the crucial opening letters her sensible grasp of reality is just to the comic side of Clarissa's gathering seriousness. Her apt generalization about the Harlowes—"You are all too rich to be happy, child" (1:41)—involves a confident irony about social and moral determinants that Clarissa carefully avoids. Anna writes with an ironic vivacity proper to worldly-wise heroines such as Congreve's Millamant and Angelica. Her amused skepticism when Clarissa tells her that she would not be in love with Lovelace displays an epigrammatic view of feminine instabilities that is at home in comic drama: "Well but, if you have not the throbs and glows, you have not; and are not in love; good reason why—because you would not be in love, and there's no more to be said; only, my dear, I shall keep a good look out upon you; and so I hope you will upon yourself; for it is no manner of argument that because you would not be in love, you therefore are not" (1:49). After all, Anna is an onlooker, and she reminds Clarissa here that "a stander-by is often a better judge of the game than those that play" (1:49). As an observer, she takes naturally to the dramatic metaphor; the advice she subsequently offers is no longer comic, but it is still structured in terms of simple dramatic transformations.

Anna proposes legal action, the simple and direct step of "resuming" the fortune left to Clarissa by her grandfather, a fortune she has put in her family's control. Anna's recommendation is plain and forceful: "You will say, you cannot do it while you are with them. I don't know that. Do you think they can use you worse than they do? And is it not your *right?* And do they not make use of your own generosity to oppress you? Your Uncle Harlowe is one trustee, your Cousin Morden is the other: insist upon your right to your uncle; and write to your Cousin Morden about it. This, I dare say, will make them alter their behaviour to you" (1 : 125). This advice is a mixture of briefly rendered scenes built around rhetorical questions, re-solved by simple facts and legal inevitabilities; it constitutes a simple scenario for Clarissa, an outline for a proto-feminist play, one is tempted to say.

But it is addressed to a Clarissa whose mode of perception is deferential to circumstances, attuned to historical complications, exquisitely analytical and argumentative in the face of the brutally simple commands of her family—resistant, in short, to any kind of dramatic simplicity, Anna's or her family's. For example, Clarissa attempts to argue with her mother, who warns her that "this won't do somewhere else. You *know* it won't" (1 : 73). That is a fearful reference to the dreaded paternal presence, who will hardly bear explicit naming, never mind being "thus dialogued with," as Mrs. Harlowe puts it. Indeed, when Mr. Harlowe condescends to speak a few pages later, Clarissa trembles at the "sternness in his looks" (1 : 75) and notes that he speaks only to his silent wife: "My dear, you are long absent. Dinner is near ready. What you had to say lay in a very little compass. Surely, you have nothing to do but to declare *your* will, and *my* will—but perhaps you may be talking of the preparations" (1 : 76). Simple and silent obedience is all that Mr. Harlowe's speeches, such as they are, call for, and his gouty generalized presence as "A JUSTLY-ENRAGED FATHER" (as he signs himself a bit later, 1 : 121) is a literary self-dramatization quite opposed to the literary-moral manner his daughter is attempting to de-velop in this opening phase of her story. For Clarissa is more than the dutiful daughter she signs herself as at times. In this opening sequence she is what deserves to be called a novelistic sensibility in the sense that she is out to explore an untenable necessity and to find a way through and around it. As the pressures mount and she becomes more and more con-stricted by a tightening family circle drawn around her, she searches for reasons, meditates on the complexities of her situation, refuses the simple (and in several senses dramatic) solutions of obedience and defiance held out by others, and rejects tragic submission, domestic pathos, or feminist comedy.

She thus achieves, I think, an impressive self-understanding. Shortly before the "elopement" with Lovelace she meditates on the sources of her moral-intellectual habits and on the origins and consequences of the neces-sity that she has slowly clarified:

I should have been very little the better for the *conversation-visits* which the good Dr. Lewen used to honour me with, and for the principles *wrought* (as I may say) into my earliest mind by my pious Mrs. Norton, founded on her reverend father's experience, as well as on her own, if I could not thus retrospect and argue, in such a strange situation as we are in. *Strange* I may well call it; for don't you see, my dear, that we seem all to be *impelled,* as it were, by a perverse fate which none of us is able to resist? And yet all arising (with a strong appearance of self-punishment) from ourselves? Do not my parents see the hopeful children, from whom they expected a perpetuity of worldly happiness to their branching family, now grown up to answer the *till* now distant hope, setting their angry faces against each other, pulling up by the roots, as I may say, that hope which was ready to be carried into a probable certainty?

Your partial love will be ready to acquit me of *capital* and *intentional* faults: but oh, my dear! my calamities have humbled me enough, to make me turn my gaudy eye inward; to make me look into myself! And what have I discovered there? Why, my dear friend, more *secret* pride and vanity than I could have thought had lain in my unexamined heart (1 : 419–20).

This extraction of the psychological and historical background of her dilemma substitutes understanding for action, indeed makes understanding a form of action as Clarissa balances external circumstances and internal will. This passage is both meditative deference and aggressive exercise of the self; it represents a perfect form of displaced self-dramatization. Such balancing of external fate and internal will as Clarissa articulates here and elsewhere is the highest form of Christian moral understanding and, as such, a form of moral action.

In formal terms, Clarissa's character is described by marking the alterations that occur in this manner of self-preservation and in its accompanying implicit understanding of the world. For much of the first two volumes or so, that understanding is a matter of deference to a tangle of moral, psychological, social, and even legal circumstances. Much of Clarissa's writing before the elopement constitutes a complicating revision of the positive and negative simplifications of her personality, as she insists that she is neither the self-willed egotist most of her family accuses her of being nor the legendary paragon of her grandfather's will. Such consistent self-effacement is easily seen as disingenuous, and Clarissa's denial of her very evident powers is in truth open to those charges of bad faith leveled against it from different perspectives by Lovelace and the Harlowes. And it is precisely that opposition and misunderstanding that make the term *novelistic* appropriate for Clarissa's stylistic identity, and in fact provoke or generate that mode.

Bella, James, and the rest claim to inhabit a psychological universe in which the individual is in full control of his will and totally aware of his motives. In place of the limiting tangle of circumstances and self Clarissa offers, they feel free to substitute a clear stage on which the individual can perform actions and make choices. The Harlowe scenario for Clarissa and for the family is both grand and simple—financial accumulation and social mobility. What they require of her is simple assent, an uncomplicated role in the drama of their emerging dynasty. Clarissa's refusal is novelistic precisely because a good part of what she does is to substitute complicated case histories for that simple plot. Her analysis exposes problems by means of an essentially retrospective historical intelligence. She understands Arabella's jealousy in terms of the family history and Lovelace's withdrawn proposal; she places James's resentment exactly in its social and psychological context; and perhaps most impressively, she locates her own problem squarely in the history of her parents' marriage: "My MOTHER has never thought fit to oppose my FATHER'S will when once he has declared himself determined. My UNCLES, stiff, unbroken, highly-prosperous bachelors, give me leave to say (though very worthy persons in the main), have as high notions of a child's duty as of a wife's obedience, in the *last* of which, my mother's meekness has confirmed them, and given them greater reason to expect the *first*" (1 : 60).

Powerful as the Harlowes are, they represent the dramatic mode at a rather elementary level, and Clarissa has little trouble coming to a full understanding of their determining circumstances (hence the special kind of fear, rage, and frustration she excites in them). To be sure, there are times when Clarissa is forced to drop her controlling novelistic discourse and under the pressure of the moment turn to a form of resistance that involves the broadest kind of theatrical speech and gesture. For example, after Mr. Harlowe has "ordered patterns of the richest silks to be sent from London" for the marriage with Solmes, Clarissa turns "silent for some time" and then tells Anna how she ran through in her mind the circumstances gathering to push her toward Solmes. "All these reflections crowding upon my remembrance; I would, madam, said I, folding my hands, with an earnestness in which my whole heart was engaged, bear the cruellest tortures, bear loss of limb, and even of life to give *you* peace. But this man, every moment I would, at your command, think of him with favour, is the more my aversion. You cannot, indeed you cannot, think how my whole soul resists him! And to talk of contracts concluded upon; of patterns; of a short day! Save me, save me, O my dearest mamma, save your child from this heavy, from this insupportable evil!" (1 : 101). But we notice that even in so extreme a rhetorical moment Clarissa is scrupulously accurate in surrounding that externality with a psychological interiority that is its effective cause. She is an instinctive novelist of her situation because she places even the broadest verbal moments in the context of their psychological determinants. The silence Clarissa summarizes so completely is full of "reflections" that trigger this outburst, and she is an honest recorder of her own feelings to give the odious Solmes a central place in these reflections: ". . . and then Mr. Solmes's disagreeable person; still more disagreeable manners; his low understanding" (1 : 101). We are in a position to account for the violence of Clarissa's outburst even more exactly than she, since we can catch the disgust and sexual fear that she expresses thereby. She, by the way, does not really deny her sexual fear and disgust for Solmes, as modern critics like to think (although she is restricted to a genteel and prudish idiom). That repugnance is part of her self-characterization, and she uses it as an important element in the complex and, to her mind, convincing argument against the insultingly simple role her family wishes her to assume.

A swelling scene such as this one looks forward, of course, to the encounters with Lovelace later on, for he provokes Clarissa far more effectively than the Harlowes and succeeds more completely in making her lose control of her discourse. He is her antagonist for any number of interesting psychological and social reasons familiar to any reader of the book: he is sexually attracted by her difficult virtue and seems to sense what we can call the sadomasochistic possibilities of their relationship, he hates the smug bourgeois perfection she represents, and so on. It is important to insist that such a description of his desires is not a reader's extrapolation but a close paraphrase of Lovelace's own analysis of the situation. He is, as many have noted, a splendidly dramatic character, a self-consciously histrionic sensibility who not only imagines himself and others in the actions and postures of an actual eighteenth-century stage but also sees himself as a powerful directorial self with the omniscient perspective of the dramatist, able to view human action as ironically recurrent and predictable. His radically dramatized personality includes a radical self-consciousness. He is much more than the traditional literary rake, and we have objective testimony from other characters right at the beginning of the book that he is a man of moral and social parts in many respects. Indeed, as Robert D. Hume has demonstrated, the theatrical rake hardly exists as a simple or "a single, definable type," but even on stage represents a set of amusing or shocking attitudes that playwrights can vary and that characters can assume within a more complicated dramatic personality.[10]

Throughout the long opening section of the novel, Lovelace does not appear in person, although he is spoken of and even quoted in the letters. Clarissa in her increasing confinement marvels at his freedom; "This man, somehow or other, knows everything that passes in our family. My confinement; Hannah's dismission; and more of the resentments and resolutions of my father, uncles, and brother that [than?] I can possibly know, and almost as soon as the things happen which he tells me of. He cannot come at these intelligences fairly" (1:121). She's right, of course, since Lovelace is employing a very theatrical expedient—a domestic spy. When Lovelace's first letter appears shortly after this, his vivacity and clarity cut through the complexities Clarissa has so painfully rendered. More is at stake in the contrast offered to the reader than the stylistic playfulness in Lovelace's "Roman style" (as Richardson identifies it in a footnote), for his style is characterized here and throughout the book by a manic dramatizing of the moment. Quite transparently when he writes to Belford and more insidiously in his conversations with Clarissa, Lovelace constructs literary moments in which he plays all the roles or anticipates all the lines and moves of others. Here, his first letter turns into energetic soliloquizing: "But is it not a confounded thing to be in love with one who is the daughter, the sister, the niece of a family I must eternally despise? And, the devil of it, that love increasing, with her—what shall I call it?—'tis not scorn: 'tis not pride: 'tis not the insolence of an adored beauty—but 'tis to *virtue*, it seems, that my difficulties are owing; and I pay for not being a sly sinner, an hypocrite; for being regardless of my reputation; for permitting slander to open its mouth against me. But is it necessary for such a one as I, who have been used to carry all before me, upon my own terms—I, who never inspired a fear, that had not a discernibly predominant mixture of love in it; to be an hypocrite?" (1 : 144–45).

Belford is little more than an excuse for Lovelace's self-dramatization. Clarissa pointedly speaks and writes to others and shuns this sort of verbal excess. Richardson is obviously anxious to show the reader just this particular difference between the two. At the end of the letter that precedes Lovelace's she falls into a series of melodramatic exclamations: "O that they did but know my heart! It shall sooner burst, than voluntarily, uncompelled, undriven, dictate a measure that shall cast a slur either upon them, or upon my sex" (1 : 143). Quickly, however, she drops that manner and asks Anna to excuse "these grave *soliloquies*, as I may call them." While Clarissa is out to efface herself and explore circumstances, to persuade others to moral accommodation, Lovelace treats the moment as an excuse for self-display and uses language as a means of self-assertion. His sensibility is defined by the denial of that complex necessity that Clarissa explores and the rejection of the deferential modes of analysis and expression that she seeks to exemplify. His theatrical models are clearly visible in his discourse, and he always places those models within the ironic brackets of his own self-consciousness about them. "I love," he says to Belford, "when I dig a pit, to have my prey tumble in with secure feet and open eyes; then a man can look down upon her, with an *O-ho, charmer, how came you there?*" (2 : 102). One could multiply examples of Lovelace's formulations of his freedom. This one exemplifies his tendency for dramatic structure, in this case a simple comic scene that is the generic opposite for Clarissa's meditative complication of events in which she always stays, as it were, within the circumstances she presents and tries to avoid controlling imagery such as Lovelace's.[11]

And yet for all his dramatic virtuosity, Lovelace always seems to understand that the attraction between him and Clarissa is grounded in the problematical and the contradictory, rooted in psychosocial factors that he is well aware of and that resist the simplifications of the heroic drama and the romantic wit-comedy that are his models. "Thou knowest my heart, if any man living does," he writes in that first letter to Belford. "As far as I know it myself, thou knowest it. But 'tis a cursed deceiver; for it has many and many a time imposed upon its master—*master*, did I say? That am I not now; nor have I been from the moment I beheld this angel of a woman" (1:145). Lovelace goes so far as to construct in this letter an elaborate psychological theory to account for his obsession. Whether or not he is telling the truth about that "quality-jilt" who has driven him from his early manhood "to revenge upon as many of the sex as shall come into [his] power" is immaterial, for what results in the letter is his backing away from introspection and self-analysis into self-dramatization. Lovelace's dramatic imagination operates consistently as a means of organizing his own contradictions and instability. His opening letter turns into soliloquy and resorts to a series of vignettes with him at the center of each. If Clarissa's analytic intelligence is her way of resisting the simple Harlowe scenario and of revising her own dangerously simplified legend as moral paragon, then Lovelace's histrionics are a means of resisting the discoveries of his own formidably analytic mind. Both of them display, in short, capacities for dramatic and novelistic self-understanding, and they are the results of those choices of emphasis and style (in the broadest sense) that enforce their identities. In the beginning, the formal structure of the book at its simplest is an opposition between Clarissa's novelistic meditations and Lovelace's dramatic manipulations. As the book progresses, that structure grows more complex and involves a transformation of these terms into a new opposition.

The long, slow pivot of the book deserves, I think, to be called a dialectical transformation of Clarissa and Lovelace in terms of the interaction between the novelistic and the dramatic modes. "Dialectical" is appropriate in this case, since these characters and the modes they choose for their self-presentation collide and simultaneously repel and interpenetrate, each revealing the presence of a form of itself in the other, discovering itself in a new and transformed manner in the process, and transforming the other even as it transforms itself. We end with two new terms (characters in this case), each of which has been crucially modified by an interaction with the other in which it has discovered a truth about itself. This dialectic in *Clarissa* has a specifically literary form, and the transformations the characters undergo are properly described by the transformations in the literary modes they employ.

Clarissa's attempt to arbitrate between personal will and external circumstance is interrupted by Lovelace literally shifting the scene and altering the dominant tone of the discourse. The elopement itself, of course, is deliberately staged—a Lovelace production right down to the props and the imaginary actors. Clarissa perceives it in retrospect as the result of her tactical error in meeting Lovelace alone, but she experiences it and renders it for Anna as a mixture of spontaneous compulsion and neatly arranged dramatic tableau. "Now behind me, now before me, now on this side, now on that, turned I my affrighted face in the same moment; expecting a furious brother here, armed servants there, an enraged sister screaming, and a father armed with terror in his countenance more dreadful than even the drawn sword which I saw, or those I apprehended. I ran as fast as he; yet knew not that I ran; my fears adding wings to my feet, at the same time that they took all power of thinking from me" (1:484). This passage marks a crucial shift in tone. Till now, Clarissa has negotiated in a carefully univocal and quasi-legal style, much given to citing precedents and cross-examining the discourse of others.[12] She is also forced into other styles, including that of the tragic heroine, but she is always in some kind of control of those styles, even if only in retrospective narration to Anna. When James attacks her on stylistic grounds for what he calls her "whining vocatives" and infuriates her by his condescending pedantry, Clarissa declares in her answer that she writes "in a style different from my usual, and different from what I wished to have occasion to write" (1:268). The result is, overall, an eloquence and moral reason that her family fears. As her Uncle John says, "There is no standing against your looks and language. . . . For my part, I could not read your letter to me, without being unmanned. How can you be so unmoved yourself, yet be so able to move everybody else?" (1:304). In this scene, Lovelace tricks her into entering a world of action and movement where precisely those dramatic simplifications that she has been avoiding appear with a force that she cannot resist. Instead of thinking, she imagines and visualizes in an instant what she has been refining and sifting at great length.

In this scene and in their many encounters thereafter, Clarissa struggles against the spontaneity and loss of stylistic control that Lovelace's machinations seek to induce in her. The heated and heightened language of some of their exchanges is essentially Lovelace's discourse, and while she still has her reason Clarissa charges him repeatedly with a falsifying "volubility." The accusation is apt, since Lovelace is master of many accents and styles, from the jocular conspiratorial manner of his letters to Belford, to the smooth manners he displays as outraged man of honor and deferential suitor in his early dealings with the Harlowes, to the charming self-justifier with Lord M. and his aunts, to the impassioned imperial amorist of the love duets with Clarissa. While she suspends final judgment of him partly because of this variability and notes his "impenetrableness," Lovelace sees Clarissa in wholly conventionalized roles as a female character, refusing to grant her the directorial self-consciousness of roles, types, and styles that he possesses. For him she is an embodiment (a lovely one) of generalized and essentially literary female types, tragic and comic.

In an important sense, Lovelace is right about Clarissa. She is not "acting" the way he is. As Kinkead-Weekes observes, Clarissa's stylistic lapses are governed by her invariable "moral currency" and by "the kind of integrity that makes Clarissa Clarissa."[13] Ironically, however (and dialectically), the dramatic universe forced upon her by Lovelace turns Clarissa to the divine comedy of her staged demise and transforms her at last into an icon who transcends the female types he has tried to impose or to extract. His plots and manipulations reduce the complex psychosocial world Clarissa begins with to fake situations and locations such as Mrs. Sinclair's and the elaborate Captain Tomlinson ruse. Meaningful moral analysis and accommodation to establish the novelistic mode of understanding are necessarily impossible in these artificial settings where a comic necessity controlled by Lovelace the dramatist hangs over all action and utterance. The incessant psychosexual pressure that Lovelace thus applies denies Clarissa the opportunity for revision and mediation that she enjoyed when facing her far less subtle family. Clarissa is kidnapped out of the real world, in effect, and stranded in Lovelace's formal world, given a choice only between the plots of romantic comedy and she-tragedy.

All of this happens very gradually. Initially Clarissa is well able to defend herself verbally, retaining traces of her characteristically analytic style. Lovelace's theatrical style of self-presentation is easily parried and even mocked by a Clarissa who listens to his summaries of what he has endured for her sake and remarks: "Can't you go on, sir? You see I have patience to hear you. Can't you go on, sir?" (2:78). As Lovelace takes this bait and dramatizes what he has already overdramatized in an earlier letter,[14] Clarissa's talents as a literary and moral intelligence are wonderfully evident:

> Menaces every day and defiances put into every one's mouth against me! Forced to creep about in disguises—and to watch *all hours*—And in *all weathers*, I suppose, sir—that, I remember, was once your grievance! *In all weathers*, sir! And all these hardships arising from yourself, not imposed by me [2:79].

She follows with a long and exact rebuttal of Lovelace's self-justifying speeches, modulating from irony ("O sir, sir! What sufferings have yours been!") to specific criticism of his verbal devices, exposing the shallow egotism behind them:

> . . . so that all that followed of my treatment, and your redundant *onlys*, I might thank you for principally, as you may yourself for all your *sufferings*, your *mighty* sufferings! And if, voluble sir, you have founded any merit upon them, be so good as to revoke it; and look upon *me*, with my forfeited reputation, as the only sufferer [2:80].

Lovelace's final reaction to this irrefutable analysis, this exposure of his literary unsoundness, is an outburst of passion: "Darkness, light; light, darkness; by my soul!—just as you please to have it. O charmer of my heart . . . take me, take me to yourself; mould me as you please; I am wax in your hands; give me your own impression, and seal me for ever yours" (2 : 80). Such rant seems to be provoked by the literary dead end into which Clarissa has driven Lovelace, and its only effect is to make her "perfectly frighted," wishing herself "a thousand miles distant from him." In Lovelace's own account of the scene to Belford, he qualifies the spontaneity of his outburst, giving it in retrospect an outrageous theatricality. "There was, I believe, a kind of frenzy in my manner which threw her into a panic like that of Semele perhaps, when the Thunderer, in all his majesty, sur-rounded with ten thousand celestial burning-glasses, was about to scorch her into a cinder" (2 : 98). But in the same letter he also admits that he was carried away almost too far: "It is exceedingly difficult, thou seest, for an honest man to act in disguises; as the poet says, *Thrust Nature back with a pitchfork, it will return*" (2 : 99). Lovelace's dramatization has been thrown slightly out of control, and his rapture has been the result of Clarissa's masterful elimination of his other verbal resources. What he tries to revise in retrospect as a Jovian erotic tableau and then as a self-justifying and exemplary moral-emotional moment (complete with Horatian tag!) is in fact the first of Clarissa's verbal triumphs. He is driven to react passion-ately, out of his projected dramatic sequence; he loses some of his control and becomes what Clarissa's novelistic intelligence and verbal talent show him to be rather than the overseeing dramatist he wishes to be.

But in the long struggle that ensues, Lovelace does manage to have things his own way—albeit by slow oscillations that repeat with many varia-tions the interactions of this scene. Clarissa's moral-stylistic integrity is kept intact: she not only resists Lovelace's various scenarios but exercises her powers of analysis and maintains a scrupulous record of herself that is moral and religious in motive and documentary and novelistic in effect. For Lovelace, writing is a dramatic opportunity; for Clarissa it continues to be a process for self-discovery and a means of steadying a world that she readily admits is marked by psychological instabilities. She writes down "everything of moment that befalls me; and of all I *think*, and of all I *do*, that may be of future use to me; for besides that this helps to form one to a style, and opens and expands the ductile mind, every one will find that many a good thought evaporates in thinking; many a good resolution goes off, driven out of memory perhaps by some other not so good" (2 : 128). She records not just herself but others as well with fairness and accuracy, sensing an unsoundness in the women at Mrs. Sinclair's and seeing directly through such lesser rakes as Mowbray, Belton, and Tourville. But Lovelace's compulsive stage-managing works to undermine that acuity and render it irrelevant. Clarissa is not only driven to escape, an act of shocking directness for her contemplative sensibility, but to other melodramatic and theatrical actions.

Writing to Anna from Hampstead after the escape, Clarissa shows traces of her situation in the instability of her discourse. It begins here with demonic imagery and shades off into a moralizing and hopeful allegory:

> Oh, why was the great fiend of all unchained, and permitted to assume so specious a form, and yet allowed to conceal his feet and his talons, till with the one he was ready to trample upon my honour, and to strike the other into my heart! . . .
> And is it not in my own power still, by the divine favour, to secure the great stake of all? And who knows but that this very path into which my inconsideration has thrown me, strewed as it is with briers and thorns which tear in pieces my gaudier trappings, may not be the right path to lead me into the great road to my future happiness; which might have been endangered by evil communication? [3:18]

Such imagery comes easily to a pious reader such as Clarissa, and she has turned to it before; but it is Lovelace who has provoked its new intensity and frequency. The transformation of experience by moral allegory is Clarissa's literary defense against him. When Lovelace finds her shortly after this, his comic metamorphosis from "a cursed crabbed old wretch" into "a lively gay young fellow" (3:41–42) is a secular revision of her images. Even here, however, there is a marvelous literary complexity to the scene. Since Clarissa recognizes him, Lovelace is forced to reveal himself. She in fact metamorphoses him, and he is drawn into a literary comparison that follows his source as it both glorifies and degrades him: "I threw open my great-coat, and, like the devil in Milton [an odd comparison, though!] 'I started up in my own form divine/Touch'd by the beam of her celestial eye,/More potent than Ithuriel's spear!'" (3:41). Even as he reaches for that parallel (or has it forced on him), Lovelace finds that nothing can describe Clarissa. He admits his literary failure: "Now, Belford, for a similtude—now for a likeness to illustrate the surprising scene, and the effect it had upon my charmer, and the gentlewoman!—But nothing *was* like it, or equal to it. The plain fact can only describe it, and set it off—thus then take it" (3:41).

Lovelace finds that Clarissa inhabits his dramatic universe in unexpected ways, defying his powers of representation as in the previous scene and at other times enacting with a sincerity and moral eloquence what he had hoped would be merely sexually stimulating distress. After the rape, Clarissa's disordered pages point to a scattering of her literary powers; these moving fragments are a discarded and incoherent anthology of literary possibilities for understanding a self no longer whole and encompassing those forms that Clarissa has used up to now: moral allegory, prophetic denunciation, apt quotation, and retrospective analysis (which breaks off and turns to confused self-pity). She recovers from that breakdown by appropriating Lovelace's histrionics, stealing his dramatic thunder and transforming it by sincere reenactment.

That transition can be illustrated briefly by two scenes in which Clarissa dominates and surprises Lovelace by employing two radically different methods of self-dramatization. What enforces the moral superiority and irresistible pathos she now commands is a literary contest that Lovelace identifies quite specifically as a stylistic achievement that reduces him to incoherent babble. He repeats her speeches shortly after the rape and especially notes their oratorical adjuncts: "her eyes neither fierce nor mild, but very earnest; and a fixed sedateness in her whole aspect, which seemed to be the effect of deep contemplation: and thus she accosted me, with an air and action that I never saw equalled" (3:219). Her performance here is exactly the clear and forceful opposite of what Lovelace's psychodramatic theory of behavior expected, and his summary of the scene is full of admiration for her oratorical and emotional control:

> As I told thee, I had prepared myself for high passions, raving, flying, tearing execration: these transient violences, the workings of sudden grief, and shame, and vengeance, would have set us upon a par with each other, and quitted scores. These have I been accustomed to; and, as nothing violent is lasting, with these I could have wished to encounter. But such a majestic composure—seeking me—whom yet, it is plain, by her attempt to get away, she would have avoided seeing—no Lucretia-like vengeance upon herself in her thought—yet swallowed up, her whole mind swallowed up, as I may say, by a grief so heavy, as, in her own words, to be beyond the power of speech to express—and to be able, discomposed as she was to the very morning, to put such a home question to me, as if she had penetrated my future view—how could I avoid looking like a fool, and answering, as before, in broken sentences, and confusion?
> What—what-a—what has been done—I, I, I—cannot but say—must own—must confess—hem—hem. . . .
> O Belford! Belford! whose the triumph now! HERS, or MINE?
> [3:220–21]

Like all his moods, Lovelace's admiration is temporary, and Clarissa's moral oratory and compelling gestures have to give way. But when they do, it is to an intensified tragic idiom that is equally unanswerable.

Lovelace arranges to find Clarissa's "promissory note" to Dorcas, thereby involving her in a new escape scene; he prepares to confront her with feigned anger. Clarissa emerges from her room with a full tragic dignity that collapses Lovelace's farce (her term) and substitutes a dramatic authenticity that frightens Lovelace and his whores: "The infamous mother whispered me that it were better to *make terms* with this *strange* lady, and let her go" (3:289). "Every tongue silent, every eye awed, every heart quaking, mine, in a particular manner, sunk, throbless, and twice below its usual region. . . . Such the glorious power of innocence exerted at that awful moment" (3:287). The generality Lovelace grants to Clarissa here is quite different from the demeaning female roles he has tried to assign, and, as so often in the book, Lovelace is moved against his will. Here, he watches as his dramatic project is transformed with uncanny exactness. Clarissa not only speaks in the highest tragic style, but carries a penknife held at her breast. The suicide she threatens reenacts Lovelace's reenactment of the Richard III gesture in the garden just before the elopement but with obvious differences in authenticity.[15]

What has happened is that Lovelace has slowly managed to shift the dominant discourse, to accomplish his ends by modulating the generic and stylistic emphasis toward the comedy-melodrama of seduction. But the interaction of personalities and the styles that accompany them complicate matters. Instead of simply succumbing according to one of Lovelace's lively plots, Clarissa in due course constructs a slow, massive drama of submission to fate and substitutes an eroticized religiosity for his ever-varying sexual tableaux. Deprived of the possibility of the limited freedom the novelistic mode can discover if given the chance, Clarissa's sensibility can only operate in the context of an inescapable necessity that is the negative pole of the novelistic project. Given her own compelling circumstances as a woman and as a Christian (circumstances that Lovelace's dramatic theory can only understand in self-serving or comically mechanistic terms), she may be said to reject Lovelace's literary models as ways of dealing with such facts. Instead, she diverts them into a religious spectacle of holy dying in which a stark providential pattern replaces the tangled circumstances uncovered by the novelistic mode. Clarissa passes over eventually into Lovelace's dramatic universe, but that sphere is crucially modified by the transformed remnant of her novelistic style and sensibility. Thus, she substitutes deference and submission for his assertion and manipulation, extracting the determinism implicit in the dramatic mode by replacing Lovelace, the omniscient dramatist, and his repertory of secular texts with God (the ultimate dramatist) and the Bible and other religious texts. In the dynamic of the dialectic, moreover, her sensibility has itself been redirected toward a new version of Lovelace's dramaturgy in which Clarissa is the stage manager of a spectacle but one consistent with her experience and chosen as fitting and fateful rather than invented for self-display. That is to say, Clarissa resolves matters by a death play founded on stylized gesture and movement, on scriptural quotation and religious allegory rather than on the secular models that Lovelace has obsessively in mind and that feature improvisation of gesture and language and strictly limited comic meanings.

The accomplishment of this transformation proceeds slowly through the last third or so of the novel, and it is marked by an obvious withdrawal of Clarissa from normal correspondence. More and more, she is written about by others, notably by Belford, and is thereby objectified, assuming in his reverential evocations an iconlike stillness and significance: "Up then raised the charming sufferer her lovely face; but with such a significance of woe overspreading it that I could not, for the soul of me, help being visibly affected" (3:446). When she speaks and writes, Clarissa now tends to a brevity that contrasts with her earlier prolixity, and those cryptic utterances are thoroughly informed by biblical echo and quotation. Clarissa is, of course, physically weak and emotionally drained, but she is also turning away stylistically from the personal and the psychological to the archetypal. Her discourse is pared down to pious aphorism, and she speaks in homilies that are deliberately impersonal, homilies that constitute a rejection of personal complication. For example, after a heartless and unforgiving letter from Arabella, Clarissa writes to her mother and begs forgiveness with self-depreciating self-dramatization: "No self-convicted criminal ever approached her angry and just judge with greater awe, nor with a truer contrition, than I do you by these lines" (4:83). She then passes to self-justification, but even there she is true to the dramatic attitude struck at the beginning of the letter. This summary is a deposition, a sworn statement couched in a mode that turns impersonal:

> . . . and this you will the readier believe, if the creature who never, to the best of her remembrance, told her mamma a wilful falsehood, may be credited, when she declares, as she does, in the most solemn manner, that she met the seducer with a determination not to go off with him. [4:84]

What she finally asks (on her knees like Lovelace in the woods, but with what a difference!) is a blessing in one sentence that will become her "passport to Heaven": "*Lost, unhappy wretch, I forgive you! and may God bless you! This is all! Let me, on a blessed scrap of paper, but see one sentence to this effect under your dear hand*" (4:84). The entire letter is a quasi-legal document, but Clarissa is the prisoner in the dock rather than the moral investigator of the early volumes. Legal language and dramatic spectacle are now joined, and this letter's imaginings look forward to the reading of Clarissa's will, which is really a series of moral dramatizations in which the legend of St. Clarissa is memorialized. The most striking of these scenes is a final dramatic reversal very much in Lovelace's manner: if Lovelace insists upon viewing my corpse, she writes,

> Let him behold and triumph over the wretched remains of one who has been made a victim to his barbarous perfidy: but let some good person, as by my desire, give him a paper, whilst he is viewing the ghastly spectacle, containing these few words only: "Gay, cruel heart! behold here the remains of the once ruined, yet now happy, Clarissa Harlowe! See what thou thyself must quickly be;—and REPENT!" [4:416–17]

For his part, Lovelace is subject to the transformations within the dialectic. His dramatic discourse is gradually undermined for us (and for Clarissa and Belford), as readers of his letters, by the accumulating insight that its theatricality is an inevitable expression of his personality and history rather than simply the self-conscious role that he has freely chosen. After

Clarissa escapes for good and begins her protracted death scene, Lovelace attempts to reassert his controlling grasp of the dominant discourse, imagining various resolutions—some comic, like marriage, others extravagant, like keeping Clarissa's preserved body by his side. But the comic inventiveness is gone, and in time Lovelace's persona turns into a mere person. He finds that his devices become his compulsions. In one scene after another, Lovelace's dramatic supervision is eroded, and he is surprised by emotions and pushed into language that he cannot wholly control. Quite early on, Clarissa's novelistic intelligence had placed him as a sadly predictable social and moral-psychological type, and what Lovelace thinks is his inventiveness and irrepressible freedom become by the end of the book the grim necessity appropriate to the aristocratic rake and megalomaniac. Just as he forces Clarissa into a synthesis in which the dramatic mode reinterprets and transforms her novelistic self-understanding, Lovelace stands exposed in the latter half of *Clarissa* as a novelistic character—that is, as a prey to social and psychological determinisms, a man forced to act out his grief, rage, and even his death with a theatricality no longer self-consciously assumed but imposed by that interplay of self and circumstances which is made central by the novelistic understanding. And just as Clarissa redefines the dramatic mode, negating its negation by turning it from the secular parody of divine arrangement that it is for Lovelace into an austere religious rite of submission that leads to liberation and transcendence, so, too, Lovelace in his career redefines the novelistic and makes it in the course of the novel the discovery of a theatrically rendered necessity rather than a study of the possibility of a modest freedom that Clarissa embarked upon at the beginning.

Notes

1. The references in parenthesis in the text are to the Everyman edition of *Clarissa* in four volumes (New York: Dutton, 1932).

2. Belford speaks for Richardson when he finds that Clarissa is much more convincing a tragic heroine than Calista in Rowe's *Fair Penitent*. Belford's approval of Clarissa is partly on stylistic grounds, for he finds that "whatever the ill-usage of this excellent woman is from her relations, she breaks not out into excesses" and "on every extraordinary provocation she has recourse to the Scriptures, and endeavours to regulate her vehemence by sacred precedents" (4:120). Calista commits suicide and that is not only wrong but a vulgar literary device. "But, indeed, our poets hardly know how to create a distress without horror, murder, and suicide; and must shock your soul to bring tears from your eyes" (4:119).

3. William J. Farrell has pointed out Lovelace's style derives from the tradition of the courtly love letter and that Clarissa resists his advances in the language of she-tragedy. Farrell finds that Lovelace's plain style is an affectation and his courtly one "a manifestation of his true self." Clarissa, too, finds her nobler being in tragic idiom, and her development of a "dramatic rhetoric parallels and thus emphasizes her role as the pathetic but noble victim" ("The Style and the Action in *Clarissa*," in *Samuel Richardson: A Collection of Critical Essays*, ed.

John Carroll [Englewood Cliffs, N.J.: Prentice-Hall, 1969], pp. 97, 101). Farrell's perceptive essay notes that styles are functional and expressive, but he does not emphasize the way that these styles interact, and he fails to see, I think, the radical complexity of selfhood that Clarissa and Lovelace achieve, by which style expresses personality without exhausting or fully comprising it.

4. Mark Kinkead-Weekes, *Samuel Richardson: Dramatic Novelist* (London: Methuen, 1973), pp. 434–35. Richardson's echoes of Restoration and eighteenth-century drama are surveyed in Ira Konigsberg's *Samuel Richardson and the Dramatic Novel* (Lexington, Ky.: University of Kentucky Press, 1968). Leo Hughes's "Theatrical Convention in Richardson: Some Observations on a Novelist's Technique" (in *Restoration and Eighteenth-Century Literature: Essays in Honor of Alan Dugald McKillop* [Chicago: University of Chicago Press, 1963], pp. 239–50) is an invaluable analysis of Richardson's exact employment of the stylized gestures favored on the eighteenth-century stage. Hughes notes that Richardson printed his friend Aaron Hill's *Art of Acting* and finds parallels between Hill's elaborate systems of gesture and glance and Clarissa's and Lovelace's notions of personal expressiveness (pp. 248–49). A. D. McKillop's *Samuel Richardson: Printer and Novelist* (Chapel Hill, N.C.: University of North Carolina Press, 1936) has much to say about the dramatic echoes and theatrical methods of *Clarissa* (see pp. 141–52). As McKillop notes, Ernest Bernbaum first pointed out the resemblances between the plot and characters of *Clarissa* and those of Charles Johnson's *Caelia* (*The Drama of Sensibility,* [Boston: Peter Smith, 1915], pp. 158–62, 165).

5. "The significant antecedents of *Clarissa* are to be found not in earlier prose fiction, but in the drama—in Rowe's *The Fair Penitent* and in Charles Johnson's *Caelia*. . . . Yet in neither *The Fair Penitent* nor *Caelia*, for all their preoccupation with the pathos of the heroine's situation, is there an assimilation of the tragic experience sufficiently convincing psychologically to produce high tragedy." So writes John Loftis in *Comedy and Society from Congreve to Fielding* (Stanford, Calif.: Stanford University Press, 1959), p. 137.

6. *Selected Letters of Samuel Richardson*, ed. John Carroll, (Oxford: Clarendon Press, 1964), p. 72.

7. There was a good deal of intelligent debate throughout the century on the most appropriate acting styles. Actors such as Garrick and Macklin promoted a more "natural" manner on stage that modified but by no means eliminated the declamatory and gestural style of their predecessors. See Alan S. Downer, "Nature to Advantage Dressed: Eighteenth-Century Acting," in *Restoration Drama: Modern Essays in Criticism*, ed. John Loftis (New York: Oxford University Press, 1966), pp. 339–40. Downer points out that complete psychological identification with a character was a commonplace ideal repeated by actors and theorists throughout the century (pp. 361–62). In 1783 Dr. Johnson ridiculed such a position: "Johnson, indeed, had thought more upon the subject of acting than might be generally supposed. Talking of it one day to Mr. Kemble, he said, 'Are you, Sir, one of those enthusiasts who believe yourself transformed into the very character you represent?' Upon Mr. Kemble's answering that he had never felt so strong a persuasion himself, 'To be sure not, Sir (said Johnson); the thing is impossible. And if Garrick really believed himself to be that monster, Richard the Third, he deserved to be hanged every time he performed it.'" *Life of Johnson*, eds. G. B. Hill and L. F. Powell (Oxford: Clarendon Press, 1964), 4:243–44. The point is that actors then and now are subject to the physical limitations of the stage, and mimicry and other external business are always necessary to promote whatever internal identification the actor may feel.

8. "*Clarissa*'s Richardson: An Essay to Find the Reader," in *English Literature in the Age of Disguise*, ed. M. E. Novak (Berkeley and Los Angeles: University of California Press, 1977), p. 199.

9. Eric Rothstein, *Restoration Tragedy: Form and the Process of Change* (Madison, Wisc.: University of Wisconsin Press, 1967), p. 82.

10. Robert D. Hume, "The Myth of the Rake in 'Restoration' Comedy," *Studies in the Literary Imagination* 10 (1977): 38.

11. In her *A Natural Passion: A Study of the Novels of Samuel Richardson* (Oxford: Clarendon Press, 1974), Margaret Doody says very well that Clarissa and Lovelace "might be said to live in the imagination." She goes on to note the theatrical origins of Lovelace's self-imaginings and observes that he is "more sophisticated than the characters in the dramas to which he refers, because these dramas themselves are included in the scenery of his mind; he can maintain the shifting perspectives of reader, audience, actor, director, and character in his versatile reactions to drama and to life" (pp. 104, 113–14). Doody sees Clarissa in less literary terms and remarks that "her reactions are always in terms of principle" (p. 118). My point throughout this essay is that Clarissa's principles refine Lovelace's purely literary modes but still depend upon literary expression.

12. In a way, it is hardly remarkable that style should be examined in an epistolary novel where personality is expressed by style. Clarissa is not alone in this examination of the discourse of others, but I think it can be argued that she has the most highly developed moral-literary theory in the book.

13. Kinkead-Weekes, p. 435.

14. See Lovelace's letter written in "Ivy-Cavern in the Coppice—Day but just breaking." "On one knee, kneeling with the other, I write! My feet benumbed with midnight wanderings through the heaviest dews that ever fell: my wig and my linen dripping with the hoar frost dissolving on them!" (1:327–28).

15. "You shall see, madam, what I will bear for your sake. My sword shall be put sheathed into your hands (and he offered it to me in the scabbard). My heart, if you please, clapping one hand upon his breast, shall afford a sheath to your brother's sword. Life is nothing if I lose you" (1:481).

List of Contributors

KALMAN A. BURNIM, Fletcher Professor of Drama and Oratory at Tufts University, is former chairman and now director of Graduate Studies of the Department of Drama. He is coauthor, with Philip H. Highfill, Jr. and Edward A. Langhans, of the multi-volume *Biographical Dictionary of Actors, Actresses, Musicians, Dancers, Managers, and Other Stage Personnel in London, 1660–1800*. Among his books are *David Garrick Director; The Prompter* (with William Appleton); and a six-volume edition of *The Collected Plays of George Colman the Elder*.

BRIAN CORMAN is associate professor of English at the University of Toronto. He has written on Etherege, Shadwell, Otway, and Congreve, and he is working on a study of genre and generic change in late seventeenth-century drama.

ROBERT HALSBAND, professor emeritus of English at the University of Illinois, has written biographies of Lady Mary Wortley Montagu and of Lord Hervey. He also edited Lady Mary's complete letters and her essays. His most recent book is *"The Rape of the Lock" and its Illustrations, 1714–1896*.

LUCYLE HOOK, professor of English at Barnard College, Columbia University (retired), has published articles about Restoration and eighteenth-century drama and music in various scholarly publications, including the *Shakespeare Quarterly, Theatre Notebook, Huntington Quarterly*, and the *Augustan Reprint Society*. A double biography of Elizabeth Barry and Anne Bracegirdle is scheduled by Oxford University Press for 1983.

LEO HUGHES is professor emeritus in the Department of English, University of Texas. His published works include *A Century of English Farce, The Drama's Patrons*, and editions of *Ten English Farces* (coedited with Arthur H. Scouten) and *The Plain Dealer*, as well as many articles on eighteenth-century English drama.

ROBERT D. HUME is professor of English at Pennsylvania State University. He is the author of *Dryden's Criticism, The Development of English Drama in the Late Seventeenth Century,* and *The Rakish Stage,* as well as editor of *The London Theatre World* and *Vice Chamberlain Coke's Theatrical Papers, 1706–1715* (with Judith Milhous). He is currently at work with Arthur H. Scouten and Judith Milhous on a revision of parts 1 and 2 of *The London Stage, 1660–1800.*

J. PAUL HUNTER is dean of the College of Arts and Science at the University of Rochester. His publications include *The Reluctant Pilgrim: Defoe's Emblematic Method and Quest for Form in Robinson Crusoe* and *Occasional Form: Henry Fielding and the Chains of Circumstance* as well as numerous essays on the novel and literary theory in the eighteenth century. He also edited *The Norton Introduction to Literature: Poetry.* He is currently working on a major study of the origins of the English novel.

SHIRLEY STRUM KENNY, provost of Arts and Humanities at the University of Maryland, College Park, is the editor of the Clarendon editions of *The Plays of Richard Steele* and *The Works of George Farquhar* (forthcoming), as well as other editions of eighteenth-century plays. She has published numerous articles on textual studies, theatrical history, and criticism of eighteenth-century drama.

J. MERRILL KNAPP is professor emeritus of music at Princeton University, as well as former dean of the college, chairman of the Music Department, and director of the Princeton Glee Club. He has written *Selected List of Music for Men's Voices* and *The Magic of Opera,* as well as many articles. He is a member of the executive boards of the Halle Handel Society in East Germany and the Göttingen Handel Society in West Germany.

EDWARD A. LANGHANS is chairman and professor of drama and theatre at the University of Hawaii. With Philip H. Highfill and Kalman A. Burnim, he is coauthor of *A Biographical Dictionary of Actors, Actresses, Musicians, Dancers, Managers, and Other Stage Personnel in London, 1660–1800* (eight volumes in print as of 1982). His *Restoration Promptbooks* was published in 1981.

STODDARD LINCOLN is professor of music at the City University of New York and Brooklyn College. He reconstructed a performing edition of the opera *Semele* and gave its world premiere at Oxford. His scholarship on the work of John Eccles has led him into his present project, a thematic catalogue of Restoration theatre music. A performer as well as a scholar, he performs concerts in the United States and England on the harpsichord and forte piano.

JUDITH MILHOUS is associate professor of theatre history in the Department of Communication and Theatre Arts at the University of Iowa. She is the author of *Thomas Betterton and the Management of Lincoln's Inn Fields, 1695–1708* and coeditor with Robert D. Hume of *The Frolicks* by Elizabeth Polwhele and *Vice Chamberlain Coke's Theatrical Papers*. She is currently working on a book on *The Triumvirate Management of Drury Lane, 1709–1732*.

CHARLES C. MISH, professor of English at the University of Maryland, College Park, is a leading authority on seventeenth-century English fiction. He has published *English Prose Fiction, 1600–1700: A Chronological Checklist*, as well as two anthologies of seventeenth-century fiction and numerous articles on the subject.

JOHN J. RICHETTI is professor of English at Rutgers University. He is the author of *Popular Fiction Before Richardson: Narrative Patterns 1700–1739*, *Defoe's Narratives: Situations and Structures*, and the forthcoming *Philosophical Writing: Locke, Berkeley, Hume*.

ARTHUR H. SCOUTEN is professor emeritus of English at the University of Pennsylvania. He is the editor of part 3 of *The London Stage*. He has also written *A Bibliography of the Writings of Jonathan Swift*, coauthored volume 5 of *The Revels History of Drama in English*, and coedited *Ten English Farces* (with Leo Hughes) and *The Country Gentleman* (with Robert D. Hume). His numerous articles focus on Swift, Defoe, Shakespeare, and English theatre history.